D0825227

Contemporary Japan and Popular Culture

ConsumAsiaN Book Series

edited by

Brian Moeran and *Lise Skov*

and

published by

The Curzon Press and The University of Hawai'i Press

Contemporary Japan and Popular Culture

Edited by
John Whittier Treat

UNIVERSITY OF HAWAI'I PRESS
HONOLULU

© John Whittier Treat 1996
All Rights Reserved

Published in North America by
University of Hawai'i Press
2840 Kolowalu Street
Honolulu, Hawai'i 96822

First Published in the United Kingdom by
Curzon Press
St. John's Studio, Church Road
Richmond, Surrey TW9 2QA
England

Printed in Great Britain

Library of Congress Cataloguing-in-Publication Data

Contemporary Japan and popular culture/edited by
John Whittier Treat.
p. cm.
Includes bilbiographical references and index.
ISBN 0–8248–1855–5 (alk. paper).
ISBN 0–8248–1854–7 (pbk. : alk. paper)
1. Japan – Civilization – 1945– . 2. Popular culture – Japan.
I. Treat, John Whittier.
DS822.5.C69 1996
952.04 – dc20 96-7545
CIP

Contents

IV Film, Television and Japanese Ideologies

V Popular Literature and Japan's Present

Acknowledgements

This volume is an expanded version of a symposium published in the *Journal of Japanese Studies* (Summer 1993), itself the result of a public conference on contemporary Japanese popular culture jointly sponsored in May 1991 by the Society of Japanese Studies and the Center for Japanese Studies at the University of California, Berkeley. That conference was organized by Mary Elizabeth Berry and John Whittier Treat, and attended by contributors to this volume Aoki Tamotsu, Brian Moeran, Susan Napier and Lise Skov. Also presenting were Lawrence Grossberg, Irmela Hijiya-Kirschnereit, Earl Jackson, Jr., Chalmers Johnson and William Kelly; Sandra Buckley had her paper read by Marilyn Ivy. Andrew Barshay, Stephen Snyder and Melinda Takeuchi joined in the post-conference discussion of the papers presented.

Special thanks are due Susan B. Hanley and Martha Lane Walsh of the Society for Japanese Studies in Seattle for their early endorsement of and assistance in this project; to Aiko Fujisaka and Marsha Yonemoto in Berkeley for their help with the conference arrangements; and to both those contributors who joined the project later and the anonymous referees who volunteered their labor to improve the work offered here.

Every effort has been made to trace the copyright of the illustrations reproduced in this book. Unfortunately, in some cases this has proved to be impossible. The author and publisher would be pleased to hear from any copyright holders whom they have been unable to contact, and to print due acknowledgements in the next edition.

A note on Japanese names

Japanese names appear in Japanese order, which is to say that surnames are followed by given names. The only exceptions are when an individual is better known internationally with his or her names reversed: thus 'Otomo Katsuhiro', but 'Ryuichi Sakamoto'. Note, too, that macrons have been dropped from Japanese names typically romanized without them, as they have from common words as well ('Tokyo', 'Showa').

Introduction

Japanese Studies into Cultural Studies

John Whittier Treat

Anthologies of Western academic writing on Japanese culture are not new: indeed, both the history of 'Japan studies' and its classroom pedagogy are unimaginable without them. Yet our inheritance of essays on Japanese literature and the arts, produced by those several generations of European and American scholars motivated to produce Japan as the cultural counterpart or rival (and thus both similar and different) of their own Western traditions now exists in a kind of stalled historicity. The tea ceremony, the noh theater, the lyric, the art of arranged flowers and the choreography of the martial arts – all are old, even ancient proofs of a spare and elegant culture that to the Japanese people today must seem so remote from daily life as to be as exotic as they were to the first intrepid European visitors.

Just as Japanese culture at the end of the twentieth century is hardly recognizable from the perspective of traditional aesthetics, so too have the methods and aims of those who study Japan been dramatically altered by the advent of new theories in the academy, on the one hand, and the dazzling speed of cultural change in Japan itself. Some may continue to see in, for example, the 1980s subculture of the dancing Sunday rockers in Tokyo's Yoyogi Park a reiteration of Japan's group-oriented social traditions (Littleton 1985), but such explanations no longer, if they ever did, suffice to account for a set of fluid symbolic systems and practices that enable different groups to make various kinds of sense of their lives today – lives more appropriately described, perhaps, as 'fragmented' or 'different' than as 'collective' and 'same'. We have to be skeptical whenever we think we see familiar patterns or values reemerge in a culture that has been called 'continuous' for reasons less historical than ideological. Alan Tansman's analysis in this volume of the career of the late popular *enka* singer Misora Hibari demonstrates how what we have been conditioned to think of as 'traditional' may be very recent and expedient; and indeed, how music is as subject to history and politics as it is to individual talent and passion. The essays gathered here attest both to the altered register in which the study of Japanese culture, popular or otherwise, now proceeds and to the related phenomenon of that culture's mercurial parameters: the hyper-commodification of everyday life in Japan *and* the nagging suspicion that we scholars are not innocent of that process ourselves, have made the entry of cultural studies into the field of Japanese studies as critical as it is inevitable.

Contemporary Japan and Popular Culture, however, does not present itself as an advertisement for a heretofore undiscovered Japan, or as a manifesto for a new paradigm for academic work. The points of view included here are not only various, they are often plainly incompatible with each other. This is not only unavoidable, given the persistent dichotomy of celebratory versus apocalyptic rhetoric of critical commentary on popular culture, but, to make a virtue of necessity, actually welcome. I hope that this volume will find its way into the classroom, where presumably the dissonance of debate is where effective teaching begins.

What joins these essays together is first their common curiosity about the most recent twists and turns in Japan's collectively experienced 'everyday life'. But then there is also the sense that whatever our respective disciplines, popular (or 'mass', in the careful idiom of many of the contributors) culture, and the explosion of theoretical work around the world that details and analyzes it, can be ignored within the confines of first, area studies, and second, traditional high-cultural studies, only at considerable intellectual peril. With the advent of a homogenizing 'transnational' capitalism, notes Masao Miyoshi, 'Cultural eccentricities are to be avoided. . . . National history and culture are not to intrude or not to be asserted oppositionally or even dialectically' (Miyoshi 1993:747), and so the study of Japan (one of the leading agents of such capitalism) as a discrete, much less unique, cultural instance (the erstwhile 'area' in 'area studies') is at best nostalgic, at worse ideologically complicit. When Brian Moeran, in his discussion here of the marketing of Japanese cars in Britain, notes the 'emerging mysticism of "Japan" itself in European and American advertising in the 1980s', he attests to how the notion of a national culture in the age of state-less capitalism is nowadays evermore virtual than real.

But at the same time Miyoshi's impatience with the political feebleness of popular culture under this expanding hegemony risks repeating the tactical error pointed out by Andrew Ross in his *No Respect: Intellectuals and Popular Culture*, namely that the intelligentsia has weakened itself by refusing to take popular culture seriously. Of novelist Murakami Haruki, the subject of one of this volume's essays and whose sales *and* residences are as globally dispersed as any 'transnational corporations', Miyoshi writes he 'is the poet laureate of Japan in the 1980s and 1990s. . . . [His novels are] sophisticated stylizations of trivia, flying over the boredom and irritation of everyday life' (Miyoshi 1991:235). Miyoshi associates such writing with the 'vanishing of criticism' in present-day Japan. But why should not our means for criticism now be as transformed as so much else in contemporary life? 'Today', writes Ross with a verve redolent of his theme, 'a code of intellectual activism which is not grounded in . . . the discourses of popular, commercial culture will have has much leverage over the new nomination of modern social movements as the spells of medieval witches or consultations of the *I Ching*' (Ross 1989:212–13). And in the case of Japanese popular, commercial culture, there is the added danger when critics claim that there is no other kind of culture to be found in Japan any more, and so dismiss it for its very 'popularity'. A failure to engage it seriously will mean a failure to take *Japan* seriously – not least of all in the sense that here is a place which exists not only discursively or imaginatively, but as a powerful force (either as a nation-state or as the titular headquarters of a number of Miyoshi's 'TNCs') at work in our lives worldwide.

Just who, however, is charged with taking Japanese or any other popular culture seriously is a question that demands a disciplinary apology. According to one authority, there are no 'scholars in Japan who specialize exclusively in "popular culture"' (Katō 1989:viii). The same might be said of the West, where the popular is the proprietary concern of nearly all the social sciences and the humanities, but is not the only object of study for any field. While this might appear as an opportunity for the sort of interdisciplinary work itself so 'popular' in the university today, this is probably a case of making the best of an awkward situation. If in fact popular culture is today something that we inhabit as completely and thus as often unaware as we do, say, ideology, language or the air we breathe, then each of the interpretive disciplines is, like it or not, implicated not only in its inquiry but its enactment, too.

Important distinctions nonetheless demand to be made. Despite our common cause joined in this volume, anthropology is not yet history, nor have literary studies become just one branch of sociology. 'Popular culture' has to be distinguishable from something that is neither, and unless 'Japanese popular culture' is a coherent phrase this volume is pointless. We cannot assume that histories the world over have converged (much less 'ended'), no matter how much we would like to apply the ambitious techniques used in the study of contemporary popular culture in Britain or North America to Japan. While the study of Japanese popular culture, like that of any nation's, is not an exclusively new undertaking, neither is its history all that long; perhaps more importantly, as a nation outside the West, the question of *Japan*'s popular culture inevitably invites the questions of origins, sources, influences and colonialisms both long-standing and otherwise. The inquiry into Japanese popular culture cannot be much older than the concept of the 'popular' or of 'culture', both words that in their contemporary contexts run parallel to discourses of the 'modern' and, behind them but never too far away, the 'West'. As Lise Skov claims in her essay on the reinscription of essentializing or reifying Orientalist stereotypes within avant-garde Japanese high fashion, Japan 'has been first to question the habitual identification of modernity with the West'.

This is one of the historical cleavages to be opened up by the essays in *Contemporary Japan and Popular Culture*. Others ask to be closed. Distinctions between a 'high' and a 'low' – unlike that between a 'refined' and a 'vulgar' – are, as in the case of the wedge inserted between a 'cultural' arena of life and something 'else', the product of a reconfiguration of the social along lines predicted (though hardly determined) by the reorganization of life, everyday or otherwise, that accompanied first industrial and subsequently consumer capitalism. The names most prominently associated with the study of popular culture in Japan – Yanagita Kunio, Gonda Yasunosuke, Kon Wajirō, Ōya Sōichi and Katō Hidetoshi – are names not only of the property of the twentieth century, but of the struggle among the Japanese intelligentsia, left, right and center to understand and intervene in, explicitly or implicitly, the social practices occasioned or made salient in this same turbulent and controversial century of Japan's transformation.

In my own discipline of literary studies, the ongoing twentieth-century debates in Japan over the status of *junbungaku* or 'pure literature' versus the popular are inseparable from what is at stake in Japan's modernity. When intellectuals such as Takami Jun and Itō Sei, despite their considerable differences, postulate pure literature as transcendental, non-contingent and most importantly 'unified', they yearn to take at least one kind of highly formalized fiction out of social or economic matrixes: junbungaku, like 'high culture' in much of the modern world, is a utopian gesture, a dream against the onslaught of capitalist commodification. At the same time, the complementary move, in which we disavow the ideology of aesthetic 'unity', has its own utopian inspiration, namely the isolation and identification of what would then have to be 'left' in the text: precisely those same social and economic contexts that have to be the familiar stuff of Japan's modernity.

'The term "popular"', notes Katō, 'is not popular in Japan' (Katō 1989:xvii). What he means, of course, is that the term *taishū* in Japanese reflects the political assumptions and agendas in whose interests that term (or any of its alternatives) has been deployed. In this it seems little different from the English 'popular', whose own controversial use is eschewed by some who prefer, for example, 'mass' or 'public' or simply 'culture' unqualified. One finds in Japan a split similar (but not identical) to that signified by the use of 'mass' versus 'popular' in *minshū* versus taishū: indeed, the lexical and so theoretical possibilities proliferate when one notes that Japanese social scientists such as Aoki Tamotsu use the English words *popyurā* 'popular' and *masu* 'mass' to signify a difference from the Japanese vocabulary that would otherwise confine them. Moreover there are special risks involved when describing Japanese culture with any of these adjectives, given the long-standing Orientalist penchant (one evident among Japanese as well as foreign scholars) for looking at Asian societies as homogeneous, or outside of history, in contrast to a West that reserves variety and 'individualism' for itself. What we risk, in other words, is falling victim to a collusion of imperial disdain for the 'backwardness' of non-Western collectivist cultures with a twentieth-century Marxist disdain for mass-produced cultures. When Nishibe Susumu declared Japan in the early 1980s to be 'the ultimate "Utopia of the Masses"' (Nishibe 1982:78), he chose a phrase that resonates in at least two registers: the promise of modernity and the nightmare of an Asian horde. Moreover, *Nihonjinron* – psuedo-academic books celebrating a belief in Japanese national or ethnic uniqueness predicated on Japan as populated by an undifferentiated 'mass' –

so ubiquitous in the 1970s and 1980s means that our discussion of Japanese popular culture must be careful to exercise caution in appropriating the Frankfurt School-derived dissatisfaction with mass societies, lest a legitimate criticism of modernity be mistaken for an Orientalism that attributes to Japan, in Edward Said's partial definition of the term, 'a kind of ideal and unchanging abstraction' (Said 1979:8).

Luckily we have at our disposal today ways of looking at popular culture unprecedented in their subtlety and capacity for critical self-reflection. The tremendous attention now paid cultural studies in the academy has been inspired, first, by the widespread intuition that 'culture' is now better a term to work within when investigating how people live there lives than 'society', given the former's capacity to include the fact of a human inventiveness and resilience that affirms a promise largely lost to the latter. (The North American city where I live is fond of 'cultural festivals', but I've not heard of any pending 'social festivals'.) Second, cultural studies is inspired by the common consensus today that popular culture is no longer – if it ever was – limited to the catalogue of baser forms of entertainment or other leisure activities enjoyed by the working classes, but is in fact some convenient shorthand for the myriad ways in which modern people experience what makes them 'modern' or even 'people'. This attention has made certain assertions about popular culture nearly axiomatic in those places, Tokyo among them, where Antonio Gramsci, Roland Barthes, Louis Althusser, Raymond Williams and the Birmingham School have been read sympathetically.

Any axiom, of course, is an irresistible invitation to discover otherwise. The most recent theorizing seems ready to dispense with the 'production, text, and appropriation' paradigm for analysis deeply rooted in cultural studies in favor of one less mechanical. What Lawrence Grossberg has criticized as the 'communications model' in popular cultural studies, where even if the 'message' of culture is variable the structural source of its encoding and the site of its decoding are not, is now faced with describing, in addition to 'meaning', 'the complexity of effects and relations circulating through and around culture' (Grossberg 1992:45). At the conference that inaugurated this volume, and where Grossberg provided such theoretical admonitions, Japan anthropologist William Kelly already noted that 'the notion of multiple zones seems more promising than the tendency of popular culture theorists to presume a simple dichotomy between the elite producers of goods and messages and the mass of consumers'.

Popular culture, a phrase that will not really do any longer but which has yet to be supplanted, is now held to be both material and immaterial, real and iconic; it is actively constitutive of experience as well as passively reflective of it. As Andrew Painter argues here in his essay on Japanese daytime television, 'Television, in Japan as elsewhere, does not merely reflect society – it transforms it'. At the same time culture is always a plural, a set of cultures, some of which we are born into, some we design for ourselves, some we reject, and some we inhabit ambiguously; indeed, the corollary is that that 'we' is created in and by these multiple cultures, as well as existing prior to them. My own essay in this volume, a look at what can only problematically be called the 'subculture' of adolescent Japanese women within recent fiction, makes the point that not only is Japanese popular culture much more variegated than is typically conceded, but that this heterogeneity is what allows the social subject to work *against* ideology at times, with it at others. What finally emerges as the delicate object of study for those of us interested in the popular are the fluid relationships among these various moments, planes and experiences – each of which may be articulated with the other, but none of which could ever reliably predict or guarantee those links.

If this is indeed our newly complicated register for the study of Japanese popular culture, it is at odds with what has been long-standing pedagogic practice. The history of the teaching of Japanese culture in North America has, as governed by the legacy of Orientalism on the one hand, and the social scientific logic of postwar 'area studies' on the other, stubbornly subscribed to the ideologem that every Japanese cultural practice – if not every Japanese *person* – is nothing but a whole example of what is discursively named 'Japan'. The subordinate relationship of the cultural to the social or historical often implied in the titles of such college courses as 'Japan in Literature' or 'Japan Through Film' has, in theory at any rate, been superceded by more subtle and exasperating complex formations of culture as the social and the historical – and thus as much the Japanese work ethic or voting patterns as it is the novels of Mishima. Recently an American-made documentary video entitled *The Japanese Version* has been marketed to classroom teachers of Japanese studies. 'Version' here refers to the appropriation by Japan of the American pop cultural originals (the wedding cake, the country-western bar, etc.), but it is an appropriation that students have been known to react to with ridicule. The filmmakers' techniques risk making their Japanese subjects look infantile for sake of a 'mimicry' that our own Western narcissism so often both demands and derides. (Figure 1) Such classroom aids are the latest installment in the history of our Western penchant for pegging Japan as a set of corrupted duplicates of foreign prototypes, which, as Joseph J. Tobin has put it, 'tend to produce unflattering views of the Japanese as passive victims of first Chinese and then Western cultural combinations or, alternatively, as active, underhanded agents of plagiarism' (Tobin 1992:3).

The danger, of course, is that updated representations of the Japanese as hapless imitators of the United States is validated both by historical habit and a vengeful impulse of much more recent vintage: namely that despite all their economic successes, the Japanese remain stunted in other, cultural ways. Of course, one could survey, as some have, the endless variety of Japan's 'love hotels' and permutations of its 'Western cuisine' and arrive at the opposite conclusion: that the Japanese are perennially playful, preeminently creative in their elaboration of practices and things naively 'borrowed' from abroad. Either tack, however, leads to a reductive reading of how culture is created, experienced and transmitted, and both are received truisms that cultural studies, focused internationally as well as locally, should seek to confound. Culture is now the name we give that 'contested ground' which is structured and restructured by its own institutions, habits, play, imaginations, and even sheer accident. But it would be a mistake to cite the perhaps necessary polymorphousness of this definition as reason enough to reject the analysis of popular culture as unworkably vague or impractical, and thus inconsequential. On the contrary, the growing awareness that, for example, the shows we watch and the novels we read are not escapes from the tedium of everyday life, but are implicated in how that life is constructed and experienced, dictates that popular culture be taken seriously indeed.

There is, of course, a particular historical and institutional moment that has produced this nexus of Japanese studies with cultural studies. The crisis in literary studies precipitated by the shift in our literacy away from the printed word and towards other varieties of signifiers, and to a lesser extent the crises brought on by contending methods in history, sociology and anthropology, parallel the disruption of multidisciplinary area studies in the wake

Figure 1 From a brochure advertising the documentary video *The Japanese Version*: This cowboy may be smiling, but the Rising Sun suggests a less happy story

of both a post-Cold War world and one where the naturalness of even a place name ('Japan') is questioned by the ascendancy of theories of discourse and difference. More specifically, the prominence of work in the field of popular culture in the West over the past two decades may have something to do with the particular Anglo-American refocus on the experience of everyday life, a refocus that has benefited from and inspired anew a wealth of corresponding intellectual inquiry. In Japan, that same refocus may also be the result of a heightened sense of ill ease, even panic, among intellectuals increasingly estranged from their own society's production of that same oddly evacuated everyday life.

In his essay included here on the literary works of Murakami Haruki, anthropologist Aoki Tamotsu states that what distinguishes 1980s Japan is not just its affluence, but its production of a nostalgia for an earlier age that was not. It is, in Aoki's phrase, a culture of 'maturation and forfeiture'. Susan Napier likewise reviews the history of postwar Japanese science fiction to discover that the celebration of utopia has, in the 1980s and coordinate with Japan's changed status within the global economy, given way to one of dystopia. Such findings should not surprise Western readers, who are probably familiar with reports of similar shifts in their own cultures. When Nakamori Akio dubs Japan's 1980s the 'era of the idol', one in which the media invented and promoted new singing acts not for their talent, but for their very lack of it – a lack that allows for an unprecedented identification between audience and performer (Nakamori 1991) – Americans can surely counter with examples drawn from their own entertainment industries which increasingly both manipulate public taste and enforce a regimen of narcissistic products (e.g., *Roseanne*, *The Simpsons*) to satisfy it. Surely Nakajima Takeo's description of contemporary Japanese culture as fragmented, decentered, virtual, 'retro' and, inevitably, 'postmodern' might well have been said of many others (Nakajima 1991).

That Nakajima bemoans his country's current culture as a 'black hole' incapable of all but the passive absorption of Western fashions and trends is a finding that many of the essays gathered here contest and, to my mind, decisively refute. But that does not mean that the international synchrony one can see in his list of attributes has no implications for us. While each essay here is careful to point to the specificity of contemporary Japanese cultural practices, the relative youth of the contributors to this volume means that much they remark of Japan comes with ample analogies in America or Britain: the 'we' so commonly deployed in English-language scholarship on Japan no longer refers so automatically to the presumed non-Japanese audience, but rather to the collective citizenry of a world increasingly organized by a global, or at least international, late capitalist popular culture.

What this means is that we have our own good reasons for wanting to mediate the distance between the typical panic over the depressing predictability of a mass-produced culture and the typical celebration of the democratic potential of a public culture uncapped by elites. If from North America or Western Europe, we grew up in a popular culture not wholly dissimilar from Japan's – which is not to say that we cannot be dispirited by it, or blind to the utopian promise in it. If works of mass culture 'cannot manage anxieties about the social order unless they have first revived them and given them rudimentary expression' (Jameson 1979:139), then we are guaranteed the ambiguity that many of the contributors to this volume identify in their views on the question of Japanese popular culture's implications for human development and freedom.

Thus the mutual obsession, both East and West, with what might be a hegemonizing postmodernity; an obsession that means the most basic structures of social existences, whether 'ours' or 'theirs', have been reinterpreted against a 'cultural logic' locally modulated but universally applied. Note, for example, the conspicuous flows of capital, cultural and financial, between Japan and the West (Madonna's concerts sell out in Tokyo, but Sony buys a big piece of Hollywood). It makes ever less sense as we approach an unprecedented cultural convergence, and as the epistemic distance that once so clearly separated Japan from its students abroad, to conceive of popular culture as anything other than a way of viewing 'culture' itself – a word once again under fierce pressure to mean something both more and less than it might once have.

One might argue that in the world in which we North Americans, Japanese and West Europeans live today, where so much of our experience is commodified and therefore 'mass', that the 'popular' really only exists as a methodological wedge, a way of disclosing the many, and often incompatible 'common senses' (pluralized by Stuart Hall) about the complex forms that any quotidian life assumes. To worry about the relation of the popular to high or official culture is to think about the perennial problem of value: perennial first because value is so exasperatingly mercurial (consider how Tokugawa bourgeois culture, such as the kabuki theater, is now officially sanctioned 'high culture'), and second because its determination only deflects us from understanding how cultures high, low and in-between exist in discursive and material relations of exchange, negotiation and conflict with each other. Indeed, our work in the study of popular culture, be it that of Japan or elsewhere, is initially to separate our inquiries from the project of determining value ('good' cultural practices versus 'bad' ones) – or rather, to understand that that project is itself a 'high cultural' reflex – and consequently to bypass the probably irresolvable conflict of looking at culture as either exclusively 'popular' (implying a 'bottom-to-top' percolation of discourses and practices) or 'mass' (implying a 'top-to-bottom' imposition of same). We have to explore instead how we simultaneously and variously position ourselves – or are, via the work of ideology or forces more literally coercive, position*ed* – in reproductive, indifferent, or resistant relations with the cultural structures that comprise the social formation, and from there govern our sense of daily experience.

It remains necessary, of course, to keep in mind that speaking of *Japanese* popular culture must entail certain specificities, and historical and methodological obligations, that speaking of popular cultures in the West may not. The burden we thus assume should not deter us: as Gayatri Spivak insists, cultural studies must be *transnational* cultural studies, lest our 'highly sophisticated vocabulary for cultural descriptions' in the English-speaking West 'sanction a kind of global ignorance' (Spivak 1993:278). Knowledge will presumably flow several ways. Anthropologist John G. Russell discloses in his essay on the representation of the 'Black Other' in Japanese popular culture that those images are imaginable only within the context of 'Western ethnocentrism and cultural hegemony'; just how those forces work at home as well as abroad is illuminated by his findings. Similarly, Leo Ching asks in his essay on the discourse of the influence of Japanese popular culture in Taiwan, 'What is the effect on the cultural pattern of the society when a Taiwanese youth sings a Chinese song with a *karaoke* machine from Japan?' Or when, as is now the case, Nintendo's video game character Super Mario is better known in the United States than Mickey Mouse? Just what *does* 'Japanese popular culture' mean when all three terms, 'Japanese' included, function ironically in the breaches that have opened up in the complexes of contemporary life? Naoki Sakai has demonstrated how 'the discursive object called Japan' is only awkwardly constructed atop provincial Western historical narratives (Sakai 1989:96); Raymond Williams tells us that 'popular' has long been tagged with connotations both favorable and unfavorable (Williams 1976:198–99); and while Kogawa Tetsuo has told us that the Japanese word '*bunka* covers the whole semantic extent of "culture"' (Kogawa 1988:54), just what is that extent? In light of Williams' citation of 'culture' as 'one of the two or three most complicated words in the English language' (Williams 1976:76)? And complicated further for us, when its Japanese equivalent is inextricably bound together with the West and with modernization?

We work today in light of the fact, as articulated by Arjun Appadurai, that 'our very models of cultural shape will have to alter, as configurations of people, place and heritage lose all semblance of isomorphism' (Appadurai 1990:3). Brian Currid, writing here on just what 'world' can mean in Japanese 'world music', uses the varied career of Ryuichi Sakamoto to indicate 'the complicity and complexity of the transnational practices of "world musics" as multiple ways of organizing temporality, geography, and identity'. 'Japaneseness', in this collection of essays as well as those produced by earlier generations of Japan scholars, is a subject of debate, if not longer within *sumi-e* painting and the *Tale of Genji.* It is now impossible to write or even conceive of 'Japanese' popular culture without involving the much of the rest of the world, just as we have never been able to isolate the 'popular' or 'culture' itself outside of its complements: and it is with that warning, that the '(im)possibility of cultural studies' of which Spivak speaks begins.

Although each essay in this volume has chosen to define and explore its own piece of Japanese popular culture, collectively they take up the issues which culture and ideology at the end of the twentieth century make paramount in Japan, and do so in registers that are broadly historical, political and economic. They make wide use of a variety of Japanese and non-Japanese critics and disciplines to configure the words 'Japanese', 'popular' and 'culture' in complex and, among ourselves, admittedly contradictory relations of determination and articulation. More importantly, they are the start, I hope, of more work by those of us trained in a traditional discipline but who are now interested in the potential of a multidisciplinary, transnational cultural studies that might better capture our experience of how the world, including Japan, has changed.

References

Appadurai, Arjun 1990 'Disjuncture and difference in the global cultural economy,' p. 1–24 in *Public Culture* 2 (2).

Grossberg, Lawrence 1992 *We Gotta Get Out of This Place: popular conservatism and postmodern culture*, New York and London: Routledge.

Jameson, Fredric 1979 'Reification and utopia', p. 130–48 in *Social Text* 1.

Katō Hidetoshi 1989 'Some thoughts on Japanese popular culture', p. xvii–xviii in R. Powers and H. Katō (eds.) *Handbook of Japanese Popular Culture*, Westport: Greenwood Press.

Kogawa Tetsuo 1988 'New trends in Japanese popular culture', p. 54–66 in G. McCormack and Y. Sugimoto (eds.), *The Japanese Trajectory: modernization and beyond*, New York: Cambridge University Press.

Littleton, C. Scott 1985 'Tokyo rock and role', p. 49–56 in *Natural History* 94 (8).

Miyoshi, Masao 1993 'A borderless world? From colonialism to transnationalism and the decline of the nation state', p. 726–51 in *Critical Inquiry* 19.

—— 1991 *Off Center: power and culture relations between Japan and the United States*, Cambridge: Harvard University Press.

Nakajima Takeo 1991 *Karagenki no Jidai: hachijū-nendai bunkaron* (*An Age That Only Looks Robust: culture in the 1980s*), Tōkyō: Asahi Shimbun Sha.

Nakamori Akio 1991 'Pink Lady no 80-nendai ron' (Pink Lady and the 1980s), p. 149–75 in Ōtsuka Eiji (ed.), *Shōjo Zasshi Ron* (Essays on Teenaged Women's Magazines), Tokyo: Tōkyō Shoseki.

Nishibe Susumu 1982 'Japan as a highly developed mass society: an appraisal', p. 73–96 in *Journal of Japanese Studies* 8 (1).

Ross, Andrew 1989 *No Respect: intellectuals and popular culture*, London: Routledge.

Sakai, Naoki 1989 'Modernity and its critique: the problem of universalism and particularism,' p. 93–122, in M. Miyoshi and H. D. Harootunian (eds.), *Postmodernism and Japan*, Durham: Duke University Press.

Said, Edward W. 1979 *Orientalism*, New York: Vintage Books.

Spivak, Gayatri Chakravorty 1993 *Outside in the Teaching Machine*, New York and London: Routledge.

Tobin, Joseph J. (ed.), 1992 *Re-made in Japan: everyday life and consumer taste in a changing society*, New Haven: Yale University Press.

Williams, Raymond 1976 *Keywords*, New York: Oxford University Press.

Part I

Hermeneutics of the Image in Japanese Popular Culture

1

Race and Reflexivity

The Black Other in Contemporary Japanese Mass Culture

John G. Russell

Two days before we left Loo Choo the commodore gave still another farewell banquet for Loo Choo's regent. Our 'Ethiopian minstrels' put on an evening of theatrical entertainment afterward. The guests seemed well pleased – they laughed a lot – but why?

William Heine, *With Perry to Japan* (1856)

Why won't black mothers let their children play in the sandbox?

Because the cats keep covering them up.

Dave Spector, *It's Only A Joke!* (1984)

On September 22, 1986, in remarks widely reported in the American press, Japanese Prime Minister Nakasone Yasuhiro, addressing a National Study Council meeting of his ruling Liberal Democratic Party, blamed the presence of blacks, Puerto Ricans and Mexicans for the decline of 'American intelligence levels'. In the same address, Nakasone praised Japan as a 'high-level information society' (*kōdo jōhō shakai*) on the cutting edge of the information age. Unfortunately the Prime Minister was silent on the question of the source and quality of that information, as his comments on American intelligence levels and subsequent remarks by Watanabe Michio in 1988, at yet another party meeting accusing blacks of being indifferent to bankruptcy, strongly suggest. Whether callous or calumnious, these statements are not isolated incidents, for they are embedded in a negative view of blacks that permeates virtually all aspects of Japanese discourse on the Black Other.

American furor over these comments focused on Japanese arrogance, ethnocentrism and antiblack racism; almost overnight Americans came to see Japanese 'homogeneity' – a myth embraced by many Japanese and Americans alike – as a weakness, with Op-Ed columns and ads singing self-congratulatory paeans to the strength of American racial diversity and problematizing Japan's shabby treatment of its own – suddenly visible – minorities. What many of American commentators ignored was the contiguity of Japanese and Western antiblack racism.

As Marilyn Ivy points out in her dissection of the speech, Nakasone's is a 'classically paranoic attempt to confirm Japanese world parity in an increasingly fragmented international and domestic milieu, to restore the honor of the Japanese by comparing it to other races' (1989:23). It is worth noting that in these attempts the Japanese have been aided by a view of the world – particularly the nonwhite world – heavily indebted to Western discourse on the theme of race and difference. Nakasone's comments came as no surprise to those familiar with the theories of Arthur Jensen and William Shockley or purveyors of the Morton Downey, Jr. show and late-night radio talk programs. There, blacks (and other minorities) are cast as modern Vandals crashing the gates of American Empire and whose growing visibility within those gates is treated as symbolic of a collapse of American social order. Nor, given the informational exchange between the USA and Japan, should it have surprised Americans that Nakasone would borrow this idiom as an omen of what would take place in Japan were it to replace its official ideology of 'monoracialism' (*tan'itsu minzoku*) with American-style pluralism, and that he would merely recapitulate (apparently for domestic consumption only) the fears of the American bourgeoisie.

Naoki Sakai's observations on the *Nihonjinron* ('treatise on the Japanese') genre, of which Nakasone's statement is part, seem appropriate here. Nakasone's insistence on asserting Japanese difference from the West 'embodies a nagging urge to see the self from the viewpoint of the [white] Other'. Not only does this 'positing of Japan's identity in Western terms' establish 'the centrality of the West as the universal point of reference' (1989:105) in defining the parameters of Japanese difference, but it also privileges Western discourse on the Black Other.

Japanese literary and visual representation of blacks rely heavily on imagery derived from Western conventions. Such representations function to familiarize Japanese with the Black Other, to preserve its alienness by ascribing to it certain standardized traits which mark its as Other. Yet they also serve the reflexive function of allowing Japanese to meditate on their racial and cultural identity in the face of challenges by Western modernity, cultural authority, and power.

An analysis of the visual and literary conventions used to represent blacks in Japan reveals their striking resemblance to those which prevailed in the West and whose influence in shaping Japanese perceptions of blacks can be detected as early as the sixteenth century. True, in Japan as in Europe the color black has traditionally carried negative symbolic connotations (e.g., corruption, death, evil, illness, impurity), and certainly aesthetic tastes in Japan's classical court culture leave no doubt as to the value associated with white skin. Japanese proverbs testify to the positive aesthetic valuation of the color white as a marker of beauty: 'iro no shiroi wa shichinan kakusu' (white skin compensates for many deficiencies), 'kome no meshi to onna wa shiroi hodo yoi' (in rice and women, the whiter the better), and 'Fujisan no mieru kuni ni bijin nashi', the last conveying the notion that women who live in the overcast, snowy northern prefectures of Shimane, Niigata and Akita are pale-skinned beauties compared to those who live in warmer, sunnier climes, a view that survives today in such expressions as *Akita bijin* (an Akita beauty).

Nonetheless, it does not follow that the *racial* characteristics Japanese ascribe to dark-complexioned races, particularly blacks, ought necessarily to parallel Western ones, which they do all too frequently. Indeed, the evidence suggests that in ascribing certain of these characteristics to blacks, the Japanese have been heavily influenced by Western values and racial paradigms, imported along with Dutch learning (*Rangaku*) and Western science in their rush to catch up with the West. In a word, Japanese views of blacks have taken as their model distorted images derived from Western ethnocentrism and cultural hegemony. That the Japanese had, as historian John Dower points out, their own indigenous racial paradigm based on Tokugawa Confucian notions of 'proper place' is not denied; what is suggested, however, and conveniently overlooked by many Western commentators on Japanese antiblack racism, is that the position blacks have come to occupy in the Japanese hierarchy of races not only echoes Western racist paradigms but is borrowed from them.

In the postwar period in particular, with the rise of American hegemony, these perdurable stereotypes of the Black Other have been in large part reinforced by the centrality of American discourse on the non-white Other in Japan. With the cultural authority and the distributive currency of American mass media and popular culture, this has resulted in Japan's uncritical acceptance and indigenization of the racial hierarchies they project. One sees in these representations of Black Otherness a repetition of the discursive strategies (e.g., the domestication of the exotic, familiarization, stereotyped conceits) employed by the West in its construction of The Orient. In both cases '[s]omething foreign and distant acquires . . . a status more rather than less familiar . . . [and is seen] as a version of things previously known' (Said 1978:55).

A Genealogy of the Black Other

Derogatory references to Africans appear early in the history of Japanese contacts with blacks. Metaphors equating blacks with animals and subhumans can be traced to sixteenth and seventeenth centuries and Japan's initial contacts with the African and East Indian servants who accompanied Portuguese and Dutch traders to Japanese ports in Nagasaki. Japanese envoys dispatched to America in 1860 to establish ambassadorial relations accepted the institution of black slavery as a fact of life. They viewed the African slaves they encountered as timid ape-like creatures or as subhumans whom they equated with Japan's own outcasts, the *burakumin* (Wagatsuma and Yoneyama 1980; Miyoshi 1979). References to blacks in diaries kept by the delegation are more or less contemptuous and unsympathetic, describing them as pitifully stupid, grotesque, dirty, unmannered, and physically repulsive. In some cases, it appears these views were prompted by the comments of their white guides, as one such diary suggests: 'The faces of these natives are black, as if painted with ink and resemble those of monkeys. According to the Americans, they are the incarnations of apes' (Wagatsuma and Yoneyama 1980:64).

Contemporary literary representation of the Black Other has generally adhered to these early impressions. A brief survey of literary and visual representation of blacks in contemporary Japan reveals the persistence of racial stereotypes which ascribe to blacks the following characteristics: 1)infantilism 2) primitivism 3) hypersexuality, 4) bestiality, 5) natural athletic prowess or physical stamina, 6) mental inferiority, 7) psychological weakness, and 8) emotional volatility. But this tendency to dehumanize and belittle blacks disguises another tendency, particularly in literary works, to employ the Black Other as a reflexive symbol through which Japanese attempt deal with their own ambiguous racio-cultural status in a Eurocentric world where such hierarchies have been largely (and literally) conceived in terms of polarizations between black and white. Within these hierarchies Japanese, as Asians, have traditionally occupied a liminal state – a grey area – 'betwixt and between' the 'Civilized White' and the 'Barbarous Black' Other.

For the most part, Japan's image of the Black Other is deeply ensconced in the cushy deliriums of Euro-American supremacy. The dichotomy that the West had drawn between 'European Culture and Civilization' on the one hand and 'African Barbarity and Savagery' on the other, a paradigmatic hierarchy justified by the theological theory of the Great Chain of Being and the Social Darwinism of nineteenth-century anthropology and intellectual discourse, provided a conceptual base upon which Japan could erect its own hierarchy of racial otherness, but one in which its own position tenuously mediated color boundaries while maintaining Western centrality. The conventional wisdom, adopted by Japanese scholars, was to retain this hierarchy, placing Japan and its Asia neighbors between the two extremes. Thus Fukuzawa Yukichi in his *Outline of Civilization* (Bunmei-ron no Gairyaku, 1875) holds up an idealized West as the apex of 'civilization' (*bunmei*), deems Japan and its Asian neighbors 'semi-civilized' (*hankai*) and positions the African continent at its nadir, as a land of naked 'savages' (*yabanjin*) mired in barbarity. This hierarchy was consistent with contemporary Euro-American discourse that placed the 'Mongol race' between, as one nineteenth-century scholar wrote, 'the lowly blacks and the lofty whites'. Such attitudes about Africa were replicated in the imaginative geographies and stories about Africa written by Japanese during the nineteenth and early twentieth centuries. Their authors, adopting the vocabulary of their colonial mentors, refer to Africa as the 'Dark Continent' (*ankoku tairiku*), 'primitive' (*mikai; genshi*) and to Africans themselves with a large number of pejorative terms for 'native' or 'primitive' never applied to whites. (See Shirashi 1983:171–197 for a discussion of the impact of the nineteenth and early twentieth-century Western discourse on Africa in Japan.)

Modern Japanese narratives reproduce these tropes. For example, Endō Shūsaku's *Nigger* (Kuronbō, 1971), set in sixteenth-century Japan, is the fictional tale of Tsumpa, an African brought to Japan by a Jesuit missionary who has purchased him for slave traders out of compassion and taken him on as a man-servant. As the two make their way through Kyoto, the unfamiliar sight of a black man causes such a public uproar that daimyō Oda Nobunaga dispatches his retainers to investigate. Tsumpa and the missionary are brought before the daimyō and the African is made to perform for him.

> The missionaries were perplexed. Knowing the kind of man Nobunaga was, they knew they could not refuse his order. They knew that if the Negro humiliated Nobunaga, they would face his wrath. But they did not know what, if anything, the Negro could do. Until then they had only used him to carry their belongings and for his labor.
>
> 'What can he do?' Nobunaga asked. Valegnani [one of the missionaries] was completely nonplused. Organtin [another missionary] whispered Nobunaga's order to the Negro.
>
> Unexpectedly, the Negro laughed, revealing his white teeth. And beaming like a child, shouted. . . .
>
> The Negro made tapping gestures with his hands. 'Is it possible to borrow a drum . . .?'
>
> Organtin asked.
>
> A retainer quickly ran to fetch one.
>
> The Negro took up the drum and gazed on it happily like a child. After tapping experimentally on it with his fingers two and three times, his body began to sway and he started to sing in an unfamiliar language.
>
> Nobunaga watched the strange dance. The Negro was violently swaying back and forth, jumping up, and then – and then suddenly in front of the powerful Nobunaga something unheard of happened.
>
> Bu, bu, bu
>
> Pu, pu, pu
>
> At first, none knew where the sounds were coming from. But after a while, realization dawned. The two missionaries blanched. The sounds were being emitted from the Negro's buttocks. In rhythmic tones, high and low, strong and weak, [the Negro] was farting.
>
> (1973:20–21)

The sixteenth-century Japanese in this novel act as diary accounts from the period suggest they in fact did upon seeing Africans for the first time. They see Tsumpa as a dirty, semi-human creation, an *oni* (demon) – though one strikingly different from and inferior to the 'southern barbarians' (*nanbanjin*) to whom they have more or less grown accustomed. Indeed, upon first seeing the African, Nobunaga orders his retainers to bathe him to see whether his black skin will wash off.[1] What is problematic is not so much these depictions – which reflect contemporary narratives – as the character of Tsumpa as rendered by the modern-day, omniscient third-person narrator, a narrative tone which resurrects in a Japanese setting the Western stereotype of the African as a primitive, if in some cases saintly, Noble Savage. Although Tsumpa is described as a twenty-five year-old adult, his behavior throughout the novel is consistently rendered as infantile. He is a powerful giant, yet he seems more comfortable among the children he befriends. The image Endō presents in these scenes is one of gentle playmate and clown. The modern, ironic sensibility which pervades most of the novel and its depiction of feudal intrigue and political machinations does not extend to its portrait of the African, who emerges in the end as little more than an oversized child.

It is noteworthy that black characters often appear in Japanese stories in connection with children. Such juxtapositions are symbolically suggestive. On the one hand, the Black Other is often employed as a symbol of childhood alienation. Like his adolescent companions, the Black Other in these narratives is a tragic man-child, and it is through their association and identification with him that the Japanese adolescents in these narratives attempt to resolve some internal crisis and assume the burden of adult responsibilities. Both Ōe Kenzaburō's story 'The Catch' (Shiiku, 1958) and Itsuki Hiroyuki's 'Johnny Who Saw the Sea' (Umi o Mite Ita Johnny, 1966) describe relationships between Japanese male youths and black American GIs. These narratives, including Endō's *Nigger*, would seem to borrow the American literary convention of using the Black Other as a means of introducing an adolescent non-black protagonist to an unjust world of adults, marking their loss of innocence and naivete, as, for example, in Twain's *Huckleberry Finn*, Faulkner's *The Rievers*, or Carson McCuller's *Member of the Wedding*.

However, on another level, these narratives depict the Black Other as himself (black women rarely appear as major characters in Japanese fiction) child-like, as a weak, pitiful being whose confused and impotent attempts to master his environment are defeated in the end by forces beyond his control. This trope consistently appears in fictional works in which blacks figure, from Ariyoshi Sawako's *Not Because of Color* (Hishoku, 1967), to more recent works, such as Yamada Eimi's *Bedtime Eyes* (1987) and Morimura Shōichi's *Proof of the Man* (Ningen no Shōmei, 1977). In short, the Black Other is victim and underdog. The equation of blacks with children is implicit in the use of the diminutizing suffixes *-bō* and *-chan* employed to belittle blacks, as in such expressions as kuronbō and *kuro-chan* ('nigger'), the suffixes themselves connoting emotional immaturity and less than full adult status.[2]

The popularity of child and animal tropes is not limited to literary narratives. The association of blacks with children as 'playmates' also finds expression in consumer goods, such as the Dakko-chan doll popular during the 1960s and the recent line of Sambo products marketed in Japan, products which often blur the boundary between human – or perhaps more accurately homunculoid – and animal. For example, black character dolls are sometimes placed next to stuffed apes and other stuffed animal toys in shops. Indeed, when shown photographs of some of these goods, some Japanese interviewed for this study contended they thought they were not blacks but animals, apes of some kind; few seemed disturbed by their admission. Boundary blurring is also suggested by a line of floor mats called 'Animal Mats' that come in the shape of various animals, but which include two in the form of a black male and female domestic. Nor are popular media immune: In the Japanese-dubbed version of the television series *The A-Team* the black character played by Mr. T is renamed 'Kong'. Finally, there is the story of a black woman on a suburban Tokyo train where a little girl reportedly pointed to her in fascination and asked her father, 'Daddy, what is that?' The embarrassed father, trying to satisfy her curiosity by reminding her of the Chinese fable *Journey to the West* (Saiyūki), prods her to recall Songoku, the simian hero of the tale (*Los Angeles Times*, 1 January 1990).

Japan, The West, and the Search for Identity

As I mentioned previously, Japanese images of blacks are inextricably linked to Japan's unequal relationship with the West. With the importation of Dutch learning, Japanese acquired not only a taste for Western science but also for Western prejudices against blacks and other subjected races. The stereotype of the black as comic jester and quintessential entertainer was introduced to the Japanese as early as 1854 when Commodore Matthew Perry, returning to Edo

Bay to conclude a trade treaty with Japan, treated Japanese negotiators to an 'Ethiopian' minstrel show, performed by white crew members in black-face ('a serenade of pseudo-darkies', as one witness to the performance put it) aboard the flagship *Powhatan*. According to crew diaries, the Japanese were quite delighted by the comical, cavorting 'blacks' (Barr 1965:37, Heine 1990:169).

European art trends and American films also influenced the way Japanese came to perceive and depict the Black Other.[3] An example of the influence and longevity of Western stereotypes is the Calpis beverage company's popular 'kuronbō minstrel' trademark, designed in 1923 by German artist Otto Dünkelsbühler and which adorned bottles of the soft-drink in Japan until 1989.[4] While certainly more stylish than similar black caricatures, Dünkelsbühler's black minstrel evokes European modernism's fascination with 'Negro primitivism'. The influence of his design is evident in an illustration which appears in a 1987 English conversation text, though the original's fashionable black dandy has been replaced by a less sophisticated 'aboriginal' cousin.

The legacy of such Western conventions is further evident in the work of twentieth century Japanese illustrators. The black 'primitives' (*bankō*) the child-king Dankichi encounters in Shimada Keizō's popular children's book *The Adventuresome Dankichi* (Bōken Dankichi), serialized from July 1933 to February 1939 (Figure 1), are in the Sambo mode. They are comical entities with bulging eyes, misshapen ears, and bulbous white lips, a depiction not noticeably different from that which prevailed in American animated cartoons of the same period. A more direct influence can be observed in the work of Tezuka Osamu, the 'Walt Disney of Japan,' whose black 'primitives' in such works as *Jungle Emperor* (Janguru Taitei), serialized in comic book form from February 1950 to April 1954, show the stylistic signature of his namesake, as well as Shimada's, whose work he admired. Like Shimada, Tezuka follows the imaginary geography laid down by the Western view of Africa and its inhabitants, borrowing inspiration from the popularity of the Tarzan films of the 1930s and 1940s, a genre he attempted to imitate in such early works as *Jungle World of Devils* (Janguru Makyō, 1948), *Tarzan's Secret Base* (Tarzan no Himitsu Kichi, 1948) and in subsequent works.

In *Jungle Emperor* Tezuka replaces the Shimada's child-king Dankichi with Leo, the white lion cub protagonist. Like his predecessor, Tezuka's narrative condescends to the Africans; two of its

Figure 1 'Black' savages, Shimada Keizō's *The Adventurous Dankichi* circa 1933

recurring human protagonists – the Tarzan-like Japanese youth Ken'ichi and the white Mary, whom the Africans have enthroned as their Queen/Goddess – are depicted as superior to the Africans. Within this fabulous landscape, the author combines three processes: 1) the anthropomorphization of the story's animal protagonist; 2) the deification of its non-black protagonists; and 3) the subhumanization of the black Africans, who are depicted as less civilized and far more inept than the creatures with whom they share their jungle habitat.

Helen Bannerman's *The Story of Little Black Sambo* (1899) sees the continuation of this stylistic legacy, though it is important to note that while introduced to Japan during the Meiji Period (1868–1912), it did not obtain widespread recognition until 1953 when a new version, complete with 'pickaninny' illustrations, was published by Iwanami Shoten as part of a new line of children books. Although published well after the convention of representing blacks in the Western stereotypical mode had taken root, its popularity (120 versions have appeared since) and influence in shaping the Japanese image of the Black Other should not be underestimated.

As I suggested earlier, the Black Other serves as a repository for certain negatively sanctioned values ('impurity', 'primitivism', 'laziness,' techno-cultural 'underdevelopment' and 'backwardness'), yet it also serves as a convenient instrument for the search for Japanese racial identity. In some ways the Black Other occupies the same symbolic space and function as do burakumin and Koreans, two categories of Other with which blacks are often equated (Ohnuki-Tierney 1987). While the former serve reflexively to remind Japanese of their identity as Japanese, the Black Other serves as a reflexive symbol through which Japanese attempt to reappraise their status vis-à-vis whites and the symbolic power (e.g., modernity, enlightenment, European-style civility and High Culture) they are seen to represent; that is, it is employed as a category mediating White Otherness and Japanese Selfhood, forcing Japanese, particularly those who have lived abroad, to rethink their identification with whites and valorization of Eurocentric aesthetic and cultural values. Such reflexive use of the blacks expresses itself in two ways: 1) The Japanese agent/narrator may continue to accept the racial status quo and see oneself as an excluded and inferior other vis-à-vis Euro-American norms but attempt to compensate for the perceived deficiencies by elevating him or herself above other 'backward' groups; 2) He/she may identify with the Black Other, asserting solidarity with non-whites in general as a fellow *yūshokujin* (person of color), and reject the racial status quo.

An example of the former can be found in Endō Shūsaku's *Up to Aden* (Aden Made, 1954) which is noteworthy for the negative symbology it attaches to the color black and the author's frank admission of his own feelings of inferiority toward whites. In one scene the narrator, returning home by ship from study abroad in France after an ill-fated love affair with a French woman, shares a fourth-class cabin with an dying African woman.

> Lying down in the fourth class cabin, I stare at the feverish brown body of the sick [African] woman before me. I truly feel her skin color is ugly. The color black is ugly, yellow even more so. This black woman and I both belong eternally to ugly races. I have no idea how or why only the skin of white people became the standard of beauty, nor how or why the standard of human beauty in sculpture and painting are all derived from the white bodies of the Greeks and remains

so today. But I am certain that with regard to the body, those like myself and this black woman can never forget the miserable feelings of inferiority in front of white people, however disturbing such an admission may be.

(1971:161)

An example of the latter reflexive use is provided by the nonfiction works of photo-journalist Yoshida Ruiko, particularly in her debut work *Hot Harlem Days* (Haremu no Atsui Hibi, 1967), an account of her experiences living in New York's Harlem during the heyday of the Black Power movement and a provocative critique of American racial hierarchies.

But why did I, a Japanese, want to continue to photograph blacks? Of course, the environment in which I happened to be placed was a factor, as well as the discovery that I could capture [their] beautiful images. But now back in Japan I realize that was not all. Their continued history of struggle and oppression and reawakening to their blackness, unconsciously compelled me to project my own identity as a yellow person placed among other races in a racist national state [*jinshushugi kokka*]. A desperate defiance as a yellow woman placed between black and white [*kuro to shiro no aida ni okareta kiiroi josei*] was also a factor. Whenever I took photographs of [their] dazzling, shiny black skin, I felt as if some yellow fluid like mustard were seeping from my skin.

(1979:216)

Concluding her book Yoshida writes:

Hot Harlem Days is a coming-of-age record of the maturation of one yellow-skinned woman's [*kiiroi hada no onna*] life in an American black ghetto in the 1960s At the same time, it is also a journal of one person's search for self-identity, a person who – like blacks – is a minority in American society.

(1979:226)

Yoshida's use of terms like *ōshokujin* (yellow person) and *hada no kiiroi onna* (yellow-skinned woman) and her identification of herself as a 'minority' is a deliberate statement of her solidarity with other people of color, a consciousness she tells the reader she did not possess until her experiences in America. In this and subsequent works, Yoshida rejects Western racial hierarchies, while criticizing her compatriots, particularly the Japanese intelligentsia, for their uncritical embrace of them and oppression of minorities at home.

Western hegemony and Japan's subordinate relation to the West have had a profound effect on the Japanese self-image as well as their image of the non-white Other. The West has played a pivotal role not only in introducing Japan to the Black Other but in defining the parameters of culture and civilization in general. Given Western hegemony and cultural authority and its lavish display of modernity and material power in Japan and elsewhere, it is not surprising that in its attempt to catch up with the West Japan began to identify with it. At the same time, it has peripheralized cultural links with its Asian neighbors whose influence on Japan waned with the expansion of Euro-American power in the Pacific.

This alignment can be detected in the 'Caucasianization' of Japanese as Western fashion and aesthetic sensibilities begin to take root, flowering in the Meiji Period and again in the 1920s in the form of *moga* and *mobo*, 'modern girls and boys'. Epitomized by the character of Naomi in Tanizaki Jun'ichirō's *Naomi* (Chijin no Ai, 1924), these youth modeled their appearance on contemporary Western silent film stars. Nor did the anti-Western rhetoric of the Second World War prevent Japanese from depicting themselves as Caucasian in physical appearance, in effect, '[distancing] themselves physically from the "darker" peoples of Asia' (Dower 1986:209). This is a convention that survives today in comics and animated cartoons. According to Dower, the anti-white, anti-Western rhetoric of the war years was 'reactive' and had 'no clear counterpart in the racism of white supremacists' (1986:204). Japanese racism was preoccupied with elevating the Japanese and with 'wrestling with what it really meant to be Japanese' (1986:205). While the 'reactive' nature of Japanese racism may account in part for the anti-white racism of the war years, neither it nor theories which link Japanese racial attitudes to culturally informed prejudices regarding skin color adequately explains anti-black racism in Japan. To account for the latter, one must recognize the impact of Western hegemony and the other factor Dower cites specifically, namely the Japanese preoccupation with racial elevation and desire to distance themselves from races subjected by Western power and whose plight Japan hoped to avoid by acquiring the accoutrements – material and intellectual – of a powerful, implacable colossus.

This attempt to distance the 'Japanese' self from the darker Other, is nicely described in Endō Shūsaku's autobiographical novel, *Studies Abroad* (Ryūgaku, 1965). Early in the novel the protagonist is invited to a party at a restaurant in Lyons by a Japanese friend. Also in attendance are a Roman Catholic priest, several French women and two black Moroccan students, Paulin and Magiro, who have been studying in Paris. Symbolically, Paulin represents what author V.S. Naipaul has termed a 'mimic man', a non-white who attempts to ingratiate himself with whites by adopting Western ways as his own but whom whites find humorous. Even the narrator finds the African, with his coarse hair slicked down with oil and parted in the middle in imitation of a French gentleman, a wretched, pitiful figure.

In one telling scene the priest introduces the protagonist's companion to Paulin, but the Japanese student is so startled by the contrast between the pink palms and black skin of African's extended hand that he pulls back his own in an involuntary reflex of physical repulsion. Later, one of the women requests that one of the African students sing a 'traditional' song for them. Both the Japanese protagonist and the French view the singing African as a miserable if unintentionally comic figure.

> Paulin spread his legs wide and began to clap out a beat. His body swayed as he sang. His voice was shrill and the exaggerated movements of his body were enough to embarrass the onlookers. The Catholic priest chewed his pipe stifling a laugh and the women, unable to bear it all, turned away. It was clear to Kudō that the women did not find his dancing and singing attractive. Yet Paulin continued to sing anyway. He was deliberately planning to endear himself with these women.
>
> Kudō, trying his best not to look in their direction, averted his eyes. As the student named Paulin sang, he knew almost too painfully what his true motives were. The Negro is singing that stupid song to ingratiate himself with the white women. He thinks that will endear them to him.
>
> After Paulin had finished singing, the priest, his pipe still fixed in his mouth, placed his hand on Paulin's shoulder. The brown brow and cheeks of the Negro student dripped with sweat, the sweat of a slave forced to perform hard labor.
>
> 'Do the Japanese go in for such singing and dancing?'
>
> Kudō glared at the priest and blurted, 'Absolutely not! We . . .'

> The priest had not understood Kudō's feelings. Somewhat nonplussed, he said quietly, 'No, no, of course. I only meant we'd heard that Japanese songs are artistic'.
>
> (1968:34–35)

Aside from the suggestion of an implicit sexual rivalry between the Japanese and the African for the attention of the white women, the scene suggests that for Kudō the black is an uncomfortable reminder of his own insecure status to whites. Kudō's strong reaction to the priest's innocent suggestion that Japanese might have something in common with these Africans prompts his angry outburst and would seem to indicate that the presence of these dark, unsophisticated interlopers has shattered his delusive identification with European culture.

A rather remarkable but by no means exceptional example of distancing in the form of racio-cultural one-upmanship – where Japanese hoist whites on their own supremacist petard by elevating themselves above whites but at the expense of other non-whites – is evident in the following excerpt from psychiatrist Ōhara Kenshirō's popular study of mental depression, *The Age of Depression* (Utsubyō no Jidai, 1981).

> It is well known that compared to America the number of suicides in our country is high and I have already touched upon the close relationship between depression and suicide. In fact, one cannot think of them without reference to self-punishment and guilt. Dr Kraines, an authority on depression, in comparing the suicide and homicide rates of whites and black Americans has suggested that suicide among whites is higher and that a reason for this is that whites tend to direct aggression internally upon the self in contrast to blacks who tend to direct their aggression externally. He has suggested that the level of culture of whites is higher than blacks. Following this premise, the Japanese, who have a higher suicide rate than white Americans, have a higher level of culture than Americans.
>
> (1981: 173–74)

In connection with distancing and elevation, I would like briefly to discuss two other related processes: 'negrofictation' and 'primitization'. In both the image of the Black Other is forced to conform to certain stylized, Procrustean categories – preconditioned 'pictures in the head', as Walter Lippman aptly referred to stereotypes – that serve to maintain a conceptual distance between Self and Other. In short, the integrity of the stereotype must be preserved despite contradictory evidence; external reality made to conform to the internal dictates of representational conceits so that the conceptual center holds.

In Japan, negrofictation manifests itself both visually and vocally. Visual negrofictation is evident in the caricatures of Carl Lewis, Ben Johnson, and the Tanzanian runner Jima Ikanga in an illustration that appeared in the 1988 Seoul Olympics edition of the television program guide *TelePal* and in the grossly deformed black mannequins that appeared in front of a Tokyo department store in 1988 (Figure 2).

Such grotesqueries run the fine line between caricature and stereotype. Whereas caricatures exaggerate existing personal characteristics. negrofictation substitutes exaggerated racial features – here markers of pseudo-negritude (e.g., thick, bulbous lips, banjo-eyes, flaring nostrils) – where they do not objectively apply to the individual who serves as model, thus forcing a fit where one is absent. The distinction is a subtle one, but one which must be kept

Figure 2 Black mannequins pose 'stylishly' in front of a Tokyo department store (*Washington Post*, 22 July 1988)

in mind given the proliferation and popularity in Japan of *mono-mane* (comical mimicry), caricature and stylized portraiture in which popular Japanese celebrities are rendered in ways that might strike an outside observer as racist had a non-Japanese done them. The pervasiveness of these markers of pseudo-negritude has made it virtually impossible for some Japanese even to conceive of representing blacks non-stereotypically. For example, some Japanese informants interviewed for this study suggested that without them they would be unable to identify such figures as black; in such light, non-stereotyped representation seems to be regarded as oxymoronic. Visual negrofictation seems to be a twentieth-century phenomenon. Edo and Meiji-period prints render black-skinned servants in the same 'Tengu' mode (i.e., with long, narrow faces dominated by elongated phallic noses) used for white foreigners, distinguishing them from their white masters by costume (many are bare-footed), hair texture, and black or grayish skin color. Indeed, the black Africans in the Yokohama Prints of Meiji artist Hashimoto Sadahide are rendered with dignity and sympathy (Figure 3). And it would appear that the convention of representing dark-skinned people in the Sambo-mold favored in the West is not standardized until the turn of the century.

Vocal negrofictation frequently occurs when the voices of blacks are dubbed into Japanese. It is not an uncommon practice among Japanese TV producers to substitute coarse, deep-throated, or high-pitched, whinny voices – often rich in dialect – for those of black males even when the speakers' original voices are otherwise race-neutral and dialect-free. The standardization of voices to 'fit' certain categories of Other is not limited to blacks. One encounters it in quiz and news programs where stylized vocalizations, substituting for the foreigner's original voice, are used to impose essentialistic qualities (*rashisa*) based on the speaker's perceived class, gender, and age.

Primitization of the Black Other is a ubiquitous feature of Japanese documentaries/game shows. 'Primitives' and rural villages are frequently chosen as objects for presentation and comparison and made to fill the role. A recent example is the case of N'Xkau, the South African !Kung and 'star' of *The Gods Must be Crazy* (1979) who, following the popularity of the film in Japan and a subsequent Japanese television feature on his life in the South African 'bush', was invited to Japan. Whatever the producer's intent, the result was to juxtapose the !Kung's 'endearing primitiveness' against

Figure 3 Yokohama print of black servants by Meiji artist Hashimoto Sadahide circa 1860

the 'modernity' and 'sophistication' of urban Tokyo. Indeed, N'Xkau treatment and Japanese reaction to him recalls a scene from *Nigger* in which the Tsumpa becomes a sideshow attraction. Producers may also request that their 'primitives' appear in traditional (i.e. 'tribal') wear despite the fact that Western attire is not unknown to them. If genuine primitives are unavailable, they can be manufactured and their reactions orchestrated, as when a group from a Kenyan village (again, attired natively) were invited to Japan a few years back and directed by the studio sponsoring them to display before the cameras bemusement and wonder at the marvels of hi-tech Tokyo, since apparently that was what viewers should expect from real exotics.

Transvaluation

Recent trends in Japanese literary representation of the Black Other tend to portray blacks as sexual objects, studs, fashion accessories and quintessential performers, images that imported American media reinforce daily. Consider the following passage from a Japanese guidebook to New York's ethnic diversity:

> At parties thrown by whites, just having a fashionable black guest who dances skillfully adds life to party. This effect is so well known in New York that [whites] boast that they have stylish black friends. In fact, when [white] New Yorkers assemble with their friends to sing, dance, and drink, if there are just a few blacks the party will come to life. They may be natural entertainers. However, more than anything else the blacks themselves seem to enjoy playing the role of entertainer.
>
> (Nagasawa and Miyamoto 1986:136)

Just as the image of the Black Other in the West as bumbling Stepin Fetchit and contented domestic was eventually replaced with the threatening superstuds of 1970s blaxploitation films, such as *Shaft* and *Superfly*, a similar transvaluation seems to have taken place in Japanese mass culture. Though stereotypes of blacks as sexual athletes and born entertainers are not new, they were perhaps given greater distributive currency during the Occupation and the Korean War with the influx of black GIs and American popular culture and through Japanese exposure to racist white GIs who were not above spreading the seeds of their racism overseas: once warned by government propaganda of the propensities of Americans for rape and carnage, Japanese were now being told similar horror stories about blacks by white American GIs.[5]

With the Vietnam War, the rise of the counter-culture and the influx of black popular music and culture, disaffected Japanese youth came to see the African American as a counter to the values of the Japanese establishment and the Black Other was adopted as a symbol of defiance, forbidden fruit, and their own alienation from the Japanese mainstream.

This change in attitude is suggested in Murakami Ryū's Akutagawa Prize-winning novel *Almost Transparent Blue* (Kagirinaku Tōmei ni Chikai Burū, 1976), an explicit tale of decadence that graphically depicts the sexual exploits of a group of disaffected Japanese youths involved with black GIs stationed at Yokota Air Base. Drug use, orgies, and human debasement dominate this novel of sexual excess in which stereotypes of black sexuality abound.[6]

The trope of the African American male as sexual athlete and priapic paramour acquires a masturbatory redundancy in the works of Yamada Eimi, a prolific young writer whose sexually graphic fictions consistently take as their theme torrid love affairs between Japanese women and black GIs. Her debut novel *Bedtime Eyes* explores the relationship between Kim, a naive Japanese club singer and Joseph 'Spoon' Johnson, a Harlem-born GI who has gone AWOL and who is secretly selling military secrets to an unidentified foreign power.

'Spoon' – the nickname resonates with phallic symbolism – is the ultimate priapic stud, a smooth operator, and stylish hustler. Their relationship is a purely physical one. Some Japanese reviewers of the novel have praised Yamada for the frankness of her descriptions, her refusal to substitute flowery euphemisms for the sex act. Instead she invests her novel with Anglo-Saxon vulgarisms and a dry, almost clinical naturalism.

Yamada's other works, as well as images of blacks found in American films, have sparked a renewed media interest in, nearly a preoccupation with, black sexuality.[7] The result has been a breakdown of the boundaries between private and public culture. What had once been a taboo subject, the relations between black GIs and Japanese women, suddenly became a topic fit for open discussion, sensational serials in Japanese magazines, late-night television debate, and underground cinema. It is worth noting that only a few decades before the publication of *Bedtime Eyes*, Yoshida Ruiko complained of the preoccupation of Japanese colleagues who would take her aside to ask whether she had slept with blacks or, assuming that she had, to ask that she rate their sexual performance. By 1984, however, TV stations were sending crews to Roppongi and American bases in Yokota and Yokosuka to ask Japanese women dating black men the same questions and broadcasting their responses for inquiring minds at home.

Conclusion

The representation of blacks follows conventions largely derived from Western racial categories and hierarchies. Contemporary images – more old wine in new bottles or, better put, old stereotypes in new media – continue to rely on Western conventions, though some of these conventions, as in the case of the Sambo imagery, may have passed out of usage in the West itself. While Japanese themselves often fail to recognize these images as racist (a response not unlike that of whites when first confronted with their black stereotypes), Japanese representation of blacks tends to be condescending and to debase, dehumanize, exoticize, and peripheralize the Black Other, who at once serves as a symbolic counterpoint to modernity, rationalism, and civility – and as an uncomfortable reminder of the insecurities and ambiguity of Japanese racial and cultural identity vis-à-vis an idealized West.

Notes

Research for this paper was supported by a grant from the Japan Foundation, 1989–1990. All translations are mine.

1 In many ways Tsumpa the African is a black counterpart to Gaston, the titular 'wonderful fool' of Endō's novel of the same name, *Obakasan* (1959). Both are fish out of water, clown/mediators (see Ohnuki-Tierney 1987), whose misadventures in Japan satirize Japanese foibles. Gaston's is the face of reasoned civilization, Tsumpa's that of primitive, uncultured innocence: the African's black skin inspires scatological associations. Indeed, at the beginning of the novel Tsumpa's arrival is predicted by an old fortune-teller whose predictions are inspired by inspecting his client's feces. Upon inspecting the feces of a young woman client the fortune-teller informs her that she will soon meet a strange man who will pass in front of her house. The prediction proves correct, for the next day Tsumpa and company arrive in town. Shimada Keizō's *Bōken Dankichi* offers a variation of the scene in *Kuronbō* where Tsumpa is ordered to bathe to demonstrate to Nobunaga that his skin color is natural and not a deception. In Shimada's inverted version, the Japanese child-king covers his body in mud to pass as a native in order to escape from cannibals, only to have his deception ruined, predictably, by a sudden rain storm. The equation of blacks with dirt in both is obvious.

2 One reason for the popularity in Japan of Bannerman's *The Story of Little Black Sambo* may owe, in part, to the coincidential affinity the character's name has with other terms which employ the dimunitizing *-bō* suffix (*kuronbō*, 'nigger', 'a darkie', 'little black one'; *akanbō*, 'a baby', 'little red one'; *okorinbō*, or a person who easily angers, 'a little petulant one'), and may explain why many Japanese, who are unaware of its racist etymology, regard the term as cute and endearing.

3 Contemporary images of blacks in Japan are more or less variations of archetypes derived from American cinema. For example, Tarzan-like characters, complete with 'savage natives', are a staple of Japanese animation. *Gone with the Wind* still enjoys tremendous popularity in Japan on video and in theatrical revival and a musical version is part of the repertoire of the all-woman Takarazuka musical revue. Donald Bogle in his much overlooked *Toms, Coons, Mulattoes, Mammies and*

Bucks (1973) notes that American cinematic stereotypes of blacks are multivalent and often contradictory, stereotypes of blacks as 'pickaninnies', slow-witted 'coons', and timorous 'darkies' co-existing with those of threatening subhumans, lascivious rapists, and domesticated militants. These ambivalent images are presently embodied in the personas of the Child-Eunuch Michael Jackson and the Priapic Prince, both of whom fall within Bogle's tragic mulatto category. On the other hand, rap images revolts against the desexualization and mulattoization of the black male.

Although on its surface the iconography of posturing black macho would seem consistent with the stereotype of the threatening black male, the subtext is largely subversive, using it to promote a positive, uncompromising black self-image. However, the popularity of rap music among Japanese youth would seem to lie less in the subversive content of its socio-political message than in its counter-fashion (*han-seisō*) statements and danceability (*nori ga ii*), all of which ultimately serving to confirm black stereotypes.

4 Negative reaction in America and the efforts of Japanese activists prompted many Japanese companies to cease production of stereotypical black character goods and company trademarks. In 1988 Iwanami Shoten ceased publication of the book; other publishers followed suit. Calpis and Takara (the manufacturer of Dakko-chan) abandoned use of their black character trademarks in 1989.

5 The Occupation not only helped export antiblack racism to Japan, it also gave the Japanese the means of reproducing it for white consumption back in the States by encouraging production of stereotyped black figurines under the 'Made in Occupied Japan' label. Other stereotypes are not so benign. The image of the black GI as rapist has become something of a staple of Japanese pornography and films about the Occupation (Buruma 1984:57). The black rapist trope also appears in Matsumoto Seichō's short-story *Kuroji no E* (Picture on Black Cloth, 1965) and in adult comic books.

6 The film version, directed by Murakami, soft-peddles the novel's explicit interracial sex scenes and is tame even by the censor-sensitive standards of Japanese visual pornography. Only one orgy scene survives; the partially clad black actors engage in stylized writhing atop their Japanese partners, yet never so much as even kiss them, as if the director believed such intimate contact contaminating.

7 Reviewers frequently apply such terms as *mondai sakuhin* or *mondai shōsetsu* (controversial novel) to Yamada's works, stressing their 'shock value' and 'taboo-breaking' content. Yet given the ubiquity of the black rapist trope, the shock value of her books would seem to owe less to their miscegenational themes than to the suggestion that Japanese women would willfully select blacks as sexual partners.

References

Ariyoshi Sawako 1967 *Hishoku* (Not Because of Color), Tokyo: Kadokawa Shoten.

Bannerman, Helen 1899 *The Story of Little Black Sambo*, London: Grant Richards; Okabe Furuhiko, trans. 1953 *Chibikuro Sambo*, Tokyo: Iwanami Shoten.
Barr, Patricia 1967 *The Coming of the Barbarians*. London: Penguin.
Bogle, Donald 1973 *Toms, Coons, Mulattoes, Mammies and Bucks*, New York: Viking Press.
Buruma, Ian 1984 *Behind the Mask*, New York: New American Library.
Dower, John W. 1986 *War without Mercy*, New York: Pantheon.
Endō Shūsaku 1973 [1971] *Kuronbō* (Nigger), Tokyo: Kadokawa Bunko.
—— 1968 [1965] *Ryūgaku* (Studies Abroad), Tokyo: Shinchō Bunko.
—— 1954 'Aden made' (Up to Aden), p. 151–179 in 1971 *Shiroi Hito/Kiiroi Hito* (*White People/Yellow People*), Tokyo: Kōdansha Bunko.
Heine, William 1990 [1856] *With Perry to Japan*, Honolulu: University of Hawaii Press.
Itsuki Hiroyuki 1966 *Umi o mite ita Johnny* (Johnny Who Saw the Sea), Tokyo: Kōdansha Bunko.
Ivy, Marilyn 1989 'Critical texts, mass artifacts: the consumption of knowledge in postmodern Japan', p. 24–46 in M. Miyoshi and H.D. Harootunian (eds.) 1989 *Postmodernism and Japan*, Durham: Duke University Press.
Matsumoto Seichō 1965 *Kuroji no E* (Picture on black cloth), p. 69–129 in 1965 *Kuroji no E: meisaku tanpenshū II* (*Picture on Black Cloth: the collected stories of Matsumoto Seichō Vol. II*), Tokyo: Shinchō Bunko.
Morimura Shōichi 1977 *Ningen no Shōmei* (*Proof of the Man*), Tokyo: Kōdansha Bunko.
Murakami Ryū 1976 *Kagirinaku Tōmei ni Chikai Burū* (*Almost Transparent Blue*), Tokyo: Kōdansha Bunko.
Miyoshi, Masao 1979 *As We Saw Them*, Berkeley: University of California Press.
Miyoshi, Masao and H.D. Harootunian (eds.) 1989 *Postmodernism and Japan*, Durham: Duke University Press.
Nagasawa Makoto and Miyamoto Michiko 1986 *I Love New York*, Tokyo: Bunshun Bunko.
Naipaul, V.S. 1967 *The Mimic Men*, Harmondsworth: Penguin.
Ōe Kenzaburō 1958 'Shiiku' (The catch), p. 73–129 in 1959 *Shisha no Ogori – Shiiku* ('The Extravagance of the Dead' and 'The Catch'), Tokyo: Shinchō Bunko.
Ōhara Kenshirō. 1981 *Utsubyō no Jidai* (*The Age of Depression*), Tokyo: Kōdansha Gendai Shinsho.
Ohnuki-Tierney, Emiko 1987 *The Monkey as Mirror*, Princeton: Princeton University Press.
Said, Edward W. 1978 *Orientalism*, New York: Pantheon.
Sakai, Naoki 1989 'Modernity and its critique: the problem of universalism and particularism', p. 93–122 in M. Miyoshi and H.D. Harootunian (eds.) 1989 *Postmodernism and Japan*, Durham: Duke University Press.
Shimada Keizō 1933–39 *Bōken Dankichi* (*The Adventurous Dankichi*), Tokyo: Shogakkan.
Shiraishi Kenji 1983 'Kindai Nihon no Afurika ninshiki shikiron' (A preliminary essay on modern Japan's knowledge of Africa), p. 171–197 in

Ōsaka Ni-Futsu Sentâ (ed.) *Seiō Afurika vs. Nippon* (Western Europe and Africa vs. Japan), Tokyo: Daisan Shokan.
Spector, Dave 1984 *It's Only a Joke!*, Tokyo: Ark.
Wagatsuma Hiroshi 1967 'The social perception of skin color in Japan,' p. 407–43 in *Daedalus* (Spring).
Wagatsuma Hiroshi and Yoneyama Toshinao 1980 *Henken no Kōzō* (*The Structure of Prejudice*), Tokyo: NHK Books.
Yamada Eimi 1987 *Bedtime Eyes*, Tokyo: Kawade Bunko.
Yoshida Ruiko 1979 [1967] *Haremu no Atsui Hibi* (*Hot Harlem Days*), Tokyo: Kōdansha.

2

In Pursuit of Perfection

The Discourse of Cars and Transposition of Signs in Two Advertising Campaigns

Brian Moeran

Introducing Road Signs

The successful economic development of most industrialized countries has depended much on the successful manufacture of automobiles. The spread in the ownership and use of cars has not only led to the development of massive dependent industries, but to the deskilling of labour, the creation of road-systems, the transformation of cities and of society as a whole (Wernick 1991:72). As an invention of industrialization and mass production, the automobile was soon the object of pre-planned technological and stylistic obsolescence as a means of promoting and sustaining a consumption ethic. This first occurred in the United States in the mid-1920s (Marchand 1985:156–158). In Japan, mass aspiration for car ownership came with that for colour television sets and coolers (air conditioners) in the early 1960s (the so-called 'age of the 3 Cs'). Still, in 1962, when the first 'product planned' car in Europe, the Ford Cortina, was launched, the Japanese automobile industry was able to export just one thousand cars a year to Europe (Bailey 1986:87). Now, as we are all aware, that figure has multiplied by more than a thousand times, so that Japanese car manufacturers have become the focus of economic and political attention in a global economy.

At the same time, 'more than any other manufactured product, the car enshrines and projects the values of the culture which created it' (Bailey 1986:101) – whether about consumption (Marchand 1985:157), consumers (Williamson 1978:52–53; Marchand 1985:137–140), the manufacturer himself (Marchand 1985:306), sex (Williamson 1978:85, 121; Posener 1982; Bailey 1986; Moeran 1990), family (Vestergaard and Schrøder 1983:135–136; Marchand

1985:161; Wernick 1991:72), art (Marchand 1985:128–129, 141), technology (Wernick 1991:70–91), the relationship generally between machines and nature (Williamson 1978:129–131), and so on.

This paper is about the creation and communication of values such as these in two print media advertising campaigns for cars in Britain and Japan. In Japan as elsewhere, the rise of popular culture is linked to the decline in the relative prestige and visibility of high culture during the latter half of the 20th century, and this decline is itself closely connected with the increased size and importance of the culture industries (Crane 1992:34). One such industry is, of course, advertising – one of whose major clients in Japan has been the automobile industry, and whose total turnover in Japan alone increased ten times between 1956 and 1970, doubled again between 1970 and 1977, and doubled yet again between 1977 and 1986, before expanding yet further into the 1990s.[1] It is precisely during this period that serious discussion of advertising as a popular cultural form has begun to take place.

It has been pointed out that those writing about advertising have a tendency to mimic the object of their study and try to attract attention by making exaggerated claims which the product on offer cannot possibly measure up to (Sinclair 1989:1). Hopefully, the claims made here are rather modest: namely, that there are two drawbacks to the kind of hermeneutic (structural and post-structural) interpretations of advertisements (and, indeed, of other popular cultural forms) generally practised by academic analysts. Firstly, they address ads (and, by extension, popular cultural forms) as single semiotic entities and finished products, and secondly, they fail to consider the marketing strategies and social processes involved in their creation.

Much of the postwar work on advertising (for example, Barthes 1977 or Williamson 1978) has picked out for comment particular advertisements for particular products (Panzani Italian food, for example, or Good Year tyres) to illustrate a particular theoretical argument (the relation between denoted and connoted messages, or the existence of 'referent systems'). Although commentators may be aware of the fact that products exist as part of a whole range of other products – either of the same type (e.g. perfumes) or marketed under the same label (e.g. various cosmetics products by Chanel) – and are thus given their identity both singly and in groups (Williamson 1978:28), they still tend to analyse advertisements as separate entities. So readings tend to be selective, not just in *how* they interpret relations between signifiers and signifieds, but in *which* ads are chosen for interpretation and which are ignored (Leiss et al 1990:225). In order to overcome such selectivity and to build on the semiotic approach, I wish to start from the fact that every advertisement is part of a *series* of similar advertisements which themselves constitute a total *sales*, and not just advertising, campaign, the usual aim of which is to sell a product, brand,[2] or corporate image. As such, ads are likely to achieve their meanings by referring to earlier advertisements for the same product, or across product lines (Wernick 1991:92–93).[3] In order to understand the meaning of individual advertisements for a particular product, therefore, I think it helps if we take account of the *campaign* as a whole, of present and past campaigns for that product, and of the advertising of similar, but competing products. It is this self-referring quality of advertising which allows us to talk of *intertextuality* or the 'transposition' of one or more sign systems with one another (Kristeva 1984:59–60).

Which brings me to a second, related point. Precisely because 'advertising is a discourse through and about objects which bonds together images of persons, products, and well-being' (Leiss et al 1990:5; see also Jhally 1990:1), it helps if we can move away from seeing advertisements as bounded semiotic *products* and look, instead, at why and how such products are created. In other words, we should try, wherever possible, to take account of the marketing problems and aims faced by a particular advertiser and underlying a particular campaign. At the same time, if we have the good fortune to be able to observe the social *processes* that go into a campaign, we can arrive at a broader understanding of what precisely this 'discourse through and about objects' is trying to communicate. Here I am referring to the ways in which advertisements are actually put together by people in an advertising agency, whose main concerns are with client liaison, market research, creative work, and media planning.[4] Although I have partly addressed this issue elsewhere (Moeran 1993a), I wish here to take two advertisements in order to illustrate how different kinds of knowledge of each campaign as a whole affect our reading of the individual ads concerned.

Toyota and the Perfect Car

Let us start with an advertisement by Toyota which appeared in a number of different general interest magazines in England during the late summer and autumn of 1989, and try to read it off in the standard hermeneutic manner (Figure 1).

The headline, 'Why we'll never make a perfect car', makes it clear that this particular advertisement is concerned with the idea of 'perfection' – an idea reinforced by the Chinese character *kan*, which on its own means 'perfect', but which is here glossed in English as: 'If perfection could be attained, it would not be worth having'. The idea of perfection is also presumably intimated by the visual of a Toyota Supra Turbo placed in the middle of what the body copy refers to as 'the old Zen garden'.

In what does this total concept of perfection consist? Of three basic elements. On the one hand, perfection – or, since perfection itself is impossible, near perfection – is seen by Toyota to be a result of its *technological* achievements. Such achievements – the body copy informs us – have won the car manufacturer 'the Japanese Society of Mechanical Engineers' Award for engine design four years in a row', and include such innovations as 'catalytic converters, platinum spark plugs, galvanealed steel, Excelite' and various other – to the layman, incomprehensible – bits and pieces that go into the construction of advanced technological wizardry to which we are becoming accustomed, if not necessarily attuned.

On the other hand, perfection is *aesthetic*. The Toyota Supra Turbo is photographed in the middle of 'the old Zen garden' – probably an imitation of the Ryōanji rock garden in the Western suburbs of Kyoto. The colour of the car is more or less the same as that of the rocks surrounding it. As with the other rocks in the photograph, the sand around the coupé has been carefully raked so that the car itself comes to seem like a rock – as immobile, as old, and as permanent as the Zen garden itself. The fact that this kind of garden is usually seen as an art form in Japan suggests that Toyota regards its cars not as commodities, but as art objects which do not lose, but gain, value with time. In this respect, the automobile manufacturer appears to be participating in the elevation of 'rubbish' to 'art' along the lines so amusingly described by Thompson (1979).

Thirdly, the two extremes of technology and aesthetic perfection are mediated by a *spiritual* element, for the concept of perfection is linked with Zen Buddhism (which also makes an aesthetic issue of imperfection in the array of rocks in the garden). After proudly describing its technical achievements in the body copy of the ad,

WHY WE'LL NEVER MAKE A PERFECT CAR.

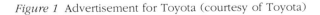

完

"If perfection could be attained, it would not be worth having."

TOYOTA

Figure 1 Advertisement for Toyota (courtesy of Toyota)

Toyota mentions how it has designed noise out of its Supra Turbo engine in an 'effort to achieve the sound of one hand clapping' – that famous Zen *mondō* described and analysed at length by such scholars as Suzuki Daisetsu (1969:89, 109). What is really important to Toyota, however, is not the engine itself so much as 'the attitude that went into its making: a way of looking at things that owes much to Zen'. This spiritual attitude consists of 'total concentration, minute attention to detail and a refusal to accept that there is such a thing as perfection'. In other words, the striving for perfection is neither purely materialistic (in its search for technological perfection), nor aesthetic (in its creation of beauty), but *social*. It is the Toyota worker's attitude which finally determines the quality of his company's finished products.

Such signifying elements themselves produce certain extensions to the semiotic process. One underlying theme of this advertisement is that it is only in a *Japanese* company – and, by implication, only in *Japanese* society as a whole – that people are spiritually prepared to strive for perfection; only by means of a specifically Japanese form of capitalism that near-perfect commodities can be produced for a near-perfect world. Given that the advertisement was placed in a British magazine, and given that it is workers in the United Kingdom who are generally seen to lack the 'spiritual' attitude necessary for good work, and who thus suffer from what the Japanese like to call the 'English disease' (*Eikoku-byō*), Toyota appears to be delivering a tough message: 'This is the way in which the Japanese were able to come back from total defeat in the Second World War to lead the world in the production of high-quality goods. This is why Toyota is the Number One car manufacturer in the world. Supported by the essentially Japanese philosophy of Zen Buddhism, the Japanese economy has become superior to all other capitalist economies. You, too, can be as successful as we are, provided that you adopt the same set of ideals about perfection as ourselves. The choice is yours.'

But this choice with which we are presented may prefer another, less convoluted, line of intepretation. Perhaps the whole point of the visual is that a car is not a rock, that it can never become one, and that is why neither the car itself nor the garden in the photograph is perfect. In the context of this visual, if Toyota were able to make the perfect car, it would in fact change into a rock – and that, of course, would be rather silly! At the same time, by placing one of its coupés in the middle of an 'old Zen garden',

Toyota is consciously destroying the near perfection of traditional Japanese aesthetics, while at the same time – ironically – contributing to the Zen aesthetic of imperfection. Perhaps the advertisement is an allegory about Japan's own historic development in the face of 'contaminating' Western influences, and the tension that has continued to exist between 'tradition' and 'modernity'.

Or perhaps the visual of this ad is playing on a problem of *representation* itself: on the fact that those involved in the creation of still photographs of cars in advertising have tremendous difficulty in representing motion. Conscious of this difficulty, Toyota's advertising agency has decided to add an ironical twist to the visual by placing a clearly mobile machine in an immobile setting. The rocks thus serve to emphasize the potential speed and motion of the car, whose mobility is enhanced by the carefully raked lines of sand around it. In this way, the visual perhaps attempts to overcome the consumer's knowledge that the car has long been outmoded by faster forms of transport (Wernick 1991:73).

PKW and Superior Quality

Let us now examine a second ad which was prepared by a Tokyo advertising agency for its European client, PKW, during the course of a competitive presentation made in the autumn of 1990 (Figure 2).[5] Here we see a large-sized PKW car parked in front of a thatched roof building, whose *noren* flapping in the summer breeze with its Chinese characters and *hiragana* syllabary clearly betrays the fact that the setting is Japan. The headline of the advertisement reads: 'Superior quality does not court people's changing tastes' (*sugureta hinshitsu wa, hito ni kobinai mono desu*),[6] while the closing phrase proclaims that: 'The essence of PKW is character' (*PKW no honshitsu wa, hinshitsu desu*).

How are we to 'read' this ad? By placing its car in a specifically Japanese environment, PKW (or, more strictly speaking, its advertising agency) seems to wish to appeal to the kind of 'Japaneseness' asserted by Toyota a year or so earlier at the start of its UK campaign. However, there is an important difference in this 'exoticization' of the product. While PKW places a European product in a Japanese environment for a Japanese audience, Toyota placed its Japanese product in a Japanese environment for a European audience. The exoticism or (counter-)Orientalism (Moeran 1993b), such as it is, differs somewhat in character.[7]

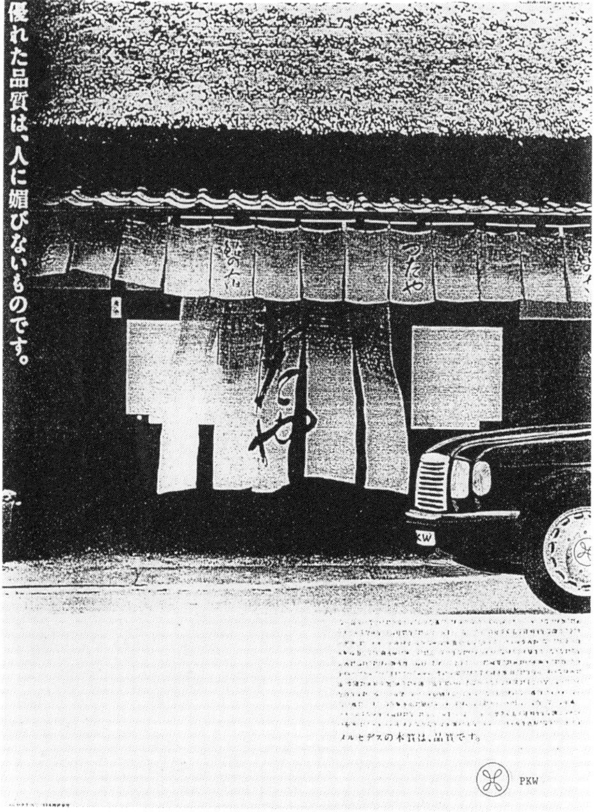

Figure 2 Proposed Advertisement for PKW

Perhaps we should adopt a different approach. PKW cars can be said to embody some of the most up-to-date and sophisticated aspects of European car technology (and the 'purity' of its engineering can be seen, no doubt, in the white paintwork of the car portrayed in the other ads that make up this brand ad series). By placing its product in a Japanese environment, the European automobile manufacturer could be said to be challenging the assumption that Japanese cars are always technologically superior (and thereby counter-challenging Toyota's challenge to the British automobile industry). This it attempts to achieve by certain subtle means. For example, by focussing on 'traditional' aspects of Japanese architecture – thatched roof, a wooden construction, noren – the visual portrays Japan as a 'traditional', rather than modern, 'country'.[8] Mindful of our earlier interpretation regarding the tension between mobility and immobility in the Toyota ads, we could say that it is *European* industry which is on the move, Western manufacturing which is ahead. This is what 'quality' and 'character' are all about.

Another partial reading along this line might note the apparent *harmony* of the European car in a Japanese setting. This suggests that PKW has, perhaps, managed to overcome the so-called 'trade barriers' that are seen to characterize so many parts of the Japanese domestic market and which often occupy the vocal chords – if not always what M. Poirot refers to as 'the little grey cells' – of European and American politicians. At the same time, however, this harmony stems from Japanese nature – as is made more than clear by the two other ads that make up the series, where the same car is seen in what appears to be a sand-raked *kara sansui* Japanese garden surrounded by hydrangeas in full bloom, or being driven along the kind of white-walled lane that typifies such areas as the north western suburbs of Kyoto. The fact that it is Western technology which is in harmony with Japanese nature suggests that PKW has in fact usurped this most precious of symbols about 'Japanese' ontology and made it its own. Toyota! Toyota! Wherefore art thou, Toyota?

This harmony, however, can also be said to be imbued with a certain tension that comes from the noren flapping in the summer breeze. Something is happening between the apparently motionless car and the still building behind it, and we realize that we do not really know what this traditional piece of architecture is being used for. Is it a Japanese inn, perhaps, out in the country? Or an exclusive restaurant set in a historical part of town? Or just an old merchant's store where one can purchase bales of hand-woven cloth? Nothing is clear. This sense of mystery is epitomised in the deep, dark entrance to the building with its mask-like facade. From the inside, perhaps, one can look out on the world, but from outside where the photograph is taken, it is impossible to know what is going on behind the noren. There is a hidden quality about the scene, a certain sense of mystery that may relate to the idea mentioned in the closing phrase of the ad that the essence of PKW is quality.

Reading a Campaign

It is clear that there are a number of possible interpretations which, as an interested consumer, I can adopt in trying to 'explain' the two advertisements presented here.[9] However, unlike Roland Barthes in his analysis of the Panzani ad, or Judith Williamson in hers of Catherine Deneuve and Chanel No 5, I am unable to come up with a single all-embracing theory that fully 'explains' either the Toyota or the PKW advertisement. Have I then failed to synthesize the various levels of interpretation to produce an underlying 'structural' message of the kind favoured by Leymore (1975)? Or does this failure have something to do with my own inadequate training in semiotic analysis? In other words, do I merely lack the necessary imagination to be able to use semiology as a really creative tool and thus emulate the more perceptive work of Barthes and Williamson (Leiss et al 1990:214)? Or is there more to it than this?

To answer these questions, I want to start by looking at the visuals and copy of other advertisements which appeared in the Toyota campaign. Each made use of the same basic design: headline in large letters along the top and one side of the central photograph of a Toyota car; body copy under the visual; and a single Chinese character in red at the top, or more usually bottom, left hand corner, glossed with a lengthy explanatory phrase in English, and colour matched with the name of the advertiser at the bottom right of the photograph.[10]

Another ad placed at this time for the Toyota Carina (July 1989) reads: 'What's a few cracks in the M25 to a car built for an earthquake zone?', and is reinforced by the Chinese character for 'shake' or 'tremor', which is glossed as 'Great strength is forged from great adversity'. The explanation in the body copy is that a Toyota Carina must be strong enough to withstand the 7,300 earth tremors that the Japanese experience every year; hence its 'extremely strong steel chassis and rigid safety cage' and the attribution of such strength to 'the steels of medieval Japan, from which were forged famous swords, so sharp they would slice drifting petals'.

We can see here that Japanese traditions – this time, craft traditions – are again used to support and explain the present-day success of Toyota. Once more, too, nature is seen to be pitted against man's technology – this time in the guise of earthquakes rather than of an old Zen garden. Finally, the allusion to strength being forged from adversity can also be interpreted as a sly allusion to Japan's defeat in the Pacific War. It was this set-back which spurred on the Japanese and led them to their present technological and economic superiority over other industrialized societies in Europe and America. A further dig at British workmanship can be seen in the topical allusion to the cracks which appeared in the road surface of one of England's newest motorways soon after it was opened.

This second advertisement reinforces, then, the idea that Toyota cars are technologically superior to those manufactured by its competitors, but this time attributes this achievement to *tradition* rather than to some kind of *spiritual* element as such, although the two are easily assimilated. Still, the failure to refer to 'aesthetic' perfection in the Carina ad suggests that we need to adjust our earlier interpretation about all Toyota cars being art objects rather than mere commodities. Nevertheless, one clear aim of the advertising campaign at this point would seem to be to stress the advanced technology that goes into every Toyota product. This is 'proved' by such material benefits as catalytic converters and strong steel chassis, on the one hand, and is supported by the less immediately tangible benefits of a Zen-like attitude and a long historical tradition of steel-making, on the other.

At the same time, the further allusion to bad workmanship and the 'English disease' suggests that a supporting aim of the campaign is to criticise obliquely the British automobile industry and to imply that it can never match Toyota's technological superiority. Finally, perhaps, we should note that – by placing one of its cars motionless in the middle of a road more or less destroyed by an earthquake – Toyota has once again stressed the problem of representation referred to earlier. As before, we find ourselves trying to come to terms with a tension between mobility and immobility. Is it that this tension is to be related to the sluggishness of the British economy vis-à-vis the ever surging energy of Japan's?

The next advertisement in the series appeared in autumn 1990. Its headline, 'The new landcruisers. Better protection from the elements', together with its visual of a Welsh or Scottish snow-clad mountain valley, repeats the 'force of nature' element found in the previous ad. Although the character *jun* (literally 'shield', but glossed as 'Even the strongest soldier needs a shield') can be said to maintain the element of aggression, the body copy as such is totally devoid of reference to British workmanship, Japanese spirit or craft traditions. Instead, it focusses almost entirely on the technological wizardry of the two landcruisers pictured, before adding a short paragraph on their environmental friendliness.

This 'eco-feature' of Toyota cars was also featured in its spring 1991 Carina ad ('Never mind the engine, at Toyota we even tune the doors') where, once again superior quality – this time characterized by *ga* (or 'elegance', glossed as 'Compromise is the enemy of achievement') – is the sole focus of the body copy. An advertisement for the Toyota MR2 put out at this time ('For perfect balance there's only one place to put the engine') retains the emphasis on technology (which it ironically referred to as 'techno-babble') and continues the series' habit of providing a lengthy gloss on the Chinese character by describing *ho* ('protect') as 'Harmony flows naturally from a state of equilibrium'. At the same time, the visual depicts the Toyota MR2 balanced on top of its own engine against a backdrop of Hokusai's 'Great Wave' woodblock print. Once again, by situating technology in the middle of a Japanese art form, the campaign emphasizes the 'Japaneseness' of the product, together with its superior aesthetic qualities.

Taken as a whole, therefore, the campaign seems to have aimed first and foremost at emphasizing technological superiority and the extreme attention to detail that goes into the manufacture of all Toyota cars. By stressing these two points the campaign was clearly designed to turn Toyota's products into brands, and, to this end, the Supra Turbo and MR2 were given added aesthetic values. While the campaign started out by directly attacking rival products, particularly British-made cars, it proceeded to play on the then current eco-fashion (Skov 1995) for a cleaner environment (with, for example, its 'to protect our planet the Landcruisers' diesel engines reduce the amount of lead (Pb) getting into the atmosphere'), before ending – perhaps rather lamely – with further 'techno-babble'.[11] We should also recognize that the different products advertised in this campaign are almost certainly targeted at different consumers in different income brackets and with different lifestyles. Thus, while the Carina is intended for the 'middle of the road' family man whose main concerns are good value for money, safety and reliability, both the Supra Turbo and Landcruiser models are targeted at a higher income group of consumers who are more likely to appreciate, even own, art objects and have a weekend home in the country. In other words, although my analysis of the campaign as a whole reveals intertextual elements that help to reinforce certain dominant meanings in each advertisement, the fact that different ads in the series addressed different targeted audiences (and were possibly affected by an unanticipated, but topical, cultural pre-occupation with environmental issues) precludes the unveiling of one single underlying structure of significance.

Anchoring PKW in Japan's Import Car Market

What we have seen so far is that the semiotic interpretation of single ads can be a little misleading in the context of a campaign as a whole. I wish now to turn to the PKW advertisement in order to examine the marketing premises underlying the selection of this particular visual, and to comment on some of the social processes which gave rise to the advertising product.

According to the presentation document prepared for PKW Japan by the Tokyo advertising agency appointed to handle its account, PKW's immediate challenge was to develop its export market in Japan. The European automobile manufacturer had set itself a sales objective of several tens of thousands of units a year by 1995, and planned to develop an expanded service network and sales force to cope with its new customers. However, as the Agency pointed out in its presentation, such expansion would present PKW with a paradox since one of the appeals of its cars in Japan was their scarcity value. By increasing its sales, therefore, PKW was in fact challenging its own overall brand image. In the Agency's opinion, one important aim of the proposed campaign should be to seek ways of overcoming this paradox.[12]

The import car market in Japan grew rapidly from 1986, registering a sustained growth from 98,000 units in 1987 to an estimated 245,000 units in 1990. Of these, an increasing proportion was in large size cars (LSC), but at the end of the 1980s the LSC segment of the import car market began to lose its share of the Japanese LSC market as a whole because of the aggressive sale of domestic models like Cima, Maxima, Celsior and Infiniti. This point was important because it was PKW's large size car (the Maxi) which was primarily responsible for the company's brand image as a whole, and yet which was losing out to Japanese competitors. Thus, even though total sales had increased, PKW's market share was on the decline. Somehow the proposed campaign also had to rectify this problem.[13]

By conducting careful research into consumer perceptions of different cars – the characteristics they attributed to them and thus the way in which they themselves segmented the car market – the Agency was able to carry out what it called a 'market structure audit'. Surprisingly, this revealed that, even though consumers sharply distinguished between PKW and competing products in terms both of performance imagery (comfort, size, safety, reliability, technology) and user/emotional imagery (elite status, sportiness, sexiness, driving pleasure), they placed them all together in the same product class when looking at the market as a whole. People divided cars into three different product classes. Firstly, there was what the Agency called the 'Euro' group of compact, middle sized cars (VW Golf, Renault, Rover, Citroen, and so on) which appealed to a large number of first time buyers of imported cars in Japan. Then there was the 'Mystical' group of middle or large size luxury cars that boasted a non-Japanese heritage (PKW, Mercedes-Benz, BMW, Jaguar, Volvo, and – partially separate – Cadillac and Pontiac). Finally, there was the so-called 'Predictable' group of Japanese cars that were functional, safe, reliable, with one model for each socio-economic level of potential buyers. This group was subdivided into one set of 'standard' models (such as Galant, Prelude, Skyline and Accord) and another of cars like Cima and Infiniti which were designed to offset the inroads made by foreign manufacturers in Japan.

This kind of market segmentation meant that: firstly, luxury cars like PKW's in the Mystical group would lose their scarcity value as their numbers increased; and secondly, that the new breed of Japanese luxury cars with their 'new technology' would probably redefine consumers' expectations with regard to all foreign cars. In short, the Agency reasoned, it seemed likely that in the near future the three groups would be redefined as 'Mystical' (BMW, Mercedes-Benz, Jaguar, etc.), 'Neo-Mystical' (Cima, Celsior, Infiniti, etc.), and 'The Rest' (including Golf, Jetta, Lancia, Rover, on the one hand, and Galant, Skyline, Prelude and Accord, on the other). What PKW needed to do, therefore, was establish its own separate category. This meant both creating an effective distinction between its own and rivals' products, and redefining the competition, while at the same time ensuring that PKW's qualities as *the* car for Japanese to buy were further emphasized.

Having analysed the market thus far, the Agency's account team preparing for the presentation then had its work cut out trying to decide precisely what it was that made a PKW car unique! In the end, those concerned came up with the argument that there was no single quality – like superior engineering, manufacture, design, or aesthetics, – that made a PKW so special. Rather, it was a combination of all of these. PKW quality derived from a 'State of Mind' which focussed on perfection, creativity, excellence, achievement and what – in a poetic moment the account executive in charge of the presentation called – 'the quest for the best'!

Having worked out the problems and opportunities that PKW presented the Agency, the account team was able to write its overall positioning statement. This was divided into brand positioning, on the one hand, and product positioning on the other. The brand positioning statement claimed that PKW was more than just a car.[14] The company had its own philosophy and blended to perfection engineering, emotional and trend values, thereby providing its customers with a special satisfaction or experience that they could not obtain from any other car in the world. It was ultimately this philosophy which placed PKW in a unique category, separate from and superior to its rivals which all relied on singular claims in their marketing.[15]

Relaying the 'Hidden Qualities' of Advertising Messages

The creative 'platform' of the Agency's campaign for PKW was to communicate the idea of its client's 'State of Mind'. This meant focussing in particular on the unique sense of satisfaction and special experience that only PKW as manufacturer could deliver to its customers, on the one hand, and that PKW drivers alone could taste as consumers, on the other. The aim, therefore, was to transplant the manufacturer's 'state of mind' into the consumer's consciousness, thereby indissolubly linking the two in permanent harmony and making the purchase and ownership of a PKW itself a 'state of mind'. To this end, the creative team – consisting of several groups of copywriters and designers, each working on a particular model or brand – devised four advertising approaches. These were titled: Hidden Quality, Theory and Practice, Dialogue between PKW and Customer, and PKW Philosophy. The basic structure of each approach consisted of a set of (usually three) brand ads, accompanied by three different sets of (three or four) product ads (for the large size Maxi, medium size Midi, and small size Mini).

Let us now look again at the advertisement with which we began this examination of the PKW campaign (see Figure 2). In fact, this ad acted as one of the brand ads in the *Hidden Quality* series which was designed to depict the philosophy underlying the PKW approach to car manufacturing, research and development, as well as the technology which put that philosophy into practice. The brand ads tried to bring out a notion of 'genuine' quality by placing PKW cars in typical scenes that reminded people of what it meant to be Japanese. In an age when quality tended to be presented in an extremely superficial manner, the creative director explained, PKW asked what a truly timeless and borderless quality might be.

This market-based explanation helps us partly understand now why a PKW was placed in a Japanese setting in front of a traditional Japanese restaurant. It helps us realize, too, that my reading of the ad in terms of the superiority of Western technology over Japanese 'tradition' was definitely not relevant to the advertiser's market strategy. The use of the thatched roof in the visual was designed to symbolize timelessness; and the fact that it was a *Japanese* thatched roof, PKW's sense of being 'beyond cultural confines' (or 'borderless'). The ad was supposed to appeal directly to Japanese consumers by placing the European car in the kind of setting that they would typically associate with the 'real' Japan. As such, PKW would become 'real' by assimilation. Each had a long tradition, a certain 'spirit' (or state of mind) that set it apart – from other car manufacturers in the case of PKW, and from other industrialized Western nations in the case of Japan.

The idea of 'hidden quality' can also be seen in the way in which the car itself is represented in this ad. The designer's intention in showing but a part of the car was to insinuate that the PKW brand was so distinctive that it could be recognized anywhere, even though more than half of it might be hidden from view. At the same time, now that we have examined the marketing background to the creative ideas, it is possible to argue that the representation of only part of the car in the visual may be related to the proportion of the domestic car market taken up by imported cars in Japan. The advertisement can thus be seen as an allegory for the Japanese car market as a whole.

The product ads in this same series differed according to each of the models advertised, but the idea was to show particular hidden qualities in each of the different car classes.[16] With the medium size Midi, for example, visuals highlighted the car's dynamic silhouette in various ways, leaving the main body of the car in deep darkness. With the small size Mini, visuals focussed in close-up on the car's steering wheel, dashboard, gear shift, and other stylistic 'hidden qualities'. And why were such images used? Firstly, the Agency wanted to attack the commonly held consumer perception of the Mini as a 'poor man's PKW'; and secondly, to show that the Mini was in fact just as 'sporty' and 'sexy' as its main product rival marketed by another European manufacturer. In other words, even though the Mini was a small and comparatively cheap version of the Maxi, it still contained all the qualities traditionally expected of the PKW name, and was a viable alternative to the rival product.

Transposing Social Processes into Advertising

We can see, then, that it was marketing strategies which underlay the choice of images for the series of ads which the Agency prepared for its client PKW, and that it is knowledge of these marketing strategies which allow us to decypher further a particular advertisement. The study of such 'marketing moves' also enables us to go beyond structuralist and post-structuralist analyses by examining both the production and consumption of social communication which exist prior to and outside particular examples of advertising (Sinclair 1989:61–62). In this way, I have tried to take account of Fine and Leopold's argument (1993:195) that the study of advertising should deal with both horizontal and vertical analytical perspectives which explore different commodities in relation to their social and cultural contexts, on the one hand, and as part of independent systems of production, distribution, retailing and advertising, on the other.

Of course, it is virtually impossible to produce a comprehensive picture of advertising. There are just too many variables that need to be taken into account. Thus Fine and Leopold (1993:219–244) themselves fail to provide a 'horizontal' analytical perspective in their discussion of clothing and food advertising, while Leiss et al (1990:219), in arguing for a combination of semiology and content analysis, ignore the 'vertical' systems of provision advocated by Fine and Leopold. It is here, perhaps, that the anthropologist who has had the good fortune to work in an advertising agency (albeit for a limited period) can make a useful contribution which also takes into account social processes as well as semiology, content analysis, and marketing moves.

Usually, an advertising campaign makes use of different media to address certain groups of consumers who have been carefully analysed, targeted and selected. However, an advertising agency also has to take its client's likes and dislikes into account when preparing advertisements. In other words, even though the account and creative teams may talk a lot about consumer targets, they are also very aware of the fact that they have to sell their campaign to their client first, and that each client company consists of a number of different types of people (from advertising or sales department managers up to senior executives on the board of directors). One of the main tasks facing all agencies preparing for a competitive presentation, therefore, is to work out the particular likes and dislikes of certain key figures in the client company who will attend the presentation and take the final decision on which agency should handle its account.

In the case of PKW, there were two figures in particular who had to be shown that the Agency knew what it was about. One was a senior sales executive from Europe; the other a vice president of PKW in Tokyo. Although not too much information was forthcoming about the former, the account executive in charge of the agency's presentation did know that he was nervous about negative consumer perceptions of PKW (its 'arrogance', for example) and that consequently he was very keen on promoting his company's brand image. It was for this reason that the Agency dreamed up the idea of 'a state of mind' linking PKW to consumers; for this reason, too, that almost all the advertisements in the campaign focussed strongly on brand image.

The vice president of PKW, Tokyo, was also responsible for an unusual feature of the advertisements shown at the presentation: the placing of a PKW car in a Japanese setting. Although the Agency had already been handling the PKW account for several years, it had never before used a specifically Japanese scene to advertise the products of its European client. Yet a number of series made use of this idea. Why? For the very simple reason that the account director had overheard the PKW vice president saying that he thought that PKW should try to integrate itself more fully into the Japanese car market as a whole. In his opinion, there was no reason why the European car manufacturer should always appear so obviously 'foreign'. This important hint allowed the Agency to create a number of ads – like the one analysed here – which placed a PKW car in an obviously Japanese environment. But was this 'reading' of a situation any more or less 'correct' than that of an academic trying to interpret a completed ad? Of course, we do not know (although the vice president *looked* reasonably pleased when the ad ideas in question were shown at the presentation). All we do know is that advertising agencies themselves provide 'commentaries' on perceived 'signs' – commentaries which then give rise to further academic commentaries (such as this paper) that together form a 'discourse'.

The fact that all advertising agencies make use of similar kinds of strategy in preparing their presentations has further consequences for our understanding of the 'meaning' of ads. In the first place, there is not always agreement among agency personnel about how exactly a campaign should be created and presented. Moreover, when an agency is awarded an account, its client usually demands changes to copy and design (and possibly overall concepts) of the series presented, and, like an advertising agency, may in the process find that arguments break out between the different departments involved. In other words, there is likely to be conflict both within each of the organizations concerned and between them.[17] As a result, it is virtually impossible for either agency or advertiser to create of its own accord the kind of 'preferred' reading usually practised by consumers (whether they be people in the street or specialist academics), because there is rarely complete cohesion of visual, linguistic and technical strategies that allows such an interpretation during the processes of an advertising campaign's production.[18]

Concluding Traffic Signals

All this, of course, bears on the 'determinants' of decyphering or reading ads. One of the problems in limiting ourselves to a purely semiological analysis of advertising, or of other products of popular culture, is that such deliberate persuasive strategies as those outlined above, as well as production practices, tend to be overlooked. By knowing a little about the social practices and personalities involved in the Agency's presentation, we understand better why PKW's brand image and Japanese scenes were emphasized. By learning about the problems faced by PKW in Japan's import car market, we have been able to see, for example, how ads for the Mini were created with specific reference to PKW's major European rival. As Myers (1983:216) points out, such readings cannot be found within the form and structure of the ads themselves. Rather, they must also be sought in the marketing strategy of the client concerned. This is, of course, no easy task since an advertiser may think it in its interests not to reveal its marketing strategy. Moreover, we need to beware of the 'intentional fallacy', in the sense that consumers need not necessarily read or accept an ad in the way intended by an advertiser (witness their graffiti responses to posters in Posener 1982). Still, by overlooking the fact that advertising is part of a total sales and marketing campaign, analysts like Barthes and Williamson, for all their interpretive brilliance, are merely acting in the same way as do all consumers when they look at ads. As such, their readings may be attributed a certain authority, but – caught as they are in the trap of analysing finished products (advertisements), rather than the social processes that surround the creation of such products (advertising) – they are merely taking consumerism one step further.

As in literary criticism and in art, advertising is in many respects concerned with its own 'intertextuality'. Ads are not characterized by some 'ineffable individuality', but are part of an 'open network' of cultural signs, participating in what Culler (1981:103) has referred to as 'the discursive space of a culture'. It is this 'discursive space' which allows certain transpositions of sign systems to intermingle with one another. For example, the Toyota campaign discussed here had already made use of Chinese characters and English glosses in a billboard campaign in south east England a year or two earlier, while its decision to present some of its products in the context of Japanese art forms coincided with similar visuals put forward by other Japanese corporations in the mid to late 1980s (see Moeran 1993b). This emphasis on 'Japaneseness' was then adopted by another Japanese automobile manufacturer, Daihatsu, in its UK print media campaign a year or two later.[19] At a totally different level of intertextuality, in the creation of ads, the Agency's PKW account team made use of visual elements from PKW public relations materials, as well as general photography annuals, design books and even other ads (a cloud formation borrowed from a photography bank appeared, more or less simultaneously, in a Japanese magazine advertisement for a new religious organization). At the same time, by a further curious quirk of coincidence, PKW itself began using a philosopher's quotation series of advertisements in its German advertising just one week prior to the Agency's presentation in which it revealed its own

'Philosophy' series with a similar eye-catching feature. Finally, of course, advertising is always creating intertextual links through language and the use of 'keywords' (Moeran 1989; Tanaka 1990).[20]

Thus 'intertextuality' does not always refer only to the existence and importance of prior ads; nor does it just show how prior ads contribute to a code of 'signification', as Culler argues. Intertextuality in advertising at least is concerned with a completely different level of interpretation – that of marketing. As a result, a hermeneutic reading can be made stronger and more plausible if it also brings in 'the author', if only as 'guest' (Barthes 1977:161), because it is the advertiser alone who can explain (admittedly his own view of) the marketing strategies behind an advertising campaign's texts and visual imagery. This is a point that can usefully be taken into account by academics studying other popular cultural forms.

Finally, the transposition of sign systems has a bearing on car advertising generally and on 'Japaneseness' itself. In his discussion of the way in which technology was re-imaged in English language car advertising in the 1980s, Wernick (1991:81) argues that the automobile became projected as 'a kind of wrap-around experience, or even as a mystical inner trip'. This re-imaging coincides with the emerging mysticism of 'Japan' itself in European and American advertising in the 1980s, so that the shift 'from outer to inner space' in car advertising can be said to parallel a shift from Western 'conquest' to oriental 'experience'. The emergence of 'Japan' as an advertising image thus neatly dovetailed with the interiorization of car advertising at this time.

These days there is a tendency for advertisers to choose 'Japanese' elements more or less at random, and occasionally to juxtapose them with 'Western' elements in a single ad. this suggests that any discussion of 'Japaneseness' should take place in terms of the overall creation of images in contemporary society. How is it that 'Japanese' images are used – not just in advertising, but in cartoons, fashion, film, architecture, videogames, and all those other forms of media and popular culture that engage our attention today? I ask because there seems to be a curious phenomenon (dare one call it 'postmodern'?) whereby images are being detached by consumers from their cultural signifieds. Once upon a time a Zen garden, or noren flapping at the entrance to a thatched roof house, would have been generally accepted as being 'quintessentially Japanese'. It would not have occurred to people that a noren might equally well be placed across the entrance of a London art museum, or that a zen garden should be used to decorate the window of a New York department store. Similarly, a *deux chevaux* Citroen driving along a straight, cobbled road lined by tall poplar trees could only have been seen as 'French', while a well-built young man with suntan, even-toothed smile, blonde hair and surfboard *had* to be 'Californian'.

Nowadays, however, these images are not necessarily so firmly anchored in advertising or other popular cultural forms. A European car can be depicted parked outside a traditional thatched house somewhere in Japan; a Japanese girl can be photographed painting a cobbled street in Montmartre, and a sumo wrestler skate-boarding through Golden Gate Park. There is nothing 'quintessentially' anything about juxtapositions that now worry nobody but certain cultural purists (such as those employed in 'Japanese Studies'). In other words, signifier and signified appear to be in the process of becoming free-floating elements, ready to attach themselves, however briefly, to anything that happens to pass them by. Thus – to mention but two recent Japanese advertisements – Bourjois mascara can be transformed into an image of Hokusai's 'Great Wave', while a Japanese model can be portrayed as Mona Lisa with a cup of Café de Colombia in one hand, stepping out of her frame before the astonished eyes of a museum guard. As described by Lise Skov later in this volume, in the early 1980s Japanese designers' adaptations of Japanese worker clothes, textiles and kimono adorned Western models striding down the catwalks of Parisian ready-to-wear fashion shows. A few years later, another Western model was adorned in formal kimono to advertise something referred to as 'La Kyushu' for All Nippon Airways. In this way, signifiers and signifieds create new 'signs' whose symboilic lives appear as transient as the lights of a flickering firefly or the rasping voice of a *semi* cicada. Alternately wrenched apart and reconstituted in different combinations, these free-floating elements now seem closer to Saussure's concept of the 'arbitrary' nature of the sign than they ever were before. In such an unanchored context the idea of 'Japaneseness', too, is now itself equally arbitrary, and therefore 'meaningless' – at least in the sense that it has hitherto been used.

Notes

1 In 1961, no Japanese automobile manufacturer featured in the list of Japan's top twenty advertisers. By 1970, however, Nissan and Toyota were third and fourth heaviest spenders in advertising, followed by Honda in eighth position. In 1980, Nissan was the country's foremost advertiser, with an annual expenditure of ¥34.33 billion, followed by Toyota (¥21.18b) in third place and Honda (¥15.43b) in tenth, each of whom had more than doubled its advertising appropriation during that decade. In 1990, Toyota was the leading car advertiser (¥44.71b), followed by Mitsubishi Motor Corporation (9, ¥34.5b), Nissan (10, ¥31.86b), Honda (14, ¥27.96b) and Matsuda (19, ¥26.16b) (Fujitake and Yamamoto 1993:233–234).

2 As Davidson (1992:23) points out, the difference between a *product* and a *brand* is crucial, because advertising is designed to change the former into the latter. Thus, 'brands are products with something extra. All brands are products, but not all products are brands, and the difference is advertising'.

3 I have myself discussed such referencing across product lines by means of linguistic sounding in Moeran (1989:122–131).

4 See, for example, Arlen's (1981) pithy account of the making of a television commercial. By suggesting that we also try to read the language of advertising in the advertiser's own terms, I am taking up – albeit slightly differently – De Certeau's distinction (1984) between decipherment and reading in an attempt to tease out the dialectical relationship between practice and system, *langue* and *parole*, that exists in all popular cultural forms.

5 For reasons of confidentiality, I have been obliged to change the names of those organizations mentioned in this paper, make minor amendments to factual data and alter the image of the car concerned. I would, nevertheless, like to thank the Agency in which I conducted my anthropological 'fieldwork' for permission to reproduce the artwork printed here.

I would also like to take this opportunity to thank the Japan Foundation for awarding me a one year Fellowship in 1990 to carry out research on the production, consumption and appraisal of Japanese advertising.

6 All translations of advertisements are those put out by the advertising agency involved in the presentation. They are not meant to be strictly accurate translations, but were designed to put across creative ideas in English copy form for the purposes of the Agency's presentation to PKW.

7 This difference may be related to nostalgia for a perceived 'tradition' as described, for example, by Martinez (1990).

8 This theme is emphasized by a second brand ad in the same series, the headline of which reads: 'Quality that adulates an age cannot break ahead of its age' (*Jidai ni geigō suru hinshitsu wa, jidai o koeraremasen*).

9 Indeed, I have analysed the Toyota advertisement in the context of a

discussion of Orientalism and Japan's 'counter-Orientalism' (see Moeran 1993b:92–93).

10 It should be noted that, as with all advertising campaigns, design variations can be found. For example, the headline and Chinese character of the Supra Turbo advertisement start either at the bottom left, or top left, of the visual, with corresponding adjustment of body copy placement. This is partly due to the size and format of the print media in which such ads are placed.

11 For comment on the 'green watershed' in the Audi 'Vorsprung durch Technik' campaign between spring and October 1989, see Davidson (1992:89–93).

12 This paradoxical relationship between perceptions of quality and mass production is, of course, not new. At the turn of the century, Japan itself was victim of the kind of thinking that equates modernization with – in this case, overall cultural – deterioration after its successful participation in the Louisiana Purchase Exposition at St. Louis in 1904 (See Harris 1990:29–55).

13 For most advertisers, in both Japan and the United States, it is not an increase in their products' consumption *per se* at which they aim so much as an increase in their market share at the expense of a rival business' share. In this respect, as Schudson (1984:24) points out, advertising becomes a defensive strategy.

14 Advertising campaigns may focus on either brand or product image, depending on the perceived marketing problems and advertising aims, or – as with PKW – on a combination of the two. The product positioning statements each consisted of a brief outline of problems affecting sales of a particular PKW model sold in Japan, together with perceived market requirements.

15 These singular claims were seen to be: BMW, sportiness; Mercedes-Benz, status; Jaguar, driving pleasure; Volvo, safety; and Infiniti, contemporary technology. Compare this with a British advertising agency's early 80s perception of Porsche as representing evolutionary engineering; Mercedes quality engineering; BMW driving engineering; and Audi innovative engineering (Bailey 1986:96).

16 The Agency's creative team was acutely conscious of the need to make its client's representatives realize that they were being presented with a coordinated campaign, rather than with a selection of disparate advertising ideas, and so made use of the same visual tone and closing phrase for each class of car in the product ads. This is what is known in the trade as 'synergy effect'.

17 This is discussed in greater detail in my monograph on a Japanese advertising agency (Moeran 1996).

18 This fact also casts doubt on the possibility of the kind of conscious manipulation and organization of consumers that such 'intentionality' suggests to some interpreters (e.g. Adorno and Horkheimer 1986: 120–167).

19 Thereby totally subverting campaigns by Japanese manufacturers like Toyota which in 1982 specifically eschewed its Japanese origin by Americanizing its products (see Wernick 1991:91).

20 In view of my earlier emphasis on the political implications of keywords in Japan's 'internal cultural debate', I should perhaps add here that I now believe such keywords to have a primarily economic function.

References

Adorno, Theodor and Max Horkheimer, 1986 *Dialectic of Enlightenment*, London: Verso.

Arlen, Michael 1981 *Thirty Seconds*, New York: Penguin Books.

Bailey, Stephen 1986 *Sex, Drink and Fast Cars: the creation and consumption of images*, London: Faber & Faber.

Barthes, Roland 1977 *Image-Music-Text*, London: Fontana.

Crane, Diana 1992 *The Production of Culture: media and the urban arts*, Foundations of Popular Culture, Vol. 1, London: Sage.

Culler, Jonathan 1981 *The Pursuit of Signs: semiotics, literature, deconstruction*, London: Routledge and Kegan Paul.

Davidson, Martin 1992 *The Consumerist Manifesto: advertising in postmodern times*, London: Routledge.

De Certeau, Michel 1984 *The Practice of Everyday Life*, Berkeley: University of California Press.

Fine, Ben and Leopold, Ellen 1993 *The World of Consumption*, London: Routledge.

Fujitake Tsutomu and Yamamoto Akira 1993 *Nihon no Masu Komyunikeshon* (Mass Communications in Japan), Tokyo: NHK Books.

Harris, Neil 1990 *Cultural Excursions: marketing appetites and cultural tastes in modern America*, Chicago: Chicago University Press.

Jhally, sut 1990 *The Codes of Advertising: fetishism and the political economy of meaning in consumer society*, New York: Routledge.

Kristeva, Julia 1984 *Revolution in Poetic Language*, New York: Columbia University Press.

Leiss, William *et al.* 1990 *Social Communication in Advertising: persons, products and images of well-being*, London: Routledge (Second edition).

Leymore, Varda 1975 *Hidden Myth: structure and symbolism in advertising*, London: Heinemann.

Marchand, Roland 1985 *Advertising the American Dream: making way for modernity, 1920–1940*, Berkeley and Los Angeles: University of California Press.

Martinez, D.P. 1990 'Tourism and the ama: the search for a real Japan', p. 97–116 in E. Ben-Ari *et al.* (eds.) *Unwrapping Japan: society and culture in anthropological perspective*, Manchester: Manchester University Press.

Moeran, Brian 1996 *A Japanese Advertising Agency*, London: Curzon Press.

—— 1993a 'A tournament of value: strategies of presentation in Japanese advertising', p. 73–94 in *Ethnos* 58:1–2.

—— 1993b 'The Orient strikes back: advertising and imagining Japan', p. 77–110 in *Supplement to the Gazette* 50:1, The University of Hong Kong.

—— 1990 'Consuming passions', p. 28–31 in *Encounter* 74:4.

—— 1989 *Language and Popular Culture In Japan*, Manchester: Manchester University Press.

Myers, Kathy 1983 'Understanding Advertisers', p. 205–225 in H. Davis and P. Walton (eds.), *Language, Image, Media*, Oxford: Basil Blackwell.

Posener, Jill 1982 *Spray it Loud*, London: Routledge and Kegan Paul.

Schudson, Michael 1984 *Advertising: the uneasy persuasion*, New York: Basic Books.

Sinclair, John 1989 *Images Incorporated: advertising as industry and ideology*, London: Routledge.

Skov, Lise 1995 '"Ecology" 1990: cycles of consumption', p. 170–96 in L. Skov and B. Moeran (eds.) *Women, Media and Consumption in Japan*, London: Curzon.

Suzuki, Daisetsu 1969 *Introduction to Zen Buddhism*, London: Rider.

Tanaka, Keiko 1990 'Intelligent Elegance: women in Japanese advertising', p. 78–96 in E. Ben-Ari *et al.* (eds.) *Unwrapping Japan: society and culture in anthropological perspective*, Manchester: Manchester University Press.

Thompson, Michael 1979 *Rubbish Theory: the creation and destruction of value*, Oxford: Oxford University Press.

Vestergaard, Torben and Schrøder, Kim 1983 *The Language of Advertising*, Oxford: Basil Blackwell.

Wernick, Andrew 1991 *Promotional Culture: advertising, ideology and symbolic expression*, London: Sage Publications.

Williamson, Judith 1978 *Decoding Advertisements*, London: Marion Boyars.

Part II

Music, Place, History

3

'FINALLY, I REACH TO AFRICA'

RYUICHI SAKAMOTO AND SOUNDING JAPAN(ESE)

Brian Currid

Reading World Beat(s)

In recent years the academy has been taken with a fascination for that most 'post-modern' of popular musics, so called 'world music' or 'world beat'.[1] The extant literature on world beat has most often read this music as metonymically representational. In this view, world beat re-stages inter-national relations within the highly over-determined, well-traversed microcosm of the recording studio. But these metonymic readings have largely refused to interrogate how relationships between geography and subjectivity are politically formed and transformed within these musical practices, and have depended on a discourse of stardom which fails to describe the historical contingency of the star as institution or apparatus; that is to say the terms of the debate have not allowed a critical investigation of the ways world beat might be differently understood as productive of relations of transnationality rather than merely representational. Much of the literature traces the self-characterizations of world beat's Western proponents and stars (Paul Simon, Peter Gabriel, David Byrne) and their new world beat careers. Other critical interrogations of world beat center on a 'political economic' approach pivoting around a logic of compensation and 'just' treatment: in this narrative, we read of the authorship rights on *Graceland*, or the financial transactions 'behind' a world beat product. Furthermore, most of the research on world beat has focused its attention exclusively on the interaction of African and Euroamerican recording artists. I want to begin here an examination of another 'world music', in two senses: another 'music', another 'world'. A productive approach to world beat might involve an examination of the ways world beat is alternatively occupied in differently located histories of international popular music and popular stardom. The music of Ryuichi Sakamoto, a Japanese world beat star, enables different relations to place and subjectivity[2] than the 'world musics' of Gabriel, Simon, or Byrne; by examining this difference, I hope to begin to disturb the unproblematic invocation of both artistic authorship and globality that has characterized recent readings of world beat and indeed the coherence of world beat itself as an object of critical investigation.

Ryuichi Sakamoto[3] has become of late something of an icon for ethnicity as it is conceived in the post-modern. Sakamoto's name is primarily associated with a number of film scores, beginning with his work on Ōshima Nagisa's *Merry Christmas, Mr. Lawrence*. Most recently in the spotlight for his soundtrack to Bertolucci's *Little Buddha*, Sakamoto won an Oscar for his work with David Byrne and Cong Su on the soundtrack for an earlier Bertolucci film, *The Last Emperor*. Sakamoto has worked as well with Pedro Almodóvar, composing a 'Spanish' soundtrack for his film *High Heels*, and he was the composer of the soundtrack for the recent film *Tokyo Decadence*. Through these various projects, Sakamoto has become a peculiar kind of transnational institution, symbolizing the processing of the 'ethnic' in the recording studio and tracing the various relationships to ethnicity across time and space that characterize a transnational post-modernity. I will read here the ways Sakamoto's music traces divergent relationships to the politics of location and ethnicity, not only in his recent world beat releases, but, attempting to set these releases in a more specific context, I will also be reading Sakamoto's pre-world beat career in the 1980s. Looking at three examples, first his early album *B-2 Unit*, second the film *Merry Christmas, Mr. Lawrence*, and finally his 1990 album *Beauty*, I hope to trace the ways in which Sakamoto 'sounds' Japan(ese) within three quite distinct soundscapes, each of which places Japan differently within an international or transnational frame.

World beat in Japan is sited at the end of a differently configured history; an examination of Sakamoto's relationship to other forms of transnational art and popular musics will allow an investigation of the specificities of world beat within a national narrative in many ways distinct from those of the West. Additionally, it is crucial to retool any analysis of exoticism and its relationship to histories of appropriation and domination in speaking about modern Japan; a reading of Sakamoto must not only look to the ways in which his world beat is made intelligible through the re-deployment of a European imperialist exoticism. In order to understand not only how world beat operates to articulate capitalist relations of domination between Japanese finance and the so called 'Third World', but, moreover, to begin to examine the ways in which Sakamoto himself, as commodity, is exoticized in Western practices of musical consumption, we should look as well to the ways Sakamoto himself differs from other world beat stars due to his ambivalent location within these discourses of exoticism.

The analytic strategies appropriate to a critical examination of world beat (in Japan or in the West) are not at all clear. Steven Feld has suggested that a useful analysis of world beat might be an 'archaeological stylistic stratigraphy showing layers and varieties of appropriation, circulation, and traffic in musical grooves' (1988:36). He argues that the musical practices that characterize world beat operate across two systems of discourse: a discourse of roots' and a discourse of 'rip-offs'. The discourse of 'roots' reads the turn to African music and musicians by Anglo-American recording artists as constituting a declaration of homage and as a narration of history which configures African music as its genesis. The work of world beat is then not appropriation, but reclamation, returning North American and European popular musics to their roots. However, this 'melody of admiration' (Feld 1988:31) is set in counterpoint to a melody of power. Feld argues that the discourse of 'rip-offs' reconfigures the meaning of the same musical, personal, international relations as technologies of hegemony, by which the performative genitive in 'our music' conceals the asymmetries of power through which a capitalist music industry functions, and in so doing guarantees their reproduction. By untangling the traffic in sounds and symbols that moves across the surface of the world beat CD, Feld hopes to trace the contours of both these discursive practices in order to trace the 'meaning' of world beat as a global phenomenon.

I would suggest, however, that a prior step needs to be made: before we can understand the configuration of hegemony and the enactment of resistance as they may or may not be located on the space of the recorded sound object, we need to entertain the possibility that the very subjectivities on which these activities are predicated need to be seen as themselves produced within the traffic of sounds and symbols, rather than as the unmediated agents behind the materiality of musical exchange. The tensions and echoes between the 'discourse of 'roots' and the 'discourse of rip-offs' figure very differently when the star artist traffics in the symbols of a musical exoticism only in so far as she herself is labeled and consumed as exotic. In addition, Feld's suggestions seem to take the 'world' in world beat for granted. The figuring of the transnational in Sakamoto's world beat is distinct from that of Byrne, Gabriel, or Simon, and it is the nature of this distinction that I seek here to investigate. The 'roots' and 'rip-offs' of Ryuichi Sakamoto can be traced through a history of imagining, sounding Japan, from a late nineteenth century colonialist modernism to the fashioning of 'Exotic Japan' in the 1980s (Ivy 1988). Additionally, I want to use this opportunity to think about the various ways in which Sakamoto functions as transnational recording star. What kind of ideological work does 'Sakamoto' effect?[4] And how is the world in Sakamoto's 'world beat' differently spaced than that 'world' mobilized by Sakamoto's counterparts in 'the West'? Finally, looking at, flirting with the queerness that I will argue inheres in Sakamoto's star-text, I will examine briefly the way Sakamoto functions in a sexualized economy of dialectically constitutive exoticism and nationalism, asking the two related questions: How does the queerness in Sakamoto's star text inflect his operation as transnational; how does transnationality inflect his operation as queer?

Sakamoto's Career

Sakamoto was born in Tokyo in 1952, during the American Occupation of Japan. He began studying composition at the early age of ten in 1962 under Matsumoto Taminosuke. While his early compositions were presumably modeled after the trends prevalent in postwar Japanese art music, his high school and early college years were dominated by an interest in the Euro-American avant-garde, including John Cage, John Coltrane, Jean-Luc Godard and Pasolini. At university in the 1970s, Sakamoto studied the work of Ravel, Debussy, and Steve Reich, and received a degree in composition.

In 1974 he began to study electronic and 'ethnic' music, and embarked upon his career as a recording musician. Sakamoto's career might be traced along a history of technological change, the late 1960s and early 1970s being the period when the studio gained its dominance of pop music, as reflected in the work of pop artists like Brian Eno and David Bowie. He and two other musicians,

Takahashi Yukihiro and Hosono Haruomi, formed the Yellow Magic Orchestra in 1978, and in that same year, he released his first solo album, *Thousand Knives*. By the next year, YMO had gained a considerable cult following and went on world tour. YMO was noted for its fresh approach to European synth-pop, a style which it integrated with an eclectic mix of other material, including 1920s Hollywood musical music. Meanwhile, Sakamoto became a producer, intensifying his connection to the studio production of the recordings. His second album, *B-2 Unit*, was released in 1980.

Sakamoto is generally styled as a Japanese Renaissance man. His career in film began in 1983, when he co-starred with David Bowie in *Merry Christmas, Mr. Lawrence*. The soundtrack Sakamoto composed for the film was released as a commercial recording both as it appeared in the film, and as a 'piano' version (*Coda*). That same year, Yellow Magic Orchestra disbanded, leaving Sakamoto free to pursue his various projects in film and solo work.

While working on this film, Sakamoto befriended David Sylvian, an English pop musician and member of the band Japan. Sylvian and Sakamoto collaborated on part of the soundtrack to Ōshima's *Merry Christmas, Mr. Lawrence*, and additionally on a single, 'Bamboo Houses', in 1983. The pair continued to have a close association, most notably evidenced on Sylvian's 1987 album, *Secrets of the Beehive*, where Sakamoto arranged the strings and woodwinds and played keyboards. Parenthetically, the collaboration with Sylvian is particularly intriguing when one considers the surprising level of success the band experienced in Japan. Mitsui Tōru has argued in his article, 'Japan in Japan: some notes on an aspect of the popular music record industry in Japan', that the success of Japan, a band whose music was marked in the West as 'art rock', achieved an inordinate amount of success in Japan due to the popularity of their visual image among young Japanese girls (1983:116). Inexpensive to Japanese record companies due to their relative unpopularity in the West, Japan's success in Japan represents an odd twist on the all-too-easily expected relationship between 'appropriation' and the traffic of musics between the phantasmatic poles of a geopolitical series, East and West, and presents a particularly interesting backdrop to Sakamoto's later career in world beat.[5]

In 1985 his work focused on collaborations with Thomas Dolby and Kisagi Koharu. At the same time, Sakamoto himself was the focus of a French documentary, 'Tokyo Melody', produced by

French national television. In the West, the increasingly successful Sakamoto will be styled as the 'Tokyo melody', the musician of Japan producing the sounds of Japan, serving to symbolize the culture of a 'new', cosmopolitan Japanese people. A review of Sakamoto's more recent work which appeared in the Australian popular press makes this point clear: 'In his native land Sakamoto . . . is a popular icon of what's best about a postwar culture seeking to escape its past through identification with things foreign' (Prendergast 1990). The author's insertion, 'in his native land', attempts to displace how the iconicity here is working: Sakamoto, of course, serves in the West as an icon for a 'post war culture' trying to 'escape its past'. Who is escaping which past?

The highlights of the period from 1986 to the present included work with the Neo Geo Ensemble, a group of international musicians playing 'international' instruments. This drive toward 'internationalization' was also reflected in his work on *The Last Emperor* soundtrack. His 1990 album *Beauty* represents in many ways the pinnacle of Sakamoto's new involvement with 'ethnic musics', as he collaborated not only with Western musicians but also with Youssou N'Dour, the Senegalese pop star, himself a key icon of the rising popularity of world beat as a genre of international pop music. *Heartbeat*, released in 1991, represents in some ways a turning away from the world beat formulation of *Beauty*: Featuring Jungle DJ Towa Towa and DJ Dmitiri from 'world-clique' Deee-Lite, this more recent album accesses a certain kind of cosmopolitan glamour with its house-inflected beats and its club quality recording levels. But N'Dour appears on this album as well, as do the familiar David Sylvian and Arto Lindsay (who had also appeared on *Beauty*). *Heartbeat* in some sense begs the question of world beat by citing a new kind of 'world music', the music of a 'world clique'.

Sakamoto's work throughout the 1980s seems to reflect certain trends in the Japanese milieu, specifically the Japanese trajectory toward 'dispersal', toward a post-modernism, and the various ways in which this historical trajectory has been narrated and politically mobilized. This trajectory lies as much within Japan as without, in constructions of Japanese-ness from within the nation and perceptions of Japan from the West. Sakamoto's music is key to understanding the 1980s in Japan primarily for its play with the inter-cultural space of the recording and film industries, and his use of the recording studio as a symbolic 'crucible' for the internationalization[6] (as opposed to 'Westernization') of Japan.

B-2 Unit: 'Not German, but Japanese Techno-Pop'

Sakamoto's role in world beat can be contextualized if we examine his earlier techno-pop. I want to begin my reading of Sakamoto by looking at one of his early solo projects, the techno-pop *B-2 Unit*, in order to trace through what I see as a very different logic of the transnational, perhaps better termed internationalism, made coherent by its seemingly mimetic dependence on the totalizing gestures of a European popular modernism. The topography of the recording studio as it appears in techno-pop, particularly techno-pop that is marked as Japanese, corresponds to an imagination of the global, in contradistinction to its later mobilization in world beat, as international modern. Rather than envisioning the global as a timeless multi-cultural fantasy, techno-pop insists that ethnicity is only a form of 'noise' that can be forced into the vectored organization of time and space that international modernism produces; international rather than transnational, techno-pop figures ethnicity not so much as a moment of rupture that disturbs and interrupts the temporal and spatial vectors of modernity, but rather, in its submission to the organizing principles and logics of an international modernity, ethnicity (or its traces) function as a proof of the telos which that modernism requires for its internal consistency. *B-2 Unit* argues that the space of Japan is one coterminous with a global modern, if not the space of the hyper-modern, accepting the claim to inevitable ubiquity that a Western modernism enacts (Sakai 1989:95) by producing local difference through the supposedly 'universal' expressive potential of the recording studio.

Techno-pop, most readily associated with the music of Kraftwerk and the parodies thereof ('Sprockets'), is characterized by an almost total reliance on synthesized sound. Using the studio as a musical instrument, techno-pop transmutes the performance-centered traditions of rock by refusing any direct connection between performers' bodies and the production of sound, even to the point that voice itself is revealed on the techno-pop recording as a technological artifact. Techno-pop claims the body of the singer or instrumentalist as part of the electronics of recording. Its music and lyrics display a contradictory relationship towards the technologies of recording and electronic music that make it possible. At times, techno-pop articulates an almost Adorno-esque critique of the alienating effects of industrialization and commodification. But simultaneously, with its highly sophisticated production techniques, the techno-pop record revels in its status as pure product of technology, pure commodity.

Kraftwerk's *Electric Cafe*, released in 1986, is a late version of techno-pop, indeed in many ways its farthest extension, and as such exhibits almost too perfectly techno-pop's (mis)comprehensions of the technological as either alienation or pure aesthetic. The song 'The Telephone Call' in particular highlights the interference with inter-personal communication that the very devices of communication produce. The song is composed largely of telephone sounds: rotary dialings, dial tones, touch tones, and the recorded voices of international operators speaking in various languages ('the number you have called has been disconnected'). A vocal refrain narrates an attempt to contact a lover on the telephone: 'I give you my attention and I give you my time/Trying to get a connection on the telephone line'. While on the surface it seems to narrate the alienation of the modern subject from inter-personal communication, the recording itself fetishizes the technological in its virtuosic manipulations of the electronics of recording, using pans from one speaker to the other, very precise programmed drum beats and crystalline synthesizers as its musical content. Techno-pop thus produces a fantasy world of cosmopolitan consumers, all with equal access to the technologies of sonic reproduction. Kraftwerk's 'Germanness' is obliterated[7] in the trans-national space of the recording studio and the apparatus of sonic reproduction, or so it seems. When techno-pop becomes 'Japanese' in Sakamoto's work, what is the effect? What sort of 'Japan' is re-territorialized through Sakamoto's early techno-pop?

Sakamoto explicitly considered his relation to Kraftwerk not one of imitation, but one of cross fertilization:

> [In Japan], as in the rest of the world, the uniform pressure of the Anglo-Saxon culture caused the musicians to only dedicate themselves to copying Western pop. In Japan the people only think of imitating all that comes from the West, and for myself I don't like the copies, only the originals. When we formed Yellow we took our reference from Kraftwerk, but the music we made was not German, but Japanese techno-pop (quoted in *El País*, June 1990).

Sakamoto here argues that the languages of a pop-musical modernism are trans-nationally available to produce style differentiations which depict the local on the stage of the global. Style is here configured as a system of musical connotation and denotation through which individual artistic subjectivity, 'originality', can be 'expressed'. The 'Japanese' of this 'Japanese techno-pop' serves as a marker of dialect within a more broadly conceived global system of musical signification, and Japaneseness and Germanness are differentiated only through the manipulations of a pre-given musical-symbolic material, a language.

The musical material on *B-2 Unit* enacts this claim by producing 'Asian' sounds (or sounds that are *marked* as Asian) and instrumental textures with the technological apparatus of the studio and through the genre possibilities that techno-pop allows. With titles like 'the end of europe', 'not the 6 o'clock news', 'riot in lagos', and 'warhead', the songs on this album evoke alternatively dystopic and utopic visions of global modernity and simultaneity, visions 'mastered' in the provocatively named 'Utopia studios' in London. But the electronic style signals that the space of the modern, as a historic condition, includes the possibility for a modernist internal critique.

'Not the 6 o'clock news' is dominated by a juxtaposition of the 'ethnic' and the technological, but in a way that suggests collage rather than collaboration. Sakamoto remains very clearly the artist behind this effect of collage, indeed as an effect of the collage, as he appears alone in a photograph on the back of the album jacket (Figure 1). 'Producer: Ryuichi Sakamoto.' The song begins with an 'ethnic' timbre, percussive in tone, backgrounded by radio-like noise. After a few seconds, this 'solo' is interrupted by the sound of a turntable scratching, and the song proper begins. The song is only held together as a unity by an electronically produced timbre of white noise that moves in pitch space and in literal space from speaker to speaker. Over this we hear various 'ethnically' marked sounds, set in a sequence for which there seems to be no logical order. Interspersed with these sounds are the sounds of voices from a radio; never speaking coherently, they serve to index voice as mediated through the technologies of mass dissemination rather than any privileged site of located subjectivity.

The juxtaposition of these radio signals with the sounds of the exotic, some of which seem as well to be emanating from a radio (or is it a television?), effects the illusion of Sakamoto as all-powerful producer, who manipulates the 'information' provided by the technologies of mass mediation to effect a new soundscape, a *musique concrète* for pop fans. 'Not the 6 o'clock news' thus

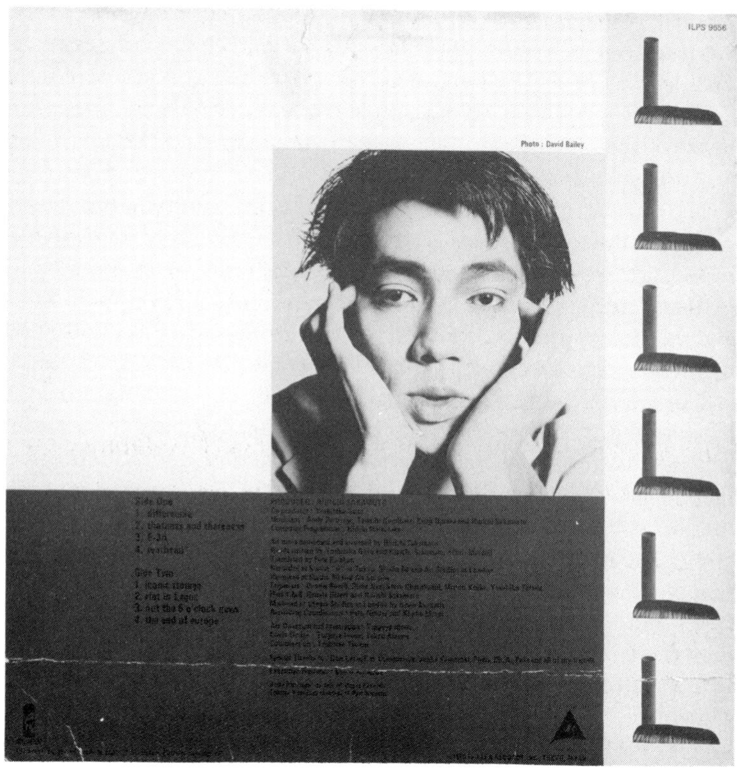

Figure 1 Back of album cover for *B-2 Unit*

positions itself self-consciously in the history of a European musical modernism, particularly that strand of modernism which begins with the Futurists and comes to fruition in both the *musique concrète* of Edgard Varèse (*Poème électronique*) and Pierre Schaeffer and the electronic music of Herbert Eimert.[8] The ethnic in this piece serves not as a site of 'roots' or nostalgia, but rather another sonic object available for the manipulations of the composer/producer, Sakamoto. The credits do not list who played these sounds – but do include the computer programmer and an extensive list of studio credits. Ethnicity is produced here as another sound-effect, whose affect as 'ethnic' is rendered unintelligible by its insertion into the 'program' of an international mix. The ethnicity of these sounds serves only to narrate place on a continuum of the modern, ethnicity as background noise amid a proliferation of other background noises. Techno-pop becomes 'Japanese' only in the sense that 'Japanese' becomes internationally modern and cosmopolitan, and Japan is re-territorialized as a space on which the drama of international modernism can continue to work itself out. This 'Japan' as utopia of progress or dystopia of modernization is radically refigured by Sakamoto's later work, when ethnicity regains its affect. Beginning with an examination of how Japan is produced as 'musically modern', as the limit (both spatial and temporal) of an international pop modernism, allows us to contextualize Sakamoto's later world beat career as a series of transformations on this space.

***Merry Christmas, Mr. Lawrence*: A Musical Neo-Japanesque?**

If *B-2 Unit* represents the imagination of Japan as a slice of a global modern, developments within more recent imaginings of Japan have narrated the history of the place of 'Japanese' within the construction of modernity itself. This sort of narration takes modernity out of the realm of the given, and begins to make the post-modern use of the modern as style and citation. Marilyn Ivy has described the phenomenon of 'neo-Japonesuku' in the Japanese mass media. In her article, 'Tradition and Difference in the Japanese Mass Media', Ivy describes a trajectory within Japanese tourism that traces political, economic, and cultural shifts within Japan, using Japan itself as a signifier for at first a primordial state of pre-modernity, and later as an icon of imagined marginality within a post-industrial world economy.

'Discover Japan', an advertising campaign of the Japan National Railways, was launched in 1970: '"Discover Japan" was the first highly visible, mass campaign urging Japanese to discover what remained of tradition in the midst of its loss' (1988:21). Travel, in this frame, serves to reclaim a lost pre-modern, pre-American self, yet used an American dialect of travel to speak the national subject: '"Discover Japan" directly mirrored the national domestic tourism campaign of the United States only three years earlier: "Discover America" . . .' (1988:23). While this search to recuperate, or perhaps to re-install an 'authentic' Japanese subjectivity in the newly reimagined place of Japan drove increasing numbers of Japanese tourists to 're-discover' Japan, the rise of consumer affluence in

1970s Japan led to an increasing encounter with the 'foreign.' No longer understanding their geo-political location as secondary to that of the United States and Western Europe, a new exotic was fabricated: this time the non-Japanese Orient and pre-war Japanese culture (Ivy 1988:23). In 1984, 'Exotic Japan' replaced 'Discover Japan' as the language of tourism. This new tourism campaign sought no longer to re-install the Japanese in a phantasmatic topography of the Japanese landscape, but rather re-packaged Japan as 'foreign, as non-native' (Ivy 1988:25). In contrast then to 'Discover Japan,' Exotic Japan is a landscape *openly* overdetermined by the production of Japanese-ness through the Western Orientalist imagination, populated by 'the triumvirate of the Japanese exotic: geisha, cherry trees, and "Fuji-Yama"' (Ivy 1988:26).

Ivy situates the *neo-Japonesuku* (the 'Neo-Japanesque') on a parallel trajectory to that outlined by 'Exotic Japan'. Referring to the revived interest in things 'Japanese' among youth culture in Japan, the neo-Japanesque designates the French interest in things not necessarily Japanese, but the creation of 'Japonaiserie', 'things in the *style* of Japan, citations of "Japan"' (Ivy 1988:28). As this term was mobilized by promoters in the 1980s, adding the (post)modernizing 'neo' to index its stylistic currency, they intended to indicate a 'neo-nostalgia', 'nostalgia in quotation marks' (Ivy 1988:28). This move de-essentializes Japaneseness as it was understood in *Nihonjinron* literature, only to transform the moment of Japan from the now into an ever-receding temporal space of tradition, distantiated from a (Japanese) post-modernity by the seemingly coherent (and politically unmotivated) movement of time.

It is in this context that I would like to place Sakamoto's soundtrack to Ōshima Nagisa's film, *Merry Christmas, Mr. Lawrence* (1983). Ōshima's film inserts itself into a history of Western wartime films in order to comment upon that cinematic tradition and the politics which it enables.[9] Set (largely) in 1942 in a Japanese prisoner of war-camp, Ōshima's film centers around the homoerotic bond that develops between Jack Celliers (David Bowie), a British POW under suspicion of guerrilla activities, and Captain Yanoi (Ryuichi Sakamoto). In so far as the film's central problem is homosexuality and its place within and across the disciplines of nationality (Japanese, Korean, Dutch, English), it narrates this problem largely through the problem of nationality within and across the discipline of the prison camp.[10] There are at least five male couples around which the narrative of the film works: Celliers and his younger brother, Lawrence and Celliers, Lawrence and Hara, Celliers and Yanoi, and finally the Korean guard and the Dutch prisoner. Each of these pairs is located at different points on an imagined continuum of difference from military homosociality (Lawrence and Celliers) to rape, or fantasized rape, in the case of the Dutch soldier and the Korean guard. The relationship between Celliers (Bowie) and Yanoi (Sakamoto) is the most charged relationship of the film, and it is this relationship whose twists and turns are most clearly narrated by Sakamoto's 'Orientalist' soundtrack.

I want to sketch out an argument that suggests Sakamoto's mobilization of an Orientalist musical style might articulate with the history of the relationship between musical Orientalisms and their labeling of the homosexual. As Philip Brett has recently argued about the music of Benjamin Britten, the musical use of Orientalism has served to displace the problem of homosexuality onto a fantasized sound(ing) of Otherness (Brett 1994: 245). In this case, however, the mobilization of these methods by a Japanese composer in a Japanese (?) film twists the logic of this operation: Empire and 'the Orient' serve not to narrate the possibility of perversion in the West; rather, different relationships to homosexuality narrate the difference between two opposed configurations of Empire (the Japanese and the English) in the same geographical locus (Indonesia). Additionally, the eroticization of Sakamoto's body in the film through the use of costume and make-up renders the relationship between composer and star open to spectatorial occupation. Captain Yanoi becomes in some sense Sakamoto, as similarly the character played by David Bowie is inseparable from the intertext of Bowie's stardom. It is in this context that the stylistic 'choices' of Sakamoto (the composer) take on an additional importance, in so far as Sakamoto's musical stardom in relation to David Bowie becomes an intrinsic part of the drama itself.

The suggestiveness of this intertext leads us back to the narration of Sakamoto's career. It is significant that Sakamoto's university degree in composition was obtained through the study of the compositional methods of French composers from the turn of the century, Maurice Ravel and Claude Debussy. These composers, and, it can be argued, composition in general at this time, occupied themselves with the discovery and application of new tonal materials. In the case of the so called French 'impressionists', one of the 'choices' for new tonality materialized in the translation of 'foreign', exotic musical materials into a musical language intelligible to the metropolitan West.[11]

> Much more than their German and Austrian neighbors, French composers also considered progress in music the result of increasing exposure to and potential assimilation of foreign idioms . . . 'All modes, old or new, European or exotic, insofar as they are capable of serving an expressive purpose, must be admitted by us and used by composers.' In the 1880s the French Ministry began supporting research trips into the provinces and abroad . . . At the Universal Exhibitions of 1889 and 1900 French composers could actually hear music from places as far away as Vietnam and Java. Debussy borrowed ideas from both these traditions.
>
> (Pasler 1991:392)

An example of the musical logic of Orientalism in this music is Debussy's *Estampes*. The title for this work 'suggests Debussy's wish to convey in those pieces the evocative and exotic qualities of Japanese prints' (Foreword 1991:xix). The first piece of this work, 'Pagodes', is most explicit in this regard. E. Robert Schmitz's guide to performing 'Pagodes' is illuminating on siting its relationship to Orientalist travelogue, bourgeois Western collecting practices, and the stuff of the 'music itself'.

> According to many books, the initial stimulus for 'Pagodes' was Debussy's entranced hearing of the Javanese gamelang [sic] orchestras at the International Expositions in Paris in 1889 and 1900. This would infer twelve to thirteen years of maturation, and a transmutation from the delight of the gamelang, and the first contact with the Orient, to the creation of a symphony of sounds transcending the Javanese scene and typifying any one of a hundred widely spaced oriental cities . . . Pagodas are consecrated temples of the Orient . . . Their architecture exhibits the same general tendency as do oriental dances. A stabilized and sober base gives rise to movemented[sic], ornate, sinuous, and shimmering superstructures. In looking at the score, you see this tendency reflected, and it is full of meaning to those who have traveled to the Orient. It embodies the oriental sense of fixity as well as the incredible teeming surface of the population.
>
> (Schmitz 1950:82)

In a footnote to this passage, Schmitz points to his extensive travel in 'the Orient', and how he was 'greatly impressed by the charm and pictorial beauty of the countries he visited: Japan, China, Indo-China, Siam . . . ' (Schmitz 1950: 82). Schmitz infers from the title of the piece that Debussy here invokes the entirety of the Orient in his transcendence of the compositional techniques he learned from gamelan. Debussy effects, according to Schmitz, the phantasmatic staging of years of travel within the piano piece, through the domestic practices of salon music, music intended for the interior of the bourgeois home.

In this gesture Schmitz outlines what Benjamin has described in his 'Paris, Capital of the Nineteenth Century': the link between the commodification of the world in the universal exhibitions of nineteenth century Paris and the staging of the bourgeois interior. At these 'popular festivals' which 'glorify the exchange value of commodities' the 'whole of nature changes into specialties' (Benjamin 1977:176). The assimilation of these specialty goods into the bourgeois interior (Japanese prints!) which is not only the 'universe, but the case [*Etui*] of the private man' (Benjamin 1977:178), allows the private man to 'represent the Universe. He collects in it the far away and the past. His salon is a *loge* in the world theatre' (Benjamin 1977:177).

In this context, Debussy's use of pentatonic scales and 'exotic' harmonies becomes symptomatic of a more general staging of the social relations of colonialism within the interior of the bourgeois home. The Japanese print on the wall, the excursion to the World exhibition: each allows the 'goods' of colonialism to become the stage on which exoticization is enacted. Debussy's 'Pagode', using pentatonic modes and saturated with parallel fourths and fifths, represents the conversion of ethnic 'thereness' into a fetish for display in the domestic sphere of the bourgeois metropole, producing the 'Orient' as a collection of musical gestures.

The techniques that these composers used to 'assimilate' the exotic, or rather, to stereotype the exotic in sound, continue in diluted form to symbolize 'exoticism' and otherness in both 'art' and popular musics in the West (Hisama 1993). But the political dynamic of this relation is significantly altered when we look at the music of Ryuichi Sakamoto. As the narration of Sakamoto's compositional training in the popular press insistently enacts his filial relation to these Orientalist composers, Sakamoto's own compositional choices should be themselves sited within this filiation, in order to make the meaning of these choices as 'citation' more clear. The music to *Merry Christmas, Mr. Lawrence* is comprised of a set of repeating leitmotifs that represent alternatively place and character within the diegesis of the film. In the opening credits, which appear following the brutal removal of the 'sodomized' Dutch soldier from the prisoner's barracks by a Japanese camp official, the primary theme of the soundtrack and the work of the camera establish the 'thereness' of the film. Behind the credits, the camera traces the passage of the guard with the Dutch soldier through the forests of Java, moving from left to right in the frame. Mobilizing the Bazinian 'realist' affect of the long take within the traditional rhetoric of Western cinema to establish 'thereness' or presence, Ōshima allows the theme music of this film to set the stakes, by configuring the space of the forest as the terrain upon which the crises of the film and its staging of male-male relations will be enacted. In the first musical example, I have illustrated the primary thematic material of this 'theme' music (Figure 2). Sakamoto has used a pentatonic melody, which he harmonizes by using parallel fourths, an Orientalist gesture familiar from Debussy. Sakamoto repeats this basic material a number of times, producing a 'cyclic' form, again familiar as an orientalizing musical trope. Sakamoto never 'ends' the theme with a resolution; rather the theme concludes with an open ended sonority. Thus, the cyclic pattern structured by the repeating motif is not brought to a close but rather a sonic ellipsis, and sets the stage for the development of place and character within the film.

While this theme serves to stand in for the scene of the film, Sakamoto uses another cyclic theme to articulate the erotic tension between Celliers and Yanoi. This theme (Figure 3) is similarly constructed from a pentatonic scale harmonized with parallel fourths. It appears at major points of development between these two characters in the film. The narration of the growing complexity of this homoerotic bond sited in the space of conflicting Empires with musical gestures that signify a citation of things Japanese allows Ōshima to make the terms through which homoeroticism is made legible precisely those which make 'Japanese-ness' legible as 'exotic' in both Japan and the West. While Debussy's music serves as a fetish behind which the social relations of nineteenth century colonialism remain unheard in the bourgeois salon, Sakamoto's citation of Debussy's compositional practice in *Merry Christmas* renders intelligible the ways in which 'Japaneseness' is produced

Figure 2 Theme from *Merry Christmas, Mr Lawrence*

through the history of colonial and orientalist technologies of domination. But at the same time, the trafficking in stereotypes of 'Japaneseness' is ambivalent in its political effects. Ōshima's staging of different relationships to homosexuality in the space of Java depends on the absence of the Javanese. In the film, Java is an empty space, filled only with the motion of history provided by the Japanese and European soldiers moving across its stage. By using Debussy's Orientalist techniques to produce 'Japaneseness' and a particularly 'Japanese' relationship to homosexuality ('Samurai aren't afraid of homosexuality', we learn at one point in the film), Sakamoto's music is embroiled in the rhetorical complexities of the neo-Japanesque.[12] 'Exotic Japan' is confined to a location in the past, and enacted indeed in a distant locale. But this 'citation' of Japaneseness across an 'empty' colonial stage relates Japan only to the West, and erases the past and recent histories of political and economic domination of Japan in East and Southeast Asia. The ironic attitude toward 'Japaneseness' here serves the distance that very formulation of ethnicity from its embroilment in a colonial history. In other words, if the history of empire only serves to stage a citation of things Japanese, there is no space to critique the notion that the history of empire itself is 'inherently' Japanese, no space to examine the historicity of Japanese imperialism, then and now. It is precisely this erasure of history which will set the stage for Japanese world beat in Sakamoto's music.

Figure 3 Theme for Celliers and Yanoi (*Merry Christmas, Mr Lawrence*)

'And finally, I reach to Africa': *Beauty* and the World Music Library

If *Merry Christmas, Mr. Lawrence* seems to parallel the development of the neo-Japanesque in 1980s Japan and to traffic within its complex logics of nationality and place, *Beauty*, Sakamoto's real foray into the international style of world beat, represents another form of the 'post-modern' invocation of Japan, described recently by Yoshimoto Mitsuhiro as the articulation of a neo-nationalism with an ideology of *kokusaika*, or inter-nationalization. Yoshimoto argues that in order

> [t]o understand the true implication of *kokusaika* ideology, we need to pay attention to the fact that the boom of *kokusaika* has occurred simultaneously as the rise of neo-nationalistic sentiment among the Japanese. We must examine the complicit relation between neo-nationalism and internationalism in which both are supplemental to each other. The development of internationalism seems inevitable when Japanese capital not only is penetrating into every corner of the global market but also is initiating the reconfiguration of the economy of the postindustrial first world countries. . . . Internationalism and neo-nationalism are merely two sides of the same coin. Both are necessary to construct a model of the world at the center of which Japan is situated. The boom of internationalization does not necessarily mean that the Japanese are now more open towards and willing to accept differences of other cultures. Since they are allowed in Japan only as pre-packaged, commodified images frequently seen on television or in flashy pictorial magazines as cata-

> logues or as actual goods themselves, other cultures, whose differences are safely contained or erased, can never have any direct impact on the Japanese.
>
> (1989:21)

Beauty articulates the relationship between a Japanese neo-nationalism and internationalization; in this final section, I will examine first the 'world music' or 'ethnic music' phenomenon as it is exhibited by the 'world music library', and proceed to think about the meaning of *Beauty* when read across such a backdrop. I will also be asking a related set of questions about the way the queerness of Sakamoto's star-text and his packaging for this project articulates with the operations of transnationality.

At least two Japanese recording companies have issued 'world music' or 'ethnic music' libraries in the 1980s, the King Record Company and JVC. Both of these collections similarly place their products on an imagined 'world map' (Figures 4 and 5) whereby each CD stands in for its place of origin. In order to sell 'ethnomusic', an advertisement from JVC sites the project of the 'ethnomusic collection' within two models of sound recording, the 'fidelity', or reproductive, model and the 'telephonic' model, or the representational (Lastra 1992).

> Remember how it feels to fall asleep on a warm evening in spring, in an open field, and to awake under a sky full of stars, feeling a part of the natural world which surrounds you. This music, with its natural rhythms, its ethnic feeling, will take you away from the city at the end of a tiring day to a calmer, more peaceful time and place.

The description illustrates a mobilization of what James Lastra has termed a representational model of sound recording, where the sound that is inscribed in the recording is utilized as a signifier for a phantasmatically prior, sonically structured event: its serves as a voice-over to a fantasy diegesis of the natural and the re-unification of the technological (the written/recorded) with the natural (the spoken/sounded). This diegesis attempts to represent (or re-member) an ontologically prior locus of 'ethnic feeling,' sited in any of the geographic areas marked on the map. Implicit in these words is that the music itself, produced through the processes of inscription that recording effects, seeks to invoke a time of 'self-presence, transparent proximity in the face-to-face countenances

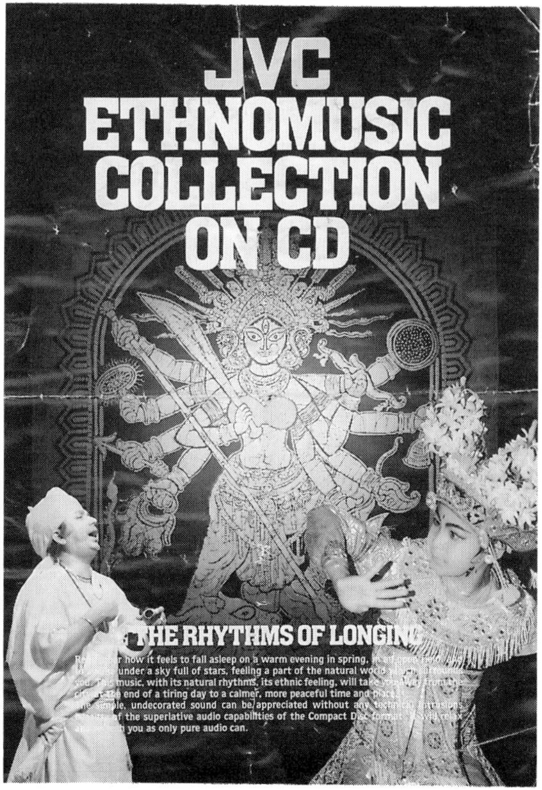

Figure 4 Advertisement for JVC Ethnomusic Library

and the immediate range of the voice' (Derrida 1976:138). This time is only made visible by its binary opposition to the worries of a modern, technological city, a city which itself has of course made this inscriptive practice possible, yet 'longs' for the edenic 'ethnic' possibilities of re-unification with the natural, where one is surrounded by the 'natural world'.

But the advertisement continues:

> This simple undecorated sound can be appreciated without any technical intrusions because of the superlative audio capabilities of the Compact Disc format. It will relax and refresh you as only pure audio can.

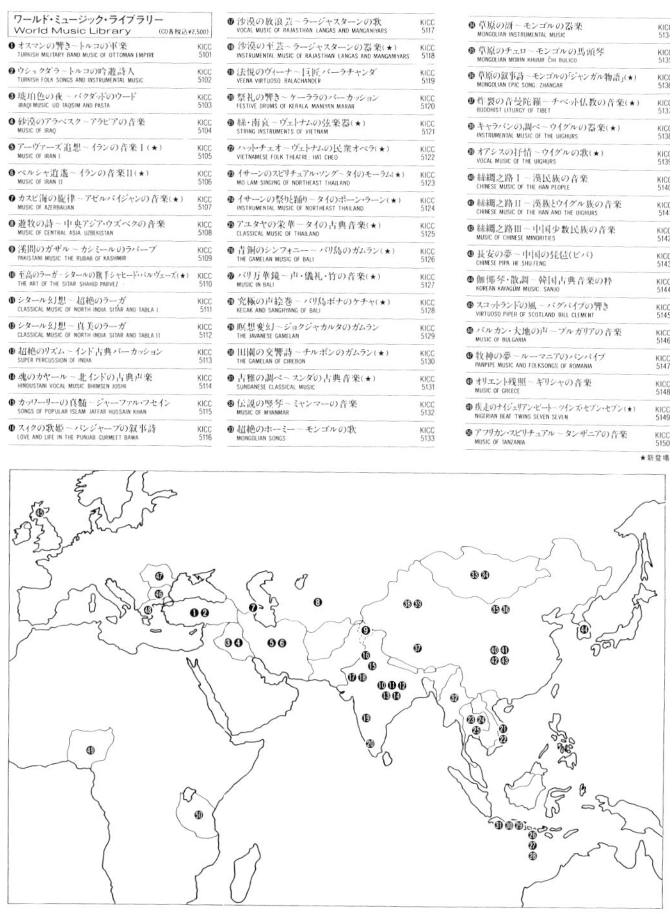

ワールド・ミュージック・ライブラリー
World Music Library (CD各税込¥2,500)

1	オスマンの響き～トルコの軍楽 TURKISH MILITARY BAND MUSIC OF OTTOMAN EMPIRE	KICC 5101
2	ウシュクダラ～トルコの吟遊詩人 TURKISH FOLK SONGS AND INSTRUMENTAL MUSIC	KICC 5102
3	琥珀色の夜～バグダッドのウード IRAQI MUSIC UD TAQSIM AND PASTA	KICC 5103
4	砂漠のアラベスク～アラビアの音楽 MUSIC OF IRAQ	KICC 5104
5	アーヴァーズ追想～イランの音楽I(★) MUSIC OF IRAN I	KICC 5105
6	ペルシャ逍遙～イランの音楽II(★) MUSIC OF IRAN II	KICC 5106
7	カスピ海の旋律～アゼルバイジャンの音楽(★) MUSIC OF AZERBAIJAN	KICC 5107
8	遊牧の詩～中央アジア・ウズベクの音楽 MUSIC OF CENTRAL ASIA UZBEKISTAN	KICC 5108
9	渓間のガザル～カシミールのラバーブ PAKISTANI MUSIC THE RUBAB OF KASHMIR	KICC 5109
10	至高のラーガ～シタールの旗手シャヒード・パルヴェーズ(★) THE ART OF THE SITAR SHAHID PARVEZ	KICC 5110
11	シタール幻想～超絶のラーガ CLASSICAL MUSIC OF NORTH INDIA SITAR AND TABLA I	KICC 5111
12	シタール幻想～真美のラーガ CLASSICAL MUSIC OF NORTH INDIA SITAR AND TABLA II	KICC 5112
13	超絶のリズム～インド古典パーカッション SUPER PERCUSSION OF INDIA	KICC 5113
14	魂のカヤール～北インドの古典声楽 HINDUSTANI VOCAL MUSIC BHIMSEN JOSHI	KICC 5114
15	カッワーリーの真髄～ジャーファル・フセイン SONGS OF POPULAR ISLAM JAFFAR HUSSAIN KHAN	KICC 5115
16	スィクの歌姫～パンジャーブの叙事詩 LOVE AND LIFE IN THE PUNJAB GURMEET BAWA	KICC 5116
17	沙漠の放浪芸～ラージャスターンの歌 VOCAL MUSIC OF RAJASTHAN LANGAS AND MANGANIYARS	KICC 5117
18	沙漠の至芸～ラージャスターンの器楽(★) INSTRUMENTAL MUSIC OF RAJASTHAN LANGAS AND MANGANIYARS	KICC 5118
19	法悦のヴィーナ～巨匠バーラチャンダ VEENA VIRTUOSO BALACHANDER	KICC 5119
20	祭礼の響き～ケーララのパーカッション FESTIVE DRUMS OF KERALA MANIYAN MARAR	KICC 5120
21	絲・南音～ヴェトナムの弦楽器(★) STRING INSTRUMENTS OF VIETNAM	KICC 5121
22	ハット・チェオ～ヴェトナムの民衆オペラ(★) VIETNAMESE FOLK THEATRE: HAT CHEO	KICC 5122
23	イサーンのスピリチュアル・ソング～タイのモーラム(★) MO LAM SINGING OF NORTHEAST THAILAND	KICC 5123
24	イサーンの祭りと踊り～タイのポーン・ラーン(★) INSTRUMENTAL MUSIC OF NORTHEAST THAILAND	KICC 5124
25	アユタヤの栄華～タイの古典音楽(★) CLASSICAL MUSIC OF THAILAND	KICC 5125
26	青銅のシンフォニー～バリ島のガムラン(★) THE GAMELAN MUSIC OF BALI	KICC 5126
27	バリ万華鏡～声・儀礼・竹の音楽(★) MUSIC IN BALI	KICC 5127
28	究極の声絵巻～バリ島ボナのケチャ(★) KECAK AND SANGHYANG OF BALI	KICC 5128
29	瞑想変幻～ジョクジャカルタのガムラン THE JAVANESE GAMELAN	KICC 5129
30	田園の交響詩～チルボンのガムラン(★) THE GAMELAN OF CIREBON	KICC 5130
31	古雅の調べ～スンダの古典音楽(★) SUNDANESE CLASSICAL MUSIC	KICC 5131
32	伝説の竪琴～ミャンマーの音楽 MUSIC OF MYANMAR	KICC 5132
33	超絶のホーミー～モンゴルの歌 MONGOLIAN SONGS	KICC 5133
34	草原の訝～モンゴルの器楽 MONGOLIAN INSTRUMENTAL MUSIC	KICC 5134
35	草原のチェロ～モンゴルの馬頭琴 MONGOLIAN MORIN KHUUR ČHI BULICO	KICC 5135
36	草原の叙事詩～モンゴルの「ジャンガル物語」(★) MONGOLIAN EPIC SONG: ZHANGAR	KICC 5136
37	炸裂の音曼陀羅～チベット仏教の音楽(★) BUDDHIST LITURGY OF TIBET	KICC 5137
38	キャラバンの調べ～ウイグルの器楽(★) INSTRUMENTAL MUSIC OF THE UIGHURS	KICC 5138
39	オアシスの抒情～ウイグルの歌(★) VOCAL MUSIC OF THE UIGHURS	KICC 5139
40	絲綢之路I～漢民族の音楽 CHINESE MUSIC OF THE HAN PEOPLE	KICC 5140
41	絲綢之路II～漢族とウイグル族の音楽 CHINESE MUSIC OF THE HAN AND THE UIGHURS	KICC 5141
42	絲綢之路III～中国少数民族の音楽 MUSIC OF CHINESE MINORITIES	KICC 5142
43	長安の夢～中国の琵琶(ピパ) CHINESE PIPA HE SHU-FENG	KICC 5143
44	伽倻琴・散調～韓国古典音楽の粋 KOREAN KAYAGŬM MUSIC: SANJO	KICC 5144
45	スコットランドの風～バグパイプの響き VIRTUOSO PIPER OF SCOTLAND BILL CLEMENT	KICC 5145
46	バルカン・大地の声～ブルガリアの音楽 MUSIC OF BULGARIA	KICC 5146
47	牧神の夢～ルーマニアのパンパイプ PANPIPE MUSIC AND FOLKSONGS OF ROMANIA	KICC 5147
48	オリエント残照～ギリシャの音楽 MUSIC OF GREECE	KICC 5148
49	疾走のナイジェリアン・ビート～ツインズ・セブン・セブン(★) NIGERIAN BEAT TWINS SEVEN SEVEN	KICC 5149
50	アフリカン・スピリチュアル～タンザニアの音楽 MUSIC OF TANZANIA	KICC 5150

★新登場

Figure 5 The King World Music Library

Here, the stakes change: the authentic prior is now to be re-produced, as 'only pure audio can'. The object of the collection is now to efface the (necessary) technical intrusions into an 'original, pure' sound event ironically by the very quality of its technology – a good inscription, then, one which realizes its place as 'secondary' to the origin. But in these words one can hear/read a discomfort, since it is clear that such a possibility, the utopic re-production of 'simple undecorated sound' remains ever unreachable, an asymptote. The technical means by which this utopic possibility is almost-attained ('the superlative audio capabilities of the Compact Disc format') remains, as technical, the very stuff which the fantasy diegesis of a natural, calming, rhythmic ethnicity represented by the JVC Ethnomusic Series needs to excise from its mise-en-scene as a guarantee of its consistency and coherence – the very forms of technology that need, by definition, to be cast always already as intrusion, to be scripted as the 'fatal accident' (Derrida 1976:135). This argument argues that the goal of the technical in recording should be to allow the originary authenticity of the sound event to 'come through' the very apparatus of inscription. But in so doing, the 'ethnics' must be sited as the 'authentic', and themselves without cities, without technology, without a history.

The stakes of mobilizing these rhetorics of recording and the 'priority' of the ethnic are raised to another degree on an example from the King 'World Music Library'. Inside the CD booklet for the King Records release, *Nigerian Beat*, there is not only a reproduction of the world library map (Figure 5) but that map is set in visual counterpoint to another visual configuration of space depicted in the booklet, that of the recording studio (Figure 6). This 'map' of the site of inscription indicates the positions of the various instruments in the ensemble and their spatial relationship to the symbolic stand in for the inscriptive apparatus, the microphone. It is intriguing as representation as much for what it fails to depict as for the information it seems to present. The microphones appear only as circles with crossing arrows pointing to the source of the sound to be recorded, and are labeled by their technological designations (MD-421, CMC 55U, U-67). There is only a depiction of that which we think we are hearing: the 'man behind the curtain' who controls the knobs and dials behind the glass of the recording booth is hidden – perhaps behind the map. This act of concealment allows the listener to imagine the performance as a 'natural' emanation of musical ethnicity in the recording studio.

This representing the installation of the musical 'source' of the CD into a placeless technological fills up the void on the world map that 'Japan' signifies/is-signified-by. The visual depiction of the act of recording pretends to be a revelation of the techniques of musical reproduction, but actually removes the studio from its historical specificity and conceals the operations that intervene between the here fetishized act of performance and the final act of audition by the metropolitan consumer. As an explorer in her own

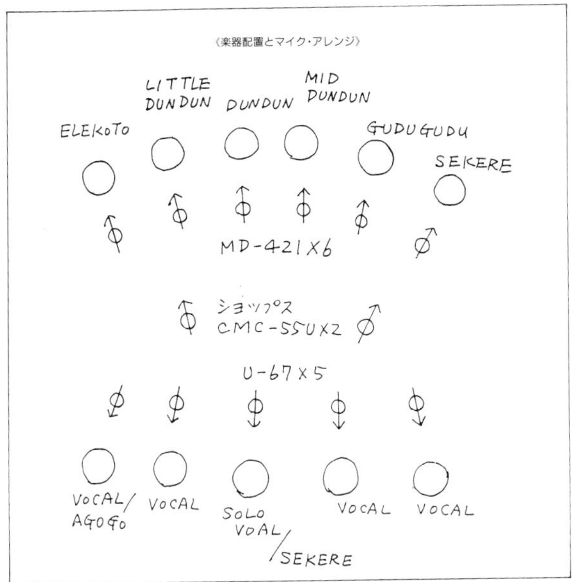

Figure 6 Another mapping: the recording studio (from *Nigerian Beat*)

home, the listener tries to imagine, both maps in hand, the relationship of these visualizations to the sonic traces on the CD, and in so doing, the 'lack' of the visual is 'filled' by the technological prowess of the reproductive apparatus. The technical 'intrusions', which would, in this logic, disrupt the fantasy of the natural, are here ironically hidden *in their very depiction*, in order that the consumer can appreciate the 'simple, undecorated sound' of the ethnic in the recording studio, can visit that place 'under the night sky'. The world map tells the listener that s/he is traveling to a distant site of origins, yet the technological mapping of the studio assures that same listener of his or her comfortable return. These 'maps' allow one to stage the originary site of musical performance, without the risk of negotiating the historical reasons that allow this recording to be possible: here specifically, the insertion of Japanese economic power into the politics of the so-called 'Third World'. Sleeping under the night sky is here not homelessness or poverty, but primordiality, pleasure. The depiction of the recording studio is not labeled as a 'place'. The recording studio refuses specificity, and masks itself as the overarching depiction of (post)modernity. Similarly, the rest of the world is that natural 'ethnic' space under a night sky, brought 'undecorated' into the home of the JVC consumer.

A 'Japan' is 'sounded' by King Records in another series of CDs, released by the same recording division as the 'World Music Library', Seven Seas, entitled 'Japanese Folk Music'. 'Packed in it is the kind of music that comes from various rich Japanese traditions found nowhere else but in Japan' (Kojima 1991:16). These liner notes, written by Kojima Tomiko, a professor at the National Museum of History and Folklore, illustrate clearly the dynamic to which Yoshimoto refers. The supposed 'internationalization' represented by the commodification of 'ethnic music' through the world music libraries of Japanese record companies inserts only a phantasmatic otherness into the space of Japan, an otherness 'whose differences are safely contained or erased [which can] never have any direct impact on the Japanese' (Yoshimoto 1989:21). The centrality of Japan staged by the world maps of these catalogues is then dialectically reinforced by the nationalist project of eradicating historicity and difference within Japan. Kojima writes that the rediscovery of 'Japanese' folk music serves to locate Japan as central in a new world order:

> Especially in the last couple of years, music in the world has been changing rapidly. The Western classical music has been appealing less to young people in Europe, and there seems to be nothing to replace it yet . . . Given such a stalemate of the present-day music scene, it is no wonder why world musicians are now looking to non-western music . . . And almost in respond [sic] to such interest from the West, non-western peoples have begun to produce new ethnic music of the first-rate quality on basis of the rich music tradition they already have. This music is what we call the 'world music'. Many of us used to think of the 'world' to mean the occidental. With the birth of the new world music, however, the meaning of the 'world' has changed . . . As this new world music has been sought after, some of us *really* sharp ones are starting to realize we have been carrying on our back our own ethnic music all this time . . . We live in a modern time, but we are at the same time at the end of a continuing line of history.
>
> (Kojima 1991:15)

In this narrative, the rediscovery of an authentic Japanese music places Japan not only as central in the new world order, but additionally that centrality has a logical place in its own national time line – it becomes indeed Japanese destiny at the end of 'a continuing line of history'. Difference within Japan is obliterated in the nationalist enunciation of the 'we': a 'we' that pretends to include in this series of CDs the music of peoples marginal to a Japanese modernity, here musicians from the Ryukyu Islands[13] and, on another CD, 'Japanese working songs!'

In the press release for *Beauty*, Sakamoto described his trajectory towards the world beat of this project through a teleo-logic that is manifestly vectored. It is difficult to read this directionality as anything but parallel to the expanding power of Japanese finance in 'Third World' economies: 'I used Japanese, Indonesian, and Chinese music . . . maybe a little bit of Indian. Now I'm moving toward the West as well – through India, Iraq, and finally, I reach to Africa.' Africa is then positioned at the end of a geographic series, the end of the earth; its place as the final 'mine' for a world beat in Sakamoto's narrative is directly opposed to the characterization of world beat common to Western stars. Feld argues that the 'discourse of roots' allows Western world beat stars to configure their celebration of African musics within a history which has long fetishized African American 'musical expression' (Feld 1988). This 'revitalization through appropriation' in the traffic between Africa and North America in the work of Paul Simon and others becomes in Sakamoto's case illegible. 'Africa' is not cited as a place of roots, but rather serves as a tool through which to 'sound' Japan through a series of appropriations 'closer to home': Korean and Okinawan musicians. Rather than producing an album which narrates the stylistic continuities between Afro-pop and international popular music styles, as Paul Simon does, Sakamoto succeeds in using the space of the international to orchestrate a newly essentialized Japanese musical difference as the 'end of history'.

Sakamoto does not describe his exploration of world beat in terms of collaboration, as Western stars often do, ignoring the politics of asymmetry that makes these collaborations legible and possible. Rather, Sakamoto describes the production of his world beat as directional from 'Japan' to 'Africa', reinforcing the logic of the 'spatial incarceration of the native' (Appadurai quoted in Gupta and Ferguson 1992:17) in an ultimately distant Africa, while importing his African talent to the metropoles of Japan and the West for 'refinement' and finally, insertion into a logic which produces the internationalization of popular music in Japan as the endpoint of a newly scripted Japanese national history. Sakamoto's music tells the story of 'culture contact' with an imperial gesture, where history remains driven by the desires and politics of the metropole, and where the agency of the 'African' being reached for is removed from the stage. Like the mapping of the recording studio and the globe in the world music library, the relations which overdetermine the importation of the 'exotic' African into the metropolitan studio are concealed in order to enact a new, transformed rhetoric of neo-nationalism.

These operations can be made even more clear by hearing their enactment in the sound world of the album. The fourth song on the CD is entitled 'Asodaya Yunta'. This song is one of four songs on the album not credited to Sakamoto, the other three being 'We Love You', a 'Japanese' rereading of the Rolling Stones song, 'Romance', a song ('Jeannie With The Light Brown Hair') composed by the nineteenth-century North American composer Stephen Foster, performed with new lyrics, and the last song on the album, 'Chinsagu No Hana', credited as 'traditional'. 'Asodaya Yunta' features Sakamoto using what he calls 'composer style' singing on the lead vocals, with a 'backup' trio of three Okinawan women, and Youssou N'Dour improvising vocals between the verses. In a feeling of two, the song serves to narrate the confluence of three styles: a 'Japanese' song (of 9 and bar phrases) inserted between 8-bar phrases familiar to the metropolitan listener as the basic building blocks of popular song, and finally N'Dour's improvisations, which appear above both these frameworks. Most of the song is arranged in a type of call and response structure, usually with Sakamoto being answered by the Okinawan trio. N'Dour remains outside of this exchange; in a sonic space with a high level of reverberation, N'Dour's voice appears to sound in an empty room. The voice of N'Dour, the voice of the 'long distance call', serves here to articulate the 'outside', the supplement to a Japanese coherence, a coherence which depends on the erasure of present and historical difference. If Okinawan voices stand in here unproblematically for 'Japanese', Sakamoto has effected not only an erasure of the economic relations which allow the phenomena of world beat, but additionally *Beauty* successfully sites itself within a master narrative of Japanese neo-nationalism: 'the more Japan is internationalized, the more it is isolated from the rest of the world' (Yoshimoto 1989:23). This dynamic is reinforced by Sakamoto's 'composer style'[14] of singing: Sakamoto on *Beauty* claims his place in an international modern by dramatizing the un-ethnic sound of his voice in comparison to the women on the album and Youssou N'Dour. Sakamoto uses his access to an international modern to authenticate his orchestration of a new Japan, 'living in a modern time but at the end of a long history'. This dynamic is literalized as the album ends with a 'traditional' Japanese song, again presumably Okinawan: serving as the open-ended site of return for an album that has begun with a 'decadent' cosmopolitanism. This concluding stroke closes the door, as it were, on the play of difference that the earlier songs on the CD suggest, without naming on whom this door is shut.

'Romance Music' enacts a string of citations which locate the recording as a meta-commentary on 'ethnicity' as produced as spectacle in popular song. The Stephen Foster song on which this piece is based, 'Jeannie With the Light Brown Hair', belongs to one of Foster's 'Irish' melodies, in contradistinction to the minstrel songs for which he is most famous. Written in 1854, 'Jeannie' appeared after Foster's success with minstrel songs in the late 1840s (Hamm 1979:217–219). Gerald Mast has argued that these 'Irish' melodies, written with the sentiments of the earlier popularizer of 'Irish' song, Thomas Moore (Hamm 1979:217), serve as the beginnings of the American 32-bar song form (1987:27). If Mast's reading is correct, it enticingly links the very form of an American musical national popular with a history of ethnic imitations and appropriations. Foster's turn towards 'Irish' material marked not a turn back to 'white song', but did mark a turn towards a different kind of national nostalgia. Turning back to Sakamoto, one can argue that his re-contextualization of Foster's ethically, racially mediated production of nostalgia on *Beauty* places Sakamoto within that Western history of popular song.

The melody of Foster's song is largely pentatonic in its pitch material. This gesture in the original song served as an imitation of supposedly Irish melodic patterns. Sakamoto's version however takes this pentatonicism and makes it mean quite differently. By arranging it for sansin and the voices of the Okinawan women on the album, and additionally by using the now familiar 'orientalizing' trope of parallel fifths in its harmonization, 'Romance' effectively re-'orients' the song to articulate a newly authenticized Japaneseness.

One would be unaware of the history of this song if not cued to its origins by the liner notes. This gesture not only dehistoricizes the meaning of the musical material, but resites the gesture towards national sentiment in the Foster song in a new Japanese context; if the 'Irishness' of Foster's late songs or 'blackness' of Foster's minstrelsy served to 'Americanize' Foster, Sakamoto redirects this gesture, by 'Japanizing' Foster through voicing this material anew. While one reading of this appropriation might have been a critique of the 'ethnic' characterizations that populate the history of Western popular music, Sakamoto uses that history rather to interpolate a different ethnicity into the authenticity and 'folkness' that the original Foster song presumably evokes in his manipulation of stereotyped 'eastern' harmonics, voices, and instrumentarium.

But these largely 'negative' readings of *Beauty* might be tempered by looking for a moment to the ways this project might work differently in the West. Hisama has critiqued the Asiophilia of popular musicians as participating in a (post) colonial regime of stereotype, that serves not only to police gender binarisms by mapping them onto an imagined geography, but also to re-produce the fantasy person of 'the china girl' as an 'exotic, fetishized object to be installed in some museum' (1993:99). The mechanism which Hisama describes is in some ways diverted by the homoerotics of Sakamoto as star. On the album cover of *Beauty* (Figure 7), we witness a new invocation of the homoeroticism familiar in Sakamoto's star text through *Merry Christmas, Mr. Lawrence*. Sakamoto's body, with his head back, displays a sort of ecstasy that is foreign to the production of masculine (heterosexual) stardom in the West. Considering his earlier role in the Ōshima film, it is difficult (for me) to see this body outside of a repertoire of photography that is explicitly homoerotic. This bodily display, when conjoined with the vocal quality of Sakamoto on this recording, the grain of his voice (Barthes 1990), leads the listener to locate this body as the site for a sensual, queer fantasy rather than as the grounding for a heteronormative imagining of the 'forceful' rock star.[15] This display of the 'world beat' artist as homo sex-symbol reconfigures the operation of the heteronormatively imagined fantasies that Hisama describes, and additionally places Sakamoto in a very different role to the decidedly non-homoerotic world beat stars to which the Western listener is accustomed. While it is crucial to describe the operation of Sakamoto within a similar structure of racial fetishization, especially in light of the history of representations of Asian

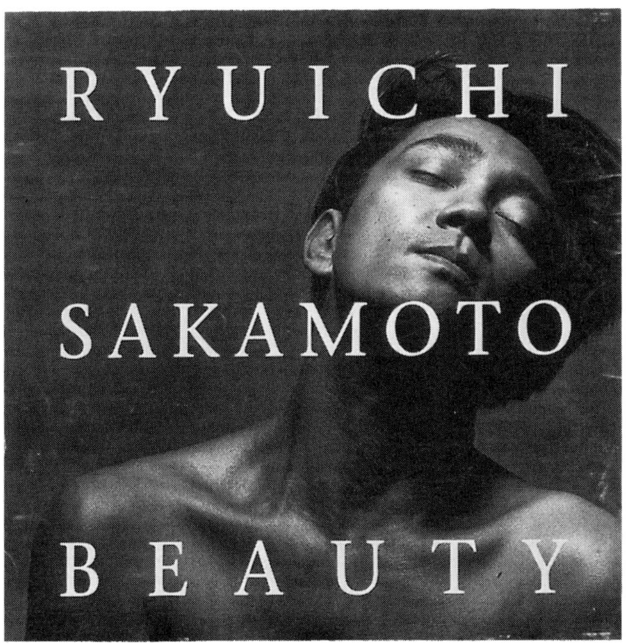

Figure 7 Album cover for *Beauty*

gay men in Western homoerotics (Fung 1991), we might want to read this work without participating in a rhetoric of prohibition.[16] That rhetoric of prohibition will in this case function all too effectively as prohibition of the queer in Orientalism, rather than the orientalism in the queer. Additionally, the Orientalisms of homo-sex in the West should not be read as mere imitation of the hetero norm (Butler 1990). Reading *Beauty* in part as a document within a history of a fantasy Japan (Barthes 1982) might allow us to see a constructive engagement with that stereotype, which might allow its operation to become both a site of pleasure *and* critique (Miller 1992:41). *Beauty* means differently when read as a neocolonialist fetishization of the 'far away' in order to essentialize the politics of the local in Japan or when used as a tool for a Western homoerotic fantasy, albeit made legible through a matrix of meaning over-determined by the histories of Orientalism. If the 'Japaneseness' of Sakamoto is read as a citation, the eroticization of that citation should not be read as a one-way fetishization, but rather a more complicated traffic in sounds and images through which differing ideological operations can be enacted. *Beauty* is simultaneously a cipher for a hidden homoerotics of fetishization in the West and a critique of their essentialization, and works through all this to articulate a Japanese (post) modernity, itself problematic for its location within the dialectic of inter-nationalization and neo-nationalism. Each of these readings is crucial to bring out the specificities of a Japanese world beat, particularly one so multi-layered and multi-styled as Sakamoto's.

Conclusion

If this reading of Sakamoto's career in the 1980s illustrates anything, I hope that it begins to indicate the complicity and complexity of the transnational practices of 'world musics' as multiple ways of organizing temporality, geography, and identity. Recent work by scholars interested in the occupation of the transnational through recorded musical practices have argued that world music is an example of the euphoric embracing of difference in itself refiguring that very difference into a kind of equivalence (Erlmann 1993:13). But I would argue that before a move is made to re-invoke the global as a site of critique, it is crucial to examine the ways in which distinct practices of transnationality in popular music configure different politics. Sakamoto's cosmopolitan techno-pop, his 'historicist' film scores, and his world beat each are the sites of different forms of pleasure, which themselves enact different forms of ideological work and contestation. Until the various forms of ideological work that these pleasures enact is more precisely laid out and critiqued, and the nature of the transnational recording star as institution and site in mass culture is more understood, the project of a critique of transnational popular musics is doomed to a reductive formalism or a totalizing political economy of 'the transnational music industry'. I hope this essay is a step towards this critique, by making the 'world' in world music a little less legible, a little less easily invoked as a starting point for critique.

Notes

I would like to thank Marilyn Ivy for her seminar on the Anthropology of Modern Japan, held at the University of Chicago in Spring, 1990, and for her insightful comments on a very early version of this essay; John

Whittier Treat for his suggestions towards its revision and his invitation to participate in this collection; David Rubinson of Kinetic Art and Business America, Inc., Ryuichi Sakamoto's international manager, for his helpful response to my inquiries; Robert C. Cook for his setting of my musical examples; and finally Wilhelm von Werthern, for both for his painstaking editing and his patience.

1 For a sampling of recent work on world music or world beat; see: Feld (1988); Meintjes (1990); Goodwin and Gore (1990); Erlmann (1993); Guilbault (1993); Garofalo (1993); Mitchell (1993).
2 On the contingency of these relations, see Gupta and Ferguson (1992).
3 I am using this ordering of names intentionally, since the name designates Sakamoto as star apparatus, institution, and as such, in the West he is always 'Ryuichi Sakamoto'.
4 The notion that a musical star is an apparatus, technology, or institution has not been that widely explored. On stardom in film as an 'industry of desire', see the collection edited by Christine Gledhill (1991).
5 Japan uses in their music traditionally legible strategies of the 'Japanese' stereotype in the West, but these stereotypes were twisted by their mass market success in Japan into something quite different. Japan's success begs the questions I will examine in relation to Sakamoto. Who is appropriating whom, and how can these 'appropriations' be traced in any meaningful way? The complications of this relationship seem indexical for the course Sakamoto's career will take in the West. See Mitsui (1983).
6 On the internationalization of pop styles in Japan, see Mitsui (1983); Herd (1983).
7 Though interestingly, the Sprockets spoof on Saturday Night Live redirects this envisioning of modernity as hyper-German. 'Now is ze time ven ve tanz'.
8 For an overview of the historical development of electronic music and *musique concrète*, see Robert Morgan's brief but lucid description (1991:461f.).
9 This point is discussed in some detail in Miyoshi's examination of the film. See Miyoshi (1991:177 ff).
10 Earl Jackson's article, appearing at about the time I was finishing this chapter, looks at a number of similar issues with a somewhat different perspective in a quite divergent context. See Jackson (1994).
11 Richard Mueller (1986) has traced the stylistic implications of Debussy's 'encounter with the exotic' in Debussy's *Fantaisie* for piano and orchestra, arguing that 'the cyclic theme of the *Fantaisie* is based on a Javanese melody' (1986:158).
12 The rhetorical complexity of the citationality of Japaneseness made legible through the mobilization of homosexuality is made more complicated by the historic linkage of the Japanese discursive production of homosexuality and the encounter and engagement with European forms of nationalist (or nationalizing) modernity. Brad

Borevitz explores this linkage in an unpublished manuscript entitled, 'Iwata's History of Homosexuality and the Discourse on Homosex in Interwar Japan', presented as a paper at Inside/Out, the Third National Graduate Student Conference in Queer Studies, held at the University of Minnesota in April, 1993.

13 The Ryukyu Islanders have, like the Okinawans, Koreans, and the Ainu, been victims of Japanese modernization and 'internal' colonialism.

14 The term is used in Sakamoto's press to describe his tentative, un-virtuosic singing style, as an apologia.

15 This reading of course presumes a queer (male) reading. While such a rude presumption might also be invoked in readings of other world beat artists, such readings do not seem as invited by these othjer star-texts as that of Sakamoto.

15 Kobena Mercer (1991) has argued that the right wing mobilization of a rhetoric of prohibition in the Mapplethorpe debates necessitated a reconsideration of his earlier critique of the racial politics of Mapplethorpe's representations of black bodies. I would suggest here that any critique of what Hisama terms 'Asiophilia' in the case of Sakamoto's homoeroticism should be made with a similar caution.

References

Appadurai, Arjun 1990 'Disjuncture and difference in the global cultural economy', p. 295–310 in *Theory, Culture, and Society* 7.

Barthes, Roland 1982 *Empire of Signs*, New York: Hill and Wang.

Barthes, Roland 1990 'The grain of the voice', p. 301–314 in Simon Frith and Andrew Goodwin (eds.) 1990 *On Record: Rock, Pop, and the Written Word*, New York: Pantheon Books.

Benjamin, Walter 1977 'Paris, die Hauptstadt des XIX. Jahrhunderts (Paris, capital of the nineteenth century)', p. 170–184 in *Illuminationen*, Frankfurt a. M.: Suhrkamp Verlag.

Borevitz, Brad 1994 'Iwata's history of homosexuality and the discourse on homosex in inter-war Japan', Unpublished paper, Department of East Asian Languages and Civilizations, University of Chicago.

Brett, Philip 1994 'Eros and Orientalism in Britten's operas', p. 235–256 in Philip Brett, Elizabeth Wood and Gary Thomas (eds.) 1994 *Queering the Pitch: the new gay and lesbian musicology*, New York and London: Routledge.

Butler, Judith 1990 *Gender Trouble: feminism and the subversion of identity*, New York and London: Routledge.

Derrida, Jacques 1976 *Of Grammatology*, Baltimore: The Johns Hopkins University Press.

Erlmann, Veit 1993 'The politics and aesthetics of transnational musics', p. 3–15 in *The World of Music* 35 (2).

Feld, Steven 1988 'Notes on world beat', p. 31–37 in *Public Culture* 1 (1).

'Foreword' 1991 p. vii–xii in *Oeuvres Complètes de Claude Debussy, Série 1, Volume 3*, Paris: Durand et Costallat.

Fung, Richard 1991 'Looking for my penis: the eroticized Asian in gay video porn', p. 145–160 in Bad Object-Choices (eds.) 1991 *How Do I Look?: queer film and video*, Seattle: Bay Press.

Garofalo, Reebee 1993 'Whose world, what beat: the transnational music industry, identity, and cultural imperialism', p. 16–32 in *The World of Music* 35 (2).

Gledhill, Christine ed. 1991 *Stardom: industry of desire*, New York and London: Routledge.

Goodwin, Andrew and Joe Gore 1990 'World beat and the cultural imperialism debate', p. 63–80 in *Socialist Review* 20 (3).

Guilbault, Jocelyne 1993 'On redefining the "local" through world music', p. 33–47 in *The World of Music* 35 (2).

Gupta, Akhil and James Ferguson 1992 'Beyond "culture": space, identity and the politics of difference', p. 6–23 in *Cultural Anthropology* 7 (1).

Hamm, Charles 1978 *Yesterdays: popular song in America*, New York and London: W.W. Norton and Company.

Herd, Judith Ann 1984 'Trends and taste in Japanese popular music: a case-study of the 1982 Yamaha World Popular Music Festival', p. 75–96 in *Popular Music* 4.

Hisama, Ellie M. 1993 'Postcolonialism on the make: the music of John Mellencamp, David Bowie and John Zorn', p. 91–104 in *Popular Music* 12 (2).

Ivy, Marilyn 1989 'Critical texts, mass artifacts: the consumption of knowledge in postmodern Japan', p. 21–47 in Masao Miyoshi and H.D. Harootunian (eds.) 1989 *Postmodernism and Japan*, Durham and London: Duke University Press.

—— 1988 'Tradition and Difference in the Japanese mass media', p. 21–29 in *Public Culture* 1 (1).

Jackson, Earl Jr. 1994 'Desire at cross(-cultural) purposes: *Hiroshima, Mon Amour* and *Merry Christmas, Mr. Lawrence*', p. 133–174 in *positions: east asia cultures critique* 2 (1).

Kojima Tomiko 1991 'Did you know of such an interesting Japanese music?', p. 15–16 in *Music of Amami: music of Japanese people* (CD liner notes) KICH 2027 Tokyo: King Record Co., Ltd.

Lastra, James 1992 'Reading, writing, and recording sound', p. 65–86 in Rick Altman (ed.) 1992 *Sound Theory/Sound Practice*, New York and London: Routledge.

Mast, Gerald 1987 *Can't Help Singin': the American musical on stage and screen*, Woodstock: The Overlook Press.

Meintjes, Louise 1990 'Paul Simon's *Graceland*, South Africa, and the mediation of musical meaning', p. 37–73 in *Ethnomusicology* 34 (1).

Mercer, Kobena 1991 'Skin head sex thing: racial difference and the homoerotic imaginary', p. 169–210 in Bad Object-Choices (eds.) 1991 *How Do I Look?: queer film and video*, Seattle: Bay Press.

Miller, D.A. 1992 *Bringing Out Roland Barthes*, Berkeley and Oxford: University of California Press.

Mitchell, Tony 1993 'World music and the popular music industry: an Australian view', p. 309–338 in *Ethnomusicology* 37 (3).

Mitsui Tōru 1983 'Japan in Japan: notes on an aspect of the popular music record industry in Japan', p. 107–120 in *Popular Music* 3.

Miyoshi, Masao 1991 *Off Center: power and culture relations between Japan and the United States*, Cambridge, Mass. and London: Harvard University Press.

Morgan, Robert 1991 *Twentieth Century Music: a history of musical style in modern Europe and America*, New York and London: W.W. Norton and Company.

Mueller, Richard 1986 'Javanese influences on Debussy's *Fantaisie* and beyond', p. 157–86 in *19th-Century Music* 10 (2).

Najita, Tetsuo 1989 'On culture and technology in postmodern Japan', p. 3–20 in Masao Miyoshi and H.D. Harootunian (eds.) 1989 *Postmodernism and Japan*, Durham and London: Duke University Press.

Ogawa Hisao 1991 'Music of Amami', p. 18–22 in *Music of Amami: music of Japanese people* (CD liner notes) KICH 2027, Tokyo: King Record Co., Ltd.

El Pas 1990 'Ryuichi Sakamoto: "Mi música es el resultado de todo lo que me gusta"' (My music is the combined result of everything that I like), June 12 (Madrid).

Pasler, Jann 1991 'Paris: conflicting notions of progress', p. 389–416 in Jim Samson (ed.) 1991 *The Late Romantic Era*, Englewood Cliffs: Prentice Hall.

Prendergast, Mark 1990 'Ryuichi Sakamoto. Japanese artist/world musician', p. 58–60 in *Sound on Sound* (September).

Sakai, Naoki 1989 'Modernity and Its Critique: the problem of universalism and particularism', p. 93–122 in Masao Miyoshi and H.D. Harootunian (eds.) 1989 *Postmodernism and Japan*, Durham and London: Duke University Press.

Yoshimoto Mitsuhiro 1989 'The postmodern and mass images in Japan', p. 8–25 in *Public Culture* 1 (2).

Material has also been drawn from a press release for the album *Beauty*, sent to me by Sakamoto's manager, David Rubinson.

Discography

Kraftwerk 1986 *Electric Cafe*, Elektra 25525-2.

Music of Amami: music of Japanese people, King Records (Japan) KICH 2027.

Sakamoto, Ryuichi 1980 *B-2 Unit*, Island ILPS 9656.

Sakamoto, Ryuichi 1983 *Coda*, London Records (Japan) L25N 1016.

Sakamoto, Ryuichi 1989 *Beauty*, Virgin Records America, Inc. 91294–2.

Sakamoto, Ryuichi 1991 *Heartbeat*, Virgin Records America, Inc. V2-86291.

Sylvian, David 1987 *Secrets of the Beehive*, Virgin Records Limited (U.K.) V2471.

Twins Seven-Seven 1991 *Nigerian Beat (World Music Library)*, King Records (Japan) KICC 5149.

4

Mournful Tears and *Sake*

The Postwar Myth of Misora Hibari

Alan M. Tansman

In 1987, toward the end of the Showa era (1926–1989), the great postwar Japanese singer Misora Hibari entered the hospital for a four-month stay. To millions of loyal fans the media presented these months of suffering as a closing chapter in the life of a persona they had helped create – a persona embodying pain and perseverance. Nearing death, wracked by pain, Hibari asked her long-time friend and collaborator Funamura Tōru to write her a song, for she needed, she said, to sing once again before she died. He wrote *Tangled Hair* (Midaregami), in which he likened her to a lone lighthouse overlooking a powerful ocean. Funamura worried that his melody might be too difficult for her to sing, and Hibari was concerned that she might be too weak to carry it off. Yet she insisted, and the biographies of her life reveal that he held nothing back. Her performance of this song in 1988, six months before she died, was her last public singing appearance. When she sang it before 50,000 people in the Tokyo Dome, Hibari lifted herself to the glittering heights of schmaltz – or to the pinnacle of spiritual resonance, depending upon one's taste. Bedecked in black and silver feathers swathing her body like a protective nest, a feathered glittering black headdress shooting four feet into the air, Hibari, her shoulders clad in armor, became a bird, a creature from another planet ready to take off, or be transformed, like Yamato Takeru, the mythological Japanese hero, into a white bird-god. Neither male nor female, old nor young, she was now beyond this world.

The scene at the concert is extravagantly, audaciously artificial, yet also deeply sincere. 'Hibari', she says, her voice quivering, truly as if in pain, as if speaking of a being not of her own making, 'supported by your love, can today again lift her wings; today I give these feelings of gratitude to song and sing to the very end' (NHK

1989). Lush strings accompany clarinets and a single lonely guitar as her feathered figures is projected onto a massive screen high above her head. There is great pain in her face, a heavy burden that weighs her down as she seems ready to lift off.

「みなさんの愛に支えられ、ひばりはまた、はばたくことができ
ます……」と、ステージから挨拶する言葉がくぐもった。そし
て最後の 人生一路 を歌い終わると、白い花道をゆっくりと
歩いて消えた。

When Hibari sang in 1949 at age twelve in her film debut, she sang to nobody but a future she faced with defiance and lightness of heart. Here, after all her losses, after seven years of illness, at the close of Showa she again sings to nobody at all. The narrative of her life, which her fans had been reading and listening to from the start of her career in 1949, now transforms the light breeze wafting across her childhood song into a sad wind giving her song depth and gravity. She concludes the number shaking with the words originally written for her as she lay in her sickbed: 'Do not die' (*shinanai de okure*). To whom does she sing 'do not die'? To herself? To her countless, nameless fans, as they were often called? To a sad, Japanese, minor pentatonic spirit of lament? Her final words express a longing for what once was, what might have been, and perhaps what can be – for the world of *enka*, the genre of short melancholy Japanese songs employing Western instruments and a minor pentatonic scale, that she sang best.

By her death in 1989 Hibari's reputation as Japan's greatest postwar singer had ascended to the level of myth. Her voice, wrote one critic and fan in 1990, sang

> of a confession with nobody to confess to. Within her song there is a certain something wrapped in an ancient silence older than even existence: the magnificent speech of flowers, in a garden deep in the night, which nobody knows the meaning of; the steady gaze of nature. Are not hers the original sounds of all living beings, the songs of ancient birth itself, older than our existence? To whom does her song belong? The singer? Or the listeners nearby? From where does her song emanate? From the singer? Or from the trembling bodies of the listeners?
>
> (Furuzawa 1990:154)[1]

By the end of her life Hibari had acquired a shaman-like aura. To her fans, she was a being grounded in everyday life but touched by a higher power. She was a salve soothing postwar wounds. In her final performance in 1988, even as she stood on stage she seemed 'supported on air like a spirit' (Furuzawa 1990:158). Yet many Japanese felt as ambivalent about Hibari at her death as they always had. She continues, even now, to be a sort of Japanese Elvis, loved by some and reviled by others. 'American culture has never permitted itself to be exemplified by Elvis Presley, and it never will' (Marcus 1991:59). Japan, too, will continue its uneasy relationship with Hibari, at one extreme seeing in her the atavistic grip of native sensibility, the uneasy reminder of a gloomy past better left behind, the queasy schmaltz of an outdated culture; at the other extreme finding in her the essence of a much-vaunted Japanese spirit of forbearance – specifically, of postwar forbearance. To this day, Japanese who struggled after the war hope to forget the hard times Hibari's songs of endurance have kept alive, but need to remember those times that are so fundamental to their identities. This ambivalence accounts for the passionate responses – both disdain and awe – of the Japanese to her. Hibari's popularity, like that of enka, has never waned. It submerges periodically only to reemerge, like a repressed myth (Mita 1992:80–95).

Hibari as the People's Singer

The nation mourned when Hibari died of pneumonia on May 24, 1989, four months after the death of Emperor Hirohito. Hibari's final hours were reported with the same care and accuracy as were his: news reports and documentaries filled the airwaves, and the newspapers, from the loud pages of the *Nikkan Sports* to the national dailies *Asahi*, *Yomiuri*, *Mainichi*, *Sankei*, and *Nikkei*, ran front page stories of her death. All spoke of her as having sung with and for the spirit of postwar Japanese. Some lamented the death of that spirit's demise; others editorialized that it, like her, would never die: she was an 'immortal bird' (*hibari* means skylark; *misora* means beautiful skies) still inflight. Record stores sold out of her recordings, thousands stood vigil through the night by her home in Yokohama, and thousands more lined the streets to watch her hears pass by. Many shed the same tears of awe and gratitude they had for their emperor.

With the deaths of Hibari and Hirohito the narrative that had plotted Japan within the postwar era now finally – after-repeated pronouncements over the course of three decades – concluded. The nation's preoccupation with recovery, healing, and growth had already given way in the 1980s to concerns with global power, consumerism, and internationalism. Now, the coffin was closed: by the political nail of the death of the emperor, the economic nail of the death of Matsushita Konnosuke, the founder of Matsushita ('Panasonic'), and the cultural nail of the death of Misora Hibari.

Hibari had come to symbolize postwar Japan. When she died in the last year of Showa and the first of the new Heisei era she was transformed with Showa Japan into myth: 'When history is personified', writes Greil Marcus of Elvis Presley, 'and the person behind that history dies, history itself is no longer real' (1991:8). Hibari's death, like that of Presley, has become a handy cultural marker, a symbol of the end of an age. Yet her death, which seemed to symbolize the passing of an old-fashioned temperament, paradoxically ensured the survival of that temperament by transforming it into myth. The myth could be fully born, that is, only when freed from its material embodiment.

With Hibari's death, a chapter of history seemed to end. But whose history? To many, including the popular writer Sawaki Hidae, Misora Hibari's history 'is our history, the people's history'. From her debut in 1949 at age twelve 'Hibari expressed the fundamentals of postwar life, and with her death closed the entire Showa era, leaving behind the image of Showa women, who were allowed such little happiness'. The power of Hibari's voice belongs to 'all the nameless fans', and the universal power of her songs derives from the 'authority of common feeling possessed by all the nameless' (Nippon Geinō 1990).

It was in the voice of a melancholy and defiant singer that Hibari, with the anguish of a Billie Holiday and the gift to transmute that anguish, held in thrall an audience comparable in size and sociology to that of Elvis Presley. The passion for Hibari, hardly unabated today, belongs to fans who still respond to her, as fans do to Elvis, as if she belongs to their own lives. Fans see in her, as they do in him, a stoicism and endurance, an honesty and sincerity that betrays no ambiguity or irony. They see a performer and a person who is loyal to the images they have constructed and the feelings they have projected onto their star. Hibari was, in this sense, transparent. She was not afraid to stand naked before an audience. She had the gift of an Otis Reding: to make her listeners care about her. She performed, like Elvis (the later, commercialized Elvis, not the wild working-class Elvis at Sun Records), 'to bind people (or a people) together, and to confirm their identity – not, as in the most vital pop moments, to divide people and thus to force them to question who they really are' (Marcus 1991:64).[2]

Like country and western stars, Hibari created a bond with her working-class audience – an irony, considering that Japanese fans of American country music, going back to rockabilly in the 1950s, have always been the children of urban elites (Mitsui 1993). It was her ability to express 'communal sentiment' (*kyōdōtaiteki na kyōtsūkanjō*), in the novelist Hisashi Inoue's words, that made Hibari a genius (Hisashi 1990:22). Hibari's fame began in the immediate postwar years of economic uncertainty – characterized by Marilyn Ivy as 'an intensely fragmented, individualized sense of consciousness' (1993:245) – and reached its height in the early 1950s, when an increased mass sensibility and a new cultural conservatism were beginning to overshadow the drama of 'intense fragmentation'. Hibari's charisma brought fragmented individuals into a mass audience during a time of social and economic uncertainty, and continued to remind that audience of the staying power of their Japanese spirit of perseverance through adversity.

Hibari reminded them of what was 'authentically' Japanese. With the signing of a peace treaty with the United States and the end of the American Occupation in 1952 many in Japan came to feel a greater ease with native traditions and a need to peel back the artificial layer of American-imposed ideologies. The culture critic Isoda Kōichi has described the mid-1950s as a time when all the gods of immediate postwar Japanese thought – revolution, individualism, freedom, democracy – had died. There was now a feeling of 'cultural security', as Yoshimoto Takaaki put it then (Yoshimoto 1965:312). Writers and intellectuals debated the meaning of and need for a 'people's literature'. The poet and critic Yamamoto Kenkichi argued for a renewed link between the artist and 'the rules that bind communal society' (Yamamoto 1957:3) at a time when Hibari was already binding communal society with her voice. It is certainly no coincidence that her celebrity peaked when the novelist Kōda Aya's reputation did: both were conservative cultural icons seen to be preserving traditional sensibilities and languages tied to the people and the past.

One might thus understand Hibari's rise to stardom as due in part to her being an image that embodied central but threatened values. If, as Whitney Balliet says, jazz is the 'sound of surprise', Hibari's songs – enka – are the sound of familiar but penetrating recognition. Hibari's charismatic appeal, and that of enka, was especially strong because the social order seemed uncertain or ambiguous.

Hibari's charisma depended as well on her ability to embody contradictory images (Dyer 1991:58). In her hundreds of acting, singing, and biographical roles, she played adults as well as children, men as well as women, the poor and the rich, the countrified and the urbane; she was giddy and mournful, hopeful and despondent. She projected a sincerity not only persuasive to her fans but respected by her fellow professionals: "What she sings 'Mournful Sake', says Miyako Harumi, Hibari's only rival for genius in the postwar singing world, 'there's no "Mournful Sake" first, and then Misora Hibari later: Misora Hibari and "Mournful Sake" are one' (Miyako 1990:135).

Hibari's sincerity was part of a persona constructed by the star industry through records, movies, television, fan magazines, and concerts. Her image was both molded and guarded. To her audience, she has always been the 'Tokyo Kid' from the 1950 film of the same name: a ragamuffin whose genius makes her the object of upper-class enchantment (mingled with curiosity and disgust), whose loyalties nevertheless remain with the poor and hardworking people. After achieving great fame and financial success, Hibari often insisted that she belonged to 'the people', not to the entertainment industry. In *Tokyo Kid* she sings her hit song in the most common of postwar locales, an empty lot, as well-dressed bourgeoisie run to hear her.[3] The soundtrack's lush orchestration virtually drowns out the guitar accompanied of her long-time costar and friend, Kawade Kiyohisa. But Kawade's presence reminds her viewers that though Hibari may be part of the entertainment industry, she still belongs to the simple world of the people, to the street singer and the single string accompaniment, to the world of authentic enka.[4]

Tearful Songs of Nostalgia and Resistance

It was Hibari's persona and image that allowed her to become a cultural marker, but above all it was her voice and the songs she sang that gave her such dramatic cultural presence. From 1940 until the war ended in 1945 the monochromatic songs of war and sacrifice repressed the dazzling array of prewar musical styles of popular Japanese song. Immediately after the war, however, the association of war songs with feudalism, nationalism, and defeat made them culturally taboo. Now, the stoic melancholy of Japanese-sounding songs gave way to lighter, Western melodies of hope. The first postwar hit, 'The Apple Song' (Ringo no Uta), in 1946, was a tonic allowing Japanese to endure defeat, destruction, and famine, and to look to the future with hope. In the first and final verses, sunny days were here again:

Putting my lips to the red apple
I quietly look at the blue sky.
The apple says nothing, but
I know how the apple feels.

Shall we sing the apple song?
If the two of us sing together, it'll be even more fun,

If we all sing together, we'll be even more happy!
Shall I tell you of the apple's feelings?
The apple is so cute, how cute the apple is!
(Ongaku no Tomosha 1977b:10–11)

The greatest outpouring after the war of joyous (and, some would say, 'un-Japanese') energy came from the frenetic performances of 'boogie queen' Kasagi Shizuko singing the boogie woogie rhythms of Hattori Ryōichi. Kasagi, her skirt hitched up high, would rush through a song with a hysterical and joyous abandon – an almost American élan – that made one forget the day's doldrums and lose oneself in a dazzle of quick rhythms and a jumble of ecstatic lyrics. 'Tokyo Boogie Woogie' sang of hope for a future in which the universal language of song would be all that mattered (and Japaneseness would nowhere be found):

Tokyo boogie woogie, rhythm uki uki
heart zuki zuki waku waku
resounds and echoes in the ocean.
Tokyo boogie woogie
the boogie dance is a world dance
the song, a dream of two.
Let's whistle to the melody of love and boogie
the song of burning hearts, with a voice of sweet love,
let's dance together tonight under the moon.
Tokyo boogie woogie
rhythm uki uki, hear zuki zuki waku waku.
The song of the century, the song of the heart,
Tokyo boogie woogie, hey!

In 'Shopping Boogie' Kasagi transformed the growling of empty stomachs into the joy of words on which the imagination, at least, might feast:

Carrots, radishes, burdocks, lotus root, Popeye's favourite spinach, tomato, cabbage, nappa, cucumbers, lilies, stupid eggplant, watermelon, Tokyo negi negi, boogie woogie button and ribbon, shaddock, matches, cider, cigarettes, jintan mints yayakoshi [what a bother] yayakoshi yayakoshi yayakoshi aah! yayakoshhi

Hey ossan [uncle], how are you? Hey ossan, how much is this?
Hey ossan, are you there? Hey ossan, how much is this?

Osan, ossan, how much is this? Ossan, how many for how much?
Ossan ossan ossan ossan ossan ossan ossan ossan
ossan ossan ossan ossan ossan
I can't hear you
and I really don't care
and I really don't care
Ahhhhhhh, tough life. (Kasagi 1990)

These boogies were Kasagi's songs, and when Hibari recorded one in 1954 she caused a minor scandal, earning the wrath of the older singer and the disdain of critics who decried her as a mere mimic. Not that Kasagi had much to worry about. When Hibari leaves her metier, the melancholy enka, and tries to sing with abandon, as she does in the 1952 'Mambo Festival' (Manbo matsuri) her performance seems as stiff as her forced smile or festive exclamations of 'wasshoi wasshoi'. The festive atmosphere she projects is not infectious. Her greatest successes were always with enka, the people's defiant but melancholy music.

It was only in the late 1960s and early 1970s that the term enka came to refer to sad Japanese-flavored ballads, rooted in popular songs (*kayōkyoku*), sung with complex and dramatic melismas. Enka were sung by women in kimono or evening dresses and men in tuxedos, to middle-aged, working class audiences that listened to the music on media commonly consumed by them, such as karaoke and AM radio. Amidst the growth of new folk and rock music, enka provided an alternative for the over-thirty set looking for its own musical niche.

Listening to enka provided an alternative to imported musical styles and represented 'authentic' Japanese experience. Yet though audiences claim that enka sounds and feels authentically Japanese, in reality, like all so-called authentic myths, it is an impure amalgam of forms. Enka is a hybrid musical style that can be traced to the important of Western musical education. In 1872, a repertory of choral 'school songs' (*shōka*) became a compulsory part of school curricula. Collected and edited by Isawa Shūji (1851–1917), who brought back with him from Lowell, Massachussetts, a teacher of music and a new philosophy of musical education, these school songs were short ditties that borrowed Irish and Scottish folk melodies. Like Japanese folk songs, the melodies were in pentatonic scales – accounting for the astounding popularity to this day in Japan of 'Auld Lang Syne' (*Hotaru no Hikari*) – to which were added Japanese lyrics. Often the songs were accompanied by organ, which had been used in Protestant churches. Musical educators fused Western and Japanese musical scales, resulting in a scale without the fourth and seventh notes (*yonanuki*). Early enka synthesized this scale with the popular melodies of Edo Japan.

The term enka originally referred to songs of political resistance, and later to songs of social and personal lament that told of the pain of separation in love through images of harbors, rain, and tears. Enka began as protest songs performed on street corners in the 'people's rights movement' of the 1870s and 1880s. In response to government repression against political protest, singing gradually became a guerilla tactic: enka referred to *enzetsu*, or speeches, and like many of today's rap songs, were a chanted form of social protest. The 'Dynamite Dong Ditty' in 1885 called for liberty and threatened 'the roar of dynamite':

> Whatever happens to me
> if we can have liberty in this country
> I'll strive for the good and welfare of the people.
> If we cannot, there will be the roar of dynamite.
>
> (Mitsui 1989:64)

Enka as politics faded in 1890, with the convening of a national legislature (signaling a success for the people's rights movement), and in 1895, with victory in the Sino-Japanese war. The only national enka club disbanded in 1901, after which enka came to refer to light satirical songs known as 'student enka' (*shosei enka*):

> Tinkle, tinkle, ringing the bell
> here comes a dandy on a bicycle
> trying to show off his trick cycling
> with both his hands off the handlebars.
> Look out, don't go that way
> look out, don't come this way
> now you have fallen off, you see
> high-falutin' girls with gold-rimmed spectacles
> the students of the West End college.
> Poems by Byron and Goethe in hand
> they chant about something to do with Naturalism
> when rustle the rice plants of Waseda College
> gently blows the breeze of love.
>
> (Mitsui 1989:64–65)

When politics faded, enka singers took to the streets with violins (the first violin accompaniment is said to have appeared in 1907) to sing the news set to melodies. The songs continued, however, to snub authority and the pretensions of the educated elites, a quality that would last through Hibari's career in the 1980s. Such early enka disappeared as a genre by the late 1920s when songs of love and loss – though not referred to as enka – became popular. The 1920s saw the birth of mass popular music, or *ryūkōka*, the generic term created by Japan's first record companies, Victor and Columbia, to refer to popular music that sounded Western. The popularity of these songs grew because they accompanied silent films, the singer performing at the side of the stage. They then were heard over the radio in 1925 and on records in 1928. In the 1920s, most songs sold only a few thousand copies, but in 1929 Nakayama Shimpei's 'Tokyo March' (Tōkyō Kōshinkyoku) sold 300,000, necessitating the establishment of copyright and royalty laws (Mitsui 1994). The first hit songs 'The Song of Katiusha' (kachusha no Uta) – sung in a Japanese performance of Tolstoy's *Resurrection* and then recorded in 1915 – and 'Boatman's Ditty (Sendō Kouta), also composed by Nakayama Shimpei in 1921 – represent the earliest forerunners, both musically and lyrically, of what is now known as enka.

Enka went on to adopt elements from a variety of musical styles. The dramatic vocal flourishes, or melismas, that characterize enka were strongly influenced by *rōkyoku*, the sentimental narrative chanting of love and duty born as Osaka popular street entertainment (*naniwabushi*) in the eighteenth century, then performed in the late nineteenth century in portable huts. Rōkyoku produced Japan's first recording stars, Tochuken Kumoemon and Yoshida Naramaru, in the jubilant years after Japan's victory over Russia in 1905. During the 1930s and through the war, rōkyoku was given official government sanction because it was seen as promoting nationalistic sentiment. It fell into disfavor after the war, only to reemerge in the 1960s. Kōga Masao's 1948 'Elegy of the Night Town' (Yū no Machi Elegy) is an example of eclectic rōkyoku, combining guitar and rōkyoku melodies with eighteenth century parlor songs (Fujie 1985:11).

Besides rōkyoku, other popular musical styles have influenced enka: Japanese folk and street entertainment, chanson, tango, rock, blues, swing, country and western ('Tennessee Waltz', sung in English, was a hit in the 1950s). Acculturation of musical forms in Japan has been a complex process, in which genre names have often lost their original meanings. Before the war, all foreign styles of popular music were referred to as jazz (though 'real' jazz did boom in the 1950s), or 'blues', which first entered Japan in 1923. ('Saint Louis Blues' was recorded numerous times in the 1930s.) 'Blues' came to refer to a slow fox-trot dance rhythm, a sad ballad with a Western flavor, rather than to an African-American song of pain and lament. The minor scale and slow rhythm of 'blues' songs like 'The Parting Blues' (Wakare no Blues), composed by Hattori Ryōichi and sung by Awaya Noriko in 1937, helped lay the foundation for postwar enka:

> If I open the window I can see the port,
> the meriken wharf's light I can see.
> The night breeze, the sea breeze
> carrying the breeze of love.
> Where will today's ship depart for?
> The stifling heart, ephemeral love,
> the sentimental dancing blues.
>
> Carving a tattoo of chains on her arm,
> Madras, who can withstand the yakuza,
> although speaking a different language,
> sobs from the weakness of love.
> Two hearts that can never meet again,
> the sentimental dancing blues.
>
> (Ongaku no Tomosha 1977a:108–109)

Postwar Japanese song offered its practitioners a profusion of styles, and Hibari sang the entire range. It was a rich melange – as complex and varied as the literary styles available to writers in late nineteenth century of Japan – of the most contemporary foreign imports and the oldest Japanese folk melodies. Hibari's renditions of American jazz classics put her on a par with her American counterparts, and her English-language version of Edith Piaf's 'La Vie en Rose' places her in comfortable company with the best *chanson* singers.[5] Various styles could appear even within one composition, sometimes resulting in combinations either charmingly creative or absurdly silly, depending on one's taste. In the 1956 *Sword Slashing* (Chanbara Kenpo) Hibari is a brave young samurai, slashing her sword through a group of nasty ruffians to the tune of a rockabilly number.

Yet Hibari's greatest successes, and the songs that most convinced her fans of her authenticity, were the melancholy enka. After the Japanese public's drunken craze with American inspired boogie-woogie in the 1940s, nostalgic enka returned (with a Kōga Masao revival) in the mid-1950s to reassert its parochial, lachrymose longing in the Japanese popular imagination. It was perhaps Hibari more than anyone else who restored this melancholy voice to Japan, at a time of rapid economic growth and generally conservative cultural renaissance – or retrenchment, depending on one's point of view (Takeuchi 1987:148; Mita 1992:115).

It was the songs of Kōga Masao that provided Hibari her melancholy vehicle. The song one most associates with Hibari was written after the war, but comes from a musical mold cast in the 1930s. 'Mournful Sake' (Kanashii Sake) was composed by kōga in 1966, yet belongs to a song style that he took to its greatest artistic and commercial heights thirty years before, during the same period when Japanese intellectuals were searching for authenticity in Japanese culture.[6] songs like his 1931 'Yearning for her Shadow' (Kage o Shitaite), which sold 400,000 records at the time, remain among the century's most popular. Having attained the status of classics, his songs have been absorbed into the tradition so thoroughly that they seem like folk songs (though they are far more sentimental) by unnamed composers, and they fell to their audience natively authentic. With classics like 'Sake: Tears or Sighs?' (Sake wa Namida ka Tameiki ka), Kōga so suffused the 1930s world of Japanese popular music with tearful song that the decade became known as 'the age of Kōga':

> Sake: tears or sighs?
> Where I throw away my heart's sorrows.
> The pain of my nightly dream
> of that person, to whom I am bound by ties of love.
> Sake: tear or sighs?
> Where I throw away my mournful love.
> What shall I do with the lingering feelings,
> for that person, whom I should have forgotten?
> (Ongaku no Tomosha 1977a:50–51)

Kōga Masao's songs of the 1930s, though not at the time referred to as such, are enka's prototype. Like postwar enka, his songs express the pain of the elemental struggle of everyday existence, though its world is not as raw as the nitty-gritty reality of physical hardship evoked by the 'bluesteel and rawhide textures' of blues.

Like blues, enka evokes the elemental emotion of pain that comes from loss – the pain belonging to a world distant 'from the cloud-like realms of abstraction and fantasy', in Albert Murray's words. (1976:51, 68). As Hibari sings in 'Madras Hibari' (Hibari no Madorosu-san):

> The white fog at night
> that drearily drenches the lamp of the boat,
> the pier where flows the fog,
> the sailor in the striped jacket puffs on his pipe,
> and oh! ascends the ramp.
>
> The steam whistle that chokingly whispers 'Good bye!'
> is a sign of our parting.
> For whom is it a keepsake,
> the sailor's stylish muffler,
> ah! streaming in the night wind?
>
> Cryout and you won't be able to raise the parting ship's anchor.
> Just like a man! The sailor who
> raises the anchor with a smiling face, and leaves the port,
> feels the sorrow of parting in the broken paper streamers.
> (Ongaku no Tomosha 1977b:98)

Like the blues, enka is taken by fans as an authentic expression of emotion, but like the blues, enka can be artfully contrived, elegantly playful, and heroic. It has its mythic places – the *roji*, or alleyway, the harbor, the train station, the provincial town – and its poetic disposition: to persevere. The authenticity fans perceived in Hibari's singing and in her persona rests ultimately on a foundation of art – the art of the singing, crying, enka-mask.

By the time Kōga Masao's songs had popularized the sentimental enka melody (though the term did not refer to his songs at the time) in the late 1920s and early 1930s, with lone guitar, violin, or ukulele accompaniment, its motifs – lament for lost love, homelessness and nostalgia, longing for a lost past (*miren*) or for an unattained future (*akogare*), devotion, a life of wandering and impermanence – had been set in stone, as they have remained in postwar song. The imagery standing for these motifs (many drawn from a centuries-old store of poetic images) – clouds, geese, the moon, train stations, harbors, flowing waters and the foam upon them, shadows, the sound of insects, the moon, the world of dreams, to name a few – had also became shop-worn cliches, as they continue to be today.

The greatest of these cliches, certainly, has always been tears. Within the history of popular Japanese song, the most tearful years (other than 1905, during the Russo-Japanese War), were between 1937 and 1940, as Japan rushed into war and hardship (Mita 1992:48). In the 1930s, tears – of mothers grieving for lost sons, wives seeing husbands off to battle, soldiers longing for their homes far away – were colored by the war, the songs often having been solicited by the military. Themes of devotion and sacrifice easily fed into such militaristic uses, and indeed, teary Japanese melodies have become associated with a conservative strain of popular culture. Devotion, however, can cut two ways: in Hibari's enka, personal devotion and isolated grieving can overshadow patriotism and communal loss (Yamanaka 1985).

Hibari as the People's Voice

To many fans, like the popular writer Sawaki Hidae who lived after the war as an orphan with no work or food, Hibari's child's voice not only touched a tender chord but also gave succour. The image of Hibari as emotional nurse was shaped not only in song but on screen. In the 1951 film *Dearest Dad* (Chichi Koishi), Hibari stands on a bridge as she gives a gentle smile to the man who has asked her – indeed, beseeched her – to sing 'I am a Child of the City' (Watashi wa Machi no Ko), which she does to the accompaniment of an accordion. In the 1952 film *The Maiden of the Apple Farm* (Ringo Goen no Shōjo), Hibari mournfully sings what was to become one of the most loved songs of the entire Showa era, 'The Apple Melody' (Ringo Oiwake), for a man at a piano, who looks at her not only mesmerized but soothed:

> The petals of the apple blossoms
> scattered by the wind
> on a moonlit night, on a moonlit night, gently, yes . . .
> The Tsugaru maiden cried,
> weeping at the painful parting,
> the petals of the apple blossoms
> scattered by the wind, ah . . . .
>
> (Ongaku no Tomosha 1977b:10)

Hibari's role as giver of succour was a persona created by the entertainment industry. Yet though she may have been a 'publicly constructed rumor' she was more than that (Gandhy and Thomas

1991:119). She worked not only from under an imposed mask, but through one of her own making. She convinced her audience to see a real woman in her persona, or convinced them to see no difference between the two. She knew her audience, and could articulate her connection to them. She had not far to look in the postwar intellectual and political quest for 'the people' (Gluck 1993:85). 'The people [*shomin*]', Hibari said, 'are those who don't need to wear sunglasses in front of others. The people [*taishū*] are those who can talk looking straight into their companion's eyes' (Takeuchi 1987:146–147).

Hibari's eyes were never hidden from 'the people'. Her eyes glistened through tears that reflected to her audience the history of their lives in Showa Japan. Her songs, like Frank Sinatra's, seemed to a certain generation and class not only her autobiography, but theirs as well (Rockwell 1984:22). Ralph Ellison has called America the 'land of masking jokers', but the Japanese people could see Hibari in a variety of masks without losing sight of her real face (O'Meally 1991:92).

Hibari could reflect history because she was an infinitely protean performer and wore so many masks. In her 158 films, she played a cast of characters that cut across history, gender, and mood: she was a poor street kid, boy and girl (her mother, fearing her voice would change in adolescence, procured her male roles), a rough young samurai, a samurai wife, a geisha, a gangster, a happy teenager, a dancing girl in Kawabata Yasunari's novel *The Izu Dancer* (Izu no Odoriko), and a maid in Higuchi Ichiyō's short story *Growing Up* (Takekurabe).

In all these roles she was a singer for the 'nameless' people. The romance of the 'nameless' with Hibari began in 1949 in the rubble of war-scarred Japan, with the debut of a preternaturally precocious singer a mere twelve years of age in the film *Mournful Whistle* (Kanashiki Kuchibue). It was this film, featuring Hibari as a ragamuffin turned enchantress of the upper-classes, which first turned her into a hero of the people: the song sold 50,000 records, and found a permanent place in many hearts. More than forty years later, the playwright Terayama Shūji wrote a memoir called *Mournful Whistle*. The song reminded him of parting from his mother at a provincial train station. 'For me', he wrote, 'Misora Hibari's song reflected all of life' (Terayama 1993:76). It was in this movie, singing this song, that the first of Hibari's many tears appeared. A savior of the poor, in one scene she gives an apple to a hungry beggar, then returns home and announces to her older sister that she has completed the chores. As she peels her onions and sings the song 'Mournful Whistle', she begins to cry. Perhaps the onion was a device necessary to create her crying persona, for her youthfulness then may not have justified convincingly real tears:

> The hotel on the hill,
> when even its red lights
> and even the light in my heart have gone out,
> like the harbor rain drizzling,
> the whistling – even its melody is sad –
> flows forth past the street corner of love,
> and the bare, narrow road.
>
> We'll meet again sometime,
> pledging by hooking our little fingers,
> laughing as we part, but
> the loveliness of your delicate, white little finger
> is unforgettable.
> Singing of that unforgettable loneliness in a song
> and praying,
> the heart's pitifulness.
>
> The vividly colored flower of love,
> with a burning red color redder than that of
> wine in a glass of the night.
> The rose flower that I placed to my lips and
> presented to you,
> trembling to the echoing of the gong
> – oh, such sorrow!
> Scattered with my dreams.
>
> (Ongaku no Tomosha 1977b:92–93)

The film clearly parallels Hibari's life. Embodying the hopes of struggling Japanese, the maiden's star is on the rise. She sings first and foremost for those struggling, on a barren plot of land before makeshift hovels by a dank pond, with joy and abandon (like the peeing-boy statue in the pond, tinkling beside her, as if in accompaniment?). With absolute confidence in her voice and movements, she faces away from the hovels and the people working by them, looking across the pond and toward the camera, at her fans watching the film, and into a better future.

The danger of Hibari's genius was that it could elevate her above her fans and away from the people to the world of cultured elites. In *Mournful Whistle*, when an elegantly attired orchestra strikes up an accompaniment to Hibari's song, one fears she has left the people. But as if invoking the power of the past, a blind violinist – like the unlettered violinists who first accompanied enka singers on the streets in the 1920s – stands up and plays the opening notes of the song, and we are brought back, as in the 1950 *Tokyo Kid*, to the authentic enka moment.

In *Tokyo Kid*, Hibari reminds her audience with a wink that she has never really left them. In one scene she is elegantly fitted in tuxedo and top hat as she gracefully swings a black cane and taps, struts, and swings around a sprouting fountain, singing to a refined but stiff aristocratic audience. Her listeners are mesmerized by her titillating gyrations, but suddenly, the thirteen year-old Hibari spots her friends, the people, standing behind a railing, like prisoners behind their bars. A fancy gentleman offers her wine, but she playfully refuses (preferring, perhaps, the more authentic sake?), and continues to strut and glide lithely around her enraptured audience, her lips in a defiant but teasing pout. She seems cocky, as if challenging them. She picks up a flower and gracefully brings it to her lips, then offers ti to an elegant lady, who is enthralled; but she is slyly pulls it away, throwing it into the fountain. The camera lingers on the floating blossom, evoking, in this cliche of Japanese cliches, the poor people behind the railing, whose lives, too, are as fleeting as flowers upon the water. As the camera immediately cuts to the assembled hoipolloi, we see they are unkempt, gap-toothed, and ragged.

When a friend of the young Hibari tries to push his way forward from behind the railing, he is stopped by the barrier that separates the haves from the have-nots. Now Hibari throws him, and the others with him, a kiss. A man picks up a harmonica to play, as if he can't help play her sad but hopeful song. The man wants to join in with Hibari – as if merely to do so would suffuse him with her liberating energy – but a friend stops him. Hibari dances on, tapping ostensibly for the aristocrats, but actually for the gritty faces behind the railings and the working people in the audience. She approaches an elegantly clad kissing couple, but dances away from them disapprovingly, bringing to the dance floor the enthralled and elegant lady she had just passed.

The allegory may be unintentional, but in this film it is unmistakable. Despite Hibari's claim to be of the people, she dances with the beaumonde. The child's appeal to class solidarity in the movie comes from across a divide, and is based on her separation from those on the other side. Her popularity depends, ultimately on her difference from the people. She is, like Elvis, of the people, but she is also their royalty.

The loyalty Hibari received from the people was so strong that this difference could be forgiven. Their identification and the corrupting influence of non-Japanese – and other obsessions of postwar life – about Japanese self-definition and racial spirit – barely enter the discourse of enka. The people and Hibari are so ensconced within the Japanese enka world, and so threatened in it by the non-enka Japanese world, that they have little room for these other concerns. Their inside and outside is that narrowly circumscribed.

Hibari was loved by the 'nameless' common people belonging to the enka world to whom she was connected in her songs through emotion and pain. But she was also scorned by intellectuals.[7] Even in her heyday in the early 1950s she 'smelled old' to the educated elite. Her fans were numerous and passionate about her, but as the chroniclers of her life constantly remind us, she also encountered criticism, coldness, and dismissal. She was popular, they say, but never appreciated. Perhaps, some suggest, her lack of education and her family troubles shaped the upper-class view of her. Only poor, hard-working, long-suffering people from unfortunate circumstances could give her unconditional love.

This image of Hibari as working-class singer was constructed through film and song, then reinforced by adoring fans whose feelings for her were recycled back into film and song. By relishing Hibari's status as victim and object of scorn, her fans have maintained their dogged loyalty. By fostering this image, Hibari guaranteed her fans' devotion. She will always be unscarred, will never leave them completely for a more elegant world. The obsession among Hibari loyalists with the open contempt for her shown by intellectuals seems like the obsession of those who feel slighted by the ultimate arbiters of taste. The resistance of the people, in Hibari's case, never fully escapes the bitter taste of sour grapes. The condescension of intellectuals, who raise to the status of genius an Astaire, an Armstrong, a Chaplain, or a Hibari only posthumously, is a bitter pill for fans to swallow. 'We must remember', writes Lawrence Levine, 'that for most of this century [popular stars] could be shared by all of the people only when they were devalued and rendered non-threatening as "popular" art' (Levine 1988:234). One can understand the hagiographic and fawning quality of almost all writing and documentaries on Hibari. It grows from a desire by loyal insiders to hold on to a possession that outsiders, who only came to appreciate its value too late, threaten to take away.

From the beginning, Hibari was a hero of, for, and by the people – though of, for, and by the people in their resistance to the 'democratic' ideal seen to have been imposed by American on a defeated Japan: 'Her singing voice', wrote one critic, 'will undoubtedly be a powerful tool in resisting our artistic colonialization.' When the American Occupation of Japan ended in 1952, her rendition of the popular 'Apple Melody' 'returned to postwar society that which belongs to the people [*minshūteki naru mono*]' (Takeuchi 1987:186). The sad sweet melody sold a postwar record-breaking 70,000 records, sending Hibari to her peak of fame at age fifteen and to her first important live recital at Tokyo's Kabukiza theater. With its melancholy tones and lyrics about the pain of separation felt by a young girl in her country home, the song also crystallizes the motifs of enka:

> The petals of the apple blossoms
> scattered by the wind
> on a moonlit night, on a moonlit night,
> gently, yes. . . .
> The Tsugaru maiden cried,
> she wept at the painful parting.
> The petals of the apple blossoms
> scattered by the wind, ah. . . .
>
> The white, cotton clouds drift lightly, like fleece,
> past the summit of Mt. Iwaki.
> The peach blossoms are blooming,
> the cherry blossoms are blooming.
> Since then, our most enjoyable season has been
> when the early-blooming little apple blossoms come out.
> But when the unfeeling rain pours,
> scattering the white flower petals about,
> I, I recall my mother's death in Tokyo then,
> I, I . . .
>
> The Tsugaru maiden cried,
> she wept at the painful parting.

The petals of the apple blossoms
scattered by the wind, ah . . .
(Ongaku no Tomosha 1977b:74–75)

The mere mention of Tsugaru, an Appalachia-like region of intense pre-war poverty, raises the specter of provincial degradation and hardship. The biographies, documentaries, fan magazines, and news reports transformed Hibari into a provincial maiden (from humble beginnings in a fishmonger's store in Yokohama) who weeps at painful partings. Portraits recall her as a four year-old in the streets of militarized Yokohama, singing with her father's amateur band to those off to war and to those seeing them off, or at munitions plants singing to those working for the war. The public narrative of her life has her born amid crisis in 1937, surrounded by economic uncertainty, with the radio sounds of military music and the plaintive songs of Kōga Masao in the background. Hibari's rendition of 'The Mother of Kudan' (Kudan no Haha) at age four creates the image of mythic beginnings: she sings of a mother visiting the military cemetery at Yasunkuni Shrine (then and later the object of military affection and right-wing devotion) to grieve for her dead son.

Though one might be tempted to draw a parallel, Hibari was never a Shirley Temple, bringing to the poor lost charms of innocent childhood. She has always been described as the 'genius maiden' (*tensai shōjo*) – rebuked by some for her adult voice – and the very model of a hardworking child, the *gambariya*, studying with her home tutor. She has always been portrayed as a heroine: when the war ended, she worked hard, singing in the ruins of a destroyed Yokohama, performing the hits she made in movies before ramshackle postwar audiences in burned-out cities. She was, in the media and the popular imagination, like her name, the 'skylark of beautiful skies', bringing new life to a defeated nation.

Hibari's fans grew up with her, and as they aged she always remained the 'genius maiden'. Her songs of the late 1940s and early 1950s became part of her concert repertoire in the 1960s, 1970s and 1980s. Documentaries inevitably cut from Hibari's early performances (usually in movies) to clips of her singing the same songs later in life. To her fans, this conveyed continuity across time. Her performance of 'The homeland Tsugaru' in 1985 – a crowd of old women calling out to her in the diminutive of her childhood: 'Hibari-*chan*!' – evokes the same passion it did in 1953.

From her debut Hibari was, and for decades continued to be, an emotional support for working women. This role, too, became part of her public image. Documentaries and books inevitably wave the banner of her fans' letters: one woman, for example, working as a sales girl in 1958, describes Hibari as her 'only joy in life', her 'source of inspiration to work hard' (Nippon Geinō 1990). In the public mind Hibari always remained the child who sang for the trainloads of junior high-school graduates in the early 1950s, arriving at Ueno Station in Tokyo from the hinterlands of Aomori, sacks of apples on their backs, to begin working at small factories and stores. This mass exodus from the country to the city in 1953 and 1954 also found its way into her songs that sang about the lost home. She sang for the anxiety of those youths adrift in Tokyo, parted from their parents and all that was familiar.

But as Hibari continued to sing of enduring the anguish of lost love and of painful partings, in the mournful melodies of the minor pentatonic scale, her boozy sensibility no longer spoke, in a 1960s Japan buoyed by economic success, to as many as it once had. Though she had suffered with the people in the ruins of postwar Japan, many had moved on, and fewer needed her.

The future (though not the past) has always evaded enka. The 1960s belonged to the Beatles and Beatles-inspired 'group-sounds', bands like the Blue Comets and the Tigers; the 1970s to Happy End, the Brain Police (Zuinō Keisatsu) and Ostracize (Murahachibu); the 1980s to the Yellow Magic Orchestra, Michael Jackson and Madonna. In the 1970s enka became formally frozen as a genre for the middle-aged and old, a distinct category of music separate from other forms of popular song (Mitsui 1989: 11–13, Fujie 1989).

To intellectuals, liberals and the young, enka was now the denigrated song of drunken businessmen letting loose with karaoke machines in tiny urban bars, belting lyrics to the syrupy sounds of trumpet, electric bass, piano, and strings, with electric guitars and saxes playing the schmaltzy obligatos reminiscent of Portuguese *fado*. Enka had become an embarrassment. To some, Hibari's enka were now 'the music of a dead nation' (Takeuchi 1987:237). Yet that dead nation has continued to live – in the memory of postwar suffering, in the longing for imagined home-towns, in the ache to preserve an 'authentic' past. At the end of Hibari's life in the 1980s, the speeches of politicians, the disputations of intellectuals, and the advertising of the travel industry exalted the virtues of the 'hometown' of 'authentic' Japan in the provinces. Hibari's world had become an official ideal.

When posthumously became firmly situated within the seat of officialdom. By putting a final seal of approval on her career, officialdom may have intended to rein in the potentially anti-establishment energies of 'the people' for whom she sang.

Mournful Sake and the People's Tears

When Hibari sang 'Mournful Sake' in 1966, she was singing a song of protest against a future that promised economic well-being and threatened to erase the past and its troubles – she was singing a song out of her time (Takeuchi 1987:335). By 1966 Hibari and Japan – like Sinatra and America in the 1960s – had already begun to drift apart. (Rockwell 1984:202). 'Even in the 1960s', writes one critic, 'she gave off the aroma of the farm, of the trainloads of pupils transported to Tokyo en masse to work (*shūdan shūshoku ressha*)' (Hayashi 1990:134). Songs like 'Mournful Sake' now reeked of Hibari.

Every time Hibari performed 'Mournful Sake' she spoke the very same words and cried at the very same moment in her monologue stanza. In this song Hibari reveals the kitsch genius of a performer who makes staged emotion seem real, and, indeed, feels it to be real. Watching her perform, the viewer shuttles between the extravagant illusion created by sets, lights, costume, make-up, and lyric cliche, and the intensely felt emotion that makes Hibari appear truly sincere to her fans – as sincere as Judy Garland, who after a life of misfortune, cried when she sang 'Over the Rainbow'.

In her seminal performance of 'Mournful Sake' in 1986 Hibari seemed to have perfected a mythic persona that strips away all artifice while reveling in sheer staginess. Draped in blue silk and bathed in white light, standing against a pitch black background, she clutches her microphone like a talisman, bites her quivering lips, and looks down in intense and sad concentration as if steeling herself against a lifetime of pain. To the lonely plucking of a single guitar, she raises her head defiantly towards a white beam of light, and begins to sing in a gently shaking voice,

Alone at the sake bar,
the sake I drink
tastes of the tears of parting.

I wish to drink and discard
that image,
but when I drink, it floats up again inside my glass.

'Mournful Sake' shows a Hibari pulled apart yet moving ever forward. She spits out the word 'tears', her head shaking with pain, acceptance, and defiance. She caresses every breath, every vowel and consonant, and when she sing 'I wish to drink and discard that image' she gazes fearfully at her hand, as if at herself. she is rebellious as she sings 'when I drink', but then seems to break apart again as she lingers transfixed on the 'glass' that holds the image of what she has lost. When the image 'floats up again' she sinks even deeper into her pain, sustaining the final note with her mouth clenched in an anguished glissando.

Her tears come after the first verse when she slips out of her mythic singing persona, holds her arm across her body as if holding in her anguish, and speaks, her eyes glistening. By the time she arrives at her monologue she almost seems spent. With a deep sigh she begins,

> Ah, the regret that comes after parting!
> Full of lingering desire,
> that person's face.
> So as to forget my loneliness,
> I am drinking, and yet,
> even tonight, she sake makes me sad.
> Oh sake! What, how should I give up that person?
>
> O sake! If you have a heart,
> extinguish the agony in my heart for me!
> When I am drunk from the sake that has become sad,
> and cry,
> that too is for the sake of love.
>
> Beneath the heart that said,
> 'I like being alone!'
> I am crying,
> crying in bitterness for the world
> of the one whom I love but cannot follow.
> The night deepens,
> alone at the sake bar, the sake I drink. . . .
>
> (Ongaku no Tomosha 1977b: 182–183)

The dam has now broken: as she intones 'alone' (*hitoribotchi*) tears stream down her face and drop off her chin, making her nearly choke on her words. But the tears cease as she sings of 'the world . . . I cannot follow' (*soenai yo*), leaving traces of defiance in streaks on her cheek. The night darkens as she looks on in 'bitterness' (*urande*), a lyric she deepens and extends as if tenaciously holding on to her only remaining source of angry strength. The 'night' (*yo*) last even longer but sounds gentler and more accepting as Hibari lifts her head in a strong, elegant gesture. Hibari's interpretations of these phrases are the mark of a master. She saves the final breath – we are made to feel now that it comes from some bottomless inner chamber of power – for the final night that 'deepens' (*fukeru*). Quivering, she lowers the microphone and still shaking, bites her lip.

Hibari has a remarkable ability to move rapidly between the sweetest, most fragile high registers, where she seems on the verge of tears, and the darkest, most resilient low registers, where she seems unshakeably stoic. She shifts fluidly from her natural voice (*jigoe*), in which she speaks to her audience as one of them, breathing from her chest, to her falsetto voice (*uragoe*), in which she produces dramatic melismas and throbbing vibratos (*yuri*), drawing breath from much deeper down. Such fluidity bespeaks the idiosyncratic flourishes of an artist controlling her fate by imposing her style on the world.

The waxing and waning of her voice, with its dramatic build-ups, peaks, and lapses into silence, work physiologically on her listeners. It is not only working class Japanese women who (after forty years of listening to Hibari) feel their chests constrict or stomachs drop when she reaches her climaxes: it can happen also after only a few serious listenings. By creating dramatic tension and then abruptly releasing the listener, Hibari not only depicts the emotions of which she sings but also replicates them in the listener. She becomes the embodiment of feeling and will, a mythic being evoking and transmitting power (Hiraoka 1990:86, 146).[8]

To be sure, her singing performance borders on pure melo-drama. Hibari trod a fine line between the real and the artificial. Like Judy Garland, she would not merely render a song. She would create it, delivering mawkish lyrics with conviction, revealing sincere emotions beneath a surface of musical and lyrical cliches. Like Billie Holiday's haunting rendition of 'Strange Fruit', Hibari fills 'Mournful Sake' with her genuine pain, but her artistic goal, like Holiday's, was also to act with her voice, to transmute pain. 'Adversity may have stimulated her genius', writes William Chilton of Holiday in words he could have written about Hibari, 'but it never overshadowed, or distorted her singing' (1975:225). Billie Holiday 'was not the woman on the stool holding the glass of gin and looking downcast and pained. Or she was not *only* that figure, even at the last'. And Hibari was not *only* the tear-drenched woman staring into an imaginary sake cup at the ghost of the departed. Like Billie Holiday, she transformed 'what she could use of her sorrows into the pure gold of her singing' (O'Mealley 1991:13).

Like Jimi Hendrix – or Kurt Cobain – Hibari was hero and victim of a musical form and audience that demanded she resist the corruption of commercialization yet also made her a successful commercial enterprise.[9] Both artists were creations – and this point cannot be stressed enough – of an industry and an audience that made them rich and famous while insisting they not sell out. Wielding his guitar against the world, Hendrix cuts a more Byronic figure than Hibari with her dramatic melismas and extravagant high and low notes. Like Hendrix, she resists the intellectual and the elite. Yet she calls upon the people to join with her in a community of pain. To many fans, Misora Hibari's voice seemed to snub those who hurt and rejected her and what she stood for, and her tears – her Japanese tears – seemed an authentic resistance to those who would wipe them away and paint on her face a boogie-woogie smile of American élan.

Hibari's music was a dirge for what was threatening to die. When she sang 'Mournful Sake' to the people, she cried not only for the death of her own mother, who had devoted her life to her daughter, indeed, who is said to have 'created Misora Hibari'. She cried also for her dead brother, to whom she always remained loyal, though his troubles with organized crime, guns, and drugs sent him to jail and made her taboo to the entertainment world (she was temporarily banned from the annual New Year's Eve television songfest, the pop music world's grandest night of promotion). She cried too for her divorce and for her painful and protracted bone disease that threatened to end her singing. To the generation of Japanese that grew up with Hibari the extreme highs and lows of 'Mournful Sake' spoke the unspoken words of the 'nameless' people. They saw that she had made it through and survived – that her life mirrored their lives, that she had persevered without complaint and maintained her dignity in defeat. In the tears she shed in 'Mournful Sake', a generation of Japanese have claimed to see their suffering, forbearance and hope.

Hibari's authenticity could seem both sincere and constructed. Perhaps among her fans there were those who recognized this, valued her talent for dissimulation, and remained loyal to her not merely because she was like them but because she was above them. Perhaps there were fans who admired her as an artist. Hibari never said why she cried every time she sang 'Mournful Sale'. Perhaps her silence lent the song its aura.

Given all the tears she shed in her career, and in this song, why did Hibari shed no tears during her last performance of 'Mournful Sake'? Why had that mysterious place 'older than our existence' disappeared? All that remained in her performance, according to Furuzawa Taku, was 'a blank self-abstraction born from exhaustion and collapse, a prayer like water, the silence of her body, the figure of a simple and plain physical being that says "I am still alive"' (1990:165). Hibari was now pure physical suffering and pure myth. She was with her fans, but high above them.

The tears Hibari shed as she sang Kōga's song in 1966 were tears of fortitude, reminding one of the watery songs of the 1930s that depicted floating boats and expressed a desire to allow oneself and one's pain to float along with them into another world, history, or fate (Mita 1992:96–113). This water could taste of brute politics, for floating along with fate could mean drifting into sacrifice to war. Hibari's tears were both more innocent and more complex than that. They expressed the strength and resistance of her fans – the people – to the social, economic, and intellectual elite of the day, to the erasing of traditions, to artistic colonialization. They offered an alternative to the life of the mind, a misty vision to oppose the clarity of ratiocination.

Upon her death, 'Mournful Sake' disappeared from the Japanese popular music repertoire. Writes one critic:

> Among the over 1000 songs recorded by Misora Hibari in her fifty-two-year career, only this one song must never be sung outside the physical being of Hibari. Because this song could only have been nurtured by Misora Hibari, it could only have been cultivated by her remorse. Because this song was the landscape of Misora Hibari's love, of all that lay outside her being; this song was the only landscape that could heal 'Misora Hibari'.
>
> (Furuzawa 1990:165)

To her fans, Misora Hibari remains a vibration from the past that echoes into the future. Funamura Tōru wrote 'Waterfront of Sorrow' (Aishū Hatoba) in 1960 thinking of her. To him she was the light of a buoy, crying into the mist, and the waves of the sea, murmuring a song 'filled with memories, whose sounds linger and will not disappear' (Nippon Geinō 1990).

As long as the substratum of memory and longing survives in postwar Japan, as long as there lingers a sentimental attachment to suffering, doubts about moving too quickly into the future, and a shred of attachment of Japanese sounds, Hibari and enka will not fade for these fans. When Hibari died 'Mournful Sake', so tied to her own pain and to Japan itself, vanished with her from history and the vale of tears into a realm of eternal and disembodied myth.

Notes

1 Translations of quotes and lyrics are mine.

2 Another example of such a woman singer is the Egyptian Umm Kulthum (1910–1975). See Fernea (1986:135–165).

3 For a discussion of these spaces in literature see Okuno (1972:71–120).

4 My discussion of the history of enka draws on numerous sources, including Fujie 1989; Hiraoka 1990; Honda 1977; Hosokawa 1991; Ikeda 1985; Kata 1981; Kayama 1991; Koizumi 1984; Mitsui 1992; Shindō 1977; Sonobe 1962; Takeuchi 1987; Torisu 1990; Watanabe 1990.

5 It is, however, disconcerting to hear her singing 'when our *rub* was new', instead of 'when our *love* was new', in Hoagy Charmichael's *Stardust*.

6 In his 1936 essay, *Japanese Bridges*, Yasuda Yojūrō, the spiritual center and inspiration of the literary coterie known as the Japanese Romantic School, expressed a longing for a transformation of Japanese life through the creation of an authentic Japanese language. Yasuda put his hope for this transformation in the appearance of a genius of the Japanese language. At the end of the essay, blinded by his own 'stupid tears', he thinks about that genius. Yasuda sheds tears in awe before the women who appear in his essay, wet with tears as they see their husbands off to war or sacrifice their own children's lives; he is in awe before the authentic language of a young mother who naturally possesses the authentic language he seeks to master but from which he is forever barred by the machinations of his intellect. The publication of *Japanese Bridges* in 1936 came only one year before the birth of Misora Hibari, a woman many would later come to see, through her tears, as just this singer of authentic song.

7 There are exceptions. See Yoshimoto (1990).

8 Hibari had, like Wagner 'a way of emotionally engulfing listeners, taking control of their sentient lives for the duration – and becoming, for all practical purposes, noumenal music, the music of ultimate (well, virtual) reality' (See Taruskin 1944:34).

9 On the tension between commercialization and sincerity in popular music, see Frith (1981:11).

References

Chilton, John 1975 *Billie's Blues*, New York: Da Capo Press.

Dyer, Richard 1991 'Charisma', p. 57–59 in C. Gledhill (ed.) *Stardom: industry of desire*, London: Routledge.

Fernea, Elizabeth 'Umm Kulthum', p. 135–165 in *Middle Eastern Muslim Women Speak*, Austin: University of Texas Press.

Frith, Simon 1981 *Sound Effects: youth, leisure, and the politics of rock and roll*, New York: Pantheon.

Fujie, Linda 1989 'Popular Music', p. 197–220 in R. Powers and H. Kato (eds.) *Handbook of Japanese Popular Culture*, New York; Greenwood Press.

Furuzawa Taku 1990 'Inori: Ikiisogu Bara' (Prayer for the Living Rose), p. 152–165 in Bungei Shunjū (ed.) *Misora Hibari: 'utau joō' no subete* (*Misora Hibari: The Singing Queen*), Tokyo: Bungei Shunjū.

Gandhy, Behroze and Thomas, Rosie 1991 'Three Indian film stars', p. 107–131 in C. Gledhill (ed.) *Stardom: industry of desire*, London: Routledge.

Giddens, Gary 1988 *Satchmo*, New York: Doubleday.

Harumi Miyako 1991 'Uta to itta ni narikireta Misora Hibari-san' (Misora Hibari, who became one with her song), p. 118–139 in Bungei Shunjū (ed.) *Misora Hibari: 'utau joō' no subete* (Misora Hibari: The Singing Queen), Tokyo: Bungei Shunjū.

Hayashi Mariko 1991 'Sayonara Misora Hibari-san' (Goodbye Misora Hibari), p. 24–41 in Bungei Shunjū (ed.) *Misora Hibari: 'utau joō' no subete*.

Hiraoka Masaaki 1990 *Misora Hibari no Geijutsu* (Misora Hibari's art), Tokyo: Nesco.

Hisashi Inoue 1993 'Kojiin de kitta "Kanashiki kuchibue", (The 'Mournful Whistle' I heard at the orphanage), p. 6–24 in Bungei Shunjū (ed.) *Misora Hibari: 'utau joō' no subete*.

Honda Yasuharu 1977 *Sengo: Misora Hibari to sono Jidai* (The Postwar: Misora Hibari and Her Age), Tokyo: Kōdansha.

Hosokawa Shūhei and Matsumura Hiroshi 1991 *A Guide to Popular Music in Japan*, Tokyo: IASPM.

Ikeda Kenichi 1985 *Shōwa Ryūkōka* (Showa Popular Song), Tokyo: Hakuchō Shuppan.

Ivy, Marilyn 1993 'Formations of mass culture', p. 239–258 in *Postwar Japan as History*, A. Gordon (ed.) Berkeley: University of California Press.

Gluck, Carol 1993 'The Past in the present', p. 64–95 in *Postwar Japan as History*, A. Gordon (ed.) Berkeley: University of California Press.

Kasagi Shizuko 1990 *Kasagi Shizuko*, Tōkyō: Columbia Records (compact disc).

Kata Kōji 1981 *Ryūkōka Ron* (On Popular Song), Tokyo: Tōkyō Shoseki.

Kayama Kōichirō 1991 *Ōjo-Gomen* (Princess: I'm Sorry!), Tokyo: Kindai Eigasha.

Koizumi Fumio 1984 *Kayōkyoku no Kōzō* (The Structure of Popular Song), Tokyo: Tojūsha.

Levine, Lawrence 1988 *Highbrow Lowbrow: the emergence of cultural hierarchy in America*, Cambridge, MA: Harvard University Press.

Marcus, Greil 1991 *Dead Elvis: a chronicle of a cultural obsession*, New York: Doubleday.

Misora Hibari 1990 *Kawa no Nagare no Yō ni* (Like the Flow of the River), Tokyo: Shūeisha.

—— 1971 *Hibari Jiden* (Hibari Autobiography), Tokyo: Sōsōsha.

Mita Sōsuke 1992 (1968) *Kindai Nihon no Shinjō no Rekishi* (*A History of Emotions in Modern Japan*), Tokyo: Kōdansha.

Mitsui Tōru 1993 'The reception of the music of American southern whites in Japan', in N. V. Rosenberg (ed.) *Transforming Tradition*, Urbana: University of Illinois Press.

—— 1992 'The interactions of imported and indigenous musics in Japan: a historical overview of popular music and its industry', in A. Ewbank and F. Papageorgiou (eds.) forthcoming, *Whose Master's Voice?* Westport: Greenwood Press.

—— 1989 'The French Revolution and the emergence of a new form of popular song in Japan 1789–1989', in *Musique, Histoire, Democratie* vol. I, Paris: Editions de la Maison des Sciences de l'Homme.

Murray, Albert 1976 *Stomping the Blues*, New York: De Capo Press.

Murray, Charles Shaar 1989 *Crosstown Traffic: Jimi Hendrix and the rock n' roll revolution*, New York: St Martin's Press.

NHK 1989 *Misora Hibari-san: takusan no uta o arigatō* (Misora Hibari: thank you for all the songs), Tokyo: NHK. (videotape)

Nippon Geinō Retsudan 1990 *Misora Hibari o Kataru* (Speaking of Misora Hibari), Tokyo: Nippon Geinō Retsudan. (videotape)

Okuno Takeo 1972 *Bungaku ni okeru Genfūkei* (Fundamental Places in Literature), Tokyo: Shūeisha.

O'Meally, Robert 1991 *Lady Day: the many faces of Billie Holiday*, New York: Little, Brown and Company.

Ongaku no Tomosha (ed.) 1977a *Shōwa kayōshi: Shōwa gannen-Shōwa 20* (A History of Showa Popular Song: 1926–1945), Tokyo: Ongaku no Tomosha.

—— 1977b *Shōwa Kayōshi: Shōwa 21-Shōwa 51* (A History of Showa Popular Song; 1956–1976), Tokyo: Ongaku no Tomosha.

Rockwell, John 1984 *Sinatra*, New York: Rolling Stone Press.

Shindō Ken 1977 *Sengo Kayōkyoku* (Postwar Song), Tokyo: San'ichi Shobō.

Sonobe Saburō 1962 *Nihon Minshū Kayōshiron* (*A History of Japanese People's Music*), Tokyo: Asahi Shinbunsha.

Takeuchi Rō 1987 *Misora Hibari* (Misora Hibari), Tokyo: Asahi Shinbunsha.

Taruskin, Richard 1994 'The golden age of kitsch: the seductions and betrayals of Wagnerian opera', p. 28–38 in *The New Republic*.

Terayama Shūji 1993 *Kanashiki Kuchibue* (Mournful Whistle), Tokyo: Tachikaze Shobō.

Torisu Kiyonori 1990 *Misora Hibari: saiki no 795 hi* (Misora Hibari: the final 795 days), Tokyo: Magajinsu.

Watanabe Yasuko 1990 *Ototogisu Densetsu* (The Myth of the Cuckoo), Tokyo: Shufu no Tomosha.

Yamamoto Kenkichi 1957 *Koten to Gendai Bungaku* (The Classics and Modern Literature), Tokyo: Kōdansha.

Yamanaka Hisashi 1985 *Bokura Shokokumin to Sensō Ojōka* (Our People and Songs of War), Tokyo: Ongaku no Tomosha.

Yoshimoto Takaaki 1991 'Tensai dake ga enzuru higeki' (A Tragedy only a genius could perform), p. 140–151 in Bungei Shunjū (ed.) *Misora Hibari: 'utau joō no subete* (Misora Hibari: the singing queen), Tokyo: Bungei Shunjū.

—— 1965 *Gengo ni Totte wa Bi to wa Nani ka* (What is Beauty in Language?), Tokyo: Keisō Shobō.

Part III

Japanese Popular Culture in the World Economy

5

Fashion Trends, Japonisme and Postmodernism, or 'What is so Japanese About Comme Des Garçons?'

Lise Skov

Rei Kawakubo first showed her Comme des Garçons collections at the international level in the ready-to-wear fashion shows in Paris in 1981, at which time her design created a scandal of a kind that in international fashion is half way to success. Some editors and journalists, especially those writing for the American *Women's Wear Daily*, considered Kawakubo's collection to be an enormous provocation because she made use of fabrics that looked torn and faded. They took this aestheticization of rags as a slap in the face of the exclusive luxury that high fashion to their mind ought to promote. They compared Comme des Garçons models to street people and bag ladies, and dubbed Kawakubo 'Japan's answer to the atom bomb'.

The Comme des Garçons collection was certainly different from most. Models strolled down the catwalk under a strong, flashing neon light, and the music which accompanied them was abruptly switched on and off. But the main reason for the attention was that the clothes did not look like normal fashion clothes at all. The whole collection consisted of natural materials and dark colours, and the garments themselves were loose so that the fabrics could move around the models, concealing rather than highlighting their bodies. More unconventional than this was the fact that it was not easy to see how the clothes could be put on in the first place. For example, there was a sweater with four sleeves, so that it was up to the wearer to choose which two to put her arms through, and to use the remaining two as a shawl. There was also a dress with four holes, leaving the wearer to decide which to use for armholes and neckline. Nor were the clothes symmetrical: often sleeves were not of the same length, nor armholes of the same height. At the Paris collections, the whole *mise-en-scene* was, of course, supervised by

Kawakubo herself. But as soon as the clothes were out on sale in the shops, it was up to individuals to decide how to put them on.

During the years following her first collection in Paris, Rei Kawakubo had an enormous influence on women's fashion throughout the world. Her international success coincided with that of Yohji Yamamoto and Issey Miyake, and together the three designers' styles came to be known as 'Japanese fashion',[1] characterised by off-black oversize garments, the use of holes in the material as a form of decoration, asymmetrical cuts, and crumpled textiles which were treated to look as if their colours had run. Rei Kawakubo has also influenced other designers, some of whom, like Romeo Gigli, have even made their way up in ready-to-wear fashion largely by copying her style. This has in turn made him a popular designer in Japan, so that today Romeo Gigli is funded by the Japanese department store, Takashimaya, which also has exclusive rights to sales of his clothes in Japan (Fairchild 1989:29–30).

What was new about Kawakubo's emergence on the international fashion scene was not that a temporal style in women's fashion was labeled 'Japanese'. After all, this had already occurred in the late nineteenth century when Japonisme in fashion was connected with the S-shaped silhouette, perceived as similar to that of the kimono, as well as with off-blueish and purple colours (*Mode no Japonisme* 1994; Dalby 1993:106–7; Wichmann 1981:19). Since that time, fashion designers such as Paul Poiret have, along with other artists, drawn inspiration from Japanese garments, arts or export products in putting together styles which have become known as 'Japanese'. In its first sense, then, Japonisme is a name given to a passing style in Western consumer culture. The notion of 'Japan' as mere exotica was in fact partially revived in the 1980s by some fashion editors as a means to defuse the challenge posed by Kawakubo and other Japanese designers to high fashion.

Nor was it unprecedented in the 1980s for an individual Japanese designer to became widely recognised as an international fashion innovator. Although he does not present his collections in Japan, Kenzo, for example, has produced well-received ready-to-wear in Paris since the 1960s. So what was new about the 'Japanese' trend was that the style and individual Japanese designers were directly linked together. This was a new kind of Japonisme in which the country, its designers and consumers were all brought into a higher degree of interdependence with their Western counterparts.

In the fashion press, Kawakubo was seen as a member of a group that supposedly represented Japan as a nation, or at least something distinctly 'Japanese'. The international popularity of these designers gave rise to a number of simplistic attempts to connect their design closely with Japanese culture. Such attempts tended to conflate the media interest in Japanese designers who made an international hit with qualities supposedly found in the actual designer garments – which for Comme des Garçons, at least, have tended to be stylistically anonymous, yet innovative, in a way that has appealed to women across national boundaries. It is ironical that Japanese designers' influence on international, and until then mainly Western, fashion also helped to popularise an Orientalist discourse which seems less adequate than ever in providing an understanding of contemporary transnational processes of popular culture.

Japonisme is one of the key concepts used in this discussion of transnational flows of trends, images and goods. The other is that of postmodernism – a concept which has been employed to diagnose contemporary culture in the light of the growth of the media and increased globalization. Postmodernism has been seen to signify a collapse of symbolic hierarchies (Featherstone 1991) and a blending of cultural forms, especially between art and popular culture (Huyssen 1986). This, at least, has been the promise of postmodernism and so seems a good starting point for an analysis of Kawakubo who created a panic when she entered the establishment of Paris fashion. At first sight at least, her case seems to provide a perfect example to match the notions of a plurality of voices speaking from a previously univocal institution.

Kawakubo's dark, baggy outfits were stretched between the global and the local as they entered many different localities where their different meanings were contested. Both terms, Japonisme and postmodernism, signify ideas and styles that travel, and hence decentredness and instability. Both concepts are ambivalent, indicating that even if they appear as a binary opposition in which a trend is oscillating, the positive and negative poles are interchangeable. 'Japanese' fashion is thus caught simultaneously between the conventional idea of Japonisme as exotica and postmodernism's promise of a collapse of cultural hierarchies – between Japonisme as the promotion of a genuine interest in Japan and postmodernism as an almost mechanical celebration of difference without a difference – between postmodernism as a dream of a decentred world and Japonisme as firmly relocating cultural exchange in terms of the Orientalist couple Japan and the West.

Postmodernism, however, does not just serve as a contrasting concept here, for I have found it appropriate to anchor my analysis in a concept that became fashionable in the social sciences at the same time as information about Kawakubo's design disseminated through the global media. The point here is not to recover the origin, or nature, of postmodernism – whether the term is used to stage the fin-du-siecle crisis of Western rationality (Turner 1990) or rewrite the history of Edo as a consumer society (Iwatake 1993). Instead, I focus on the synchronism of a number of occurrences which can be loosely grouped around the concept. In adopting such an empiricism, I can hardly say that my intentions are not polemical.

It should also be noted that this is not the first attempt to see a connection between Comme des Garçons and intellectual trends. In an article in the New Yorker, for example, Holly Brubach interpreted Kawakubo's work as a kind of deconstruction of high fashion, parallel to the deconstruction going on in university departments (1989:107; Kondo 1992:185). While this is one perfectly valid interpretation, my interest here is rather in contributing to the complex history of Japanese and/or transnational popular culture in the 1980s. As I will show, it is impossible in this case to make a clear distinction between Japan and the transnationalism.

Recently the up-market English department store Harvey Nichols put out an advertisement with the headline 'postmodernity©' (Figure 1). The catchphrase complete with a copyright marker at the end seemed to encapsulate the confusion of the free flow of ideas on the one hand, and their careful control, on the other – an ambivalence which itself provides the background for an academic concept appearing in an advertisement for a deparment store. More interesting in this context was the fact that across from from the headline was a photograph of a dark-clad model in front of a machine in a factory hall, presented in exactly the same style as Peter Lindbergh's Comme des Garçons photographs in 1988. The intellectual designer, as Kawakubo has come to be known, obviously seems a good match for the intellectual headline of this advertisement. The contradictory term postmodernity is also carefully paralleled in Lindbergh's citation of the futurism of an earlier industrial era, a black and white belief in technology and progress. In the 1980s this was already a self-conscious nostalgia for a time

Figure 1 Postmodernity – indicating, perhaps, that it is time to look back to the fashion of the 1980s

when we could look to the future with optimism. Now the future is not only nostalgic; it is coming to us recycled through the fashions of the last decade, connoting, perhaps, that in the mid-1990s it is time to look back to the fashions of the 1980s.

Due to the very nature of fashion, a trend-setting effect like Kawakubo's only lasted a few years. Just as the focus of international fashion has shifted now away from 'Japan', so has Kawakubo's design changed, and the collections that she is presenting in Tokyo and Paris these days are quite different from her 1980s collections. Furthermore she is now also well-known for her men's collections, for her furniture design, and for the montage style of Six, the Comme des Garçons brand magazine (Sudjic 1990). The topic of this paper is not the ongoing creativity of an individual designer, however, but the intersection between a particular point in time and a particular fashion trend.

Firstly, in addressing the perceived dominance of Paris fashion, I will analyse what geographical displacements of international fashion were brought about by the emergence of successful Japanese designers. Secondly, I will criticize the attempts to understand Comme des Garçons on the basis of the question 'what is so Japanese about it?'. After that I will take a look at Kawakubo's designs to discuss to what extent they were influenced by Japanese aesthetics and to what extent they deviated from both Japanese and Western fashion conventions. Then I will go on to analyze the way in which the trend was received both by the fashion press and by women consumers around the world – which leads me to take a closer look at the way in which certain parts of the fashion press have attempted to explain away 'Japanese fashion' as merely an exotic influence on the genuinely Western institution of fashion. By way of conclusion I will summarize the changes brought about by the 'Japanese' trend.

Centre and Displacement

It has been said that in the dissemination of fashion one can discover a cultural hierarchy which in its roughest version reads as the dominance of the city over the country, middle over working-class, and Western countries over the rest of the world. Perceiving such 'dominance structures' as the cause of a strong standardization of lifestyles, cultural critics – following the Frankfurt School – have put forward the pessimistic theory that the world-wide spread of the 'culture industry' is in the process of levelling out local differences, so that people's lives become more and more similar. This line of thought has been applied to studies of consumption in industrialized societies, including that of Japan (Miyoshi and Harootunian 1989a) and, in recent years, has also been thoroughly criticized from a number of different perspectives (Wilson 1987: 64–66; Leopold 1992). However, as most writing on fashion has taken its location within Western culture for granted, little has as yet been said about the spread of fashion at the global level.

The first question to be asked here is whether it is possible to point to a single centre of global fashion from which the master copies of future clothing are issued. The obvious place to look, of course, is Paris, but its status is ambivalent. Already at the time when Parisian *haute couture* was established in the second half of the nineteenth century, it bore historical reference to the French royal court which, until the revolution in 1789, had been the centre of fashion for more than three hundred years. Thus what Norbert Elias (1983:9–10) has called the separation of the centre of taste from the centre of power is a condition of modern fashion. It would simply be a misunderstanding to relate the popularity of Paris fashion to the political hegemony of the French government! Rather, Paris couture is only available for an elite, and signifies a luxurious style which exists over and above the clothes produced for the middleclass and workingclass markets. This is the way it has spread not only throughout Europe, but also in America and Asia.

It is hardly a criticism to say that Paris fashion is but a myth, because this is in fact one of its strongest selling points. The haute couture houses – which for many signify the superiority of Paris fashion because here every single garment is made-to-measure – have experienced severe economic difficulties in the last decades. Most of them have been bought up by international, including some Japanese, cosmetics companies, and have thereby been saved from bancruptcy. The only customers for haute couture are members of royalty and other similar celebrities, as well as the wives of Middle Eastern millionaires, so the collections can rather be seen as well-established promotional activities which usually do not yield any profit. Instead, fashion houses make their money on perfumes, cosmetics and accessories – items that sell precisely because the mythical place of their origin, 'Paris', is part of their logo. The innovative and financial centre of high fashion has long since shifted to industrially produced ready-to-wear collections which are shown to buyers and to the press, rather than to potential wearers. Similar collections, however, are also shown in a number of other cities so that, although Paris may still be the most prestigious centre of fashion, it is no longer unmatched.

From *More* to *Ryūkō Tsūshin*, Japanese fashion magazines usually list Paris, Milan, New York, London and Tokyo as the five 'capitals of fashion'. But every now and then the ready-to-wear collections of, for instance, Osaka, Dusseldorf, Seoul or Hong Kong are also featured in their pages. Sometimes the Western fashion press leaves out Tokyo in spite of the fact that Japan has by far the biggest market for high fashion. They are to some extent justified in doing so because Tokyo-based designers who address European and American markets all make sure to present their designs in one of the Western ready-to-wear collections. Before 1981, Kawakubo had already worked under the Comme des Garçons brand name for more than ten years in Tokyo without attracting any attention from the international press. Her breakthrough in Paris as a 'Japanese designer', therefore, can not simply be interpreted as a sign that the era of Paris fashion was over unless we simultaneously recognize a reinforcement of the Western centre in the fact that Tokyo designers still had (and have) to make it in Paris in order to be recognized as international designers. As Sudjic has pointed out, in doing so they actually provide buyers with fresh reasons to go to France twice a year (1990:84).

In turn, the widespread popularity of the 'Japanese fashion' in the 1980s was a decisive factor in placing Tokyo on the list of international fashion capitals. A number of Japanese designers, including Kawakubo, established the Tokyo Designers' Council in the early 1980s to handle the inflow of foreign editors covering the local collections. The Tokyo Designers' Council now serves as a co-ordinator and contact centre for the international press during the biannual Tokyo collections.[2]

In looking for reasons why Japanese designers suddenly caught the attention of the international fashion press, we should first note the parallel between the success of the Tokyo designers in the early 1980s with Japan's role on the world political stage at that time as an upstart economic superpower. My point here is not to reduce fashion to economic trends, but to remind readers that Japan's industrial power has brought about in most Western countries a certain sense of instability along with an ambivalent fascination. Indeed, Japan has been the first capitalist and democratic non-

Western country to question the habitual identification of modernity with the West. As Japan further began to challenge the global dominance of the West, in particular the United States, it was hardly surprising that in the early 1980s international trend-setters looked to Japan for new styles to adopt for Western consumers.

The economic grounds for the popularity of Japanese fashion designers are even more obvious when we examine the international fashion industries at that time. From the beginning of the 1970s, the Japanese domestic market had been growing fast, and consumer lifestyles were proliferating. Women, in particular, enjoyed a growing personal consumption of goods, experiences and media, in particular women's magazines which helped to co-ordinate everything into trends and lifestyles (Skov and Moeran 1995). By 1980, Japanese women had combined their unforeseen buying power with a great appetite for Western high-class goods, including fashion garments, accessories and cosmetics. For European and American ready-to-wear designers, the growing sales to Japan conveniently coincided with a period when the interest in high fashion in the West was low due to the by then already permanent economic crisis. Consequently the high fashion market in Japan in the 1980s became not only the biggest in the world, but also the one where new trends were subsumed the fastest.

Japanese women's enthusiastic support for Paris fashion – which has helped to secure its prestige as well as its economic well-being – also gave rise to a market in Europe addressed specifically to Japanese tourists. The French travel bag company Louis Vuitton estimates that 65 per cent of its sales in France goes to Japanese customers for whom a trip to Paris is combined with shopping for specific brand name goods (JIJ 1992). Some Japanese fashion designers, such as Hiroko Koshino, even present their collections in Paris without having a real market abroad. The single Hiroko Koshino shop in Paris, filled with garments in Asian sizes only, caters to Japanese tourists rather than to locals. Thus the name 'Paris' added to Hiroko Koshino's brand name serves primarily to distinguish her clothes on the domestic Japanese fashion market rather than to establish her name internationally.

In Japan, the kind of 'self-centred'[3] consumption engaged in especially by young has often been seen as 'foreign' or 'Western', as opposed to native 'Japanese'.[4] Thus the cute look that dominated young Japanese's fashion in the late 1970s was adopted explicitly as a rejection of 'typically Japanese' style (Kinsella 1995). The 'native'-'foreign' distinction in consumer culture represents an axis in a cultural hierarchy *within* Japan which tends to position 'Japanese' with high culture and 'Western' with consumer culture, although imported designer fashion and other brand name goods tend to have a high status ranking. To exemplify: a Japanese woman may choose to wear either kimono or 'Western' couture dress at, for instance, a wedding reception, and even though dress codes are rarely mixed at the individual level, they appear side by side on such formal occasions. Kimono is often seen as a special style, but it is still within reach of a consumer choice (Goldstein-Gidoni 1993).[5]

The term 'Western clothes' may ultimately refer to the fact that modern dressmaking techniques were invented in Europe in the thirteenth century, but in this sense it seems to be obsolete in a period when the bulk of the worlds' garment production is located in Asia and Latin America, and when the majority of the world's population wears some form of 'Western clothes'. In the last decade the Japanese have even come to dress in more exclusive and fashionable 'Western clothes' than most Westerners. The Japanese *salary-man* wears business suit, white shirt and silk tie, while the Japanese woman trend-consciously combines different 'Western' brand names in her outfit: Thierry Mugler suit, Charles Jourdan shoes, Hermés scarf, Louis Vuitton bag, Chanel perfume and Lancôme make-up. There is no doubt that the term 'Western' will continue to be used in this narrow sense related to style. But at the same time as the presence of 'Western' consumer culture is strongly felt in Japan, there are also movements in the opposite direction. Thus, while Japanese women are buying up the products of Parisian fashion houses, European women for their part are dreaming of clothes from Comme des Garçons, Issey Miyake and other 'Japanese' brands.

What is so Japanese about Comme des Garçons?

So far I have delineated some geographical displacements in international high fashion, thereby showing that contemporary fashion is more complex than any global 'trickle down' theory can account for. The absence of a single centre, the heterogeneous flow of images, and the complexity of meanings all seem to reiterate some of the writings on postmodernism. Andreas

Huyssen, for example, sees postmodernism as the breakdown of Western cultural hierarchies, thereby giving way to a multiplicity of voices which have been repressed or ignored, in particular the voices of women and ethnic minorities (1986:198).

The notion that postmodernism holds special possibilities for women has been thoroughly criticized by some feminists (Wilson 1989), while others have been more optimistic about its gender political potential (Tijssen 1993). Although these discussions as they stand have been slippery enough, the question of postmodernism as an end to white Western dominance seems to lead us into even more trackless landscapes. Even though, for example, a single centre is replaced by several centres, their basic dominance over the peripheries may not be much affected. This is exactly what Miyoshi and Harootunian talk about when they say that Japan's wealth and power oscillates between decentering the West and willingly co-opting itself into the capitalist elite, thereby essentially reinforcing Western dominance (1989b:ix–x). Given the complexity of the issue, it is hardly surprising that some post-modernist writing has come to simplify these changes.

James Clifford, for example, in his critique of Orientalism (1988; Said 1978), describes the postmodern condition as '"the other" speaking back at the West', and here that anthropological 'other' is Japan. But if we celebrate 'Japanese designers' as 'speaking back at' Paris fashion, do we not then reduce complex changes in both the fashion industry and global consumer patterns to a simplified 'East versus West' model? If we argue that 'Japanese style' has outdone 'Western style', do we not simply perpetuate an Orientalist dream in which two gigantic cultural entities engage in combat, rather than contribute to breaking down the borders between 'East' and 'West'? In doing so, we ignore the rest of the world as if the transnational economic and cultural changes of the 1980s were really a matter between Japan and the West only. The exaggerated attention to what is Japanese and what is Western seems to conceal the fact that Japan is, after all, a country of alarm clocks, commuter traffic and saving accounts, more like Western Europe and north America than most other non-Western countries.

Furthermore, preoccupation with the 'otherness' of Japan seems particularly inadequate in the study of fashion which is produced in a complex dynamics where haute couture and ready-to-wear, high fashion and mass fashion, national and regional differences, along with competition between fashion capitals, all play off on one another. In this game, the Japanese designers have been particularly skillful in positioning themselves in the global market place. In terms of consumption, fashion further enters a no less complex field which is structured by social parameters such as status, class, gender, age, ethnicity, nationality, race, and as we move down to the micro level of dressing up – occasion and individual taste. This whole dynamic field, which is crucial for an understanding of popular culture, is usually left out when the 'East – West' dichotomies come in.

To clarify these problems I wish to examine the position of Dorinne Kondo (1992). The background of her article on Japanese high fashion is a study of identity, defined as strategic positionings in power relations, in a Japanese workplace. The title of her book, *Crafted Selves* (1990), delivers a metaphor for her argument, at the same time as it also matches the constructivist terms today increasingly used by fashion magazines and other commercial media to address their audience. In other words, it is her interest in the politics of identity that has led Kondo to Japanese high fashion which she analyzes from the point of view of two shifting power axes – one of East and West, the other of gender.

In her discussion of the 'Japaneseness' found in Japanese fashions designers' work, Kondo is aware of the 'Orientalist' danger of essentializing culture, but at the same time she seems to overlook what Clifford defines as the other crucial aspect of Orientalism: homogenization (1988: 258). Unlike in the writings of the Frankfurt School in which 'homogenization' is perceived as a real, social process, the term here refers to an academic perspective which ignores all actual differences within a certain country or region. In this, Clifford's concept of 'homogenization' is similar to what Hannerz has called 'the replication of uniformity' (1992:16). When, for instance, Kondo argues that Japanese designers are engaged in creating Japanese identity, she essentially ignores the interaction of market forces and lifestyles which is a precondition for fashion design, and which makes it more than likely that designers of whatever nationality more or less consciously address their design, not to national communities, but to certain enclaves of taste, which in Kawakubo's case has certainly transcended national boundaries.

Considerations along these lines are conspicuously absent from Kondo's argument, which consequently presents Japan as a homogeneous entity, as if Japanese fashion designers produced Japanese identity through their clothes on behalf of Japanese women. The immediate questions that arise are: for whom do the designers fabricate 'Japanese identity'? Are they simply engaged in an attempt to create their own individual identity as 'Japanese designers' in the international fashion world – in which case 'Japaneseness' is not necessarily to be found in the actual design? Or should we rather link 'Japanese identity' to the individual Comme des Garçons wearer who strides along the streets of Tokyo in her black baggy outfit – in which case she is hardly different from a New York woman wearing Comme des Garçons? Or do 'Japanese designers' create identity on behalf of the whole nation of Japanese who can appreciate the success of their countrymen and women in an international setting – which again turns the focus away from the actual garments? Questions like these are not answered simply by saying that fashion is a way of fabricating identity or, in Kondo's terminology, 'crafting selves' (1992:189), for as I have argued, even at the individual level of the sartorial identity of fashion, many axes intersect. And even though nationality can be important among these, it has never completely overridden such others as gender, age, social class and lifestyle.

Kondo's article can in fact be read as a meditation on the question of 'What is so Japanese about Japanese fashion?', a question which epitomises the kind of inquiry typical of Japanese studies.[6] Furthermore, at the time of the international success of Kawakubo in the early 1980s, the same question came to be widely asked by fashion editors and designers who had no previous interest in Japanology. Straight sociological facts can provide us with one kind of answer: that Rei Kawakubo is a Japanese citizen, living in Tokyo; that her company, Comme des Garçons, is organized like most Japanese companies; and that most of its sales are made in the domestic market.[7] But the question 'What is so Japanese about Comme des Garçons?' implies that there must be more to 'Japaneseness' than the *made in Japan* label in designer clothes. It seems to presume a cultural purity that is hardly to be found in modern international fashion. What are the consequences if a profound 'Japaneseness' is sought for in every seem and every dye?

One answer can be read in interviews with Yohji Yamamoto from the years immediately after his international breakthrough. Yamamoto – clearly more eloquent than Kawakubo – showed himself willing to discuss his work with the press in ideological and nationalist terms. He has stated, for example, that there is a connection between Japanese religion and his design. Very often such ideas have led to some blatant Orientalist statements, such as 'When a cowboy wears blue jeans in the field it is not fashion. In that meaning when Japanese women wear my clothes it is not fashion' (Koren 1984:94)'. The reader is left to put two and two together and come to the realization that when Western women wear his clothes, it is fashion. Yamamoto's line of thought seems to be a particularly reductive version of the *mingei* (folk craft) movement's (problematic) distinction between functional clothes and fashion clothes – a distinction which values crafted, and supposedly traditional and beautiful, goods over those that are industrially produced and distributed on the market. When Yamamoto applies it on an 'East'-'West' axis, the distinction is at best meaningless, at worst nonsense. He implies that Japan, misrepresented as a small-scale peasant community, allows no room for individual tastes and preferences – in short, no room for *fashion* – which, of course, is simply not true.

It is ironical that Yamamoto, in the above quotation, indirectly places himself – an individual designer whose personal signature, in Roman handwriting, serves as the Yohji Yamamoto company logo – in the position of a guarantor for a national culture which, to his mind, rules out individual creativity. What we find is a stark discrepancy between Yamamoto's idea of 'Japanese culture' and his own working conditions as a high fashion designer who turns out biannual collections for a highly competitive domestic market where new products are targeted well into the future to match rapidly changing consumer tastes. It is thus a little sad to find that even some fashion designers have greater faith in reductive ideas of 'Japaneseness' than in the particular medium in which they themselves are working.

To do justice to Yohji Yamamoto, it must be added that in recent years he has distanced himself from ideas about especially privileged connections between 'Japaneseness' and his design. Now he refers to himself not so much as having a Japanese as a Tokyo identity, seeing himself as a denizen of great cities. He tends to explain his earlier statements with reference to the pressure he felt right after his international breakthrough, when the press wanted to get to grips with this supposed 'Japaneseness' which had taken high fashion by surprise. In Wim Wender's film *Notebook on Cities and Clothes* (1989), Yamamoto says:

> There is no nationality in my clothes. . . . They are: not for Japanese, not for French, not for Americans. My clothes shouldn't have any nation. But when I first came to Paris I realized, and I was pushed to realize, that I am Japanese because I was told 'You are here representing *mode japonaise*'. Naturally, I am Japanese because I was born in Japan. I am simply not representing Japanese fashion. But this single pride in me was very big.

Yamamoto's statement points to the fact that the search for 'Japaneseness' sprang from social confrontations in the fashion world, rather than from qualities in the designs themselves. In the search for an explanation, the pseudo-anthropological discourse about Japan-as-different then offered itself to designers and journalists alike who were looking for a way to explain the changes in fashion.

Comme des Garçons Garments

What was it about Kawakubo's design that enabled it to become so popular and to be interpreted in such different ways? Even though, as I have shown, the fashion environment played a crucial role in the definition of 'Japanese fashion' based on well-established stereotypes of Japan, it would not be reasonable to ignore the garments themselves. Let us take a closer look, then, at the Comme des Garçons garments to discuss how they can be seen both in relation to Japanese aesthetics and to high fashion (Figure 2).

The most striking feature of Kawakubo's design is, as already mentioned, its austerity and somber colours. Such puritanism can be seen as a part of an ongoing struggle between plainness and ornamentation – not as categorical oppositions, but as an eclectic game with numerable variations in which the two are defined vis-à-vis each other. This has been going on both in East Asian history – in the early Confucianism's austere opposition to gaudy Buddhism in China (Goody 1993:383), and in the Japanese adoption of Zen Buddhism at the end of the colour-conscious Heian period – and in Western history – in the Spanish court's adoption of black, later taken up the by puritan bourgeoisie which thereby contrasted itself to the then (again) gaudy nobility.

For more than a century the division of black and white, on the one hand, and sumptuary colours, on the other, made up the relative definition of masculinity and femininity in fashion, and has

Figure 2 *Women's Wear Daily* dubbed Kawakubo 'Japan's answer to the atom bomb'

thereby turned gender distinctions into a key issue in any study of fashion. However, in spite of the brand name under which she has chosen to work, Kawakubo seems to have been less concerned with blurring gender differences than with reworking the conventions of high fashion against which she pitched the austerity of Comme des Garçons garments. A typical crossover of the 1980s, perhaps, is that while postmodernists in art and architecture claimed the right to express current trends in a colourful and ornamental manner, avantgarde designers of fashion – the art form which has been the most closely tied to the flow of time – moved towards plainness.

It should also be noted that material holds a central position in Kawakubo's design, and that the feel of a particular garment is as important as the look of it. In her own words:

> The machines that make fabric are more and more making uniform, flawless textures. I like it when something is *off* – not perfect. Hand weaving is the best way to achieve this. Since this isn't always possible, we loosen a screw of the machines here and there so they can't do exactly what they're supposed to do.
>
> (Koren 1984:117)

The preference for handmade goods over industrial products here stated is typical of a persistent brand of Japanese aesthetics, most prominently represented recently by the folk craft movement. In Kawakubo's first international collections we find elements of Japanese peasants' and fishermen's clothes in her use of natural fibres and multiple indigo dyes – where the colour is no longer blue, but almost black. In Japan, the late 1970s were marked by an interest in the rural tradition which involved a 'going back to the country', at least on bus tours, and an appreciation of traditional crafts, resulting in a booming market for pottery, for example (Moeran 1984; Ivy 1988). It is hard to imagine that Kawakubo should not have been influenced by this ongoing consumption of tradition in Japan. She might also consciously have chosen to make use of some stylistic elements, widely recognized as 'really Japanese', when she went international. But it is also important to note that such an eclectic inspiration in itself does not make Comme des Garçons garments a form of folk craft.

Following the rhetoric of fashion, Kawakubo tends to state what she *likes* when interviewed, rather than refer to (often problematic) principles of aesthetic production, as employed by, for example, folk craft potters (Moeran 1984:182–214). Tradition – however selective it may be – is not the authoritative model for Kawakubo's design which is, of course, not recognized as mingei either. Also, Comme des Garçons outfits have mainly been associated with a cosmopolitan setting, as in Kawakubo's own statement that she makes clothes for independent, working women who can look after themselves. Its fashion photography, mostly by Western photographers, is often done in urban or industrial settings.

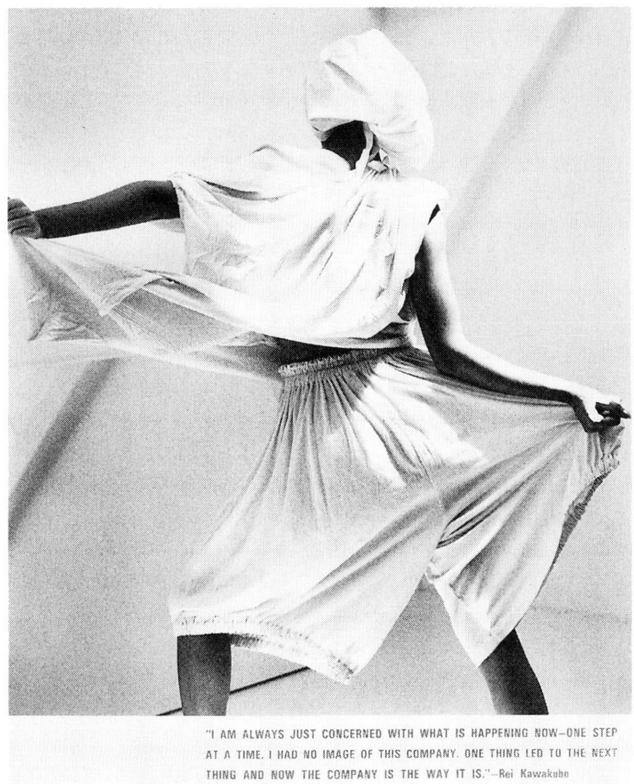

"I AM ALWAYS JUST CONCERNED WITH WHAT IS HAPPENING NOW–ONE STEP AT A TIME. I HAD NO IMAGE OF THIS COMPANY. ONE THING LED TO THE NEXT THING AND NOW THE COMPANY IS THE WAY IT IS."–Rei Kawakubo

Figure 3 Comme des Garçons – a kind of sexuality to be explored in the way loose fabrics move over a moving body

The emphasis on materials, often leading to their unexpected use over the human body, is considered to be one of the emblems of 'Japanese fashion', but different designers' intentions with regard to this emphasis and actual results naturally differ. So while Issey Miyake has been a technological innovator who has developed new weaving techniques, Kawakubo pays homage to the material by her subtle cutting, and often makes complicated garments out of very few pieces. The clothes of the 1980s' collections were not cut to fit the shape of the body and often were quite loose. This in turn gave rise to conceptualizations of the space between body and garment, a novel discovery in international fashion (Craik 1994:41). But again, it is difficult to connect this directly to Japanese costume history.[8] Some traditional work clothes are loose, whereas others are not and, though stitched together from rectangular and triangular pieces, they are fitted tightly around the body by aid of belts and straps. There is no draped material as in South Asian garments. Even modern garments tend to have a close fit as in the ubiquitous business suits that Japanese women wear in public places or on formal occasions, or in the short clingy dresses of the early 1990s, popularly known as *body-con* (body conscious).

One thing that from the early 1980s made Kawakubo's garments very special was that she did not stipulate beforehand how a woman was to wear her clothes, so that final decisions regarding design were not made until the moment a woman put on a piece of clothing – as with the sweater with four sleeves, or the coat from which the lining can be removed and worn alone as a cardigan. This highlighted an aspect of fashion which has often beed ignored: the pleasure a wearer can experience with certain clothes. My argument here is that Kawakubo's first international collections emphasized the way in which wearing certain clothes is *experienced*, rather than the way women *look* in certain clothes.

Again, it would be wrong to interpret the focus on this overlooked, but not exactly absent, aspect of fashion as something specifically Japanese, simply because it turned some Western ideas of femininity upside-down. Even though nudity, and hence the shape of the body, has not been important in Japanese aesthetics, we nevertheless find within the kimono dress code an alternative hierarchy of female body parts seen to be particularly alluring – most prominently the nape of the neck which is revealed when the neckline of the kimono is pulled down. The overall emphasis is thus still on women's appearance.

While emphasizing the feel rather than the look, baggy Comme des Garçons clothes seemed indifferent to the body they adorned. Even when garments did reveal a part of the body through a hole or an opening, it was not necessarily a part that was charged with prior sexual meanings, according to either Western or Japanese codes. Because it was only when a woman put on the clothes that the exact positioning of the holes was decided, the latter might very well end up revealing random parts of her body. In this respect Evans and Thornton (1989:159) argue that Kawakubo's collections from the early 1980s went against the fragmentation of the female body usually seen in fashion: 'crucially, as Kawakubo demonstrates, seeing the body whole is never simple'. Instead of putting the female body on display as a skillful combination of body parts and consumer goods, Kawakubo treated it discreetly, wrapped it in loose garments as if to argue that it is the individual, not the shape of the dressed body, that ought to be the centre of attention. One nineteen year-old consumer, Sue Naoko, commented:

> With Comme des Garçons you hide your skin, but at the same time your nature comes out. I don't know why – it's very strange. Even if you have very short hair and don't look like a girl, these clothes bring femininity out from the inside of you. (Koren 1984:172)

In contrast to this sense of femininity from within, the British fashion writer Nicholas Coleridge, clearly not a fan of Kawakubo's, describes her garments as deprived of all sexuality and calls them 'fashion for nuns', before wondering how it is possible 'to seduce a woman dressed like that' (1989:76). Although his attitude towards Kawakubo's designs is condescending, his point encapsulates some relevant aspects, both in terms of Kawakubo's avoidance of exhibiting the body as overtly sexual, and in terms of the confusion and distaste experienced by the world of high fashion when a style that so obviously resisted description by the usual fashion vocabulary nevertheless made an unavoidable hit. But as we know, sexuality is not a fixed set of desires and looks. Rather it is unstable and sometimes contradictory, and it would indeed be difficult to deny that in the 1980s there was a kind of sexuality to be explored in the way loose fabrics moved over a moving body. (Figure 3)

Comme des Garçons garments have rarely carried any overt allusions to either a particular culture or a specific historical situation. Kawakubo has tended to empty her clothes of any recognizable connotations. Instead, as an evasive strategy, she produces minimalist designs, repeating simple themes which themselves do not have any meaning.[9] Her collections tend to have simple names, such as the 'Wrapped collection'[10] of 1982 or the 'Elastic collection' of 1983, which refer to techniques, rather than to any historical or geographical inspiration. 'I start from zero' is how Kawakubo herself describes her way of working (Sudjic 1990:10) which, needless to say, only helps to make the 'Japaneseness' discovered in her garments all the more elusive.

My point in the above discussion has not been to deny the influence of certain forms of Japanese aesthetics in Kawakubo's work, but to put them into perspective. This is a necessary move to stop all the innovative and provocative features of her design from being reduced to mere reiterations of stereotypical aspects of 'Japanese aesthetics'. When Kawakubo's cultural background is over-emphasized in an uncritical way, it becomes impossible to see that Comme des Garçons also marks a considerable deviation from that background.

The Time and the Trend

In the early to mid-80s the austere style of Kawakubo and Yamamoto was enthusiastically adopted by Japanese women. A large number of even very young women wore actual brand name garments by these designers, but there were also more affordable adaptations available on the market. Observers at the time described it as an extremely pervasive trend – one which is reflected in the visuals from street scenes and media parties in Leonard Koren's book on the trend (1984).

Today Comme des Garçons brand garments can hardly be said to be part of mainstream fashion, either in Japan or in the rest of the world. Prices are high, but approximately the same as ready-to-wear clothes by other internationally known designers in Japan. The brand is famous for its special style, and even though it is well established in the ready-to-wear market, its turnover comes to only a fraction of such popular brands as Nicole (Sudjic 1990:51). However, in Gifu in Japan, where a large number of the Comme des Garçons subcontractors are located, the brand has a group of stable customers who wear only Comme des Garçons from head to toe. The brand shop in Gifu consequently arranges parties and weekend excursions to give these fans a chance to dress up for an audience of real connoisseurs (Sudjic 1990:52). This Comme des Garçons subculture is unique, but generally the brand tends to have devoted followers. Still, the cult can only exist because Comme des Garçons is somewhat apart from mainstream fashion.

In Europe and America, the Comme des Garçons style was also diluted and spread by the fashion industries. Here, however, its success was not unlimited, perhaps for the reason that many designers and trend-setters – who fell for the style because it was so new – adapted it too immediately and roughly for their local markets. As a result, it simply came across as too avantgarde for the main-stream consumer (Raaholt 1989). The fact that the adaption process was somewhat forced paradoxically helped to ensure

Kawakubo a reputation as an intellectual designer who was only appreciated by the few, at the same time as a lot of Kawakubo-inspired dark garments ended up on store sales racks in the mid-80s.

Kondo describes the reception of 'Japanese fashion' in the United States as starting on the New York art scene from which it spread to women in academia, offering 'a change from conventionally feminine prettiness in professorial settings' (1992:199). My own experience of the years when black was the sovereign colour on the fashion palette is of Denmark. In bars and coffee-shops in Copenhagen 'black people' emerged as a group who freely mixed the diffuse Comme des Garçons style with elements from punk, such as Doc Marten's safety boots, black leather and unconventional, but elaborate hairstyles. These two experiences match the fact that throughout the world 'Japanese fashion' tended to have a special appeal to relatively young and relatively well-educated people with a particular, sometimes professional, interest in design and aesthetics.

Following Mike Featherstone (1991:43–47) on postmodernism and consumer culture in the 1980s, I wish to argue that Comme des Garçons-inspired styles were taken up in particular by some of the 'new cultural intermediaries' who – as opposed to the 'old petite bourgeoisie' – actively promoted popular culture as a field of intellectual analysis, thereby also legitimating a personal interest in appearances. Comme des Garçons was, of course, only one out of many things that went on in popular culture during the 1980s, and certainly was not embraced by all cultural intermediaries. Even so, the recognition that 'Japanese fashion' was distinctly different from the conventions of 'Western' high fashion – which it had managed to challenge – did, in the context, function as a reconfirmation of the notion that high fashion, elitist and pretentious, was about to break down under the pressure of a widespread call for democratization. The fact that 'Japanese fashion' was perceived as not just a fashion, but connected with a (simplistic) assumption that it could only be fully understood in relation to Japanese culture, helped to bring about a new fashion discourse in which the relation between aesthetic and social processes played a crucial part.

Along with a widespread interest in Japanese design, the knowledge of 'others' and the respect for their different cultural forms was a part of the intellectualization of knowledge about popular culture analyzed by Featherstone (1991:44). My critique is not that this knowledge was superficial and eclectic. It would, indeed, be a misunderstanding merely to hold up to the media an ideal that they should disseminate exact and detailed knowledge. Not only would this be a form of academic chauvinism, but – worse – it would hardly be an alternative to the feeling at the time that Japan could only be understood according to her own premises and hence required a very specific form of knowledge – a notion which led the media to restate and reinforce blatant Orientalist stereotypes.

What I criticize is the fact that the starting point for appreciating 'Japanese' design was always Japan's difference. Such a categorical isolation was all the more ambivalent because the styles and goods that entered Europe from Japan in the 1980s tended to have a stylistic and technological anonymity which allowed them to blend in easily on the consumer market. It is especially ironical that the 'Japanese fashion' has been interpreted with reference to simplistic ideas of Japanese culture, because of the way the style was worn, exactly as a marker of individualism. Hence, one of the meanings of 'Japan' in Western consumer culture seemed to be an 'otherness' inside people's minds, made visible through austere dress. Now I would not be one to scorn anybody for not being in total unison with her material existence in this world. But is it really necessary to express one's own sensitivity and delicate individualism with the aid of a discourse that rules out the same qualities among the Japanese?

To further enhance the ambivalence of recent Japonisme, it should also be noted that sweeping gestures like this have not been rare in postmodernist writings, such as those of Baudrillard – the new prophet in the desert (Turner 1993:10) – who plainly states that Japan is a satellite of the planet Earth: artificial, deterritorialized, weightless, beyond the real (Baudrillard 1989:76). In their global dissemination, Kawakubo's garments held together the contradictions of Japan as an imaginary 'otherness' and an increasingly real economic superpower. And more than this: dressed in dark, loose clothes, cultural intermediaries on the urban scenes could simultaneously set themselves apart from mainstream fashion and its conventional femininity, appreciate the 'cultural difference' of Japan, and mark their membership of a new postmodern stratum which was, in fact, a transnational community of taste.

Exotic Influences

It is finally time to take a closer look at the way in which parts of the fashion press have attempted to explain Kawakubo's design as an exotic influence from a country where fashion is perceived to operate according to a logic completely different from the fashion of Paris, London and New York; indeed, a country where fashion hardly exists. Exotic, in this context, stands for something not only external, but also superficial and passing, something which is not strong enough to question the terms of international fashion, even though this notion contradicts the fact that the so-called 'Japanese fashion' actually succeeded in changing the agenda of high fashion. In the light of this contradiction, the statements of the fashion press must be interpreted as a countermove against the stylistic de-centering of high fashion conventions of the female body as a consumer spectacle.

The term 'exotic' has, indeed, been used as a denigration of 'Japanese fashion'. An example is the way in which Kawakubo's design persistently has been labelled 'ethnic'. The London correspondent for *Women's Wear Daily*, for instance, had the following opinion of Comme des Garçons:

> It's ethnic, that's all. It's old National Geographic school of design. If Saint Laurent goes to Marrakesh for a long holiday you know jolly well there'll be a few jellabas knocking about in his next collection. If he went to Tokyo instead, he'd produce a stronger Japanese collection than Rei Kawakubo.
> (Coleridge 1989:77)

It is curious to notice that in the fashion press the word 'ethnic' has a meaning which is close to what is otherwise termed fashion: being bound to dissappear as quickly as it has emerged, 'ethnic' simply means a fad. 'Ethnic' styles – so goes the premise for this line of thought – are not really original, and 'ethnic' designers will not be able to keep up with the biggest demand of fashion itself: that they must change. All they can do is perpetuate the tradition of which they themselves are part, repeating the designs that have been passed down to them. The 'ethnic' is a kind of fossilized folklore, the fashion correspondent seems to say, and if it happens to be in tune with the spirit of the time, that is simply because of the insatiable appetite in the West for 'difference'. But it is bound to lose its attraction once the world moves on.

Exotica actually has a long tradition in Paris fashion – from Paul Poiret to Yves Saint Laurant, just to mention two who have been explicitly inspired by the Orient. In this tradition, the term 'ethnic' refers not so much to various ethnic forms of costume as to a distinct style, characterized by bright colours and fancy materials, large jewellery, veils and scarves, and most of all, by its mixture of different elements. However, in this sense Comme des Garçons was anything but 'ethnic'. Rather than exploring the play of colours and forms typical of 'ethnic fashion', the early 1980s collections were understated, serious and pure. Kawakubo's figures were not decorative, but austere, clad in black.

A number of other Japanese designers' styles could more easily be described as 'ethnic'. Hanae Mori, for example, the only Japanese haute couture designer, seriously and systematically promoted herself under the name of 'Madame Butterfly' when she established her fashion house in Tokyo in the 1960s – an allusion not only to the main character in Puccini's opera, the femme fatale from Nagasaki, but also to the large, colourful butterfly patterns with which she decorated her dresses. In so doing, she was obviously playing the sentimental strings of Orientalist 'ethnic design'. Another example of an 'ethnic' Japanese designer is Kenzo whose first Paris collection in the 1960s was called 'Jungle Jap'. In contrast to Mori's decorative and dramatic 'ethnic designs', Kenzo's style is characterized by a humorous mixture of different colours, patterns, fabrics, and ethnic styles, and he is not particularly devoted to Japanese traditional clothes, even though elements of kimono have sometimes emerged in his collections. A third Japanese designer who employs 'ethnic' styles is Kansai Yamamoto who consciously reworks Japanese urban costume traditions. In fashion photography from the 1980s he also created a special effect by using small-town shop-keepers and road repair men at work as models dressed in his designer clothes.

Japanese exotica does, however, offer more than colourful ornamentation, and in his attempt to explain 'Japanese fashion' as different, Nicholas Coleridge goes so far as to put together fragmented statements circulating in the press into a whole narrative about Zen Buddhism (1989) – which, of course, strongly reinforces the perceived incomprehensibility of Japan. Zen as a theme in fashion was also adopted in a number of photo editorials in fashion magazines, such as 'La Mode Zen', produced by French *Elle*, but also used in the Japanese edition of the magazine. (Figure 4) The

LA MODE
ZEN
フランス人から見た禅の表情
ELLE FRANCE

Figure 4 Zen Buddhism as interpreted by Japanese and Western fashion designers

unproblematic combination of Western and Japanese designers in the editorial, and the fact that it appeared both in Japanese and French magazines (not to mention the fact that the model is Western), firmly locate the 'Japaneseness' of Zen fashion in the play of appearances. And yet, instead of analyzing the stylistic implication of this, Coleridge takes on the old Japanological project of equating social processes with aesthetics.

Zen Buddhism is, of course, an elitist religion which is practiced by men and women, leading industrious, quiet lives in secluded monasteries and temples. Certain parts of Zen have been adopted by such popular cultural forms as the tea ceremony and flower arrangement which are practiced largely by middle class women in Japan. But even so, they emphasize prescription and repetition so that the ceremonies are far from the continual innovations of the fashion industry (cf. Watts 1957:209). Apparently ignoring this, Coleridge employs such revered concepts of Japanese aesthetics as *wabi* as the key to understanding the smash hits of fashion in the 1980s. In his journalistic account of international fashion, the chapter devoted to Japanese fashion reads more like academic Japanology than like the other chapters in the book – which in itself is rather impressive. Coleridge concludes the chapter with a conversation with Mori Aki, publisher of the Japanese edition of *Women's Wear Daily* and son of Hanae Mori. Hence we would expect him to be among the more severe critics of the 'Japanese' trend. And yes, with the authority of the insider, he assures the foreign observer that all those dark colours of 'Japanese fashion' might have been exotically different in the West, but 'for me it was nothing new' (Coleridge 1989:103). So, while one fashion writer poses as Japanologist, another is turned into a native informant!

It seems that we are back to square one where *Women's Wear Daily*'s writers and sympathizers attack Kawakubo and other designers whose innovative collections managed to question high fashion's underlying assumptions, both in relation to femininity and to luxury and exclusivity. As the above example shows, this criticism was also raised by some Japanese, but in general the press' 'Orientalization' of Japanese fashion functioned to defuse the economic re-orientation of high fashion towards the Japanese market, which again was a part of a wider economic 'threat' presented by Japan in the 1980s, and felt particularly in the United States.

The paradox of the fashion writer becoming Japanologist is

perhaps that in his attempt to explain away 'Japanese fashion', Coleridge simultaneously brought to the attention of his readers traditions of Japanese aesthetics and religion, thereby certainly doing his bit to intellectualize fashion. His account of the 'wabi lobby' is written in a self-consciously ironical style as if to indicate that the author is aware of where the logic of the Japanological discourse is taking him, but even so is not entirely convinced by it.

Conclusion

By now the 'Japanese fashion' of the 1980s is over. Garments are cut closer to the body again, and black no longer holds sway in the fashion colour spectrum. But the trend has left behind lasting effects on the way in which fashion is generally perceived and on the fashion business itself, as well as on peoples's attitudes towards Japan. Today it is hardly possible to maintain that Japanese are essentially not 'at home' with the styles and meanings of Western fashion clothes (Richie 1991:108), because the work of Japanese designers has had a profound impact on Western, or more embracing international, fashion. Today books on high fashion tend to include a chapter on Japan (Coleridge 1989; Fairchild 1989; Craik 1994). At the same time coffee-table books and films on Kawakubo, Yohji Yamamoto, Issey Miyake and other Japanese fashion designers have emerged (Miyake 1978; Koren 1984; Penn 1988; Wenders 1989; Sudjic 1990). Books on Japanese aesthetics also tend to include contemporary fashion along with kimono, woodblock prints, pottery and architecture (Tanaka and Koike 1984). And even government introductions to Japan now refer to the Tokyo designers in a separate chapter of their authorized version of 'Japanese culture' (*Japan of Today* 1989:138).

I have here described the search for the 'Japaneseness' of Japanese fashion, in which designers and journalists – Japanese, Europeans and Americans – fans and critics alike have tended to reinstate a set of reductive assumptions. The Orientalist catalogue of stereotypes has, in other words, peered from behind the backs of individual commentators so that, in spite of their different points of views, opinions and intentions, they have basically agreed about where to look for 'Japaneseness' and how to interpret it. The meaning of 'Japaneseness' was at stake in a struggle over what high fashion ought to be about – with *Women's Wear Daily* defending the institutions of high fashion, itself being one of them, on the one hand, and the postmodern cultural intermediaries celebrating a perceived democratization of fashion, on the other.

The simplistic discourse of Orientalism was multiplied by the media at the same time as Japanese products in large numbers entered Western markets, not as rare exotica, but as popular and highly competitive commodities. It is ironical that Orientalist narratives which tend to be extremely systematic were repeated with an equally extreme eclecticism and pasted together not to a self-referring whole, but to fragmented collages. It is ironical also that Rei Kawakubo, as one of the designers who brought 'Japanese fashion' to fame, simultaneously reinforced the interest in the Paris collections. By reworking the premises of international high fashion, she also gave it a new vitality which has lasted until today.

NOTES

I would like to thank Meriel Hiramoto, Brian Moeran and Steen Erik Navrbjerg for helpful comments at various stages of my work with this paper.

1 As the aim of this paper is to explore the culturally constructed meanings of 'Japaneseness' in relation to women's fashion, I will use inverted commas to emphasize 'Japanese' as a normative as opposed to descriptive term.

2 In November 1991 both Rei Kawakubo and Yohji Yamamoto left the Tokyo collections, giving as a reason that they had become too commercial.

3 The term 'self-centred' is chosen here to indicate the centrality of the self and the body in young Japanese women's consumption of media, fashion goods, experiences in cities and resorts. This kind of consumption has elsewhere been described as 'hedonist', a term which I am hesitant to use because – as anyone reading Japanese women's magazines can testify – young women's consumer lifestyles are often presented in a way that emphasizes necessity, obligation and planning rather than immediate pleasure. At the same time a lot of young women who engage in this kind of consumption are labelled exactly as being 'selfish'.

4 This is parallel to the way in which the post-war 'democratization' of consumption in a number of Western European countries by the proponents of high cultural (and sometimes nationalist) values has been described as 'Americanization', in the sense of a morally reprehensible vulgarization (Hebdige 1988:30). Carter (1984) and Willet (1989) have disentangled the Horkheimer and Adorno-inspired idea of 'Americanization' of Germany.

5 Dalby (1993:61) points out that the term kimono, signifying an integrated tradition of clothing, is actually a product of the distribution

of so-called 'Western' clothes in Japan. Before the Meiji period the word was rarely used, and did not refer to 'Japanese' clothes in the general manner it does now.

6 Take the Conference on Popular Culture in Japan held at Berkeley in the Spring of 1991 as an example. The question 'What is so Japanese about that?' was asked about every single paper given at the conference, except for one paper which addressed the question directly in that it dealt with postwar nationalism in popular culture.

7 According to Sudjic (1990:24) ten per cent of Comme des Garçons sales go abroad to Germany, France, Italy, England and the USA, in that order.

8 Indeed, Evans and Thornton (1989) compare Kawakubo to the French fashion designer, Madelaine Vionnet, who also tended to avoid cutting the material for her garments. In relation to this, it should be remembered that drapery is also a sub-tradition of Western dressmaking.

9 This is especially true of the collections from the early 1980s. In recent collections Kawakubo has also used more conventionally 'ethnic' elements such as Chinese silk brocade in her twisted versions of *cheong sam*.

10 Layers of clothing wrapped on top of one another is an example of Kawakubo's adaptation of traditional Japanese garment techniques. Since 1990, when *Unwrapping Japan* (Ben-Ari et al.) came out, wrapping has also become a popular metaphor for Japanese cultural processes. But there is little evidence to support ideas that layers of cellufoil wrapped around proccessed cheese bought in a Japanese supermarket, or the round-about forms of politeness which some Japanese like to use (Hendry 1990), are part and parcel of the same integrated cultural dynamics as layers of fashion clothing.

REFERENCES

Baudrillard, Jean 1989 *America*, London: Verso.

Ben-Ari, Eyal et al. (eds.) 1990 *Unwrapping Japan*, Manchester: Manchester University Press.

Brubach, Holly 1989 'Between Times', p. 100–107 in *New Yorker* April 24.

Carter, Erica 1984 'Alice in consumer wonderland', p. 185–214 in A. McRobbie and M. Nava (eds.) *Gender and Generation*, London: Macmillan.

Clifford, James 1988 'On Orientalism', p. 255–277 in *The Predicament of Culture*, Cambridge: Harvard University Press.

Coleridge, Nicholas 1989 *The Fashion Conspiracy*, London: Heinemann-Mandarin.

Craik, Jennifer 1994 *The Face of Fashion: cultural studies in fashion*, London: Routledge.

Dalby, Liza 1993 *Kimono: fashioning culture*, New Haven: Yale University Press.

Elias, Norbert 1983 *Die höfische Gesellschaft* (Court Society), Frankfurt: Suhrkamp.

Evans, Caroline and Thornton, Minna 1989 *Women and Fashion: a new look*, London: Quartet Books.
Fairchild, John 1989 *Chic Savages*, New York: Pocket Books.
Featherstone, Mike 1991 *Consumer Culture and Postmodernism*, London: Sage.
Goldstein-Gidoni, Ofra 1993 *Packaged Weddings, Packaged Brides: the Japanese ceremonial occasions industry*, Unpublished Doctoral Dissertation, School of Oriental and African Studies, University of London.
Goody, Jack 1993 *The Culture of Flowers*, Cambridge: Cambridge University Press.
Hannerz, Ulf 1992 *Cultural Complexity: studies in the social organization of meaning*, New York: Columbia University Press.
Hebdige, Dick 1988 *Hiding in the Light*, Routledge: London.
Hendry, Joy 1990 'Humidity, hygiene and ritual care', p. 18–35 in E. Ben-Ari et al. (eds.) *Unwrapping Japan*.
Huyssen, Andreas 1986 *After the Great Divide: modernism, mass culture, postmodernism*, Bloomington: Indiana University Press.
Ivy, Marilyn 1988 'Tradition and Difference in Japanese Mass Media', p. 21–30 in *Public Culture* (1) 1.
Iwatake, Mikako 1993 *The Tokyo Renaissance: constructing a postmodern identity in contemporary Japan*, Unpublished Doctoral Dissertation, University of Pennsylvania.
Japan of Today 1989 Ministry of Education.
JIJ: The Japan International Journal 1992 'The Kansei factor: image making in Japanese advertising', p. 18–24 (2).
Kinsella, Sharon 1995 'Cuties in Japan', p. 220–54 in L. Skov and B. Moeran (eds.) *Women, Media and Consumption in Japan*, London: Curzon.
Kondo, Dorinne 1990 *Crafting Selves: power, gender, and discourses of identity in a Japanese workplace*, Chicago: University of Chicago Press.
Kondo Dorinne 1992 'The Aesthetics and Politics of Japanese Identity in the Fashion Industry', p. 176–204 in J.J. Tobin (ed.) *Re-made in Japan*, Cambridge Mass.: Yale University Press.
Koren, Leonard 1984 *New Fashion Japan*, Tokyo: Kodansha International.
Leopold, Ellen 1992 'The manufacture of the fashion system', p. 101–17 in J. Ash and E. Wilson (eds.) *Chic Thrills: a fashion reader*, London: Pandora Press.
Miyake, Issey 1978 *East Meets West*, Tokyo: Heibonsha.
Miyoshi, Masao and Harootunian, H.D. (eds.) 1989a *Postmodernism and Japan*, Durham: Duke University Press.
—— 1989b 'Introduction', p. vii–xxi in their (eds.) *Postmodernism and Japan*.
Mode no Japonisme: kimono kara umareta yutori no bi (Japonisme in Fashion: composed beauty born of the kimono) 1994 Kyoto National Museum of Modern Art and Kyoto Costume Institute.
Moeran, Brian 1984 *Lost Innocence: folk craft potters of Onta*, Japan, Berkeley: University of California Press.
Penn, Irving 1988 *Issey Miyake: photographs by Irving Penn*, Tokyo: Libro Porte.
Raaholt, Lennart 1989 *Strømninger i form og norm* (Trends in Form and Norm), Public Lecture at Baaring Folk High School.

Richie, Donald 1991 (1981) 'The Tongue of Fashion', p. 98–113 in *A Lateral View*, Tokyo: Japan Times.
Said, Edward 1978 *Orientalism*, New York: Vintage Books.
Skov, Lise and Moeran, Brian (eds.) 1995 *Women, Media and Consumption in Japan*, London: Curzon.
Sudjic, Deyan 1990 *Rei Kawakubo and Comme des Garçons*, London: Fourth Estate & Wordsearch.
Tanaka, Ikko and Koike, Kazuko (eds.) 1984 *Japan Design: the four seasons in design*, Tokyo: Libro.
Tijssen, Lieteke van Vucht 1993 'Women between Modernity and Postmodernity', p. 147–64 in Bryan Turner (ed.) *Theories of Modernity and Postmodernity*, London: Sage.
Turner, Bryan (ed.) 1993a *Theories of Modernity and Postmodernity*.
—— 1993b 'Periodization and Politics in the Postmodern', p. 1–14 in his (ed.) Theories of Modernity and Postmodernity.
Watts, Alan 1957 *The Way of Zen*, Harmondsworth: Penguin.
Wenders, Wim 1989 *Notebook on Cities and Clothes*, Road Movies Film Production.
Wichmann, Siegfried 1981 *Japonisme: the Japanese influence on Western art in the 19th and 20th centuries*, New York: Harmony.
Willet, Ralph 1989 *The Americanization of Germany, 1945–49*, London: Routledge.
Wilson, Elizabeth 1987 *Adorned in Dreams: fashion and modernity*, London: Virago.
Wilson, Elizabeth 1989 'Rewinding the video' p. 191–210 in *Hallucinations: life in the postmodern city*, London, Hutchinson Radius.

6

Imaginings in the Empires of the Sun

Japanese Mass Culture in Asia

Leo Ching

Chen Kuo-rei slouches in his chair, absorbed intently by the images emitting from his thirty-inch Sony Trinitron set. Kuo-rei does not understand the broadcast coming through the stereo-sound speakers. Yet he recognizes the contest between two 300-pound wrestlers wearing their customary loincloth trying to push the other out of the ring – a traditional Japanese sumo match. Switching to another channel with a tap of his finger, Kuo-rei catches the well-groomed Peter Jennings reporting the world's latest on ABC's World News Tonight. And if Kuo-rei so desires, he can stay tuned for more news from Britain's BBC, Germany's ZDF, and France's A-2. Recently, this has become a familiar sight in Taiwan. From Japanese historical drama to CNN news, from Ultraman sci-fi to Tokyo's latest business report, Japan and the world are immediately accessible by the push of a button. The geographic proximity between the two countries has made the approximately 20 million people on this island free subscribers to Japan's latest technological ingenuity: BS or Broadcasting Satellite.

* * *

Edward Chuang works for one of the most popular and profitable department stores on Orchard Road: the Isetan. Clad in the latest from designers Junko Koshino and Issey Miyake, Edward has recently returned home after a year of studying Japanese in Tokyo. When he saw an ad from Isetan for a sales position, Edward jumped at the opportunity, even though it meant selling baby carts on the sixth floor. After his lunch break, Edward often ventures upstairs to the Kinokuniya bookstore where he browses through books and magazines from Japan, and his favorite, the monthly style magazine *Ryūkō Tsūshin*.

* * *

The music and laughter roaring out of her daughter's room have always perplexed Mrs. Kwok. She doesn't care much for the popular music that has driven her fifteen-year-old daughter Jenny to spend the bulk of her monthly allowance on the newest CDs and cassettes. However, what bewilders her is that these days young people like her daughter listen not only to Cantonese, Chinese, or English songs but also to popular songs from Japan! In the room, Jenny and her friends are humming and moving with the beat from her latest acquisition – Shōnentai's newest single, 'Funky Flushing'. They gossip on the most recent rumor about Japanese singer-actress Imai Miki and teen-idol Miyazawa Rie from tabloids such as the *Ming-Pao Weekly*. 'Let's play *suteki na* music, let's dance *asa made* disco, Let's make Funky night . . .' – the strange mixture of Japanese and English in the refrain enables Jenny to sing along as she convulses her body more rigorously.

* * *

Red-faced and sweating, Lee Myung-sung croons passionately with the background music of his favorite song. With his eyes fixed on the video screen in front, he closely follows the lyrics that change color with the melody, leading him along. The video, like many of those shown in MTV, are images attempting to approximate the narrative of the song. This is one of many *karaoke* or *bideoke* bars on Student Avenue in Seoul. A sing-along entertainment device, karaoke is a direct transplant from Japan and, in recent years, has gained tremendous popularity among business people and students here. As his performance ends, Myung-sung is cheered and jeered by his very drunk colleagues. Customary claps can be heard from other patrons as the next songster hurriedly grabs the silver microphone.[1]

Throughout Asia, Japan is in vogue.[2] From fashion to food to leisure, Japanese cultural commodities are ubiquitous, casting wooing glances at the Orient's nouveaux riches. This is especially prominent in the region collectively known as the NIEs (Newly Industrialized Economies) of South Korea, Taiwan, Singapore, and Hong Kong. A similar process can also be observed, although sporadically, in Southeast Asia, extending from Thailand to the Philippines. These signs of regionalization of culture suggest a cultural (or a consumerist?) integration process that transcends national boundaries but that is confined, for the moment, to a specific region of the world system. How are we to assess this cultural dominant? Is this the 'cultural logic' of Japanese economic imperialism (*Pax Nipponica*), or is it a regional manifestation of a general globalization process which weakens the cultural coherence of all nation-states? And is the discourse of cultural imperialism still an effective counter-hegemonic response to this emerging cultural formation? Asia is, contrary to the notorious dictum by the Japanese intellectual Okakura Kakuzō at the turn of the century, not one, and indigenous dependency and response to the growing Japanese cultural presence vary not only between, but also within, nations. For the present study, I have limited my analysis to Taiwan, an ex-colony of Japan in which Japanese cultural influence is perhaps most pervasive.

The emergence of Japanese cultural presence in Taiwan since the mid-1980s can be attributed to Japan's ascendancy as the world's prominent economic power and to Taiwan's own politico-economic changes. The point should be made here, however, that economic prowess does not necessarily entail cultural dominance. The narrative of capitalist culture is still coordinated by an unabating eurocentrism. Despite its waning economic presence, American mass culture is still the dominant and powerful cultural industry in the world today. Meanwhile, Japanese cultural influence is primarily constricted to Asia, and Japanese mass culture itself is still plugged into every trend of Western, especially American, pop culture. Today Japan has more American food franchises than any country outside of North America, and Japan also serves as the largest market for Hollywood films outside the United States. Japan can buy Hollywood, but it is unable to produce films with global appeal. As the United States continues to play the role of 'policeman' in the region, however, Japan has increasingly become the primary source of capital and technology for its Asian neighbors, as well as the major market for their exports of foodstuffs and raw materials. In 1991, for the first time since 1945, Japan's trade with Asia exceeded that with the United States. Japanese investment and technology have dominated the economies of Taiwan and South Korea, and Japanese manufactures have established dominant markets throughout Asia. The growing Japanese direct investments and exports, especially consumer goods, have made Japanese cultural images and commodities readily accessible in Taiwan. Nevertheless, it is also Taiwan's rapid economic growth culminating in the affluent 1980s that has created a consumer society capable of absorbing the influx of Japanese cultural goods.

Taiwan, together with the other three tigers of East Asia – South Korea, Singapore, and Hong Kong – has forged the fastest growing industrialization the world has ever seen. This economic 'miracle' is intrinsically related to, and dependent on, Japan and, of course, the United States. After the defeat by the Communists and the subsequent relocation to Taiwan in 1949, the Nationalist government became one of the largest beneficiaries of U.S. aid. It is estimated that Taiwan received $5.6 billion in massive economic and military aid from Washington (Chan 1990:28). American influence on postwar Taiwan was pervasive. As Robert Elegant writes:

> Between 1949 and 1965, American grants, commodities, subsidized loans, and technical advice . . . laid the foundation for Taiwan's present economic structure . . . American technology, channeled through the Joint Commission, altered everything from prenatal care and primary education to fertilizers, pesticides, and plows – and made Taiwan a better place to live.
>
> (1990:31)

This is only half the story, however. What Elegant in his ethnocentric posturing neglects, is the geopolitical self-interest of the United States. As the conflict between the United States and the USSR intensified in the latter half of the 1940s, the United States initiated the Marshall Plan and, later, the North Atlantic Treaty Organization to counter the perceived threat of Soviet expansion. The outbreak of the Korean War further extended American containment policy to Asia. Massive aid to Taiwan and South Korea was accompanied by a revision in policy toward Japan.[3] The Japanese economy was revamped and boosted during the Korean and the Vietnam Wars as a result of American military expenditure.

In Taiwan during the 1950s, agricultural reform and productivity were promoted to provide the foundation for industrial growth, and the policy of import substitution, a development strategy that sought to replace imports of non-durable consumer goods by labor intensive indigenous production, was implemented with sizable American aid. In the 1960s, partly under the pressure of U.S. advisers, Taiwan initiated a period of export industrialization involving the development of low technology light-industrial and labor-intensive products and the assembly of imported inputs for consumer goods such as textiles and toys to the markets of the developed countries, especially to the United States. Today, as real wages erode Taiwan's comparative advantage in labor intensive industries, the economy has gradually moved toward technology and capital intensive industries.

Export-oriented growth strategy, American aid, and the relative open trade regime have launched, and sustained, the economic growth of Taiwan. However, one should not overlook the intermediary role played by Japan in the economic success not only of Taiwan, but of the rest of the NIEs. In the 'triangle of growth', between the pivotal United States and the peripheral NIEs, Japan acts as an important economic agent. To oversimplify the process, as the United States plays the important role of providing an immense market and basic technology development (hardware), Japan imports the basic know-how and applies it to practical use (software). Subsequently Japan is able to sell/dispose of previously used 'secondhand' technology (machines and equipment) to the peripheral NIEs. The NIEs, in turn, use this 'secondhand' technology and equipment to launch their export-oriented industries (Twu 1990:25–26). Perhaps the continual economic success of the new NIEs and the economic hardship faced by the former NICs (Newly Industrialized Countries) of Latin America and southern Europe can be explained by the NICs' lack of Japan's intermediary role.

Riding on the 'triangle of growth', Taiwan's export-oriented economy has posted an impressive annual average real GDP growth of 8.7 per cent since 1952. The per capita income has increased from $215 in 1965 to over $10,000 in 1991. And today, Taiwan boasts one of the world's largest reserve of foreign currency. Since the 1980s a consumer society surrounded by 'the remarkable conspicuousness of consumption and affluence, established by the multiplication of objects, services and material goods', has been well established in Taiwan (Baudrillard 1988:29). Concurrently, Japanese cultural goods appear to be exerting a discernible influence on the cultural site of Taiwan.

The most frequent and ingenuous response to an emerging foreign cultural presence by local intellectuals is to see this as a degenerative extension of another nation's economic domination. This is no exception in Taiwan's curiously few and feeble discussions on the matter. I will examine the only two works I was able to locate on the topic. The first is an essay entitled 'Speed, Infiltration, and Occupation: The Japanese Invades Taiwanese Economy' by Chuang Shu-yu (1989:12–21). Chuang sees the growing presence of Japan in the cultural arena of Taiwan, which she describes accurately, as the direct reflection of Japanese economic dominance. As the martial terms in the title suggest, the article evokes an abhorrent and sensitive phase of Sino-Japanese relations: Japan's colonization of Taiwan after the Sino-Japanese War and its subsequent invasion of China. The article pointedly draws the analogy between Japan's colonial aggression in the early twentieth century and its postwar economic expansionism. This is especially evident in the use ofa military lexicon and warfare rhetoric in depicting the Japanese 'invasion' of Taiwan. Chuang writes,

> Japanese merchants are quietly *positioning* themselves throughout the important cities of Taiwan. With *piercing eyes* and *detailed strategy*, they are readying for *a long-standing deployment*. And the Taiwanese market has become the *fortress* and *testing ground* for the Japanese merchants' eventual *invasion* of other overseas Chinese communities in the world.
>
> (1989:14; my emphasis)

To Japanese imperial eyes, Taiwan is the launching pad to the world's 11.5 billion-Chinese market. And this scheme of incorporation, argues Chuang, follows the same logic as the Japanese army's establishment of the puppet government in Manchuria in 1932.

The success of the Japanese economic 'assailants' today, observes Chuang, is largely due to their well-coordinated strategies. Long-term planning, foresight in investing (real estate and commercial), information amassing, connection establishing, and Japanese-style customer servicing are all factors responsible for the infiltration of the Japanese business army. Quoting from Ezra Vogel, an authority on Japan, Chuang warns the people of Taiwan of the insatiability of the Japanese economic animal who 'will eat when it can' (1989:21). The underlying concern after all, concludes Chuang, is the dwindling market share of the domestic industries in the now booming Taiwanese consumer market. The locals would be impoverished if the foreigners were left unchecked. Overall, Chuang assigns a central role to economic practices and implies that these are really what are at stake and that cultural factors are instrumental in maintaining Japan's economic dominance.

This line of argument – seeing Japan as conspiring an economic takeover of the world and pitting the indigenous population as helpless victims against such a ploy – is similar to those deployed by the Western critics of Japanese economic hegemonism: the Japan bashers.[4] Since the 1960s, Japan's economic prowess and its recent conspicuous consumption of American historical landmarks and entertainment industries, such as the Rockefeller Center, MCA Inc., and Columbia Pictures, have incited public fear and resentment. Whereas Japan's Asian neighbors condemn its economic encroachment as the second-coming of Japanese military imperialism, likewise, but from the victor's vantage point, the Americans warn the Japanese of the repercussions Japan will suffer if history were to repeat itself. As Theodore White writes, 'The superlative execution of their trade tactics may provoke an incalculable reaction – as the Japanese might well remember of the course that ran from Pearl Harbor to the deck of the U.S.S. Missouri in Tokyo Bay just 40 years ago' (cited in Miyoshi 1991:63).

Obviously, I am not suggesting that the relationship between Japan and the United States is identical to that between Japan and its Asian neighbors. The power imbalance between the two is too great to ignore. The two responses to the growing Japanese economic presence may be similar, but they are embedded in very different historical contexts. Because of Japan's ambivalent status as the only non-Western colonial power that has barely escaped colonization itself, its relation and attitude toward the West and its Asian neighbors have been remarkably different. Like all non-Western imagined communities under the threat of imperialism and colonialism, Japan's encounter with the West was traumatic.[5] Western imperialist expansion throughout the non-Western world (by the 1880s, 80 per cent of the earth's surface was under European control), the coming of Commodore Perry and the 'black ships' in 1853, and the demise of the Middle Kingdom under Western aggression all aroused a sense of urgency and fear for Japan's own survival, and consequently led to its own imperial expansion into Asia in the involuntary pursuit of 'modernity'. From this perspective, Japan's aggression toward Asia *is* the direct result of Western infringement. Any criticism against Japanese imperialism and colonialism *necessarily* entails the criticism of Western imperialism and colonialism. This point has often been overlooked, especially today, as Americans accuse Japan of 'unfair' trade strategies without reflecting on the U.S.'s own imperialist and economic aggression toward countries in Central and Latin America.

It is this lack of self-reflexivity and self-criticism manifested in the chauvinistic expression of nationalism that not only reduces historical differences but also ignores the economic and political complexity inherent in today's global capitalist system. Today, Japan's economic expansion has brought fear to its Asian neighbors mainly because of the great suffering Japan has inflicted on other Asian countries during World War II and because of Japan's persisting reluctance to face up to its wartime responsibilities. These concerns are genuine in light of Japan's prevailing prejudice and insensitivity toward its neighbors. Unlike the Germans, the Japanese government has never sincerely or formally acknowledged and apologized for its wartime brutalities and atrocities. Although Japan has not categorically denied its involvement, it has meticulously attempted to gloss over and downplay its colonial past.[6] Although Emperor Akihito expressed remorse and has promised that Japan will not repeat its imperialist endeavor during his visit to Southeast Asia, one should not overlook the timing of the apology which coincides with the Asians' growing disenchantment with and resentment toward the overwhelming Japanese investment in that region.[7]

The contempt for Japan's economic buildup by its Asian neighbors is rooted in Japan's colonial legacy and in Japan's present-day prejudice against other Asians. To that extent, the protest against and the concern for Japanese economic aggression in Asia is justifiable. This sentiment, however, is diametrically different from the American response, which inevitably equates its declining hegemony with Japan's unfair, treacherous, and sneaky tactics in the global economy, where the rules have been made and dictated by the Americans since World War II. The danger of the Asian reaction, however, as I have suggested earlier, lies in the assumption that exploitation is unidirectional, imposed simply by one nation onto another without taking into account their own ever-growing involvement in the global economy. Historical analogies may be rhetorically powerful, but one must probe into why and how different historical contexts are reduced and produced. Taking sanctuary under the name of victimization and fostering an unexamined nationalism would only obscure the complex process of collaboration and justify the 'victimized' nations' victimization of other countries. Relegating her analysis to a crude 'Japan dominates Taiwan' formulation, Chuang not only reduces the complexity of today's global capitalism into a simple good and evil, but also ignores the various orders of power and domination involved.

What Chuang inserts, but fails to mention, in the article is a diagram – categorized into food-producing market, servicing market (department stores, supermarkets and convenience stores), real estate market, and leisure market – that shows sixteen Japanese service industries that have successfully penetrated the Taiwanese market. Chuang does not explain the fact that of the sixteen Japanese companies, only three are entirely funded by the Japanese, with Japanese money. Most of them are joint-ventures between Japanese and Taiwanese companies with 50 per cent or more stock shares held by the Taiwanese collaborators. Obviously, one should not emphasize the financial cooperation between foreign and domestic companies and overlook the unequal transfer of information and technologies. Despite domestic financial investment, the center for control and production often lies in Japan. What needs to be underscored, however, is what Robert Reich has perceptively argued: in the 'global web' of present day multinational capitalism, that the notions of a national economy tied to the well-being of a population and of products having national origins are becoming obsolete (1991). Companies and corporations are becoming more intrinsically interdependent globally and less connected to any single nation. The conception that different economies compete nationally with well-defined winners and losers not only oversimplifies the issue at hand but also runs the risk of inciting nationalistic and racist fervor. Late twentieth-century capitalism, in its relentless pursuit of profit, knows no national boundaries and feels no geographic constraints. Therefore, it is not surprising that Taiwan and South Korea, two ex-colonies of Japan that have been most vocal about and apprehensive of Japan's economic expansion, are themselves investing rapidly in North America and Southeast Asia. Taiwan especially has been making a substantial investment in China.[8] In the global division of labor, the 'victim' turns around and becomes the 'victimizer'. It is not the individual constituent but the system as a whole that requires careful scrutiny and criticism.

Furthermore, what makes the unidirectional domination thesis difficult to accept is the Taiwanese cultural producers' eagerness to imitate and transfer existing cultural products from Japan to generate profits. Eager to satisfy and exploit the vibrant consumer market created by rapid economic growth, proven Japanese cultural goods are imitated and imported to reduce cost and maximize profit. Nowhere is this 'postmodern mimicry' more prominent than in the cultural industry of popular music. In recent years, Taiwan has witnessed an unprecedented number of young popular singers. These highly commodified performers are young, good looking, stylish, and usually possess little or no talent at all. The prime example is Hsiao Hu Tui (Little Tiger Team), three youngsters whose popularity has created somewhat of a phenomenon since their debut in 1989. Hsiao Hu Tui is a simulacrum of the successful Japanese trio Shōnentai (The Young Team). Their young and energetic outwardness, mechanically choreographed dance steps, together with easy-to-memorize melodies, are well packaged and transmitted through various media for tens of thousands of young potential consumers. These young 'idols' (*aidoru* in Japanese, *o hsiang* in Chinese) are usually given a particular character trait – cute, naive, rebellious, or animated – most of which are variably different from their real personalities. Their individualities are completely suppressed. These performers almost never make or play their own music; their songs are written and produced by professional song writers. Each idol's potential hit song is accompanied by, and synchronized with, mechanically choreographed movements that operate with remarkable precision; specific sets of costumes and hairstyles are created so they can be easily identified with each number. The result is a formidable 'idol system' consisting of record companies, talent production companies, and electronic media that cooperatively ensure the availability and that incessantly disseminates these packaged commodities to the growing consumer market (Inamasu 1989; Ogawa 1988).[9]

A typical talent production company in Taiwan would often produce a Taiwanese version of the idol singers with Japanese blueprint. The planning department of the company keeps a close eye on the development of the Japanese music industry. Researchers are dispatched to Japan to purchase videos and records of popular Japanese idols. Cultural affinity and geographic proximity facilitate this imitating process. An already successful model is brought back, and a Taiwanese version is created, at times modified, to accommodate domestic needs. Japanese songs are also borrowed, either in complete or partial (especially the refrain) version, or songs are 'spliced' with different arrangements. This imitation and borrowing of cultural images from Japan is necessary for the financial survival of the companies. These production companies, mostly small- to medium-sized, do not have the capital or people power to invest and to create talents without risking financial loss. The Japanese culture industry provides a well-established model that minimizes the financial risk of these companies. If one project does not fare well, it can be canceled, and another one can be pursued without major financial loss. In this context, to see Japanese or Japanese-like cultural commodities as the immediate outgrowth of Japanese economic expansion imposed from Japan is to overlook the profit-seeking manipulation by Taiwan's cultural producers, or what Leslie Sklair has called the transnational capitalist class, in creating an ersatz commodified culture (1991:8).[10] I do not want to make light of Japan's economic influence over Taiwan. Japanese cultural products are transmitted by the major social-economic institutions of Japan (often with Taiwanese collaboration). There is a clear economic sense in which this process can be seen as being imposed on Taiwanese culture, since it is bound up directly with Japan's emergence as an economic power. The booming consumer market represents enormous potential profits for Japanese multi-nationals (although I have argued that this process is not unilateral). Even if the significance of an *economic* domination is to be taken for granted, however, in what sense they are a *cultural* imposition is not so clear. What are the *cultural* implications of Japanese multinational capitalism? More importantly, what are the meanings people attach to the practice of consuming Japanese cultural commodities?

The second and more 'culturally' directed analysis of Japanese influence in Taiwan is Tsan Hung-chih's *City Watching: New Language, New Contact, and New Culture* (1989). Tsan's book is the only substantial analysis on the recent proliferation of Japanese mass culture that I have been able to locate. Despite the tentative and apologetic tone – Tsan admits that he doesn't know much about Japan or its language – he nonetheless provides a perceptive and meticulous description of Japan's influence on the mass culture of Taiwan.

Tsan describes three types of new cultural 'contacts' with Japan: the informational, the quotidian, and the industrial. This recent interaction is *new* because before the mid-1980s, contact with Japanese mass culture was kept minimal, and Japanese songs and films are still officially banned in Taiwan. Books, mostly language texts and technical manuals, were scarcely available and in restricted bookstores only. The study of the Japanese language was mostly for business purposes although a large number of the elderly spoke Japanese: a legacy of colonial education. Today, despite the official ban, Japanese songs and video programs can be heard and rented in every record and video rental store; Japanese fashion and information magazines (or their Chinese versions) are readily available, even from street vendors. Today, Japanese language learning has shifted from the technical to the practical, from the pedagogical to the commonplace, suggesting a better knowledge and a stronger affiliation with contemporary Japan. Titles such as *Phrases Used by Young Japanese* and *Young People Making Friends in Japanese* are clearly targeted toward the younger Taiwanese with emphasis on playfulness, casualness, and speediness. One book claims, as one of its distinctive features, that it will enable the learner to understand Japanese on TV, radio, and dialogues on the video tape. These are all indications of the prevalence of 'Japaneseness' in Taiwan's mass culture today.

The first 'reality' of Japanese cultural presence, writes Tsan, can be seen in the form of informational flow. Tsan points out that in 1985, sales of publications in Japanese exceeded that of those in English. If one notes the strong emphasis on learning English in Taiwan's education system and the lack thereof on Japanese, this phenomenon is astounding. Furthermore, the increase in circulation of Japanese magazines and regular subscribers to more specialized journals suggests an established demand. The rising demand for Japanese publications is met by the increasing number of bookstores that sell predominantly Japanese books and magazines. Finally, videotapes of Japanese TV programs and movies accounted for 31 per cent of Taiwan's entire video rental business.

The second 'contact' with Japan, according to Tsan, can be observed in the activities of everyday life, mainly in consumption. Citing the flourishing presence of supermarkets and department stores with Japanese investment, the increasing conformity to Japanese fashion trends, the heavy imitation of Japanese industrial design, and the growing identification with the Japanese life-style (going to coffee shops, karaoke bars) as examples, Tsan calls attention to the noticeable change and effect of Japanese culture on the behavior pattern of the daily lives of Taiwanese consumers.

The third new point of contact with Japan, observes Tsan, is in the industries. Although historically Taiwanese industries have always had a long and intimate relationship with Japan, recently there have been new developments. In the past, technology imported from Japan was predominantly 'production' oriented (electronics, manufacturing), but today the introduction of 'service know-how' is gaining importance. And this further intensifies Taiwan's reliance on Japan in all sectors of industry.

Tsan's systematic description accurately points out the all-presence of Japanese cultural influence on Taiwan. What is most striking about Tsan's work, as I have mentioned, is his tentativeness. His aim, as he outlines his objective in the outset, is to 'describe', to 'categorize', and to 'classify' the phenomenon, but not to 'criticize'. Tsan attributes his inability to derive a satisfying conclusion to an ambiguous and murky 'perplexity of advantages and disadvantages'. On the striking lack of analysis by Taiwanese cultural critics (himself included) of the increasing Japanese cultural presence despite growing anxiety and concern, Tsan writes: '[Japanese cultural influence], lacking an apparent theory and nationalistic ideology, is unable to incite a counter-ideology. Therefore there are no ways to go about criticizing' (1989:21). Furthermore, Tsan observes that Japanese cultural dominance, which already subsumes China, Taiwan, and Hong Kong, will soon include the Philippines. And it would not be incorrect to say that there exists a 'Common Sphere of Japanese Modus Vivendi', an obvious insinuation to the Japanese wartime slogan: the Greater East Asian Co-Prosperity Sphere. 'From a certain perspective', Tsan writes, 'this is an aspect of "cultural imperialism"'. He is quick to add, however, that he 'has not, or is not yet ready to', employ the term to express a strong criticism, rather, he borrows the term only to 'explain the existence of this Common Sphere' (1989:23).

This caution and reluctance to employ the generic concept of cultural imperialism to examine the spread of foreign culture is in stark contrast to the response of other 'third world' media and cultural critics, especially in their analysis of American cultural influence. One of the most celebrated studies on cultural imperialism is Ariel Dorfman and Armand Mattelart's *How to Read Donald Duck: Imperialist Ideology in the Disney Comic* (1975). Unlike Tsan's claim that Japanese cultural goods have no conceivable ideology, therefore making criticism difficult, Dorfman and Mattelart's project attempts to decipher the American capitalist ideology hidden behind the seemingly innocent and harmless world of Walt Disney.

Against the common perception of Disney comics, Dorfman and Mattelart argue that these cultural commodities, which are imbued with a capitalist ideology that once consumed and internalized, can normalize and naturalize the social relations of Western capitalism in the 'third world'. Meticulously working their way through the Disney comics and revealing their inherent capitalist ideologies, such as the unquestioned submission to moral and physical repression and economic domination, the stereotypical description and deprecation of the exotic 'third world', the frantic chase after money, the insatiable consumerism in a world of magical abundance, and so on, Dorfman and Mattelart are often compelling and convincing. However, as pointed out by John Tomlinson in his study on cultural imperialism, Dorfman and Mattelart's work, despite being a politicized reading of the 'imperialist text', does not take into account the effect on or the reception of the general public, who actually consumes these cultural products on an everyday basis. Tomlinson writes:

> What is finally at stake is not the literary-critical merits of Dorfman and Mattelart's interpretations, nor indeed the correctness of their socioeconomic analysis, but the crucial question of how ordinary readers read the comics: that is, the question of if and how the text has its ideological effects.
> (1991:43)

While Dorfman and Mattelart are able to advance the *potential* manipulative power of imported cultural products, they significantly ignore the possibility of multiple readings of these cultural texts by the people and underestimate their abilities to negotiate and construct meanings within their own particular cultural contexts.

I do not think that Dorfman and Mattelart's work should therefore be dismissed. Despite the lack of analysis of the cultural 'effect' of imported cultural goods, their work must be read in light of the historical context that motivated their project. It is no coincidence that the term 'cultural imperialism' emerged during the 1960s, when decolonization and national independence of what is mostly now called the 'third world' was finally taking place. This marked the first time the hitherto underprivileged and oppressed were given a voice of their own. Albeit nations are 'imagined political communities,' they are also the necessary countermeasures and inescapable consequences of Western imperialism and colonialism. For the intellectuals of these new nations, cultural autonomy meant political independence. Against the disfiguring and distorting of their precolonial histories by the colonial regime, many intellectuals began a passionate search for a national culture that, in retrospect, was besieged with problematics. The concept of cultural imperialism, as deployed by intellectuals in the post-independent, neo-colonial 'third world', as a historical process of rehabilitation, to construct a meaningful resistance to colonial rule and to mobilize people in the name of national independence, is inevitable and powerful. Written in 1971, in the midst of the Chilean revolutionary process, *How to Read Donald Duck* was indeed a politicized manifesto against the colonial empire of the United States and its multinational corporations. Despite its shortcomings, Dorfman and Mattelart's work should be read as an emerging voice, located historically, against American dominance (political, economic, and cultural) of Chile. To criticize the book for having a specific political agenda (as if there is a 'neutral' text) and to overlook the 'real' effect of the objects in analysis is to ignore the great disparity and power imbalance between the imperialist 'first' world and the defiant 'third' world in the specific historical context.

The question still remains, however, as to why Tsan finds Japanese cultural products lacking a discernible ideology and why the phenomenon is difficult to assess? Tsan rightly observes that the cultural merchandise imported from Japan is gradually and increasingly discarding the shade of traditional Japanese culture and ethnic character. What are perceived as Japanese cultural products can easily be of American or British origins. Japan simply reassembles and packages other cultural commodities and sells them to other countries. Tsan cites Taiwanese punk as an example. Punk style, together with other youth subcultures that emerged in postwar Britain, are defiant expressions of British youth. Punk is a 'style in revolt, [a] revolting style' (Hebdige 1979:106). It is offensive, threatening, and antisocial. As punk has reached Japan, however, it has lost most of its destructiveness and effectiveness, although the style has remained similar. The Japanese punk is highly uniform and its defiance is very well regulated. Clothing is ripped in the same way, accessories are bought and put on the same place, dance steps are performed in a very controlled and unvarying manner. In Japan, punk has literally become a 'style', losing all political implications. There is nothing offensive or threatening about Japanese punksters.

It is this depoliticized, domesticated, highly uniform and trendy Japanese punk style that has found its way to Taiwan. Taiwanese styles are imitations of the Japanese; all accessories and essentials for the punk look are imported from Japan. What Taiwan has received, argues Tsan, is a repackaged secondhand cultural commodity that has no specific 'national' origin or discernible ideology. A similar observation has been made by Anthony D. Smith as he contrasts earlier 'cultural imperialism' with today's:

> [T]here is an important difference from earlier cultural imperialisms. Earlier imperialisms were usually extensions of ethnic or national sentiments and ideologies, French, British, Russian, etc. Today's imperialisms are ostensibly non-national; 'capitalism' and 'socialism', and in a different sense 'Europeanism', are by definition and intention 'supranational', if not universal. They are supported by a technological infrastructure which is truly 'cosmopolitan', in the sense that the same tele-communications base will eventually erode cultural differences and create a genuinely 'global culture' based on the properties of the media themselves, to which the 'message' will become increasingly incidental.
>
> (1990:176)

What both Tsan and Smith seem to imply is that in today's global cultural economy, cultures are becoming decontextualized and dehistoricized as they cross national boundaries with unprecedented ease and speed. In a world of transnational corporations, telecommunication, information networks, and international division of labor, 'national' cultures are in danger of becoming obsolete, resorting only to tourist sites and museums.

This new cultural configuration has two implications for the discourse of cultural imperialism and for Japan's cultural presence in Taiwan. First of all, as communication and information technology advance with blazing speed and as cultural boundaries become more fluid, any attempt to block or limit incoming and outgoing cultural flows is doomed to failure. Japanese satellite broadcasts can be received in Shanghai, Pusan, and Taipei simply by extending the antenna of the TV. The regulation of the transmission of foreign cultural images is beyond the political apparatus of the nation-state. Secondly, as intranational economic integration and interdependence intensify, the existing center-periphery model of cultural domination is no longer viable. Not only can the institution of cultural production no longer be isolated to a single 'center', but the passive reception of the 'periphery' should also be questioned. How is one to specify the 'source' of production of a dress designed and labeled by a Japanese designer living in France, and assembled in Hong Kong? What is the effect on the cultural pattern of the society when a Taiwanese youth sings a Chinese song with a *karaoke* machine from Japan?

Tsan's work, by claiming a lack of discernible ideology within the very object of analysis, escapes the deterministic ideological incorporation approach of Dorfman and Mattelart. He also recognizes that *economically* Japan's cultural invasion of Taiwan has made Taiwan both a victim and a beneficiary. In the final section, entitled 'How to Face Japanese Contacts?', he writes,

> All Taiwanese exports and sources of competition today, come from Japan. We imitate the Japanese. Although our products are less in quality, they are also cheaper; therefore, we can be quite competitive. The object of our learning is a very competitive Japan, far more than the United States. As a result, we can be as competitive as the United States by learning just a few things from Japan.
>
> (1989:26)

Taiwan becomes a quasi-Japan, expanding its influence to others. Tsan urges Taiwan to refute the role of a collaborator, to 'turn around' and 'compete with Japan'. He challenges his readers to ask themselves if they are willing to be 'members of the Common Sphere of Japanese Modus Vivendi', if they are willing to 'lose all history, culture, and independent national character' (1989:26). Tsan's conclusion is far from satisfying. First, despite his suggestion that transnational corporations are responsible for the growth of cultural production, he still holds onto the notion that national industries represent the well-being of the peoples in a nation. How is this competition possible or viable on a national scale within the system of transnational capitalism? And exactly what should the Taiwanese cultural industry compete with Japan for: to be the next hegemon of Asia, the world? Second, Tsan seems to assume that one can step outside the cultural and ideological formation by simply refusing Japanese cultural products; once Japanese cultural products are cut off, cultural imperialism will stop. Does Tsan intend to stop all flow of foreign cultural practices? Who will decide what is acceptable and what is not? Third, by not concerning himself with the effect of Japanese cultural products on the general public, Tsan falls into the determinist trap of assuming that Japanese cultural influence *necessarily* entails the annihilation of Taiwanese culture in total. What does he mean by culture? And whose history is in danger? What is and who represents the national character of Taiwan, the mainlanders, the Taiwanese, or the aborigines? Tsan's culturalism and Chuang's economism, by ignoring the complex connexion between a particular cultural practice and its actual effect (be it foreign or domestic), assume, a priori, that Japanese cultural commodities have an inherent power intrinsic to them that will alter the cultural formation of Taiwan. There is an intended meaning attached that corresponds to a particular text, and the critics have a transparent and unmediated access to it. In other words, they fetishize Japanese cultural practices. Cultural meanings are predetermined and transparent to the critics. The result is always already guaranteed.

What has been conspicuously missing in both analyses of Japanese cultural influence in Taiwan is how these cultural products are actually experienced by the people who consume them. They also fail to allow for the ambiguous, multi-layered, and at times irrelevant responses of the consumers. While Chuang underscores the economic strategies of the Japanese producers, Tsan concerns himself with the 'non-ideological' nature of the product. Both privilege the production aspect of cultural process over consumption. Both assume an unproblematized ideological effect on 'passive' consumers as they shop in a Japanese-style department store, sing in a karaoke bar, or watch Japanese TV programs via satellite. What is essential is not a separated analysis of production *or* consumption of a cultural process but an analysis of the relationship and interaction between the cultural products *and* their consumers: how they interpret, translate, articulate, and even transform their experiences and meanings of a foreign cultural practice.

In the era of transnational capitalism, as economic interests and interdependence between nations proliferate on a global scale, cultural convergence seems to be occurring at various levels. Foreign cultural products and their meanings are not only readily available but are also easily transferable. Since no one can escape the continuous exposure to the enormous range of presentation and reference to the ever differentiating and changing commodified cultural practices, the attempt to locate identifiable and stable presentations and relations has become extremely difficult, if not impossible. Do people who have taken up Japanese cultural practices actually recognize or even care about, their 'Japaneseness'?

What if they are not aware that a popular song is of Japanese origin? What if they did not know that their favorite variety show is a carbon copy of a Japanese show? This raises the difficult question regarding the relationship between the cultural critic (in this case, me) and the people who actually consume the cultural texts. As an 'informed' analyst – I have lived in both countries and am acutely aware of the trends in Japanese mass culture – I was able, with my personal and privileged experience, to recognize cultural products that were imitated or imported directly from Japan. On the other hand, a large number of people in Taiwan, who have no knowledge of Japan, are unlikely to see certain commodities as emblematic of Japanese culture at all! In this instance, it becomes almost impossible to assess the ideological effect of an alien cultural influence that both Chuang and Tsan see as detrimental to the economic and cultural well-being of Taiwan.

Furthermore, even if the 'Japaneseness' of the cultural commodities is recognized, there is no guarantee that the people would be interpellated in an unyielding or particular way. The connexion between cultural texts and their actual effects may be quite unpredictable and complex. The same text can be interpreted differently by various people. Cultural meaning is never singular, and cultural texts are at least potentially multifunctional. Therefore, it is foreseeable that people's interpretation and appropriation of certain cultural products are independent from, and not limited only to, their signifying and representational effects. Some people might prefer Japanese goods for the pragmatic reason that Japanese quality and packaging are superior to that of indigenous or American products. Japanese goods are attractive to these people because of their *functionality* and *presentation*, not because of their *representation*. It is certainly possible that if similar products were made elsewhere, people would still buy them. The cultural or national origin of the commodities alone does not motivate the consumer. Furthermore, how these cultural products are deployed and appropriated by people in their distinctive social contexts becomes invisible to critics who see cultural meanings as exclusively determined by the interpretive content of the products. A person, despite possessing a 'touristic' view of Japan, by simulating 'Japaneseness' in Taiwan, can see it as a way to differentiate him/herself from others and other forms of popular culture. This 'blind worship' becomes a way to define oneself in a rather homogenous and regulated society.

Obviously, there is a danger in sanctifying a kind of populism that seeks and finds resistance everywhere and that avoids the extradiscursive reality of economic exploitation and social injustice. The notion that people are completely 'free' and apparently autonomous agents who make choices without any ideological assumptions is itself an ideology. Individuals may have more choices than ever in the growing market economy of differences, but they do not have the choice to refuse. Furthermore, there are no other choices besides the choices that are offered by the institution of a particular society. This is not to say, however, that people do not actively construct and transform meanings from the cultural commodities (foreign or domestic) they consume. Any notion suggesting that cultural productions merely manipulate an excessively malleable audience, even if they attempt to do so, must be rejected. Constant conflicts, negotiations and articulations are taking place in the 'contact zone' (Pratt 1992:6)[11] between cultural texts and their audience. It is a site of struggle, an arena of contestation in which conflicting and competing political, economic and cultural forces collide, and the end result is never guaranteed in advance.

Today's Japanese cultural hegemony in the region is a direct result of its economic prowess *and* the recent blossoming and ever growing involvement of Asian countries in the global capitalist economy. Criticism directed against a single source of domination (in this case, Japan) is unconvincing and lacks analytical sophistication because, under the competitive imperative to minimize costs and to accumulate, transnational corporations from countries such as Taiwan and South Korea also seek production in lowest cost locations and exploit indigenous labor forces in China, Southeast Asia and even the United States. If one is to follow Chuang's and Tsan's arguments, today one can easily speak of Taiwanese cultural imperialism in China, and of Korean cultural imperialism in Indonesia. Furthermore, we must shun the naive notion that foreign cultural texts are prescribed in advance with a certain intention, without examining the point of contact where people actively choose, use, and interpret them. As the polarization between the rich and the poor becomes more distinct and their gap widens in both developing *and* developed nations, an unexamined chauvinistic expression of cultural nationalism is both repressive and futile. The enunciative position and environment of cultural imperialism must be scrutinized: who speaks, who is speaking for whom, from what particular historical specificity, and on what asymmetrical power relation is one speaking from? Finally, we must be aware of the enormous *global* destruction and economic exploitation that accompany the present cultural development in which symbolic meanings are increasingly commodified, dehistoricized, and depoliticized as they are transferred across national boundaries, and we must also insist on the contingent *local* articulations in which foreign cultural commodities and their potential multiple meanings are taken up by the people who consume them.

Postscript

This essay was originally written in 1991 as an initial attempt to map out what I perceived as an emerging cultural formation in East Asia that, at first glance, has all the attributes and contours of a second coming of an American cultural dominance, mimicried this time by the Japanese. My primary concern at that point was to argue that the radical discourse of cultural imperialism, which owes its historicity, and hence its viability, to a particular structural interpretation of the capitalist system, i.e., the center-peripheral model of dependency theory, is mired in a nationcentrism that appears to be suspiciously parochial, if not fascist, in today's reconfigured global relations under transnational capitalism. The attempt was neither to dismiss nor to rescue 'cultural imperialism' as a analytical concept that calls for either a hasty condemnation or a nostalgic moralization, but to delineate the limit of a concept, and to suggest that a new world situation requires a new category of apprehension and analysis.

What I did not theorize adequately back then is that this new cultural regionalism necessitates a reexamination, or even a redefinition, of the meaning of culture. The problematic usage of the term 'culture' is that it is so all-encompassing and abstract, that it can accommodate, if not erase, all variations in definition. The discourse of cultural imperialism, it seems to me, unproblematically conflates and opposes two different categories of 'culture' in its theorization: one that of the anthropological and the other sociological.

On the one hand, the proponents of cultural imperialism as a counterhegemonic discourse argue for the sanctity and sovereignty of a culture as they constantly evoke *our* organic or *our* particular way of life that is not only invariable, but also inaccessible. At best, this localism constructs itself as a temporary site of resistance to the homogenizing process of globalism. At worst, such practices merely reinforce transnational corporatism by concealing the local's capacity and desire to simulate, to reinvent, and to refunction in the global market place where differentiation and standardization are merely two sides of the same coin. The opponents of cultural imperialism as a critique of cultural imposition, on the other hand, dispute any kind of essentialism, and opposed to any allegation of intentionality, view cultural integration as the irreversible logic of capitalist modernity, aided and abetted by the advancement of technology. The new information and media technologies, together with the globalization of the capitalist mode of production, produce an ubiquitous consumerist culture that not only transcends national boundaries, but also in its wake generates an indistinctive global lifestyle and value system.

While not denying the foundational status of capitalism in shaping and defining modern world history, I am wary of the overarching and at times reductive generalizations that the globalization thesis connotes. What usually gets left untheorized is the fact that globalism, as with every stage of capitalist development, is always uneven, contradictory and discontinuous. The geopolitical and geocultural 'interconnectedness' generated by the process of globalism does not, and can not, necessarily result in a homogeneity of a world space without differentiations. On the contrary, globalism has entailed a variation of supranational and subnational interactions that seem to have invented or reinforced more differences and multiplicities. Regional consolidations and ethnic convulsions are only some of its manifestations. Most of the African continent, for instance, is completely excluded, at least for the time being, from the processes of globalization because of its lack of infrastructural apparatus to sustain transnational capital. And even in the enclaves of the so called 'first world', capital flight and the international division of labor have produced cultural configurations and economic conditions that are far from being homogenous or universal.

What is crucial in these two differing constructions and understandings of culture is their relation to what Etienne Balibar has called the nation form. The culture that is presumably at stake in the debate over cultural imperialism is usually defined as that of a 'national' culture, those values and practices where a communal or collective identity can be defined and constructed. It is a culture that is temporally extensive and yet spatially limited. In the anthropological sense of the term, this national culture performs an ordering and bordering ideological effect both within the national imaginary and against other national cultures. Put differently, it is through this sense of culture that national identification and differentiation are constituted and exercised. If the culture under siege in the discourse of cultural imperialism is intrinsically of the 'national' kind, the imperializing culture is inherently 'non-national, or 'transnational'. Although it may retain the content of a national production, its form is not restricted by the parameters of a particular nation. For instance, in what sense can we speak of Coca-cola or the karaoke sing-along as examples of cultural products that merit evaluation on the basis of an American or a Japanese *national* identity? This sociological definition of culture (media, fashion, entertainment, etc.), precisely because of its filiation to technological production which in itself is never nation-specific, points not to the ownership of cultural production (as national culturalists would have imagined) but to its accessibility within the circuit of capitalist commodification and accumulation. In other words, unlike the indigenous culture that is invented within the symbolic boundary of the nation, technoculture is always already potentially transnational. The emerging presence of Japanese mass culture in Asia should therefore be understood as a symptom, not of a specifically and inherently national cultural production, but of a variation of a capitalist cultural production under the reconfigured global capitalist relations where the dominant locus of symbolic productions is no longer occupied solely by Western Europe or the United States.

As long as the debate over cultural imperialism is caught within and between these undifferentiated categories of culture, the result is predictably either a cultural despair and alarmism, or a cultural exuberance and fait accompli. What would be more fruitful at this historical juncture, it seems to me, is to engage critically the inextricably dialectical and changing relationship between culture, in both of its local and global manifestations, together with the process of imperialism. All cultures, in one way or the other, are products and byproducts of imperialism and colonialism, if these processes are understood in terms of the historical stages of capitalist expropriation and exploitation for the realization of profit. The problem with cultural nationalism and cultural globalism is that their conceptual framework is embedded in the presupposition that cultures (global, national or ethnic) are pre-existing categories of analysis, rather than the forming and informing formations of the differing and continuing historical processes of imperialism. Although today most of us may no longer live in the era of high imperialism, we are also definitely not coexisting harmoniously in a postcolonial world space. If global mass culture represents the new configuration of changing capitalist relations in which a nation-centered response or resistance is no longer adequate, we need, on the one hand, to recognize that this cultural process is spatially and temporally uneven and discontinuous, and on the other hand, to be attentive to the different, at times contradictory and unintended, ways social agencies are articulated and empowered at every point of cultural practices.

Notes

1 I have compiled these episodes through my own observations, personal correspondence and stories related to me by friends.

2 This is not to say that Japanese mass culture constitutes the only influence on the symbolic values of these nations. Western, especially American, popular culture still enjoys a tremendous popularity in the region. Beginning from the early 1980s, however, there is a significant, and substantial, growth of Japanese cultural images and products in the area.

3 With the U.S. occupation authority's assistance, the conservative Liberal Democratic Party was empowered, the leftist politicians purged, the labor unions tightly regulated, and the *zaibatsu* reinstated.

4 Masao Miyoshi provides the most lucid and critical analysis on the topic to date. See his *Off Center: Power and Culture Relations between Japan and the United States*, chap. 3, 'Basher and Bashing in the World', p. 62–94.

5 I would like to underscore here that Western imperial expansion and its consequent colonial rule must be seen in the context of the whole history of capitalism on a world scale. For a general outline of the relation between capitalism and imperialism see Anthony Brewer, *Marxist Theories of Imperialism: A Critical Survey*.

6 What immediately comes to mind is the revision of Japanese history textbooks in the early 1980s, which prompted vehement protests from the Chinese and Korean governments. And recent statements by politicians Ishihara Shintarō and Watanabe Shōichi, who suggested that the 'Rape of Nanking' was a Chinese fabrication and that Japanese colonial rule of Asia 'did inflict some wrongdoings', but has overall benefited the colonial subjects. Furthermore, although the Japanese government has finally, though reluctantly, admitted its involvement with the dispatching of Korean and Chinese 'comfort women' as sex slaves for Japanese soldiers, it has firmly refused to make any reparation or compensation.

7 Furthermore, one should not overlook Japan's blatant racism and discrimination against the growing presence of other Asians *in* Japan. Japan's prejudice against Koreans has been well documented. For an overview of Koreans in Japan, see Lee Changsee and George De Vos, eds. *Koreans in Japan: Ethnic Conflict and Accomodation*, and Michael Weiner, *The Origin of the Korean Community in Japan, 1910–25*. Recent Japanese affluence has resulted in a labor shortage in sectors that the Japanese have pejoratively termed the Three Ks: *kitanai* (dirty), *kitsui* (strenuous), and *kiken* (dangerous). This labor shortage has induced an unprecedented influx of Asians to Japan seeking higher wages in factories, construction sites, and restaurants. The media often portray these aliens as inherently dangerous and responsible for the growing crime rate in Japan. These Asian laborers constantly face racist taunting and discrimination, despite their growing importance and necessity to Japan's industries. See the special report on the growing presence of Asian laborers and refugees in 'Totsuzen hikkoshitekita "Nihon no kokusaika"' (The Sudden Moving-in of Japan's Internationalism) (*Asahi Journal*, December 20, 1989, p. 11–20.)

8 In 1987, South Korean foreign investment amounted to $332.71 million, an increase of 112 per cent. Taiwan's investment amounted to $102.75 million, up 81 per cent from the previous year.

9 For analyses of Japanese *aidoru*, see Inamasu Tatsuo, *Aidoru kogaku* (Idol Engineering) and Ogawa Hiroshi, *Ongaku Suru Shakai* (Music Playing Society), esp. chap. 5, 'Aidoru genshō no tenkai' (The Development of the Idol Phenomenon). The closest analogy of the 'idol system' in the West is the Hollywood star system of the 1930s and 1940s. As Inamasu and Ogawa argue, however, the two systems differ in their medium of transmission: television and cinema, and thus their respective receptions. Through the cinematic apparatus, film stars are able to distance themselves from the 'masses', creating the necessary 'charisma' to construct and further advance the 'myths' of the stars. However, as television pervades our daily life, becoming part of our living space, the 'mysteriousness' of the stars dissipates, while more 'familiarity' is expected from the stars of television. In Japan, idols saturate TV for greater exposure. From singing programs to quiz shows, from TV dramas to variety shows, a popular idol easily carries five to ten regular programs a week! Inamasu and Ogawa attribute their popularity and success to their extensive exposure and the 'intimacy' between them and their fans.

10 Sklair defines the transnational capitalist class as 'those people who see their own interests and /or the interests of their nation, as best served by an identification with the interests of the capitalist global system, in particular the interests of the countries of the capitalist core and the transnational corporations domiciled in them' (1991:8).

11 I borrow the term from Mary Louise Pratt, who defines this 'control zone' as 'the space of colonial encounters, the space in which peoples geographically and historically separated come into contact with each other and establish ongoing relations, usually involving conditions of coercion, radical inequality, and intractable conflict' (1992:6).

References

Baudrillard, Jean 1988 *Selected Writings* in Mark Poster (ed.), Stanford: Stanford University Press.

Brewer, Anthony 1990 *Marxist Theories of Imperialism: a critical survey*, 2nd ed., New York: Routledge.

Chan, Steve 1990 *East Asian Dynamism*, Boulder: Westview Press.

Chuang, Shu-yu 1989 'Speed, Infiltration and Occupation', p. 12–21 in *Common Wealth* August (1).

De Vos, George and Lee, Chansee (ed.) 1981 *Koreans in Japan: ethnic conflict and accomodation*, Berkeley: University of California Press.

Dorfman, Ariel and Mattelart, Armand 1975 *How to Read Donald Duck: imperialist ideology in the Disney comic*, D. Kunzle (trans.), New York: I. G. Editions, Inc.

Elegant, Robert 1990 *Pacific Destiny*, New York: Crown Publishers.

Hebdige, Dick 1975 *Subculture: the meaning of style*, London: Routledge.

Inamasu Tatsuo 1989 *Aidoru Kōgaku* (Idol Engineering), Tokyo: Chikuma Shob.

Miyoshi, Masao 1991 *Off Center*, Cambridge: Harvard University Press.

Ogawa Hiroshi 1988 *Ongaku Suru Shakai* (Music Playing Society), Tokyo: Keisō

Shobō.

Pratt, Mary Louise 1992 *Imperial Eyes, Travel Writing and Transculturation*, London: Routledge.

Reich, Robert 1991 *The Work of Nations*, New York: Alfred A. Knopf.

Sklair, Leslie 1991 *Sociology of the Global System*, Baltimore: Johns Hopkins University Press.

Smith, Anthony D. 1990 'Towards a Global Culture?', p. 171–191 in M. Featherstone (ed.) *Global Culture: nationalism, globalization, and modernity*, London: Sage Publications.

Tomlinson, John 1991 *Cultural Imperialism*, Baltimore: Johns Hopkins University Press.

Tsan Hung-chih 1989 *Ch'en Shih Kuan Ch'a* (City Watching), Taipei: Yuan-liu.

Twu Jaw-Yann 1990 *Tōyō Shihonshugi* (Eastern Capitalism), Tokyo: Kōdansha.

Weiner, Michael 1989 *The Origin of the Korean Community in Japan, 1910–25*, Oxford: Manchester University Press.

Part IV

Film, Television and Japanese Ideologies

7

Japanese Daytime Televison, Popular Culture, and Ideology

Andrew A. Painter

For many first time viewers, Japanese television is both a surprise and a puzzle. Unrestrained, ingratiating, irreverent and often downright silly, Japanese TV seems to reflect little of the subtlety and refinement that, for many, are the hallmarks of Japanese culture and communication. Nonetheless, television is absolutely central to contemporary Japanese culture, and Japanese TV is much more than an imitation of TV in the West. By widening our focus beyond 'high culture' to include 'popular culture' (the distinction is often unclear in Japan anyway), we can make a start at answering the question 'What is it that makes popular Japanese TV popular?' Concentrating in particular on daytime programming, this chapter investigates how television is crafted to attracted and keep the attention of viewers in ways both culturally and ideologically significant.

Television in Japan is shaped both by general cultural patterns of communication and by certain properties (both limiting and enabling) of the technology of TV. One style or mode of appeal common to some of the most popular TV shows in Japan works to create a sort of quasi-intimate interaction between those on the screen and those who watch at home. While similar patterns can be observed in other media-saturated societies,[1] quasi-intimacy seems especially prominent in Japan: where intimate and informal face-to-face communication is usually restricted to clearly defined 'in-group' contexts. In a society where interpersonal relationships are strongly shaped by notions of status, the maintenance of group boundaries, and often elaborate politeness and formality, then, it is important for us to understand how and why popular Japanese television programs come to interact with and entertain audiences on a communicative level patterned, in part, on relations with intimates. In this chapter I argue that the development and penetration of the so-called 'mass media' has reshaped the landscape of contemporary Japanese social experience, allowing a new, thoroughly compelling form of quasi-intimate communication to flourish.

I begin by looking at the people who work together to produce television in Japan. (Questions about how actual viewers themselves use and interpret TV, though essential, are only touched on here.) Using examples from three daytime TV programs, I describe some of the ways that commercial TV producers in Japan strive to establish (as they put it) 'close' (*mijika na*), and 'familiar' (*shitashii*) relationships with their viewers. Many TV programs in Japan are best viewed as electronically created *uchi* – all purpose 'in-groups' that anyone can join simply by tuning to the right channel. While it is probably true that any group so easily joined cannot expect to capture the entire heart and soul of its membership, for commercial television producers all that is really demanded by the viewership ratings game is that people keep watching TV. At this task Japanese TV producers and directors succeed most remarkably: current statistics indicate that the average household in Japan has its television set (more often, sets) turned on for an average of between seven and a half and eight hours per day.[2]

What are some of the strategies and patterns used by Japanese TV producers to create a sense of quasi-intimacy between performers and viewers? What, if any, are the ideological implications of quasi-intimate television programming in Japan? While many of the Japanese producers and directors I worked with in 1988–89 confessed that they rarely knew for sure which shows would 'catch on' (*ukeru*) and which would 'fall down' (*kokeru*), the programs they make do follow a number of established patterns. Quasi-intimate programs, for example, often emphasize themes related to unity (national, local, cultural, or racial) and unanimity (consensus, common sense, identity) in order to create an intimate and comfortably familiar atmosphere. Another popular but different strategy involves the representation of spontaneity and play in order to simulate intimate, informal in-group interaction. Quasi-intimacy on Japanese TV, then, often revolves around representations of uniformity, unity, or playful spontaneity, or some creative combination of these.[3]

In practice, television in Japan, as elsewhere, is an often sloppy and unpredictable affair. TV producers do not have as much control over 'the popular' as they would often like to think, and often it seems that their strategies are more ad-hoc reactions to shifts in public taste than well-planned orchestrations of 'middle-class sentiments. What is more, TV producers do not themselves often articulate exactly what they are trying to accomplish with a given piece of programming; for them the observation that much of Japanese TV seems to play on the quasi-intimate aspects of televisual communication is far less relevant than would be a concrete formula for drawing in the largest possible audience. Thus, the process of representing intimacy on TV is by no means straightforward. The complexity is compounded by the fact that, as Takie Lebra has suggested in another context (1976:114), the intimate nature of any Japanese situation can be destroyed should it become either too spontaneous (that is, chaotic), or too rigidly structured toward unity. Even if a TV director consciously set out to create an 'intimate' style and atmosphere for a given show, then, he or she (usually he) is faced with a whole spectrum of possibilities – ranging from common-sensical assertions of national unity to rowdy displays of selfish abandon – for producing the desired affect. Due to the inherently indeterminate nature of televisual communication, finally, there is no way of knowing which combinations will work and which will fail. While the remainder of this chapter will focus on well established, popular programs, it is worth bearing in mind that television shows are cancelled in Japan just as regularly as anywhere else.

The following descriptive section begins with a popular morning 'wide-news' program that, in form and content, represents itself as a model of and for the unity of the Japanese nation and its seemingly homogenous culture. In ways both obvious and subtle, this program renders the whole of the Japanese archipelago as one unified uchi, marking everything else as *soto* (outside). My second example, a top-rated noontime variety/talk show called *It's All Right To Laugh* (*Waratte ii to mo*) is more outrageously complex. As the program title suggests, this show looks to informal interaction and spontaneity as a means to make a close connection with its audiences. The move is no longer to represent all of Japan as a single hierarchically-unified uchi, but instead to persuade viewers that, at least in the egalitarian context of together experiencing the program, a sort of comfortable, informal uchi can be had. By creative metonym, the program presents the Japanese TV performers and their 'world of entertainment' (*geinōkai*) as intimate, friendly, and on the best of terms – just like the millions of viewers at home. 'It's All Right To Laugh' also introduces another important element of Japanese-style quasi-intimate programming: the symbolic transgression of cultural markers such as public/private and *omote/ura* (front/back). The result is a kind of televisual voyeurism, involving the highly public treatment of what are usually very private matters. In my third and final example – an afternoon 'wide show' (*waidoshō*) – I make my strongest arguments about the cultural and ideological consequences of such electronically mediated quasi-relationships.[4] Together, it is hoped that the following interpretations of popular programs will give the reader some idea of the tone and tenor of Japanese daytime TV, will start to unravel some particular – and often peculiar – cultural and ideological dimensions, and will stimulate new thinking about the role and significance of the mass media in an increasingly 'wired' world system.

'Zoom-in Morning!': Bringing All Japan into Your Morning

'Nihonjū no minasan, ohayō gozaimasu!' (Everyone in Japan, good morning! With this ambitious interpellation of an entire nation, *Zoom-in Morning* (*Zoom-in Asa*), the Nihon News Network's (NNN) top-rated 'morning wide news' program, beings its daily broadcast.[5] In both forms and content, *Zoom-in Morning* is a striking example of how television is used to link up the diverse regions of Japan into a single, compelling whole. The style and appeal of *Zoom-in Morning* is set early on in the program opening. As rousing music plays and the superimposed program logo unfolds over a live shot of urban Japan, we are greeted by a bright 'ohayō gozaimasu!' from the anchor announcer, who is always male and almost always standing somewhere in or around Tokyo. After a few quick comments, including a mandatory recital of the day's date and the exact time, the anchor tells us that we are going to switch to so-and-so announcer in Nagoya. Pointing directly at the camera, he says in English 'zoom in!' The image quickly changes to show an announcer standing in front of a Buddhist temple outside Nagoya. She greets us 'ohayō gozaimasu!', and tells us the name of the temple. Pointing to a huge thermometer (it registers two degrees of Celsius), she comments that it is 'a bit cold' in Nagoya, but it should warm up by afternoon. Running out of time (each reporter has less than thirty seconds before the microwave feed is switched to the next location), the announcer blurts that later in the show we will visit the inside of the temple. Then, with a bright 'otanoshimi!' (look forward to it!), she points at the camera and says 'next is Osaka!' We then see two male announcers standing in front of Koshien Stadium. They greet us: 'ohayō gozaimasu!,' and then launch into a playful discussion of the hanshin Tigers baseball game of the night before. Becoming engrossed in the subject, they almost forget to mention the temperature in Osaka (we can see it clearly registered on their huge thermometer anyway) before together pointing at the camera and saying, in stereo: 'To Kumamoto TV!' We find ourselves instantaneously transported off Honshu to Mt. Aso in Kumamoto, Kyushu. A pretty young announcer greets us: 'Kumamoto desu! Ohayō gozaimasu!' She breathlessly tells us about the temperature and the expected weather in Kyushu that day, then points at the camera and says: 'Let's go to Sapporo!'

In this way, the *rirei chūkei* (relay remote reports) go on to cover almost all of Japan. Linked by a network of microwave towers and remote antennae, each reporter greets us and describes the place where he or she is standing. Interestingly, the reporters are virtually always located outside – the camera only goes inside for the national news and weather segments, which are done at the news studio in Tokyo.[6] Informational content seems relatively unimportant, as it is clearly the experience of being transported at breakneck speed all over Japan that provides the interest and entertainment. Timing is of the essence as both performers and technical staff work together to make the complex shifting of locations and images look effortless. Boundaries in space and time are collapsed together as the entire country says 'good morning' to itself via the technology of television. Here, then, is one of the clearest examples of how Japanese television produces popular representations of national unity.

TV allows us to see with our own eyes the conditions in areas far removed from the geography of our daily experience. In this sense, the experience of national unity facilitated by programs like *Zoom-in Morning* is not entirely fictitious. Nonetheless, it is not by coincidence that the areas most often featured on the show are those with at least enough size to support local TV stations – these are the source, in fact, of most of the material used on the program. The unified Japanese nation exhibited on TV is structured by the very shape of the TV network system. In this case, *Zoom-in*

Morning represents both the unity of Japan and that of the various stations belonging to the NNN network. This is not lost on the producers of the program, who see it as a prestige builder for the network, and as a venue for announcers at local stations to get some national exposure.

On *Zoom-in Morning* the unity of Japan-as-uchi is constantly reinforced by contrast with clearly soto elements. One long-popular daily feature is the 'English conversation' segment, in which a clearly foreign character called 'Wiki-san' (who is from Sri Lanka) tries to teach a different conversational phrase to a 'volunteer' each day. These segments are often hilarious, especially because Wiki-san typically has to chase people down on the street in order to get them to speak English. Perhaps eighty per cent of the time the poor Japanese person seems unable to speak, or even mimic, any English at all. This does not discourage Wiki-san, who always ends by thanking everyone while handing out autographed copies of his latest book on English conversation.

The whole segment is somewhat bizarre: what is the point of having a foreigner run around with a camera crew trying to persuade regular people to utter something in English in forty-five seconds or less? (The producers originally hoped to use a white, blue-eyed young woman to do this spot on the show, but Wicky ended up getting the job through an introduction from a TV employee who knew Wiki-san from taking English lessons with him at a conversation school.) While the ostensible goal of this 'one-point lesson' is to teach 'English conversation', the more powerful function may be instead one of demonstrating how much alike the Japanese are in being so unsuccessful in dealing with those who are culturally different. Viewers of the program feel kinship with the poor Japanese interviewees who stumble to make any sense at all in English (their attempts usually end in good natured, though unintelligible, resignation and a temporary inability to communicate even in Japanese without sounding like a total idiot), while the TV audience also enjoys a feeling of superiority by having access to translations of both the questions and answers already superimposed on their screen. The very fact that watching totally inept people blunder through the minefield of intercultural communication proves to be entertaining in Japan reflects a sort of mass commitment to the idea that 'we Japanese' are so special and different that true communication is probably not even worth trying for. This kind of ideological strategy; in which unity is represented not by focussing on what is shared, but instead on the alien nature of other ways of life, is quite common on Japanese television. (It is perhaps best exemplified by popular Japanese game shows such as Fuji TV's *Understanding The World* [Naruhodo The World], where exotic peoples and customs are 'explained' as answers to quiz questions.) We will call it simply what it is: ethnocentrism in the name of unity.

The uchi/soto contrast, which now comes to encompass Japanese/non-Japanese within its range of meanings, is made most clearly of all when *Zoom-in Morning* features live transmission from foreign cities. These scenes inevitably show an announcer standing on the street somewhere with a crowd of Japanese people in the background. While the announcer talks, the Japanese abroad wave at the camera and hold up signs with greetings to relatives back home. Often, the announcer will introduce someone from the throng, for example, a young Japanese mother holding an infant born overseas. In this way, the rare occasions when *Zoom-in Morning* ventures outside of Japan serve to reinforce all the more the image of the Japanese as a people organically and irrevocably attached to their homeland.

Zoom-in Morning is thus a most obvious example of how television technology is used in Japan to represent the nation as a unified whole. At the same time, the program makes the explicit point that the daily panoptic experience of nation as uchi is only made possible by the diligent efforts of the NNN television network. In fact, the format of the program reproduces the hierarchical organization of that network; with the Tokyo station (NTV) taking the lead and playing the largest part, followed by the Osaka station (YTV) which sometimes takes over the lead role, and finally the lesser stations which seldom do much more than report the weather. The rapid relay reports from all over the country – which always start and end in Tokyo – thus represent a characteristically Japanese sort of unity; that is, a hierarchical one.

Zoom-in Morning is seen as a prestige and morale-building show by executives in the NNN network. Certainly the program is far too expensive to serve as the model for most of daytime television in Japan. The expense is worth it, in the eyes of network programmers, because the show is successful in getting audiences to turn on their channel first thing every morning. The quasi-intimacy on *Zoom-in Morning* comes in large part from representations of unity based on a common link: Japanese nationality. The next example, a daytime talk/variety show, illustrates how a completely different style – characterized by irreverent spontaneity and extreme informality – can also be used to give Japanese TV an intimate feel.

Uchi as Informal Togetherness

Every weekday from twelve noon to twelve-thirty the highest rated program in Japan is *It's All Right to Laugh*. Filmed in front of a large studio audience of between 70 to 100 young people, the program is broadcast live nationwide on the Fuji Television Network. Unlike most housewife-oriented shows that precede it in the morning hours or follow in the afternoon, *It's All right to Laugh* has a considerable number of male viewers – including many workers on their lunch breaks – in addition to the women who make up the bulk of television audiences throughout the day in Japan. *It's All Right to Laugh* is a hodgepodge of skits, quizzes, monologues, dialogues, and performances, all held together by the program's central figure; a middle-aged *manzaishi* (comedian) known as 'Tamori'. Often clad in white pants and always wearing dark glasses, he is an emblematic figure for Japanese television. Appearing in many programs (often on different networks) and countless TV commercials, Tamori is an especially successful example of what the Japanese call a 'talent' *tarento*.[7] Ridiculous to an extreme, his main appeal stems from his self-deprecating style and his refusal to follow the norms of polite Japanese interaction. He deals with even the most respectable of guest in a way that soon leads the conversation toward outrageous subjects. To a young actress, for example, he will openly ask: 'What kind of underwear do you use? Where is it stored Is it folded neatly or just thrown into a drawer'

The motivation behind such questions is more than sexist. Tamori behaves in such a way with both men and women in order to bring them down to the common horizontal level of intimate interaction. On *It's All Right to Laugh* there are many times when viewers seem to get a glimpse of the human (*ningen-rashii*) side of stars that they would not have seen in any other context. The license implicit in the title of the program, 'it's all right to laugh,' also signifies that on Tamori's show viewers can expect to hear *urabanashi* (literally 'back region talk') that shatters the smooth front of *omote*. This deliberate and public violation of normal conventions of interaction is surely a large part of the program's appeal.

It's All Right to Laugh begins in the same way each day. Tamori appears on stage and sings an outlandish theme song while three young men (aspiring young comedians) dance and sing in accompaniment. None of them can sing or dance, and this open self-ridicule effectively levels them down to a nearly equal status with both the studio audience and, by extension, the audience at home. A series of roughly arranged skits and activities follows, and everyday people from the audience are often incorporated into the show. The program is fast-paced and lively. Because there is limited flexibility as to when commercials are to be inserted into the live broadcast, oftentimes in the middle of some activity the music signalling a commercial will start to play, causing Tamori and all on the set to groan aloud as the show is suddenly interrupted.

The centerpiece of the program is the conversation between Tamori and the 'special guest' of the day. Guests may be musicians, actors, authors, comedians, or any sort of celebrity. The unique feature of this 'talk corner' is that the guests who appear on the show are portrayed as forming an unbroken chain or network. That is, each guest is ostensibly invited to appear, live and on camera, by the special guest of the day before. Everyone appearing on the show is thus linked into a larger network of acquaintances. At the center of the main stage is a large panel with a calender full of eight-by-ten photographs of all the celebrities who have appeared on the program for the month. To emphasize the theme of correctedness even more, the set where the talk corner is filmed is often covered with flowers, cards, and telegrams from well-wishers who have gone to great trouble to congratulate their celebrity friends.

As if the message is still not clear enough, after the guest appears on the stage and begins the interview, Tamori asks him or her to recite the following verse:

Tomodachi no tomodachi wa
mina tomodachi da
Sekai ni hirogeyo
Tomodachi no wa.

The friends of friends
Are all friends (of ours)
Let's spread to the world
the circle of friends.

When the last word is reached, the entire studio audience and the visitor together shout out 'Wa!' (meaning both 'circle' and 'harmony') while putting their arms over their heads in the shape of a circle. The guest is required to recite the stanza without error and in the proper timing so that the audience will be able to synchronize itself to perform the final gesture and 'wa' at exactly the right moment. At that moment, a camera located above and behind the audience gives a view of the entire studio performing the 'wa' gesture from the most dramatic angle. If this iconic/echoic moment goes well, the guest returns to his or her seat and finishes the interview with Tamori. If not, Tamori may require that the whole routine be repeated until perfect. In this way the guest, no matter how famous or iconoclastic, is made to cooperate with the audience and to depend on them for help in completing the verse successfully.

After unity has been (re)established, Tamori and the guest sit down and talk on a variety of subjects. Tamori is a master at leading his guests into interesting areas of discussion. Although he controls most of the conversation, he does not do so in a domineering way. In fact, he often intentionally says idiotic things that are corrected or forcefully rejected by the guest. This allows Tamori to perform his trademark gesture: one arm raised to scratch the back of the head in mock embarrassment, while his face takes on an exaggerated, wry grimace. After talking on a wide variety of subjects, the guest makes a telephone call to invite a friend to be the special guest for the next day. Here too the interaction is standardized within the program format. After some small talk on the telephone (we learn that TV stars talk on the phone much like ordinary people do), Tamori asks the key question 'Ashita kite kureru ka na?' (Tomorrow you'll come, won't you?) to which the recipient of the call is expected to respond 'Ii to mo! (That's fine!).[8] The studio audience claps and the phone call is ended. Tamori wraps up the interview, the audience is signalled to begin clapping again, and the show goes on a commercial.

In this way, an unbroken series of guests is featured on *It's All Right to Laugh*; each one a good friend of the one before. This 'circle of friends' is a simple way to represent graphically the Japanese geinōkai circle of entertainers as a harmonious and interconnected community. At the same time, the participation of the audience members in welcoming each 'special guest' implies that there is no greater distinction to be made between the celebrities and the common folk: all are part of a larger circle and community known as Japanese society. Quite often the special guest of the day will come bearing presents for Tamori and for the members of the studio audience. A star who appears in a commercial for a particular shampoo may bring dozens of bottles provided by the maker, while another may bring tangerines from his native village. This pseudo-reciprocity is yet another manifestation of the stress on unity and interconnectedness that is such an important feature of Japanese television programming.

The segments of *It's All Right to Laugh* that feature the participation of amateurs as well as stars make representations of intimacy through spontaneity even more clear. On a recent show, for example, three young comedians welcomed a man on stage whose sole claim to distinction was the ability to slice raw vegetables using only a business card. After he demonstrated his skill by successfully cutting a cucumber in half and, with somewhat more difficulty, slicing a thin potato in two, it was time for three young celebrities to try to imitate his feat. They eagerly attacked a variety of vegetables with their business cards until one of them was able to duplicate the cutting of the cucumber. Making jokes among themselves, they sent the man off with a round of applause. The next volunteer was a young man dressed in a martial arts outfit. His 'skill' was to eat peanuts with chopsticks held in both hands. After he demonstrated his less than earthshaking ambidextrous ability, the three tarento again eagerly set about trying to imitate his performance. They were all able to do fairly well, and their pace (as well as that of the accompanying music in the studio) became faster still as they continued eating with both hands. Finally, one of the celebrities looked at the guest with mock pride and spoke through a mouth stuffed full of peanuts: 'so it seems that you have appeared on this show to demonstrate something that isn't special at all!' The studio audience laughed as the good-natured guest walked offstage. The three celebrities trying to imitate the amateurs seemed perfectly comfortable in doing so. (We are used to watching amateurs imitate TV stars, but how often in the United States do we see TV talent try to imitate us?) With them, there was little of the hip detachment of American stars; the Japanese celebrities did not portray themselves as cool and aloof in opposition to the normalcy of their guests. Instead, they related to the amateurs as if they were good friends. What was funny for the audience was precisely the open enthusiasm with which the celebrities did the ridiculous. This is especially entertaining in a culture where fastidious attention to rules of interpersonal decorum is usually enforced.

In Japan it seems that the people on the television screen, no matter how various in fashion, personality, or age, are not so very different from us (that is, the viewers). They laugh like us and they make jokes we can understand and enjoy. If at times it appears that Japanese television is ridiculous and unrestrained, surely we can understand and allow for these very human excesses. The outrageous behavior of Japanese celebrities, questioning authority and parodying those high up in the hierarchies of society, is entertaining precisely because it imaginatively rejects the vertical for the horizontal dimension of experience – something positively valued in Japan but often difficult to implement in practice.

Programs like *It's All Right to Laugh* appear to be virtually unplanned and ad-libbed. They may seem to lack any overt structure. In fact, however, much work goes into making the program appear to happen so effortlessly and spontaneously. Walter Ong comments:

> The open relationship between television and nontelevised actuality puts a special premium on preserving spontaneity – which in fact for television products mostly means creating spontaneity. All art forms to some degree tend to pass themselves off as in one way or another unprogrammed, spontaneously achieved actuality: *ars celare artem*. Art consists in concealing art. . . . in television the spontaneity cultivated by art is more essential than in any other art forms and more complexity artificial.
>
> (Ong 1977:320)

Just as Ong suggests, the seemingly spontaneous qualities of many Japanese television programs are by no means the result of sloppy work by the tarento or by producers and directors; on Japanese television spontaneity, amateurism, and harmonious interaction are all carefully planned.

It's All Right to Laugh is perhaps an extreme example of how spontaneity and the playful transgression of ura/omote are celebrated on Japanese television. While *It's All Right to Laugh* is always high in the ratings, it is also a regular feature on the biannual list of 'most hated programs' among Japanese parents. Not a few Japanese, it seems, do not want to see common sense etiquette blatantly violated on television. Tamori, it should be noted in this connection, in fact became popular largely due to his abrasive, iconoclastic image. *It's All Right to Laugh*, although widely watched, is too wild and controversial to serve as the archetype for daytime TV in Japan.

The dominant format on afternoon TV, the so-called wide show (waidoshō, i.e., a long show), features a softer approach to entertainment that falls somewhere in between the two examples just discussed. The wide show borrows and modifies the themes of *Zoom-in Morning* and *It's All Right to Laugh*, combining their strategies to appeal to audiences in terms of unity, informality, and the promised exposure of what is normally kept private. Let us turn to the Japanese wide show, much like American soap operas and talk shows combined in its dominance of daytime TV, for our final and most complex example of how television is socially constructed in Japan.

The Japanese Wide Show: Television and Cultural Form

Programs in the wide show genre can be found all over Japanese television, especially in the morning, late afternoon (two to four p.m.), and late night time slots. The name wide show does not refer to the content of the programs, which are certainly not broad in their scope, but instead to their protracted length: at least 60 minutes. The wide show can loosely be described as a talk show; and its cozy format has been influenced by American programs like NBC's *Today* show, among others (Stronach 1989:139). Despite these American influences, which are significant, the wide show has developed into a truly independent and distinct form – a culturally specific genre of telerepresentation.

Wide shows follow a consistent pattern, making their production easily routinized and relatively inexpensive. The most conspicuous formal feature of the wide show is the panel. Usually filmed live in front of a studio audience, these programs are made up of the 'talk' of numerous panelists on a pre-determined set of topics. The panelists may be actors, singers, comedians, Buddhist priests, or any other sort of tarento; but their function during the program is not so much to showcase their own talents (or lack of the same) as it is to take part in a consensually-oriented conversation. Usually, panelists who are 'affable' (*aiso ga ii*) are selected by program producers. Producers and directors in Japan agree that it is a mistake to include too many outspoken tarento on a panel: the ideal balance is one which allows space for followers as well as leaders. The tarento work at a public project that is characteristically Japanese: the creation (tele-representation) of consensus.

During my fieldwork within an Osaka television station, I belonged to the production staff of *The Two O'Clock Wide Show* (Ni-ji no Waidoshō): a nationwide, live program broadcast from two to three o'clock every weekday afternoon. The program varied its format and content every day, with only the host and hostess of the show appearing regularly Monday through Friday. The production staff also shifted duties from day to day; one day's director might be the producer on the following day, etc. Consider the following weekly schedule for *The Two O'clock Wide Show* as it stood during the beginning of my fieldwork in the winter of 1988.

Mondays: The Well-side Meeting (*Idobata Kaigi*).
Tuesdays: Visits to Palatial Homes (*Gotei Hōmon*).
Wednesdays: Information about the Entertainment World (*Geinō Jōhō*).
Thursdays: Marriage Emergency Hotline (*Fūfu 110-ban*).
Fridays: Kaneyama's Conversations with Beautiful Women (*Kaneyama-san no Bijo Taidan*).

While the formats are shifted periodically in order to increase ratings, these examples are relatively typical of afternoon wide shows in Japan. Presumptions about the audience held by program producers and writers, I found, have everything to do with what sort of shows get on the air. During a highly-charged program planning meeting for *The Two-O'clock Wide Show*, one of the free-lance writers firmly stated: 'The three pillars of audience interest in wide shows are voyeurism (*nozoki*), gossip (*uwasa*) and wife-mother-in-law relations (*yome-shūtome kankei*).' I looked around the room to see the entire program staff nodding in solemn agreement. Sure enough, the Tuesday, Wednesday, and Thursday program formats, based directly on the above 'three pillars', have all proven to be especially popular mainstays of *The Two O'clock Wide Show*. (By contrast, both the Monday and Friday programs were doing poorly in the ratings and were changed several times during my fieldwork. Monday's program – despite bearing a title depicting the show as an electronic version of traditional housewife 'well-side get-togethers' (*idobata kaigi*) – was disorganized and rarely fun to work on or watch. Fridays' show featured a famous ex-baseball player who would interview three different women each week; but he was a terrible speaker who was eventually cut from the program.)

Tuesdays' 'Visits to Palatial Homes' is similar to the American program *Lifestyles of the Rich and Famous*, although there are many differences. Each week a reporter visits a different home and talks about it with the people who live there. The home of a famous star or public figure is preferred, but if the house is large and fancy enough, even a totally unknown businessman's place is fine. (The producers of the program are constantly complaining that they have already filmed all the best houses in Japan, and sometimes two or even three homes must be used when there is not enough of interest in just one house.) The usual pattern is for the reporter, usually a male or female comedian, to begin outside the house by admiring its majestic exterior. Ringing the doorbell or knocking on the door, he or she is almost always greeted by the woman of the house. (The domestic sphere is, after all, her 'natural' domain.) The reporter removes his or her shoes and steps up into the entry way. The camera pans to show the entire area. Because the *genkan* (entrance area) is the face of the Japanese house, in wealthier homes there is usually some sort of art work or other imposing object on display here. Often at this point the video tape is stopped and the cameras in the live studio show us a panel of tarento who will make comments and otherwise react to the beautiful homes shown on the screen. The owner of the home is usually seated in the middle of the panel, and as the program progresses he or she is asked various questions about the house, work, and family.

'Visits to Palatial Homes' is built on the juxtaposition of video taped scenes of the homes and live conversation by studio panelists. Two of the panelists who appear regularly on the show are a well known comedy team, 'Ikuyo and Kuruyo'.[9] One is tall and thin, the other is short and plump; both are female. Their main role during the program is to make interesting conversation and to provide suitably exaggerated 'reactions' (the production staff use the English word) to the gorgeous homes. Program producers attribute the popularity of the show to the voyeuristic view it affords of huge homes and the conspicuous consumption that is so common among the 'new rich' (*narikin*) in Japan. (A typical subtitle to a Tuesday show might be 'Lady [company] President has over 30 fur coats in eight-bedroom palace!!!') The opulent homes are symbols of elite society in Japan, while the reporters who comment on them come to represent, to some extent, the typical folk who do not live in such luxury.

While the *tatemae* (superficial) presentation of the program is that of admiring and exhibiting the lifestyles of the rich, there is often a *honne* ('true' or 'inner') subtext that is critical of such conspicuous consumption. Often the comedian's lavish praise for a particular home or living room design is in fact a carefully-disguised rejection of narikin pretence. While on the level of the tatemae everything said is perfectly polite, a major source of humor and pleasure for the audience is to read the critical subtext that is not impressed by money. (Especially subtle or humorous jabs always get a laugh out of the members of the program production staff; who seem to share the comedian's general disdain for the flashy rich.) The relatively low-status background of many Japanese comedians – based largely on the traditionally low social ranking of entertainers in Japan – makes it possible for them to address the TV audience in a horizontal manner less often seen in the United States. Where the American *Lifestyles of the Rich and Famous* is a one-dimensional celebration of wealth, the Japanese version contains an interesting counter-current that reflects a quite different cultural orientation toward money and status.

Wednesday's program, 'Information about the Entertainment World' is in many ways the backbone of the wide show genre. If an important scandal or story comes to light in the entertainment world in Japan, this format can be used on any day of the week. The program absolutely thrives on scandal. An entire one-hour show is often devoted to rumors about the imminent marriage of a young Japanese aidoru *kashu* (idol singer), or to the imminent divorce of another. The topic of any wide show conversation is called a *neta*. The word is derived by reversing the syllables of *tane*, meaning 'seed' in Japanese. Like a seed, then, the neta (if introduced and nurtured properly) will grow into a thriving, healthy, and (hopefully) entertaining conversation. It is the work of all the panelists to assist in the development and flowering of the neta, and they coordinate their efforts by following the guidance of the program host and of the floor directors who signal to the panelists from behind the cameras. A neta may thus be stretched (*nobasu*) or cut (*kiru*) at the whim of the director, who is ultimately responsible for its success or failure. While a well developed neta may go on for some time, the nightmare of Japanese TV directors is for a neta grow stale (*shirakeru*) or to run out entirely (*neta-gire*).

The tarento are mediators who specialize in speaking on behalf of the imaginary and essentialized whole: what H. D. Harootunian has called the 'holonic culture' of Japan. Their situation is vicariously enjoyed by the viewers who, I think, can make real connections between the TV performances of the tarento and the performances they too must enact every day. The ability of the tarento to speak as individuals *and* as representatives of common sense is an indispensable communicative skill everyone needs to learn.[10] The subjects of the neta and the persons who talk about them on television in Japan are all members of the geinōkai. Although many members of the geinōkai are accomplished musicians, comedians, actors, or even rakugo artists, the majority of tarento in Japan are products of television itself. The idol singers, produced and discarded production-line style by the Japanese entertainment industry, are an important, if extreme, example. Although, they too, are high among the ranks of the tarento in Japan, most are acknowledged to be poor singers who are popular mainly because of their 'fashion' or 'cuteness' (*kawaisa*). Like other tarento in Japan, the young singers (usually between fifteen and nineteen years of age) are heavily dependent on talent agencies for the construction and maintenance of their *imeiji* (image) by constant exposure in the Japanese mass media. Interest in these tarento transcends their often minor performative talents, with domestic habits and romantic relationships all considered fair game. Television, which helped to produce these tarento, feeds their popularity by constantly exposing them to the public. It also feeds on their popularity by making their private lives part of the television spectacle.

Watching and working on the Japanese television while listening to how my friends and colleagues would talk about various tarento led me to see the Japanese geinōkai as a special mass-mediated universe in which both public and private issues could be openly talked about; a sort of vicarious realm that supplies the neta for topics otherwise too delicate to discuss. At the very least, making the geinōkai the subject of discussion allows more freedom for program producers to exploit the tarento who, after all, are largely dependent on mass media organizations for their livelihood. Because viewers in Japan do not see the tarento as fundamentally different from themselves, they are able to use the publicly available representations of tarento lives in order to reflect upon their own. The neta of the Japanese wideshows allow the discussion of divorce, infidelity, disease, and scandal in a perfectly safe fashion. Without such a vicarious universe, I think, many Japanese would have real trouble discussing these topics openly because they would have to relate them to actual socially connected others.[11] The quasi-interaction facilitated by television and tarento in Japan thus permits greater possibilities for interaction between persons in society. In a culture where indirectness and nuanced communication are highly valued, the geinōkai may serve as an invaluable vehicle for the expression of all sorts of more locally relevant feelings and emotions.

At the same time, as in any mass-mediated society, the tarento are clearly made special by their constant exposure on television. Their lives, mediated and made widely available for (quasi)public scrutiny from even early in childhood, become cultural icons of a peculiarly modern sort. Regular life-course transformations usually experienced on a personal level – puberty, marriage, the birth of children, middle-age, and even death – are shared by millions through the medium of television. The most spectacular examples of this are the weddings and receptions of popular Japanese performers, especially the aidoru singers. These marriages run into the millions of dollars in a sort of conspicuous consumption extreme even in Japan. Spectacular ceremonies and receptions, broadcast live with more attention and care than is the network sponsors who underwrite most of their huge cost. When the happy couple leave for their honeymoon (usually overseas), they are followed by a troop of reporters and announcers eager to document their happy first days of married life.

Wednesdays' 'Information About the Entertainment World', like all wide show, features a panel staffed with a variety of tarento. If the neta for the day is about a famous singer, often his friend will be invited to the program to give 'the inside story'. The panel is anchored by the so-called 'entertainment commentator' (*geinō hyōronka*), whose sole qualification is that he or she is extremely well-informed about many tarento and is able to talk at length about even the most insignificant of subjects. These commentators are walking dictionaries of the trite and the sordid, and they are in great demand. *The Two O'Clock Wide Show* was lucky enough to feature Mr. Katō Kōichi – a leading commentator – for several years until Mr. Katō, a heavy smoker, was finally forced to retire upon contracting (of all things) cancer of the tongue. The final irony came when the death Mr. Katō was itself taken up by the wide show as a neta; yet another commentator took his place on the panel and provided the 'inside story' about Katō's final days. Self-referencing, reflexive, and intertextualizing to an extreme, the Japanese wide show constructs a world of representations that is real and yet unreal, relevant and yet irrelevant, played for laughs and yet deadly serious.

The immensely popular wide show format known as 'Marriage Emergency Hotline' is an apt final example of Japanese TV and the representation of consensus. 'Marriage Emergency Hotline' is a personal advice style program consisting of two short dramas that recreate the domestic problems of viewers who, according to the host of the program, have called or written in with problems. Each drama is followed by a lengthy discussion by the panelists, who aim to find some sort of 'solution' (*kaitō*). It is these discussions that provide most of the interest for the show, and these take up twice as much program time as do the dramas. Not surprisingly, a commonly used word during these discussions is 'common sense' (*jōshiki*). Such common sense is the standard against which the dramas are judged, and it is also the means for redressing the domestic quarrels. It is not to be tested or modified, it is simply asserted as a given.[12] What is somewhat surprising and troubling is the fact that, despite the program's repeated claims at authenticity, over ninety per cent of the dramas presented on 'Marriage Emergency Hotline' are complete fictions.

As in most Japanese talk shows, the panelists do all of the talking on 'Marriage Emergency Hotline'. Let us consider in more detail the composition of the panel for this program. (The numbers refer to Figure 1).

1) Katsura Harunosuke. An accomplished comedian, Harunosuke-san is the only member of the panel to participate in both the drama and ensuing discussion about the conflicts presented in it. As a panel member, he is often used to lighten up the conversation if things get overly serious; while as an actor he usually plays the part of the *salary-man* husband embroiled in some sort of family conflict.

2) Okuda Hiroyuki. The host of *The Two O'clock Wide Show*, his function here is mainly to direct the conversation towards the main discussants, but he occasionally chips in. The personality of the program host is not nearly as important on Japanese wide shows as on American talk shows – the consensus among Japanese

producers being that he can do little to help a show and much to hurt it. (Thus, the directors on the program I worked on were constantly trying to get the host to stop talking!) The host is complemented by his charming assistant who sits beside him.

3) Yoshimoto Mayumi. Ms. Yoshimoto is the hostess of *The Two O'clock Wide Show*, where she plays the role of the *kikite*, or 'professional listener'. It is her job to agree with what is said by the guests or by the host, to murmur whenever appropriate to keep the rhythm of the conversation going, and finally to inform the audience in as pleasing a voice as possible that it is time for a commercial. Ms. Yoshimoto has a youthful sort of cuteness about her, and she seems to be greatly loved by the viewers of this show.

4) Miyako Chocho. Ms. Miyako is the first of three regulary-featured panelists whose sole function is to interpret the dramas and to provide (often humorous) advice to the audience. A famous manzaishi for many decades, there is absolutely no doubt that she is the main focus of the program. It is her presence which makes the whole show stick together. As one of the original producers of the 'Marriage Emergency Hotline' commented, 'We designed this program to be 'the Miyako Chocho show.' Chocho did a similar advice show on radio for many years, which set the precedent for the TV version.

While the other panelists may provide more concrete information regarding a given conflict and possible ways to resolve it, it is always Miyako Chocho who has the final word – the voice of experience speaks loudest here. Indeed, in the long-unchanged pattern of this program, it is always Miyako-san who does the wrap-up of each case considered; the final minute of the segment is left for her to sum up what she feels to be important and best in any situation. As she speaks, the camera (camera #2 from straight on) slowly zooms in to a tight close up, bringing the audience into close proximity to this sincere woman as she speaks her mind.

5) Kayaki Kansho. Mr. Kayaki supplies this program with the voice of religion. He is the president and chief priest at one of the most powerful temple complexes in Japan: the Mt. Hiei temple above Kyoto city. He is also an entertaining and funny conversationalist, which keeps his input into the discussions from becoming too esoteric. His large, heavy-set frame, shaven head and wide shoulders present a sharp contrast to the frail body of Miyako

Chocho. (This contrast is often exploited by the director who will call for a 'two-shot', where these two – the frail old woman and the husky Buddhist priest – are framed together and, more often than not, the frisky old lady is found scolding the bemused priest).[13]

6) Furukawa Atsushi. Finally, we come to a panel member who would seem absolutely essential to an American advice program – the lawyer. Much as one would expect, he provides information about the various subtleties of family law, divorce procedures, and the like. However, compared to the other members of the panel, he is clearly the least prominent in the flow of conversation. His voice, the voice of the law, is subordinate to the voices of religion and experience.

7) Mori Takeshi. Mr. Mori is a young announcer/reporter who works on several YTV programs, including the *Zoom-in Morning* show. His authority is entirely a product of his position in various news programs, and as an announcer he represents here the newest voice of all: the voice of television. His youth is often played off against the aged experience of Miyako Chocho who, when she is not bullying the Buddhist priest on some matter, is often busy upbraiding the young Mr. Mori for his lack of 'common sense'.

Now that we have some idea of the eclectic group that makes up the panel of the show, let us consider the layout of the studio. The main set area consists of a large table along which the panelists are seated so as to make filming angles easier for the cameramen. Off to the side of the panelists sit the members of the studio audience; usually between thirty and forty housewives. Although the audience is located in close proximity to the panel, actual on-camera communication between the panelists and the audience is exceedingly rare – in fourteen months of watching this show, I observed such interaction only three times. In practice, the role of the audience is the very opposite of active participation; it is strategically located in the set to serve as a backdrop for the interaction of the panelists.

When the panelists are talking, the director may order a cameraman (usually camera #1, as in the above diagram) to slide over to the right and take a 'wide shot' – including both the panelists and the audience in the frame. The resulting image on the television screen is of panelists speaking in front of a nodding (or laughing)

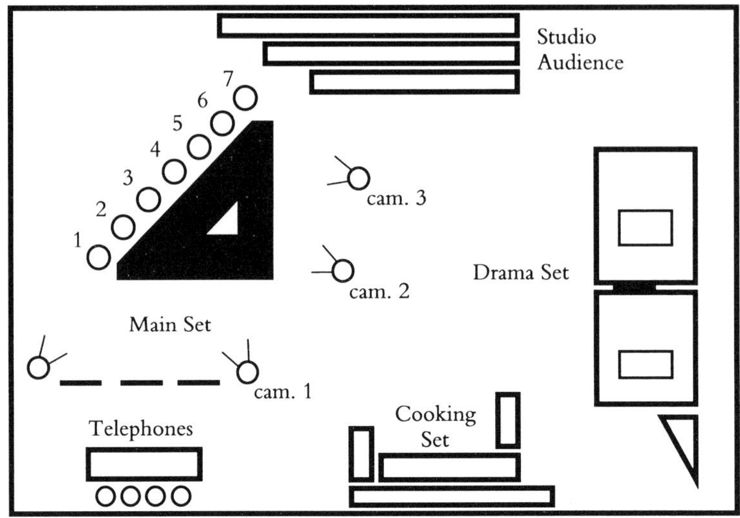

Figure 1 Studio Layout of 'Marriage Emergency Hotline'

audience. A similar effect is achieved by the use of 'reaction shots': quick, tight group shots of audience members following, but never taking part in, the conversation of the panelists. The presence of the audience members is essential to the creation of the consensual atmosphere of the program. The form of the image, with panelists as mediators who speak on a variety of common-sense topics in front of a passive studio audience, reproduces in microcosm the formal relationship between the audience at home and the tele-representations they watch. By extension, just as the passive studio audience is included in the world of the wide show, viewers at home are also included through their watching. The interpellation of viewers is often direct in these programs; with the host asking the camera/audience rhetorically 'what do you think?' or 'how do you feel about this?' or 'Isn't that shocking?'. Titles of several other wide shows are overt attempts to include the viewer in the programs: *Wide You*, *Let's Meet at Three O'clock* and *You at Three O'clock* are all popular examples.

Instead of investigating the myriad complexities that make wife/mother-in-law relations to tense in Japan today, the wide show presents sensational exaggerations that teach very little about reality. The ageing of Japanese society, the long working hours of Japanese men, and the extreme pressure on children and their mothers in Japan to succeed in the educational system are all featured in the dramas, but instead of addressing them as 'social problems' (as in the American perspective), these factors are depicted as inevitable parts of social life which all persons must adapt to. Interpersonal problems are made into entertaining neta in Japan by a process of exaggeration – faced with the dramas presented on 'Marriage Emergency Hotline', the worries of the typical housewife seem tame by comparison. Program producers told me that this is the real reason for the program's popularity: housewives like to see people in more miserable situations than themselves. This hardly flattering view of the audience is typical of wide show producers, some of whom held the brazen view that, in the final analysis, 'television is a scam' (terebi wa gomakashi nan da).

Due in part to the sensational nature of the material in the dramas, more often than not, the panelists offer no practical solutions at all. Instead, they engage in entertaining, innocuous banter for most of the program. Despite the stated goal of giving advice to viewers with problems, this seems to be the real appeal of the program for both performers and the audience. For example, consider the opening scene of a typical drama about a wife/mother-in-law conflict: this one entitled 'Demon Mother-in-law Abuses Wife Who Cannot Have Children And Forces Her Towards Divorce' (Ko o Umenu Yome o Nonoshiri, Rikon Seyo to Semaru Oni-shūtome) and translated from 'Marriage Emergency Hotline' of February 16, 1988.

> Host: First we have a wife/mother-in-law related problem. This is the complaint of a 29 year-old wife, married for six years, who – because she is yet to have children – is being pressured to divorce by her mother-in-law. . . .
> Hostess: Please watch the drama. . . .
>
> [Wife, dressed in apron, to businessman husband sitting at the breakfast table. . .]
>
> W: What time do you plan to get back from work tonight?
> H: I don't know.
> W: 'I don't know' is no good! I have to prepare things, you know?
> H: Hey, what I don't know, I don't know. There's nothing I can do about it.

W: You always get back late recently. You haven't been back once before midnight, have you?

[The mother-in-law, or shūtome (S), enters the kitchen from the next room. She addresses her son in a exaggerated, mothering way. . . .]

S: Well, after all, it's no fun to come back to a house with no children, is it Takao?
H: I'm going to be late for work. See you later.
S: Okay, give me a call if you can. . . .
H: Mom, it's cold out today, be sure not to catch a cold.
S: Thank you!

[The husband leaves and wife and mother-in-law stare at each other in quite obvious hatred.]

As this opening scene ends, the studio fills with an urgent drumming background music that complements the age-old conflict between these traditional enemies. Ensuing scenes emphasize how the husband favors his mother over his wife (something already evident in the above establishing scene), before going on to suggest that he is already engaging in an extra-marital affair with the consent of his mother, who hopes desperately for a grandchild. As if the core problem is not clear enough, the camera zooms in on the face of the housewife washing the dishes as a tape plays her voice-over in a sort of internal dialogue:

W: [voice over] Six years married and we are still unable to have a child. My expectantly waiting mother-in-law, wanting a grandchild, grows ever more aggressive in her attacks on me. . . .

The conflict finally comes to a head when the husband's infidelity is disclosed. Note how overdrawn the evil mother-in-law character is, and how much detail is included in the drama so as to foster later conversation by the panelists:

[The husband and wife are sitting on the tatami in the family room. . . .]

W: You told me that you were in Tokyo on business on the 23rd of last month, but that was a lie, wasn't it?
H: What's this all of the sudden? I was. . . . [the wife cuts in]

W: What, then, is this photograph? It came out of *your* pocket! It's Shimogawa Onsen in Izu isn't it? And the date is imprinted on the picture so you can't talk your way out of it! And, my, what a pretty woman! – Just how long have you been betraying me?!!

[The mother-in-law enters and immediately jumps in. . .]

S: What a high-and-mighty way you yell [at him]! Do you really think you have the right to talk like that to your husband?
W: What is that supposed to mean?
S: That sort of attitude from a woman who can't even bear a child. . . .
W: Am I disqualified as a wife because I haven't had kids?
S: What I am saying is just that I want to see the face of my grandchild. And you are a wife who can't even get pregnant. . . .
W: Please don't make it my sole responsibility! When we went to the hospital to check the doctor said we were *both* norma. . . .
S: But in fact no baby has been born, has it?
W: [pleadingly to husband] You, if this woman gets pregnant, do you plan to leave me?
S: That's to be decided at the time, isn't it?
W: [again desperately to husband] Why don't you say something?!
S: Shut up! So I should just break up with this girl, right? Okay, I'll do it!

[The husband gets up and leaves the room]

S: He loves children. . . . the poor boy!
W: You're encouraging him, aren't you? Why are you trying to tear us apart like this?
S: You know, since long ago people have said 'San-nen ko-naki wa saru' . . . (Three years without bearing children, and you go). . . . Perhaps it's best for you to do the same!

[The Mother-in-law laughs in triumph before leaving the room; the wife slumps to the floor in misery . . .]

[Music swells, lights dim, and the drama ends.]

The obviously exaggerated character of the mother-in-law and of the entire conflict of the drama is typical of the sorts of situations used on this show. Some other titles of featured dramas include: 'Demon-Wife Urges Old Mother-in-Law to "Make More Money!" While Putting Her to Work Day and Night'; 'Devil Mother-in-Law Has Fortune Told and Attacks Pregnant Daughter-in-Law, Telling Her "Don't Have the Baby!"; and finally 'Demon-Wife Deceives Mother-in-Law, Sells Her Land, and Kicks Her Out of Newly-Built House!'.

The extreme nature of the drama transcribed above is thus actually representative of the sort of conflicts normally used on 'Marriage Emergency Hotline'. Because the dramas make it quite clear who is in the wrong, this is rarely the main topic of talk among the panelists during their discussion. Consider the following excerpts from the panel discussion about what to do about the situation enacted in the above drama:

> [Mr. Okuda, the host, summarizes the case of] 'the mother-in-law attempting to force her daughter-in-law into divorce because she hasn't yet had children'. . . .
>
> [Camera #2 takes a tight bust shot of Miyako Chocho, who says] How very strange! This is not the age for that sort of thing.
>
> [The Buddhist priest comments,] Since the doctor said there was nothing wrong, just because they haven't had a child yet, its still not impossible. . . . Perhaps they should try making efforts together like going to soak in hot natural baths [*onsen*] and the like. . . .
>
> [Miyako Chocho] Yes, because after all, having a child is a blessing.
>
> [Kayaki] Yes, it's a blessing . . . so they should take hot baths together or try electricity treatments or, I suppose there's all sorts of things. What about that, you experienced people? Aren't there such things? [he points at Okuda, the host]
>
> [Okuda is surprised] Why do you point at me? [embarrassed laughter] Yes, well there are onsen which are famous for their fertility-giving powers. . . .
>
> [Kayaki] Maybe they could go rub against some stones or something. . .
>
> [Harunosuke, back to the priest] *You* should know about that sort of thing, why don't you recommend a good place!?

Up until this point, the focus of the panel has at least ostensibly been on giving some advice (no matter how irresponsible) to the wife. From here on, however, the conversation becomes more and more playful, and only tangentially related to the problems presented in the drama.

> [Harunosuke offers an obvious set-up line] This sort of thing, y'know, you get them [children] when you don't need them, and when you want them. . . .
>
> [Chocho jumps in] Don't tell me you made another child outside marriage again!! [she looks to the Priest for support as Harunosuke pleads] No! That's not what I mean!
>
> [Kayaki, kidding] It looks like you've added one more to your pile of worries! Shall I listen to your worries?
>
> [Harunosuke protests] I'm not talking personally, I mean in society in general. . .
>
> [Kayaki] It didn't look that way to me!
>
> [Chocho agrees] Your eyes were welling with tears!
>
> [Kayaki and Chocho continue to tease him as the studio audience laughs.]

As the playing bantering continues, we approach an interesting and somewhat unusual moment when the conversation – up until now concerned with the basically hypothetically problems of others – suddenly becomes very personal. In this moment, we can suddenly understand on a completely new level why Miyako Chocho says that having children is 'a blessing'.

> [Miyako Chocho comments] It's fate. Children must be seen as a blessing.
>
> [Kayaki, the priest, eagerly chimes in] It's a mistake from the very beginning to say that we 'made' or 'got' a child. We should say that we were 'blessed with' a child.
>
> [The rhythm between him and Chocho is unusually good today. At this point, Harunosuke interrupts with a seemingly innocent question which changes the atmosphere in the studio in the studio in a split-second.]
>
> [Harunosuke] Excuse me, but, Miyako-san, isn't it the case that

in your divorce, the fact that *you* couldn't have children was the cause [for divorce]?

[Sudden total silence in the studio, as if the air had suddenly drained out of the place . . . taken back a bit, Chocho responds.]

[Chocho] Yes, yes of course. In my case it was my body. There *are* women who physically can't have children, you know. . . . But to go on to say that that was the reason for the divorce is wrong. In my case, it was a one-to-one problem.

[Chocho switches quickly to address the imaginary wife in the TV audience] I think it's up to you. If you want to have a child, then you should try harder with your husband. You may think he got involved with another woman because of the lack of kids at home but, children or no children, I think that men are things which screw around [*Otoko wa uwaki o suru mono da*].

[Directly following this statement, the camera switches to the Buddhist priest, who is nodding in furious agreement with Chocho. She is finishing the wrap-up quite quickly now, perhaps partly to avoid talking any more about her own personal experiences.] I think that if you worry too much about what your mother-in-law says and get frustrated, then you may not be able to have the child that you would otherwise (naturally) have borne. . . .

[The camera switches to a shot of the host and hostess set to announce the next commercial.]

[Okuda comments,] Hmmm . . . how did you [the viewer] feel [about this topic]?

[Okuda expects Yoshimoto-san, as usual, to give the key-word for the commercial, but instead she adds a rare observation of her own.]

[Yoshimoto] Yes, it seems that if one is not psychologically relaxed then . . . [she intends to go on but Okuda is already cutting off her sentence]

[Okuda, hurriedly] Yes, such things are often said. . . .

[Giving up on elaboration – the hostess is not, after all, paid to forward her own ideas – Yoshimoto gives the key-word for the commercial] Yes, but before we go on, a commercial.

The goal of this 'problem solving' session is not to solve anything at all: because the drama already makes it quite clear who is wrong and who is right, the only possible advice is that everyone should behave according to the laws of 'common sense'. The simplicity of the solution, combined with the extreme nature of the dramas, allows ample time and fodder for playful discussion among the panelists. The clearly unusual case in which Miyako Chocho was forced to talk about her own personal affairs (*kibun no koto*) instead of those of an anonymous other (*hito no koto*), highlights how much of Japanese television is able to present a smooth tatemae front precisely because truly problematic issues are studiously avoided. Conflict is only made entertaining in Japan when it is exaggerated out of all proportion – only then can it be dealt with safely without calling into question the overt harmony on Japanese TV and out in society. This is radically different from how American television deals with representations of personal and social conflict. Where in Japan harmony is the norm, in the U.S. conflict often is, and this difference is absolutely crucial in understanding the differing styles and effects of television in both countries.

Consider the recent evolution of the typical American talk show. The convivial talk shows which once dominated afternoon programming, innocuous programs named after their obsequious hosts 'Merv Griffin' and 'Mike Douglas', have been displaced by a new breed of talk show. Named after their popular moderators whose colorful names reflect a new pluralistic emphasis – *Donahue*, *Oprah*, *Geraldo* – all share the same formal features. Like their Japanese counterparts, these talk shows also feature a panel. Unlike typical Japanese panels, these are composed of (so-called) experts who function to inform and incite the large, individualistic studio audience which surrounds and dwarfs them. It is clearly the audience that plays the greatest role in these talk shows; the reverse of Japanese TV, where panelists do all of the speaking. Unlike the aura of consensus which Japanese producers try to create by choosing compatible panelists and innocuous topics suited to tatemae discourse, on American television divisive, controversial topics are favored; and the best panelists are those who not only fight among themselves, but also with the audience members.

For American viewers, what is often entertaining about these shows is to see indignant audience members stand up to 'speak their piece' on some issue: 'I don't care what ya' say doc, I don't want no AIDS-infected kid in my school!' Where the Japanese wide show portrays problems as a the result of a breakdown in proper interpersonal relationships, American forum-style talk shows tend to locate problems out in society while asserting that any solutions will inevitably be *individual* ones discovered through introspection and self-discovery. Thus American talk shows ideologically align themselves with the culturally valued category of 'the individual' – all problems are caused by society and all solutions involve individual choice. Meanwhile, Japanese television aligns itself firmly with society and common sense in depicting the nation as a consensual and unified whole in which problems only arise when individuals fail to fulfil their proper roles and duties. In the United States, society is often portrayed as a realm for interpersonal conflict; in Japan, it is a unified and harmonious context that sets the ground rules for proper individual behavior.

Shaped by differing cultural models of the self and its relation to society, daytime television programs in Japan and the United States tell different kinds of stories about the world. These stories, like 'Marriage Emergency Hotline' and *Donahue*, are fascinating examples of the ways in which technology, culture, and ideology variously combine in modern societies. They teach us that television is not the same thing everywhere, and they suggest that the sorts of communication facilitated by television are far too complex to be covered by the single all-embracing term 'mass communication.' Television in Japan plays on and with fundamental cultural markers such as uchi/soto, public/private, and ura/omote in order to represent an informal and unified world of vicarious entertainment. This emphasis on quasi-intimate, harmonious interaction reflect Japanese cultural orientations just as surely as the sarcastic banter of situation comedies or the individualistic display on *Donahue* reflect American society and culture. In both cases, we need to study the wider implications of these differing orientations, including the ways they lend themselves to the operations of ideology.

On Television Technology, Culture and Ideology

I have argued that much of Japanese television produces representations of quasi-intimate communication among and between TV performers and viewers, and that this style of entertainment is patterned, in part, on informal interaction of the sort found in uchi (in-group) contexts. The process, to be sure, works both ways. For example, many of the exuberant performances used to liven up *bōnenkai* (year-end parties) and other informal get togethers in Japan are now directly borrowed from TV. While such cultural connections are significant, looking at how televisual communication differs from face-to-face interaction is also revealing. This conclusion focuses on selected technical properties of televisual communication that figure prominently in the ongoing spectacle of popular Japanese TV culture.

Firstly, televised images and events are electronically mediated, while most everyday interactions (except talking on the phone and singing karaoke) are not. More specifically, television technology allows for meaningful communication to take place between persons in contexts that are radically separated, both in space and time.[14] The spatial break seems especially crucial in Japan, where face-to-face interactions involve delicate and tactful negotiations of status, social distance, and formality. The use of tact presumes the ability to size up a particular context, to plan one's speech and behavior accordingly, and to monitor and adjust to the reactions of others. TV, due to its mediated nature, cannot work in this way. In this limited sense, then, television is indeed tactless. The Japanese case suggests that the very tactlessness of TV may even become an important reason for its popularity.

The inevitable break between those on TV and those who watch provides an important space for play: the very distance that separates contexts of television production and reception allows for the representation of a world in which time, place, status, and behavior are all flexible. Everyone can share in the close and informal relationships represented on Japanese TV precisely because those relationships are largely imaginary. While the televisual uchi is real and tangible enough to facilitate empathy and identification among viewers, it is experienced as both public (produced and circulated in society) and private (viewed inside the home) at the same time. The popularity of quasi-intimate television in Japan is thus linked to TV's ability to transcend spatial boundaries – boundaries which are always also cultural. TV is embraced by Japanese audiences not only because of its form and content, but also because of the context in which it is most often received: the domestic sphere. TV offers the Japanese a new and quintessentially modern sort of public culture that is made all the more appealing by its ambiguous positioning vis-à-vis cultural notions of public and private space and the sorts of behavior appropriate in each.

The word uchi, which has been used quite loosely in this chapter up until this point, merits closer attention. Consider Dorinne Kondo's interpretation of the term:

> . . . [*U*]*chi* describes a located perspective: the in-group, the 'us' facing outward to the world. It is the *ie* [household] or other group to which one belongs. . . . Uchi defines who you are, through shaping language, the use of space, and social interaction. . . . the uchi is the center of participatory belonging, the center from which one can create relationships with the outside world (1990:141–142).

Thus, uchi cannot be understand apart from the interconnections between spatial and social relationships in Japan. Uchi always refers to a particular location or context that may serve as the setting for 'participatory belonging'. As such, uchi specifies both a place and a particular quality of experience (Kondo uses the word 'feeling'). While the domestic sphere is not the only area where belonging and a sense of intimacy can be found in Japan (it is often quoted how salarymen may refer to their own company as *uchi no kaisha* when dealing with outsiders), one's household is certainly a key uchi domain. Because television is most often watched in the relaxed comfort of the home, then, it hardly seems surprising that the medium takes on a quasi-intimate tone. While quasi-intimacy via the media is not unique to Japan, the way in which it ties in with pre-media social patterns – such as uchi and soto – is culturally specific. At the same time, the various techniques and strategies used by Japanese TV producers to produce this quasi-intimate feeling should alert us to the fact that none of this happens naturally – Japanese telerepresentations of unity, unanimity, and spontaneity are carefully planned and engineered.

Secondly, television is a predominantly one-way instrument of communication. Unlike face-to-face or telephone-mediated conversations in Japan (both of which are rhythmically punctuated with supportive *aizuchi* utterances), on TV direct feedback is minimized. As if to make up for the lack of reciprocal interaction, television programs often include symbolic substitutes for the absent audience. Strategically placed live studio audiences, professional panelists (who do the talking and reacting on behalf of the audience at home), and eager amateurs are thus common features on Japanese TV. Although it is actually produced by a small number of highly educated cultural specialists in exclusive organizations, TV consistently represents itself as a transparent, open, and reciprocal medium that speaks on behalf of the whole of Japanese society. The goal of TV producers is not to homogenize society or to mislead viewers to serve some hidden, political purpose or class interest – the TV directors I worked with were very straightforward in saying what they hoped to accomplish: they wanted viewers to pay attention to their shows. In both Japan and the United States, TV producers seem to worry mainly about the particular 'twists' (*hineri*) and details given to their programs; they generally do not question the cultural and ideological presumptions that underlie everyday practices of television production and consumption.[15]

The one-way nature of TV communication is essential for understanding how unity and unanimity are so regularly (and seemingly natural) presented on Japanese TV. Whether or not Japan is actually as loaded with consensus as TV presents it to be, viewers certainly seem to enjoy watching such telerepresentations. Because direct feedback is minimized on TV, moreover, it is virtually impossible to disrupt or call into question such broadcasts. For many Japanese, indeed, challenging TV's images of unity probably seems a foolhardy undertaking: who doesn't already know that televisual unity, like the tatemae consensus found in many Japanese in-groups, is always partly a product of the imagination? What is significant is that Japanese people and Japanese TV continue to represent their social relationships as harmonious – for them the ontological status of these pro-social representations is largely beside the point.

Television, in Japan as elsewhere, does not merely reflect society – it transforms it. This chapter has suggested some of the ways in which Japanese culture, ideology, and technology combine to yield surprising and unusual kinds of television programming. Images of unanimity, informality and friendly spontaneity are used to unite Japanese TV audiences into an imaginary whole. This, in itself, is not a bad thing. Japanese viewers no doubt recognize that the unity offered by television is illusory, but they enjoy vicarious participation in TV's electronic uchi all the same. Still, it is important to note that not everyone is included in the harmonious electronic uchi in Japan: socially stigmatized groups, and just about anyone problematic enough to ruin the harmonious, quasi-intimate tone of Japanese TV are all invisible and excluded. In this sense, what are most ideological about Japanese TV shows are not the hidden messages contained within the programs-as-texts, but instead the problematic areas and issues that never make it onto the airwaves at all.

As ideologies depicting a friction-free future 'information society' proliferate in Japanese business circles, government rhetoric, and the mass media, it becomes all the more important to point out the gaps and inconsistencies inherent in this unified, utopic vision. In a passage that works well with the main theses of this chapter, media sociologist Watanabe Jun articulates what he sees as the fundamental contradiction within the Japanese televisual celebration of togetherness and intimacy:

> Television never directly connects those who appear [on the screen] and those who view. The relationship that forms between them is always a quasi-relationship; in reality they are absent from each other. Nonetheless, television makes it feel as if there is an extremely real and direct interaction taking place. . . . Indeed, the form of such a relationship has been made a fundamental basis for program production. Not only in terms of content, but also in the very relationship between those who appear and those who watch; television makes us realize that 'the greatest presence is simultaneously the greatest absence' (1989:129).

Despite all its contradictions, there is something universal and human about the Japanese experience of television. Japanese TV represents a positively social, even gregarious, approach to mass mediated modern life. While this may seem surprising in light of certain dominant stereotypes of the reserved and repressed Japanese, much of the spectacle of Japanese TV makes perfect cultural sense when viewed in terms of mediated quasi-intimate entertainment. Television culture, in Japan as elsewhere, is the product of a remarkable combination of technologies, institutions, practices, and publics. Learning about the ways in which TV educates, entertains, or just keeps the attention of various audiences can tell us much about the cultural and ideological dynamics of modern societies. The case of Japan suggests that TV is not the same everywhere, and also that how the medium is used and interpreted has much to do with the ways in which people see themselves and their relations with others in society. Television, in short, is both reflective and constitutive of modern societies, and for this reason it deserves the critical attention of a much wider audience.

Notes

This essay has been influenced by the input of many, including students, colleagues and TV viewers, since its initial publication in the *Journal of Japanese Studies*. Thanks go especially to David Slater for his insightful criticism.

1 Indeed, it is reasonable to expect that some kind of quasi-intimacy may develop between TV personalities and members of the viewing audience in any society where TV is usually watched in the privacy of the home. In the United States, for example, Gallup pollsters once found Walter Cronkite to be the 'most trusted man in the country', even though the vast majority of Americans only knew him through the medium of TV.

2 Source: Personal communication (September 23, 1992) from the chief of the research division at the Yomiuri Telecasting Corporation (YTV), Osaka, Japan. Other statistics, such as those provided by numerous NHK public opinion surveys, also point to the widespread positive responses to TV in Japan. For example, a 1977 survey of 'Japanese TV Viewing' found 64% of respondents agreed with the statement that 'television is something like an additional member of the family'. In the same survey 'close to 70% [of respondents] answered that [not watching TV for seven days straight] would make them "lonely"' (Nihon Hōsō Kyōkai 1983:112). On yet another survey 61% of respondents agreed that 'watching television helped them get used to talking and singing in front of people' (1983:142). Summing up the Japanese people's strong attraction to television, NHK researchers argue that it can be explained in part by the 'curiosity and love of information' shared by many Japanese, and by 'the characteristic tendency of Japanese to continually strive for togetherness [*ittaikan*] and assimilation into society' (1983:122). While the veracity of these NHK's select an already written response' surveys is certainly open to question, their data do generally support the arguments about TV and quasi-intimacy that are the subject of this paper.

3 Quasi-intimacy is but one of many features of Japanese television amenable to cultural and ideological analysis of the sort attempted here. My own writing on Japanese TV has also dealt with issues related to gender, education, and ideologies of youthful purity. What makes quasi-intimacy especially interesting, for me, is how the nature of the problem forces one to focus and refocus on the properties and characteristics of the medium of television and on the way in which context affects the meaning of TV. Thus, while it is correct to point

out that TV everywhere probably involves quasi-intimacy of some sort, the patterns and motifs involving unity and spontaneity found on much of Japanese TV are culturally specific ways of going about elaborating on the possibilities of modern communications technologies.

4 This final example, *The Two O'clock Wide Show*, is the program I know best, and is representative of a whole class of wide show programs that dominate daytime TV in Japan. Accordingly, the discussion of this program – the production staff of which I worked on for nineteen months – is more lengthy and detailed than that of the two programs that precede it.

5 Although television broadcasting in the Kansai region usually starts between five-thirty and six in the morning, the majority of viewers turn on their sets sometime around seven. *Zoom-in Morning*, which airs from seven to eight each morning, is thus the first program that many Japanese see each day. Programs offered during this same time slot on other channels are similar in form and content: Asahi Television broadcasts *Good Morning Asahi*, Mainichi Television offers *Big Morning*, and Kansai TV asks *It's Morning! What Will Happen?*.

6 This is the opposite of the American news programs, such as NBC's *Today Show*, where the set is designed to convey the cozy interior feeling of an upscale living or family room, and where ventures outside are the exception rather than the rule.

7 While the term comes from the American entertainment industry term 'talent', in Japan tarento usually means something like what in the United States is called a 'TV star' or 'TV personality'. Media sociologist Inoue Hiroshi has argued that because Japanese tarento are so often on TV in so many different capacities, what they are most often selling is not a particular character or role, but something very close to their own 'personality' (1978:70). The tarento must be charming and attractive, but not so far from the mainstream so as to distance themselves from their audiences. Describing the general differences between fan letters written to movie stars and those written to TV tarento, Inoue notes that whereas movie stars are often idolized along with the characters they play by their fans, typical letters to TV tarento tend to address them in familiar everyday terms: [these letters are] 'written with the sort of intimacy appropriate for a friend, acquaintance, or neighbor'. While to a foreigner's critical eyes many Japanese tarento seem to do a poor job at playing the various roles they do on TV – for Japanese audiences it seems that the personality of the person playing the various parts is far more important than the actual performative skill with which the job gets done.

The ultimate expression of the peculiar logic of the Japanese tarento is the so-called *aidoru* (idol) – usually a teenage singer – who is amazingly popular while young and pure, but can only remain in the entertainment world after a certain age by undergoing an *imeiji chenji* (image change): a sort of media engineered shift in person-ality (usually from young and virginal to adult and sexy) which makes the fleetingly popular aidoru into a viable life-long tarento. These aidoru are rarely good singers in the technical sense of the term, but what they sell, once again, is not skill but a kind of charisma that works all the better when it appears familiar and human.

8 It is no coincidence that the person being invited as a guest the following day is always nearby a phone and also able to be on the program. In fact, the staff of the program has already checked his schedule and phone number. It is also probably not coincidental that so many of these tarento just happen to be promoting a new film or album at the time of their appearance on the program. Friendship is fine, but business is business.

9 Both single and in their thirties, these two often use the issue of marriage as the subject for their comedy routines. They pretend to be desperate to marry, and they compete with each other over who is more popular. Their act is a playful transformation of a very real social pressure in Japan – especially for women – that is, the idea of *tekireiki*, or a marriageable age.

10 Japanese television, like communication more generally in that country, tends to stress positive echoes – repetition, agreement, complementarity – whereas in the individualistic West negative echoes convey an ironic, and thus distancing, perspective in communication (see Sperber & Wilson 1988).

11 One objection to this line of thought would be: perhaps the Japanese simply don't want or need to talk about such issues at all. Intuition tells me, however, that things are not so simple – in fact, many Japanese talk about all sorts of issues with each other once they are on truly close terms.

12 When this same sort of show was done on radio in Japan, the advice given – 'leave him' or 'get a divorce' – often seemed beyond social convention. While occasionally outlandish suggestions are made during the television program, the bounds of common sense are never really challenged.

13 Kayaki-san has appeared often on television programs on other networks; a development which distressed the production staff of *The Two O'clock Wide Show*, who worried that his religio-symbolic image would be diminished due to overexposure. We thus have the curious situation where the members of a television company are found telling a priest to be less secular and more religious and moral – an interesting reversal of the usual pattern we find in the United States!

14 This passage, indeed this entire paper, has been greatly influenced by John B. Thompson's brilliant *Studies in the Theory of Ideology* (1984) and *Ideology and Modern Culture: critical social theory in the era of mass communication* (1990).

15 The best inside-look at the ideology of American TV producers continues to be Todd Gitlin's *Inside Prime Time* (1984). His analyses of how producers rely on past precedents in creating new programming is in many ways parallel with what I found inside the Japanese TV station. In both cases, the result is a great deal of consistency in the underlying structure of TV programming.

References

Barnlund, D.C. 1989 *Communicative Styles of Japanese and Americans*, Belmont: Wadsworth.

Inoue, Hiroshi 1987 *Terebi Bunka no Shakaigaku* (The Sociology of Television Culture), Kyoto: Sekai Shisō Sha.

Gitlin, Todd 1984 *Inside Prime Time*, Berkeley: University of California Press.

Kasza, G.J. 1988 *The State and the Mass Media in Japan, 1918–1945*, Berkeley: University of California Press.

Kato, H. (ed.) 1959 *Japanese Popular Culture*, Tokyo: Tuttle.

Kondo, D.K. 1990 *Crafting Selves*, Chicago: University of Chicago Press.

Lebra, Takie S. 1976 *Japanese Patterns of Behavior*, Honolulu: University of Hawaii Press.

NNS Cooperative Council 1980 *NNSR Ripōto 19 'Shufu-muke Waidoshō to Shichōsha'* (NNSR Report 19: Housewife-Oriented Wide Shows and their Viewers). n.p.

Nihon hoso kyokai 1983 *Terebi Shichō no Sanjū-nen*. (Thirty Years of Television Viewing), Tokyo: NHK Hōsō Yoron Chōsashō.

Ong, W.J. 1977 *Interfaces of the Word*, Ithaca: Cornell University Press.

Painter, Andrew A. 1991 *The Creation of Japanese Television and Culture* (dissertation), Ann Arbor: UMI International.

Sperber, D. and D. Wilson 1988 *Relevance: Communication and Cognition*, Cambridge: Harvard University Press.

Thompson, J.B. 1990 *Ideology and Modern Culture: critical social theory in the era of mass communication*, Stanford: Stanford University Press.

—— 1988 'Mass Communication and Modern Culture: contribution to a critical theory of ideology', *Sociology* 22:3, p. 359–383.

—— 1984 *Studies in the Theory of Ideology*, Cambridge: Polity Press.

Watanabe Jun 1989 *Media no Mikuroshakaigaku* (The Microsociology of the Media), Tokyo: Chikuma Shobō.

8

Panic Sites

The Japanese Imagination of Disaster from *Godzilla* to *Akira*

Susan J. Napier

From as early as 1951, with the awarding of the Venice Festival Prize to Kurosawa Akira's *Rashōmon*, the Japanese film has long been one of Japan's most highly regarded exports. Since that time, Western art house audiences and critics have been impressed and moved by the variety and artistry of the Japanese cinematic oeuvre. In the 1950s and 1960s, this variety ranged from the subtle explorations of family life expressed in Ozu's films, to the dynamic intensity of image and narrative in Kurosawa's work. More recently, Ōshima Nagisa's controversial films such as *Realm of the Senses* (Ai no Koriida, 1976) have shocked and intrigued audiences world wide, while Itami Jūzo's brilliantly funny examination of Japanese eating habits, *Tampopo*, made it into twenty-three 'top ten' lists in American newspapers and magazines in 1987.

Despite the consistently high praise of critics and reviewers, however, the Japanese film has remained largely an elite preserve, appreciated in urban art cinemas and on university campuses. And yet, there is another side to Japanese cinema which remains largely unexamined in both Japan and the West. This is Japan's popular cinema, the often unexported movies seen by millions of ordinary Japanese citizens. For many years this popular cinema was ignored or bemoaned by critics in the West, who saw the rise of mass produced and mass marketed films as a link to a perceived decline in the quality of Japanese cinema overall.

Busy lamenting the increasingly small output of the classic directors, Western critics and reviewers have shown little interest in the mass culture items that were crowding out the art films. Donald Richie, for example, the dean of Western critics of the Japanese film, has summed up popular Japanese cinema as 'a plethora of nudity, teenage heroes, science-fiction monsters, animated cartoons,

and pictures about cute animals' (1990:80). Regrettably, this assessment is largely correct.

Recently, however, critics in both the West and Japan have begun urging a closer look at Japanese popular cinema and, at least with science fiction films, a closer glance turns out to be highly rewarding. In the case of Japanese science fiction, particularly animated science fiction, the critics are often following the lead of the fans, both Westerners and Japanese, who have turned certain movies and series of movies into major cult hits.[1] This has been true since the release of the first *Godzilla* (Gojira) monster movie in America in 1954 and has continued to this day in the overwhelming reception accorded to the 1989 science fiction blockbuster, *Akira*, an animated film based on an almost equally popular comic strip series by Otomo Katsuhiro.

Of course, not all Japanese science fiction films have been consistently popular in the West. Enough of them have inspired such intense devotion, however, as to raise intriguing questions about the reasons behind their popularity. In particular, one might ask if there are certain popular culture universalities at work here. Or is it that science fiction is a particularly international genre?

At the same time, even those works that have only been popular in Japan can be looked at from the opposite point of view: was there something 'too Japanese' about them that might inhibit their reception outside Japan? In any case, both types of films provide opportunities to understand modern Japanese culture from a new vantage point.

Indeed, the enormity of the whole science fiction phenomenon in Japan itself, including novels, fan magazines and comics for both adults and children, is well worthy of scholarly attention. This article is an attempt to deal with that phenomenon on a selective basis, an effort to use one part of the science fiction genre, the dystopian/disaster movie and related comics (*manga*), as a key towards exploring both the science fiction genre in Japan, and contemporary Japanese cultural history in general.

In fact, science fiction is a particularly appropriate vehicle for treating the complexities of the Japanese success story. The very vocabulary of the genre, that of technological, social, and cultural advancement, reflects the cultural instrumentalities that characterize modern capitalism. These instrumentalities include the rapidity of change, the ideology of progress toward some anticipated 'future', and the omnipresence of the machine.

All of these elements are treated in Japanese science fiction, usually in a way that emphasizes the darker side of modern Japanese society. While such popular culture staples as children's comics and romance novels have often supported the stereotype of Japan as a secure, peacefully middle class environment, Japanese science fiction, whether in prose, comic, or film form, has tended to revel in what Susan Sontag has called 'the imagination of disaster' (1985:451). The works examined in this article, the *Godzilla* series, *Japan Sinks* (Nippon Chinbotsu), *Akira*, and related comics and prose, all center around a vision of disaster, of social, material, and sometimes spiritual collapse, 'panic sites', as Kroker and Cook describe certain kinds of contemporary texts.

These works are not alone in their shared dystopian vision. Much of Japanese science fiction, from the turn of the century on, has had a distinctly and memorably bleak view of society, as is common with Western science fiction as well. Indeed, the twentieth century in general has long been considered the age of the anti-utopia.[2] This brings us to another intriguing aspect of science fiction, its unique ability both to reflect and comment upon modern culture. Or, as Jameson puts it, science fiction serves to 'defamiliarize and restructure our experience of our own *present* and to do so in specific ways distinct from all other forms of defamiliarization' (1982:152).

That the Japanese 'present' has often been a problematic one is clearly indicated in the development of science fiction in Japan.[3] Japanese science fiction parallels the modernization of Japan but celebrations of this modernization are notably lacking. After an initial spate of novels envisioning a techno-military utopia under the emperor, prewar science fiction limned a future where advanced technology and military success had only brought about wars, famines, and plagues, or else more sophisticated ways to oppress a passive, fearful citizenry. Much of postwar Japanese science fiction has continued this dystopian trend, often with apocalyptic touches, especially in the immensely popular writings of Komatsu Sakyō whose 1973 novel *Japan Sinks* is one of the works considered in this chapter.

The notion of disaster is of course not the only theme in Japanese popular culture, or even in Japanese science fiction.[4] It is an important one, however, with profound implications for understanding both the development of science fiction in Japan, and also the changing Japanese notion of identity. For science fiction, in its insistent concern with difference (in terms of 'alien' versus 'normal, or 'natural' versus 'artificial'), is a genre fundamentally involved with the problem of identity.

The Japanese imagination of disaster, therefore, deserves examination both on a formal level, in terms of its relationship with the science fiction genre as a whole, but also in terms of its role within the context of postwar Japanese culture. By comparing *Akira* with the earlier *Japan Sinks* and *Godzilla*, one can trace two major developments. The first is a pattern of change in terms of technique and narrative structure, from what might be called the traditional science fiction film with its convention of 'secure horror' with definitive narrative closure in both the *Godzilla* films and *Japan Sinks*, to what can well be called a post-modern privileging of narrative movement and lack of closure in *Akira*. The other pattern is what might be labelled an ideological change in terms of both the presentation of disaster and in the attitudes inscribed within the films towards disaster, from a negative portrayal of disaster in *Godzilla* and *Japan Sinks*, toward a virtual celebration of it in *Akira*. This ideological development, I would suggest, encompasses both a generational change, and also the very conception of Japan's identity as a nation in a complex contemporary world.

This conception of identity is closely linked to the role that history plays in contemporary Japanese culture. Intriguingly, history too has important links with the science fiction genre. In his essay 'Nostalgia for the present', Jameson argues that the rise of science fiction 'corresponds to the waning or blockage of . . . historicity . . . to its crisis and paralysis, its enfeeblement and repression' (1991:284). This proposition is particularly interesting in regards to Japan where science fiction began to be imported and written only a few years after the Meiji Restoration in 1867, an event which in many ways turned into an attempt to destroy or at least rewrite history rather than to 'restore' it.

Turning to contemporary Japan, the works examined in this article show a fascinating and problematic relationship with history, starting with *Godzilla*'s attempt to rewrite it, going on to *Japan Sinks*' attempt to enshrine, it and ending with *Akira*'s largely successful effort to erase it. In a sense, the *Godzilla* series, *Japan Sinks*, and *Akira* may be seen as occupying a continuum, both in Japan's imagination of destruction and ultimately in Japan's imagination of itself. This continuum spans three decades, starting in the early 1950s which spawned both *Godzilla*'s nuclear anxiety and its easy moral certainties, through the 1970s ambivalence towards Japan's own success that characterizes *Japan Sinks*, and ending with *Akira* in the late 1980s, a decade of tumultuous change, both in Japan's conception of itself and its relationship with the rest of the world.

The Ideology of Secure Horror: *Godzilla* and *Japan Sinks*

To see the changes in this continuum more clearly, let us examine the films in more detail, starting chronologically with *Godzilla*. Perhaps even now the most famous of Japanese popular culture exports, the *Godzilla* series began in 1954. The original film quickly became an enormous hit in Japan and internationally, spawning both direct progeny, in the series of *Godzilla* movies that continue to this day, and various related monster films such as *Rodan* and *Mothra*. *Godzilla*'s narrative, the chronicle of a scaly prehistoric monster who is awakened by American nuclear testing and lays waste to Tokyo until finally destroyed, both established and exemplified certain fundamental conventions of the genre.

The most universal of these conventions is that of the dangers of science, a theme as old as *Frankenstein* and one that, as will be seen, carries on importantly in *Akira*. *Godzilla* gives this theme a nationalistic twist, however, in emphasizing that it is American science which brings forth the monster. Even more significantly, it is Japanese science, personified by the humane Japanese scientist whose suicide helps destroy *Godzilla*, which ultimately saves the world.

The film can therefore be seen as operating on a number of ideological levels. First, it demonizes American nuclear science in an obvious reference to the atomic tragedies of Hiroshima and Nagasaki.[5] Secondly, it allows for the traditional happy ending (another important convention in the traditional science fiction movie genre), by allowing 'good' Japanese science to triumph against the evil monster. The film thus offered its immediate postwar Japanese audience an experience that was both cathartic and compensatory, allowing them to rewrite or at least to re-imagine their tragic wartime experiences.

Godzilla tapped into more than just the Japanese nuclear allergy, however. American audiences enjoyed it as well, partly no doubt, as a chance to work through their own nuclear age anxiety at a level that was alien and sometimes amusing in imagery, but familiar in its narrative conventions. In this regard *Godzilla* clearly belongs to the genre of what Andrew Tudor labels as 'secure horror'. In this genre the collectivity is threatened, but only from outside, and is ultimately reestablished, usually through the combined efforts of the scientists and the government. It is a fundamentally optimistic genre in which it is possible, as Tudor says, 'to imagine successful human intervention' (1989:214).

Naturally, this intervention is not finally effective until the movie's end, and therein lies the other obvious charm of *Godzilla* and its descendants: the suspenseful pleasure of watching large blocks of Tokyo real estate being crunched underfoot. This kind of cathartic/empathetic vision of destruction, which Sontag describes as 'the peculiar beauties to be found in wreaking havoc, making a mess' (1985:454), is typical of all disaster films and is the most consistent common element to be found in the works examined in this article.

While destruction is a constant in these films, the objects of destruction vary in important ways, as is clear in the second film I would like to discuss, *Japan Sinks*. Released in 1973, this four hour long evocation of the Japanese archipelago's total submersion into the ocean was an immediate and enormous domestic hit. The film's popularity is not surprising, since it was based on the famous science fiction writer Komatsu Sakyō's best seller of the same title. Interestingly, however, the movie, although released in the West, never reached any audience at all. The reasons behind this disparity in popularity may well be related to two interlocking elements, the objects destroyed in the film and the attitude taken toward this destruction.

As the title suggests, *Japan Sinks* is a movie whose narrative action is concerned solely with the destruction of Japan (due to a movement of the earth's plates in the seas underneath Japan, causing a violent series of earthquakes, volcanoes, and tidal waves). Furthermore, its predominant emotional tone is less one of excitement than of a sense of mourning for the loss of Japanese culture. As such, and despite the enjoyable, if unexceptional, special effects, the film inevitably had a limited appeal to non-Japanese audiences. From the point of view of this article, however, the film's very uniqueness of focus makes it a fascinating comparison with *Godzilla* and *Akira*.

Since the narrative of *Japan Sinks* consists entirely in following the country's process of inexorable submersion, there is little of the suspense found in a typical disaster film where the outcome remains in doubt. What suspense there is comes, not from wondering whether Japan can be saved, but whether most of its citizenry and a few remnants of its cultural artifacts can be rescued before the final disaster.

In this regard, the film narrative has a twofold focus. It includes the images of wholesale destruction typical to this genre, from massed crowds scurrying away from tidal waves, to earthquakes shaking the city apart, to fiery volcanoes spewing lava. Related to these, it also includes the frenzied efforts of the government and the scientific and military establishment to save what they can. These institutions, incidentally, are presented wholly positively, another element traditional to films in the 'secure horror' genre. Also typical of these films, the movie's main protagonists are scientists.

At the same time, however, the emphasis is less on the orgiastic joys of destruction and/or combat against that destruction, which movies in the *Godzilla* series highlight. Instead, both camera and narrative linger lovingly on the beauty and the grandeur of what is being destroyed. Not surprisingly, Mount Fuji is a prominent screen image.

In fact, some of *Japan Sinks*' most powerful scenes are ones in which destruction is only imagined. In one scene, for example, the Australian prime minister is shown gazing greedily at an exquisite statue of Kannon, the Buddhist goddess of mercy. At the same time he comments, 'I wish they'd send us more of these and fewer people!'

The above mentioned scene brings us to the ideological subtext of *Japan Sinks*, one that shows some intriguing developments from the period of time in which *Godzilla* was made. In *Godzilla*'s version of secure horror, the forces of destruction come from outside and are vanquished. The collectivity is viewed as something positive, deserving of protection, but to some extent taken for granted. The film, and subsequent films in the series, comment on Japan-American relations, but the real focus of the *Godzilla* series is on the scaly monsters themselves and the exhilarating destruction that they wreak, although only temporarily. The series' reassuring subtext remains the same throughout: even if famous monuments such as Tokyo Tower or the new Tokyo City Hall get trampled on, they can always be rebuilt.

In contrast, while *Japan Sinks* remains within the genre of secure horror, since it privileges a secure and reassuring collectivity, the film's action and ending are downbeat, emphasizing loss over success. In one evocative scene, for example, a pilot is ordered to fly over the Kinki region and relay photographic documentation of the damage caused by the recent massive earthquake activity. The scientists back at headquarters wait expectantly for the transmission of the photos but all that is relayed to them is a single image of sinister whirling clouds above an empty blue ocean. Impatient, they order the pilot to hurry on to Osaka: 'This is Osaka', comes the reply.

The scene is a quietly devastating one, conveying a sense of poignant and irrevocable loss. Other scenes are even more overt in underlining the emotional bond between Japan and her people. I use 'her' deliberately here, for this Japan is overtly personified as a female in both book and film. Thus, in one memorable moment towards the film's end, one of the scientists refuses rescue, stating that he prefers to commit a double 'love suicide' (*shinjū*) with Japan. The novel goes even further, containing a speech in which the scientist compares his love for Japan with his love for a woman.

If Japan is a female, then in *Japan Sinks* she has become a badly battered victim with no hope of recovery. This is in significant contrast to the *Godzilla*, series in which the destruction is both more impersonal and less catastrophic. Indeed, the enormity of the destruction in *Japan Sinks* is initially a surprise. This is especially so when one considers the timing of the film's appearance, a period following over a decade of double digit growth, when Japan's economic success was drawing admiration and envy. What had happened in the Japan of the early 1970s to make a film that is essentially an elegy to Japanese culture so popular?

To answer this it is necessary to go back to the 'present' of Japan in 1973 that the film so successfully defamiliarizes, and also to note the difference between generations in each film discussed here. The writer of *Japan Sinks*, Komatsu Sakyō, was born in 1931 and is therefore a full fledged member of the generation of Japanese most traumatized by the war and the collapse which followed. Perhaps even more significant than the war, however, was the combination of this initial trauma with the years of economic success in the 1960s, a period also characterized by enormous social and generational conflicts. In a culture where ephemerality has traditionally been one of the fundamental notions of existence, this success must have struck many members of Komatsu's generation as very likely to be transient. At the same time, the loss of the war and the subsequent renewed onslaught of Americanization/modernization exposed the fragility of both the physical and cultural presence of Japan.

Against this background, the popularity of *Japan Sinks* becomes more understandable. While 'high culture' Japanese cinema such as the films of Ōshima and other so-called New Wave directors profiled rebellious youth and a chaotic contemporary society in a way that disturbed many viewers,[6] *Japan Sinks* allowed its audience the melancholy pleasure of mourning the passing of traditional Japanese society. The film is essentially an elegy to a lost Japan.

In a sense slightly different from Jameson's use of the term, the film's Japan has become defamiliarized. It is literally a non-place, a place that exists only in the imagination and memory of its surviving people, now scattered throughout the world, and in its souvenirs, those cultural artifacts that have been commodified and dispersed among alien nations. Despite its vaguely near future setting, *Japan Sinks* actually looks backwards at a collectivity and a past that it eulogizes, commodifies and finally embalms.

Japan Sinks is thus a freeze frame of the Japanese citizenry in 1973 with their sense of an eroding identity and an ambivalent attitude towards power and success.[7] (Ironically, the 'oil shock' which occurred soon after the novel was published seemed for a time a frightening confirmation of what might be called a cultural 'fear of success'). As is obvious in the film, this 1973 identity combined insecurity about the state of society with pride in the traditional collectivity, a collectivity which seemed on the point of disintegrating.

Indeed, the film ends with an image of disintegration on a massive scale: It consists of a single image, a high altitude shot over the sea where Japan used to be, the names of its no longer existing cities superimposed on an empty ocean. All that remains of Japan is its history, encased in either written or collective memory.

If *Japan Sinks* is an homage to history, *Akira*, our final film to consider, celebrates history's imminent demise. Far more sophisticated in its special effects and complex story line than either the *Godzilla* series or *Japan Sinks*, *Akira* still shares with them a fascination with disaster. Indeed, *Akira* is perhaps the most vividly realized evocation of disaster to be produced in Japan thus far.

It is also an extraordinarily popular film. The year of its release it became the highest grossing movie in Japan, reaching an even wider audience than the original comic series had attained. Even more interestingly, it has met with a strong reception among both critics and the public abroad. With its narrative complexity, superb animation, and extraordinary technique, *Akira* is an important text, exemplifying certain aspects of popular culture in contemporary Japan that are well worth detailed examination.

In My End is My Beginning: *Akira*'s Celebration of the Alien

Akira begins with an ending. Taking full advantage of the special effects available in the animated cinema, the film opens in an eerie silence as the camera travels up an empty city street and a one line announcement appears on screen, 'Tokyo, July 16, 1988'. The next image is an overpowering white radiance followed by another brief announcement: '31 Years After WWIII, AD 2019, Neo Tokyo.'[8]

The film's action subsequently switches to 'Neo Tokyo' to present a grim future world: 'Old Tokyo' is now a vast bombed out crater while 'Neo Tokyo' is a place of overwhelming aesthetic and social alienation, a decaying cityscape that is physically fragmenting, at the same time as its political center is only barely held together by corrupt politicians and enigmatic military figures. Throughout the film, society seems on the brink of destruction, threatened by a variety of forces including a delinquent underclass, a mysterious resistance movement, and a group of mutants possessing terrifying psychic powers.

The viewer's initial response to *Akira* is undoubtedly a visceral one. *Akira*'s animation is cutting edge. Or, as Tony Rayns says of the film, 'a large part of the attraction is the sheer quality and vigour of the animation itself' (1991:16). Supervised with great care and expense by the comic's creator Otomo himself, *Akira* creates a future world as densely and grittily realized as the surreally bleak milieus of such Western live action SF films as *Blade Runner* (1982), *Total Recall* (1990) or *Alien* (1979). *Akira* also shares with these films a dark, hard edged visual vocabulary, indicating its membership in what Constance Penley calls Tech Noir, (1989a:122) a paradoxical genre that excoriates technology at the same times as its sophisticated special effects are implicit celebrations of technological achievement. The glossily dark surfaces of tech noir films both underline the overwhelming grimness of the visions presented, as well as create a visual style or 'world' that is as important a part of their appeal as their narrative content.

The bleak grandeur of *Akira*'s 'world' is breathtaking. Its vision of 'Neo Tokyo' combines an extrapolation of present day Shinjuku's futuristic urban skyline with the overwhelming scale of Fritz Lang's *Metropolis*. 'Neo Tokyo', in turn, is contrasted with glimpses of the immense and dark wasteland of the crater that was 'Old Tokyo'. It is this forbidding combination of dystopia and apocalypse, the inhuman immensity of the city with the equally inhuman catastrophe of the crater, that are the two central images with which both film and comic serial begin, and which underlie the entire work.

In between these forbidding images runs the gamut of life in

'Neo Tokyo', a society which, true to what Penley calls the 'critical dystopia' (1989b:188) is clearly far more of a defamiliarization of present Japanese society than a sustained extrapolation into the future. Otomo's vision thus highlights and extends some of the most obvious problems of contemporary Japan: the aimlessness of youth, especially outsiders such as motor bikers, the repression of resistance in both schools and the work place, and the increasing power of the new religions.

Although this omnipresent dystopian background is a vital element in *Akira*, what makes the film unusually interesting and lifts it beyond the category of the typical disaster movie, is the fascinating and complex narrative it foregrounds. As Tony Rayns says, '*Akira* is very probably the first animated feature with a genuinely novelistic density of incident and character' (1991:66). To summarize as briefly as possible: both film and comic focus primarily on an outlaw group of young bikers, led by two former orphan asylum inmates, Kaneda and Tetsuo, who become involved with both the resistance movement and a group of telekinetic mutants. Their involvement begins in an extraordinary early scene when Kaneda and Tetsuo, escaping a rival gang at the crater of 'Old Tokyo', encounter a bizarre looking creature with the body of a boy but the grotesquely wizened face of an old man.

The creature is, in fact, a boy, but one whose childhood was frozen in the 1980s as the result of a series of experiments which turned him into a telekinetic mutant, possessing great psychic powers but remaining mentally a child. The child is part of a group of mutants, the most powerful of whom is the mysterious *Akira*. It was experiments with *Akira*, the viewer (or reader) learns, which led to the nuclear destruction of Tokyo and ultimately to World War III.

Kaneda and Tetsuo are both drawn into the strange world of the mutants for ultimately antagonistic reasons: Kaneda, who is perhaps the closest thing to a conventional hero that the work possesses, becomes attached to Kei, a female resistance fighter who is attempting to rescue the mutants from the government, especially from the control of a man known only as the Colonel. Kaneda's interest in Kei is purely physical rather than political, and the reader/viewer never learns what the resistance specifically hopes to accomplish through revolution.

Tetsuo's fate is far more bizarre. His initial encounter with the mutants stirs up his own incipient telekenetic powers, leading him to a series of strange and graphic metamorphoses as his new powers begin to take control of him. His actions become increasingly destructive and increasingly uncontrollable, even though what appears to be the entire military-industrial complex of Japan is eventually called in to stop him. At the film's climax, he and his former friend Kaneda engage in an apocalyptic duel on the site of the old Olympic stadium in Yoyogi, a site where, ironically, a future Tokyo Olympics is planned to be held. In this duel, Tetsuo mutates back and forth between human and inhuman in a series of what must be some of the most spectacular special metamorphoses since the last few minutes of Stanley Kubrick's *2001*.

As does the Kubrick film, *Akira* ends with a beginning. Tetsuo ultimately mutates into a new being, perhaps even a new universe. The film ends with the new creation intoning the threatening words 'I am Tetsuo'.

Tetsuo is not the only threatening creature in *Akira*, however. The whole world of the film is a threatening one. From the corrupt politicians and the ominous Colonel, to the brutal teachers at the school the bikers occasionally attend, the film is notable for its lack of sympathetic characters. Unlike traditional disaster films, both in Japan and the West, *Akira* offers no moral center or even a positive alternative. Science, seen as responsible for the mutants and for World War III, appears capable only of evil while the resistance's opposition is totally uncharacterized. Even Kaneda, whose main virtue seems to lie in his bravery and deeply held gang loyalties, is only marginally more positive than anyone else.

Akira's nihilism has much in common with contemporary American films which can be classified as part of the post modern genre. These films, which include the previously mentioned Tech Noir science fiction works, or such surreal visions as David Lynch's *Wild at Heart*, have in common a fast-paced episodic narrative structure often organized around scenes of intense violence, a fascination with arresting imagery over character development, and an almost total lack of a moral center. Both narrative structure and content therefore seem to celebrate the 'constancy of uncertainty' (1989:19) that Tetsuo Najita suggests is central to the post modern experience. Or as Arthur Kroker puts it, these films 'are panic sites, just for the fun of it' (1986: 279).

Indeed *Akira*, with its visceral excitement and frenzied pace is fun at the same time as it is provocative and perhaps disturbing. In some ways the film fits into what Andrew Tudor calls the genre of 'paranoid horror', in which danger comes not from outside in the form of alien invaders (as in *Godzilla*, for example), but from one's friends, family or even oneself. As Tudor describes it, 'gone is the sense of an established social and moral order which is both worth defending and capable of defence. Gone too is the assumption that there are legitimate authorities who can demand our cooperation in exchange for their protection' (1989:22). *Akira*'s attitude toward the established order is an overtly negative one. Furthermore, the mutants and their problematic relationship with the government can be seen as exemplifying the alien within the heart of a collectivity that is itself monstrous, as is usually the case with the paranoid horror genre.

But the final impression that the audience is likely to carry away from the film is less one of horror than of exhilaration. This sense of exhilaration has to do with the ambivalent attitude toward the monstrous and towards power in general embedded in *Akira*'s subtext. The film is both a subversion of traditional power and authority and a celebration of a new kind of power, one that is linked to the issue of identity, in the form of Tetsuo's astonishing metamorphoses.[9] Unlike the traditional fixed identities that the Colonel and the politicians embody, Tetsuo's mutations epitomize the 'subject [which] has disintegrated into a flux of euphoric intensities, fragmented and disconnected' (1992:144), as Kellner summarizes the conventional view of postmodern identity.

Or, as Brent Easton Ellis says of pop singer Madonna's continuous image changes, '[her] talent lies in her willingness to transform herself and change images rapidly which seems to reflect [her] generation's conflicting interests and visions' (1990:37). At the same time, as Kellner goes on to make clear, and as Madonna's appeal exemplifies, even this fluctuating identity is still an identity, an image to be admired, even imitated. Whether Tetsuo is likely to become the next Madonna is unlikely, but it is interesting that the year after *Akira*'s release, a young film maker, Tsukamoto Shin'ya, created a critically acclaimed avant-garde film called *Tetsuo*, which he admitted was an explicit homage to *Akira*'s Tetsuo. Tsukamoto's *Tetsuo*, however, is even bleaker than *Akira*. Through an extraordinary series of grotesque, even hideous, visual images, it limns a world in which human beings turn into machines. These transformation are partly puns on the film's title, since 'Tetsuo' can also mean 'Iron Man' but they also link back to Tetsuo's metamorphoses in *Akira*. What sort of character, then, is Tetsuo?

Certainly he is not a conventionally attractive hero. His sullen, angst ridden personality is no doubt due to his having been abandoned initially by his parents to the orphanage asylum and subsequently abandoned by society to the restless existence of the biker, but it is still hard to summon much sympathy for him. As an exemplification of an outcast, he seems to exist initially as a negativity, a more sinister version of his friend, the gang leader Kaneda. It is only through his mutations and his growing arrogation of telekinetic powers that Tetsuo becomes alive to the viewer but, even then, his transformed character evokes awe rather than sympathy.

I would suggest, therefore, that Tetsuo's attraction is due to the fascination and exhilaration of his not quite controllable powers and that this attraction is to some extent generationally based: the inarticulate Tetsuo is hardly a spokesman for a generation, but he is in some ways an image of and for the younger generation of Japanese. This twentysomething generation, as the Japanese media are happy to remind us, is very different from their conservative, corporate culture parents, different enough to be given their own appellation, the so-called *shinjinrui*, or 'new beings'. How many younger Japanese actually endorse all the values of the shinjinrui is of course open to question, but there is no argument at least that there is a strong contrast between a generation that still remembers the war and hardship and a new generation that has been accustomed to a peaceful, successful Japan.

Akira's creator, Otomo, was born in 1955 and is thus no longer a member of the 'twentysomething' generation, but the audience to which *Akira* speaks and which has made it such a consistent bestseller since the comic serial's inception in 1983 is very much part of the shinjinrui, and they are only now beginning to find their own identity and own powers in contrast to the war scarred generation before them. Of course, relatively few of the younger generation Japanese subscribe to the kind of deviant behaviour that Tetsuo and his friends engage in (although antisocial trends such as bullying and delinquency have been rising), but, perhaps because Japanese society is still so inherently safe, Tetsuo's monstrousness may seem all the more appealing.[10]

Tetsuo's metamorphoses speak to the rise of a new generation that is only beginning to exercise its powers. Cutting back and forth between human and inhuman, simultaneously revelling in and rejecting his new found potential, he is both terrifying and pathetic, an adolescent unable to cope with the new powers suddenly thrust upon him. In fact, Tetsuo's mutations both encompass and go beyond the specific cultural aspects of the shinjinrui, becoming reminiscent of what Allucquere Rosanne Stone finds in contemporary American works related to 'Cyperspace', the non-physical realm of the computer where the subject loses its corporeality entirely. Or as Stone puts it, 'the discourse of virtual world builders is rife with images of imaginal bodies, freed from the constraints that the flesh imposes' (1992:113). The 'virtual world builders' Stone has in mind include George Lucas, the producer and director of Star Wars, and Douglas Trumbull, creator of special effects for *Blade Runner*, but her description could also be applied to Otomo Katsuhiro and his brilliant work in *Akira*.

The implicit connection with 'Cyperspace' is also interesting when one remembers that a large part of the audience for works dealing with Cyperspace consists of adolescent males, as does a majority of the audience for science fiction. As Stone describes it, (a fascination with) 'the experience of unlimited power' leads to the 'engagement of the adolescent male within humans of both sexes' (1992:108). Boundary crossing, another aspect of Cyberspace, and one that is well represented in Tetsuo's mutations, is another important concern of adolescence. Tetsuo's mutations can thus be seen as a metaphor for the universal changes undergone in adolescence.

The relationship with adolescence and the struggle for maturity is further underlined by the fact that Tetsuo's mutations are connected to his telekinetic powers. Freud has pointed out in *Totem and Taboo* that a belief in what he calls 'the omnipotence of thought' (1983:85) is characteristic of the phallic or exploratory stage, as the infant begins to explore his own identity vis-à-vis the world. Tetsuo's quest can be seen in overtly phallic terms, in fact, for at the beginning of his transformation he loses an arm, a displaced signifier of the phallus. Telekinetically he grows a new 'arm' and it is with this that his first mutations occur. The mutating arm, growing more grotesque with each mutation, becomes a symbol of Tetsuo's increasingly uncontrollable power.

Tetsuo's loss is interesting to compare with Luke Skywalker's loss of an arm in a fight with his father, Darth Vader, in *The Empire Strikes Back*, another science fiction cinematic exploration of adolescence. Like *Akira*, the *Star Wars* series also privileges telekinetic powers, an example of their shared grounding in adolescent fantasy. Or, as Rabkin puts it, 'formula telepath stories deal with common Oedipal anxieties, validating the reader's sense of uniqueness and his desire to change the world' (1987:92).

Of course, in the *Star Wars* series the initial sense of uniqueness is rapidly transformed into a sense of belonging. Luke's arm is promptly replaced by one that looks just the same, and he is warmly welcomed back into the collective fold, thus obviating any issues of difference before they can even arise. In Tetsuo's case however, his mutated arm grows only bigger and more grotesque, seeming to take on a life of its own, leading him to ever increasing isolation, even from his oldest friend. This isolation is exemplified in his final declaration of separateness, 'I am Tetsuo'.

Tetsuo's anguished transformations and his sense of outsiderhood are typical manifestations of adolescent angst, but they are also interesting in their inherent critique of Japanese society. Although Japanese culture celebrates the collective, it has long held a place for the outsider, from the haiku poet or the masterless samurai, to the endlessly popular image of the troubled adolescent James Dean. But Tetsuo and his friends are not outsiders by choice. They are literally orphans, rejected by society from childhood on, their only experience of collective bonding being the gang loyalties of the motorcycle group. Most nihilistic of all, the collectivity that has rejected them, the fragmented, nightmare world of 'Neo Tokyo', is itself utterly unappealing.

Akira's privileging of these desperate outcasts thus becomes an even sharper critique of the dystopian center. By contrast to the government and the educational system, the motorcycle gang, and the ragtag resistance movement, perhaps even the grotesque little group of mutants, seems almost welcoming by comparison. Indeed the movie's highlighting of telekinetic mutants is particularly interesting in terms of a cultural critique.[11] Because the mutants were initially normal children and thus should have been members in good standing of the still extant collectivity of 1988, their fate is even more tragic than that of Tetsuo and Kaneda. Frozen in childhood and taken care of by a government that is only interested in making use of their bizarre powers, they are both insider and outsider, both exploited and feared. They are, after all, indirectly responsible for World War III, that erasure of history in 1988, as well as exemplifying it by their own frozen, infantile development.

On a subliminal level the mutants are perhaps more insidiously threatening than the forlorn gang of bikers could ever be. This is signified first in their grotesque appearance, a combination of childlike and elderly that is one of both film's and comic's most disturbing visual images, and secondly through the concrete threat of their frightening telekinetic powers. Indeed, a scene involving a mutant attack on the still human Tetsuo is perhaps the most terrifying of the entire film.

In this scene, Tetsuo, who is just beginning to sense his new powers, lies on a hospital bed surrounded by a variety of children's toys, a bear, a doll and a truck. Gradually, a childish chanting sound becomes audible and the cozy looking toys begin to assume gigantic proportions. The singing reaches a crescendo as the toys converge on Tetsuo in a savage and eerie attack, but he wards them off and flees down the corridor only to keep encountering them, like ubiquitous ghosts.

The 'toys' are actually representatives, both literally and figuratively, of the mutant children, but their manifest narrative function is less terrifying than their subliminal one. To any older viewer, the attack of the cute (*kawaii*) toys beloved of young Japanese even, in the case of girls, into adolescence and beyond, suggests a potential arrogation of power by 'children', by a generation very different from the one currently in control.

Akira's insistence on the youth of both mutants and bikers is in interesting contrast to such American dystopian films as *Blade Runner* or *Alien* in which the psychological conflict occurs between adult outsiders and corporate insiders. Thus the 'hero' of *Blade Runner* is a fortyish detective while the 'hero' of *Alien* is a woman in her thirties. The emphasis on the protagonist's youth in *Akira* underlines, I believe, the specific Japanese generational tensions embodied in the film.[12]

This youthful emphasis is also intriguing in comparison with the upbeat *Star Wars* series. As previously mentioned, there too a youthful protagonist goes through an Oedipal struggle but, in the case of *Star Wars*, the older generation is by no means totally negative. Luke in fact, is helped on his development by not one but two older mentor figures, both of whom are presented completely positively.

In significant contrast, *Akira* is notable for the brutality of its authority figures such as the Colonel, the teachers at the boys' school, or the scientists whose implied cruelty is shown in their willingness to experiment on children. Tetsuo is not even allowed the Oedipal catharsis of fighting his father. As several scenes in the movie make clear, he has no positive memories of family life at all, nor are there any traditional families presented in the film.

The absent or inadequate father has long been a theme in Japanese literature from the Meiji period onwards.[13] It is also a vital theme in 'high culture' Japanese films, such as Kurosawa's 1952 *Ikiru*, whose famous flashback sequence, Satō Tadao states, 'underlines the sudden postwar collapse of paternal authority' (1982:117). Even more obvious are the works of Ozu Yasujirō, the majority of whose films, as Richie states, 'are about the dissolution of the family' (1974:5). Of course, it should be noted that in these earlier films, the point of view is usually that of the father, and the family structure is still taken as the given point of departure.

In the case of *Akira*, however, unlike their high culture counterparts, Tetsuo and Kaneda do not even seem aware of a need for a father and a mother. They deny the past as having any importance, preferring instead to build their own pathetic collectivity in the present. Ultimately, Tetsuo rejects this collectivity as well, as he revels in his new powers and turns on his old friends. Furthermore, at the film's climax, Tetsuo becomes his own father and mother; he creates himself.[14]

In its thorough-going denial or even erasure of the past and of the established order of the collectivity *Akira* is also a major change from the popular culture films previously discussed. If old Japan was a battered female victim in *Japan Sinks*, in *Akira* the remnants of the collectivity exist mainly as a group of corrupt and brutal male authority figures, existing only to be resisted. The fully sexual or maternal female is notably absent in *Akira*. There is no leavening softness in the film, no glimpse of any superior alternative or comforting escape. Indeed, aside from the rather asexual Kei, the only really important female presence in *Akira* is the menacing Lady Miyako who aligns with the male authority figure as another powerful and enigmatic leader, this time of a new religion. It is possible, perhaps, to find a female presence in the womblike architecture of the underground beneath New Tokyo where much of the film's fighting and chase scenes occur, but this too is a menacing rather than comforting presence.[15]

Architecture also exemplifies the rejection of the past, most obviously in the final climactic battle between Kaneda and Tetsuo. Taking place over the Yoyogi Olympic stadium, it becomes a clear reference to the generation before the shinjinrui, the generation which built the Olympic stadium as a proud symbol of the new

Japan. But, as Tetsuo rips the stadium apart, there is no sense of elegiac loss. Instead, the viewer responds with visceral excitement. This is indeed disaster 'for the fun of it'. For those viewers/readers who care about the past, however, this orgy of destruction can be highly disturbing.

It should be mentioned that *Akira* shares its vision of a bleakly dystopian future with a number of other popular texts. Although more conventionally upbeat SF narratives do exist, such as the popular *Gundam* series about space wars in the next century, other recent Japanese manga are notably dark. For example, Miyazaki Hayao's *Nausicaa*, another extremely popular series, is set in a dystopian future world where Earth's ecology has almost completely disintegrated, leaving the air virtually unbreathable and the land unworkable, except for a few scattered kingdoms left along the margins of the poisonous 'Sea of Corruption'. *Nausicaa*, does contain, however, a protagonist in the traditional heroic mode – a young girl, interestingly.[16] There is also at least a suggestion of a pastoral utopia in the peaceful and beautiful kingdom which she inhabits.

Totally bleak, without even the contrast of a peaceful kingdom that *Nausicaa* offers, is Tagami Yoshihisa's aptly named comic, *Grey*. This is a surpassingly dystopian work, set in a post-Apocalypse world in which computers have decided to 'help' humanity accomplish what appears to be its primary goal, its own destruction. The story's focus on menacing computers contains echoes of the American *Terminator* movies, but the Japanese comic has no pretensions to *Terminator* and its sequel's cautiously upbeat ending. Instead, its eponymous protagonist (whose other name is Death), engages in continuous bloody battles against men and machines, only to find that his final hope, to disable the supercomputer known as Big Mama, is a futile one.

Nausicaa and *Grey* both resemble *Akira* in their mutual visions of a relentlessly grim, oppressively violent future, but they also differ from *Akira* in two important respects. The first is what might be called their ideological subtext. Although the futures they envision can be called nihilistic, both works clearly present these futures as warnings. In this regard they are closer to the traditional dystopian classics such as *1984* and *Brave New World* whose aim, like their utopian opposites, was at least partly didactic: to 'teach' or at least warn their readers of the dangerous trends in contemporary society by presenting the development of these trends in a frightening but plausible future. The attitudes towards these grim futures are unambiguously negative in all these works. In *Akira*, by contrast, although it certainly satirizes some of modern Japan's most egregiously ominous trends, the sheer narrative and visual excitement tends to work against any overtly didactic message.

And yet, underneath its exhilarating postmodern surface, there may be a more subliminal 'message' in *Akira*. This message relates not only to generations within Japan but to Japan's vision of itself vis-à-vis the rest of the world. Indeed, as Douglas Kellner argues, 'the images of popular culture are also saturated with ideology' (1992:157). In the case of *Akira*, this ideology is intimately related to Japan's conception of its own identity.

Not only the generations, but the external circumstances of Japan and the world in general, have changed radically since the 1973 of *Japan Sinks*. It is in fact possible to extend our reading of *Akira* beyond its being a symbol of the new generation, to suggest that it expresses certain aspects of Japan as whole in the 1980s, a Japan whose new powers vis a vis a decaying outside world were beginning to forge a new identity for it.

In this reading, the issue of the outsider can now be seen in global terms. Masao Miyoshi and H.D. Harootunian have said that 'Japan's history is suffused with the sense of the dominant Other and its own marginality' (1989:xi), but in the 1980s the presence of a dominant Other became more ambiguous as Japan began increasingly to assert itself internationally. With this assertion came an upsurge in international hostility, and Japan began to feel itself increasingly alienated from the other great powers, especially its former protector, the United States. In the eyes of many Japanese, the United States seemed to be showing a more unappreciative, indeed jealous, attitude towards Japan's new strength. There is perhaps a foretaste of this in the previously mentioned scene in *Japan Sinks* when the Australian government officials look lasciviously at the statue of Kannon.

Japan Sinks not only anticipates Japan's outsiderhood, but privileges the country's uniqueness in its emphasis on the awesome energy that is bringing Japan to disaster. A certain melancholy pride reveals itself when the scientists speak about the immense energy going on beneath the surface of Japan, as if this unique power were somehow a positive cultural attribute.

The power that wrecks Japan in *Japan Sinks* is an almost monstrous one, one that is perhaps not so different from the energy released by Tetsuo's grotesque mutations. Like the submerging

Japan, Tetsuo is uniquely powerful and ultimately alien, even monstrous. In connection with this, it is interesting to note that the Japanese have to some extent held a love-hate attitude toward monsters in the postwar period starting with *Godzilla* himself. *Godzilla* began as the ultimate alien who, as the series continued, became a friend to Japan, an insider, 'one of us'.

Japan's sense of its uniqueness/monsterhood was no doubt compounded by the favorite epithet turned toward it in the 1960s, that of 'economic animal'. The Japanese populace took this up almost obsessively. Even more significantly, the 'animal' of the 1960s has turned into a 'terminator' in the 1980s and 1990s. A 1992 issue of *Newsweek*, for example, contains an article about resurgent Japanese competitiveness which includes a quotation describing the Japanese as the 'economic terminators of America's imaginings'. Although the article suggests that this description is inadequate, an accompanying photograph of two Japanese technicians holding a silicon wafer is captioned 'Economic terminators of the future' (Powell 1992:48).

If Japan's extraordinary successes have made it all the more monstrous to the outside world in the 1980's and 1990s, *Akira* suggests that this identity is carried now more with pride than shame. Just as Tetsuo no longer needs a father and mother, Japan no longer needs its American 'parent'. Thus, Tetsuo's no-holds-barred display of power is ultimately both frightening and exciting, suggesting both a new Japan and a new world.

In the final analysis, however, it is likely that *Akira* will be remembered less for any implicit ideological message than for this sense of excitement that it evokes in its audience. In its refusal to offer obvious heroes, its absorbtion in dizzying narrative change and overwhelming visual imagery, *Akira* offered a new world to its viewers, one that marked a change both in Japanese films but also in Western cinema as well. By comparison to *Akira*'s open-ended nihilism, the resolutely upbeat closures of such films as *Blade Runner* and *Terminator* seem almost old-fashioned.

In conclusion, we might return to the image of the continuum of disaster, on which *Akira* is the final point. In generic terms, *Akira* is in many ways an enormous leap forward from the earlier, far more conventional, disaster movies, *Godzilla* and *Japan Sinks*. *Godzilla* traced an arc of destruction that was both limited and finally contained by a secure collectivity. *Japan Sinks* privileges what might be called elegiac destruction; the destruction of Japan which it describe was total but the country survived in memory, cultural artifacts, and history. *Akira* simply privileges what David Harvey calls 'creative destruction' (1990:309) in general. The movie is a roller coaster ride of panic sights, which can be either exhilarating or disturbing but are never reassuring.

Out of *Akira*'s orgy of destruction arises a new world, but this too is not reassuring. Indeed, the film's postmodern refusal of traditional narrative closure, combined with the insistent absence of traditional Japanese culture, brings us back to one of the central questions of this chapter: the role of history in modern Japanese society. *Akira*'s narrative indicates that Japan has gone a long way in the almost four decades from the first *Godzilla* films, from victim of powerful outside forces, to becoming a powerful force in its own right. At the same time, the absence of any sort of past, be it architecturally or generationally, in the film, suggests that Japan has achieved this status through writing off its own history. The battered Tokyo that could still be repaired in *Godzilla* and became a positive collectively enshrined memory in *Japan Sinks*, has become an enormous empty crater in *Akira*.

This absence of history is a trend that is not only confined to popular culture. Modern Japanese literature also seems increasingly indifferent to history.[17] Its most obvious expression is perhaps Murakami Haruki's popular 1985 novel *Hard Boiled Wonderland and the End of the World* (Sekai no Owari to Hādo Boirudo Wandarando) whose protagonist chooses to abandon the real world for a dreamlike utopia, the chief element of which is the absence of 'shadows' or memories.

In contrast, *Godzilla* and *Japan Sinks* are haunted either overtly or implicitly by shadows of the Japanese past. The youthful protagonists of *Akira*, however, seem to have escaped the past entirely. Or have they? There may be a hint in their frantic motorcycle chases and endless mutations that they are still attempting to get away from history, or at least to transcend it.[18] Furthermore, the film's very first chase scene ends at the immense yawning crater of 'Old Tokyo', a reminder perhaps that history is not always so easy to abandon.

Notes

1 The fans have also inspired the Japanese studios. For example, *Tokyo Journal* reports that in the first six months of 1988 sixteen of the 35

films released by the three major studios, (Tōhō, Tōei and Shōchiku), were 'animated or live action features based on comics' (Bailey 1988:9).

2 See Krishan Kumar's *Utopia and Anti-Utopia in the Twentieth Century* (1987).

3 For a discussion of the development of science fiction in modern Japan, see Robert Matthew, *Japanese Science Fiction: a view of a changing society* (1989). For an overview of postwar Japanese science fiction, see Elizabeth Anne Hull and Mark Siegel, 'Science Fiction'.

4 It is possible to speculate that the very nature of the science fiction genre, one which is strongly concerned with larger than life special effects, leads to an aesthetic concentration on disaster. Certainly, science fiction films in the West as well contain their fair share of violence and chaos. At the same time, however, I would submit that Western science fiction is on the whole less nihilistic than its Japanese counterpart. In the 1970s, for example, the decade when *Japan Sinks* became an enormous domestic hit, American studios were issuing such upbeat science fiction films as George Lucas' *Star Wars* or Steven Spielberg's *Close Encounters of the Third Kind*.

5 The threat and the devastation of nuclear holocaust were also, of course, treated in many 'serious' films of the 1950s as well, such as Kurosawa's *Record of a Living Being* (Ikimono no kiroku, 1955) about an elderly man's obsession with the atom bomb.

6 For more on the New Wave and the historical events surrounding it, see David Desser, *Eros Plus Massacre: an introduction to the Japanese New Wave cinema* (1988).

7 Obviously, not all Japanese felt such insecurities about their national identity, although the suicide of the writer Mishima Yukio three years earlier may also be seen, in some respects, as a lament for a lost Japan. Other Japanese were frankly repelled by what seemed to be the virtually prewar sentiments that appeared in the book, although they are less obvious in the movie. In fact, Komatsu is hardly a nationalist in the sense that Mishima was. His attitude toward Japan is, however, decidedly 'romantic' as Yamamoto Akira describes it (1975:191–196). This romanticism is an attitude clearly shared by a large number of the Japanese reading and viewing public of the period.

8 In a bit of nihilistic humour, the day of the destruction of Tokyo in *Akira* was the same day as the film's premiere in Japan! I am indebted to Tony Rayns for pointing this out.

9 In a discussion of the animated television hero 'Ultraman' in relation to the Japanese attitude towards power, Elizabeth Anne Hull and Mark Siegel suggest that in Japan 'power should be respected, even if it is alien, and, if possible, coopted for the benefit of Japan' (1989:261). While this assertion is perhaps a little problematic in its breadth (certainly many aspects of American culture also seem to respect power), it certainly appears to apply to many of the films mentioned in this chapter.

10 My assertion as to the paradoxical appeal of Tetsuo and the other bikers is supported in Ikuya Sato's fascinating *Kamikaze Biker: parody*

and anomy in affluent Japan, a study of Japan's *bōsōzoku*, or 'violent drivers', gangs of young men on motorcycles who congregate in Japan's urban centers, in much the same way as do Tetsuo and Kaneda. Sato's study suggests that the average Japanese is fascinated by the bōsōzoku, not only because of their threat of incipient violence towards the social order but also because their behaviour and attitudes can be seen as a kind of cathartic form of 'play'. In other words, the bōsōzoku and *Akira* can be seen as related postmodern elements in contemporary Japanese culture.

11 Interestingly, works concerning telekinesis and telepathy in general surged in popularity throughout the 1980s in Japan, from children's comics and stories such as *Mai the Psychic Girl* to Tsutsui Yasutaka's satirical adult fantasy *Kazoku Hakkei* (Eight Views of Families, translated into English as *What the Maid Saw*). American popular culture also includes its share of telekinetic adolescents and children, some of which have been transferred to film. Most notable of these have been the films *Carrie* and *The Shining*, both based on Stephen King novels. *Carrie* in particular is reminiscent of *Akira* in that it too may be seen as an adolescent revenge fantasy in which the heroine uses her telekinetic powers to 'get back' at the world. Compared to Tetsuo, however, Carrie's revenge is relatively small scale, being confined to her family and high school. Furthermore, and in common with the tradition in American horror films of ultimately reinforcing the values of the collectivity, Carrie's rampage is ultimately stopped. Although the film's last scene contains the suggestion of her return from the grave, this turns out to be only a bad dream.

12 The only recent Western tech noir film that privileges youth of which I am aware is James Cameron's *Terminator II: judgment day*. Eerily, both *Akira* and *Terminator II* start with their youthful protagonists riding motorbikes and generally behaving in markedly anti-social behavior. In fascinating contrast, however, *Terminator* shows certain adults, such as the Terminator and the boy protagonist's mother, in an overwhelmingly positive light. Indeed, it is not too much to say that the entire subtext of the film concerns the search for an (adequate) father figure and the recovery of a loving mother. In comparison, *Akira*'s nihilistic vision rejects both the memory and the hope of positive parental figures.

13 For a discussion of the absent father in postwar Japanese literature, see my *Escape from the Wasteland: romanticism and realism in Mishima Yukio and Ōe Kenzaburo* (1991), p. 15–25 passim.

14 Tetsuo's self-generation after a series of metamorphoses is interesting to compare with the aforementioned Stanley Kubrick film *2001: a space odyssey*. As in that film, Tetsuo achieves an awesome new identity after a series of startling metamorphoses but with the important difference that there are no all powerful aliens behind the scenes to help him along. Once again, as with *Terminator*, the American film suggests a far greater willingness to trust in some ultimate authority figure, an intriguing difference, given the traditional stereotype of the Japanese respect for authority.

15 The absence of females in *Akira* is echoed in another comic series *Grey*. Although *Grey*'s narrative action is initially set off by the murder of Grey Death's girlfriend, there are virtually no female characters in the text itself. To some extent the absence of female characters is understandable in terms of the conventions of the action SF genre, but it is at least provocative that the computer with which Grey does battle is nicknamed 'Big Mama'. Incidentally, *Grey* also contains its share of evil aged male authority figures in the form of the 'directors' of the few remaining towns who are revealed to have been responsible for Big Mama's creation in the first place.

16 Even more interestingly, the 1980s science fiction and manga gave birth to a number of young female heroes such as 'Mai, the Psychic Girl', the space adventuring 'Dirty Pair', and the occult heroine 'Vampire Princess Miyu'. This trend may partly reflect an increased female readership, but it is also possible to see it as suggestive of a new sense of empowerment among young female readers.

17 Perhaps the most explicit statement of this rejection of history in modern Japanese literature comes at the conclusion of Mishima Yukio's *Sea of Fertility* tetralogy. In the last pages of *The Decay of the Angel* (Tennin Gosui, 1970), the protagonist enters a garden without memories to discover that his entire life, which coincides almost exactly with the span of Japanese history in the twentieth century, has either been a dream or a lie. For a discussion of Murakami and Mishima in relation to history, see Masao Miyoshi (1991:234–35). One might also mention that Japan's Ministry of Education has also occasionally 'erased' certain historical incidents in its textbooks concerning Japan's actions during the Second World War.

18 Although most of the Japanese criticisms of *Akira* that I have seen tend to emphasize its links with the future, one critic, Kamata Tōji, has attempted to relate the mysterious character of *Akira* himself to Wakanomiya, the god of the Kasuga Shrine in Kyoto (1988:54–67). Lacking expertise on Japanese religion, I am unable to say how exact the parallels are, but it is possible to see in the comic strip, at least, certain links with Japan's religious past.

References

Bailey, James 1988 'Lifting the lid on Japanese movies', p. 8–9 in *Tokyo Journal* 8.

Desser, David 1988 *Eros Plus Massacre: an introduction to the Japanese New Wave cinema*, Bloomington: Indiana University Press.

Ellis, Brent Easton 1990 'The twentysomethings: Adrift in a Pop Landscape', p. 37 in *The New York Times Book Review*, December 2.

Freud, Sigmund 1983 *Totem and Taboo*, London: Routledge and Kegan Paul.

Harvey, David 1990 *The Condition of Postmodernity*, Oxford: Basil Blackwell Publishers.

Hull, Elizabeth Anne and Siegel, Mark 1989 'Science fiction', p. 243–274 in

R. Powers and H. Kato (eds.) *Handbook of Japanese Popular Culture*, New York: Greenwood Press.

Jameson, Fredric 1982 'Progress versus utopia, or, can we imagine the future?' in *Science Fiction Studies* 9.

Jameson, Fredric 1991 *Postmodernism, or the Cultural Logic of Late Capitalism*, Durham: Duke University Press.

Kellner, Douglas 1992 'Postmodern culture and the construction of postmodern identities', p. 141–147 in S. Lash and J. Friedman (eds.) *Modernity and Identity*, Oxford: Blackwell Publishers.

Komata Tōji 1988 '"Nagare" to "chikara" no hate ni: yōdōkami *Akira* no tanjō' (At the extremity of "current" and "strength": the birth of the child-god *Akira*), p. 54–67 in *Yurika* 20 (10).

Komatsu Sakyō 1983 *Nippon Chinbotsu* (Japan Sinks), Tokyo: Tokuma Bunko.

Kroker, Arthur and Cook, David 1986 *The Postmodern Scene: excremental culture and hyper-aesthetics*, New York: St. Martin's Press.

Kumar, Krishan 1987 *Utopia and Anti-Utopia in the Twentieth Century*, Oxford: Basil Blackwell Publishers.

Matthew, Robert 1989 *Japanese Science Fiction: a view of a changing society*, Oxford: The Nissan Institute/Routledge Japanese Studies Series.

Miyoshi, Masao 1991 *Off-Center: power and culture relations between Japan and the United States*, Cambridge, MA.: Harvard University Press.

Miyoshi, Masao and Harootunian, H.D. 1989 'Introduction', p. vii–xix in Miyoshi and Harootunian (eds.) *Postmodernism and Japan*, Durham: Duke University Press.

Mishima Yukio 1977 *Tennin Gosui* (The Decay of the Angel) Tokyo: Shinchōsha.

Miyazaki Hayao 1990 *Kaze no Tani no Nausicaa* (Nausicaa of the Valley of Wind), Tokyo: Tokuma Shoten.

Murakami Haruki 1985 *Sekai no Owari to Hādoboirudo Wondarando* (The End of the World and the Hardboiled Wonderland), Tokyo: Shinchōsha.

Najita, Tetsuo 1989 'On culture and technology in modern Japan', p. 3–20 in M. Miyoshi and H.D. Harootunian (eds.) *Postmodernism and Japan*, Durham: Duke University Press.

Napier, Susan 1991 *Escape from the Wasteland: romanticism and realism in Mishima Yukio and Ōe Kenzaburo*, Cambridge, MA.: Harvard University Yenching Monograph Series.

Penley, Constance 1989a *The Future of an Illusion: film, feminism and psychoanalysis*, London: Routledge Press.

—— 1989b 'Time travel, primal scene and the critical dystopia', p. 197–212 in J. Donald (ed.) *Fantasy and Cinema*, London: The British Film Institute.

Powell, Bill 1992 'Don't write off Japan', p. 48 in *Newsweek* 919.

Rabkin, Eric 1987 'Cowboys and telepaths/formulas and phenomena', p. 88–101 in G.Slusser and E. Rabkin (eds.) *Aliens: the anthropology of science fiction*, Carbondale: Southern Illinois University Press.

Rayns, Tony 1991a '*Akira*', p. 66–67 in *Monthly Film Bulletin* 58 (686).

—— 1991b 'Apocalypse nous', p. 16 in *Time Out*, January 16.

Richie, Donald 1990 *Japanese Cinema: an introduction*, New York: Oxford University Press.

—— 1974 *Ozu*, Berkeley: University of California Press.

Sato, Ikuya 1991 *Kamikaze Biker: parody and anomy in affluent Japan*, Chicago: University of Chicago Press.

Satō Tadao 1982 *Currents in Japanese Cinema*, Tokyo: Kodansha International.

Sontag, Susan 1985 'The imagination of disaster', p. 451–65 in G. Mast and M. Cohen (eds.) *Film Theory and Criticism*, New York: Oxford University Press.

Stone, Allucquere Rosanne 1992 'Will the real body please stand up?: boundary stories about virtual cultures', p. 81–118 in M. Benedikt (ed.) *Cyberspace: first steps*, Cambridge, MA: MIT Press.

Tudor, Andrew 1989 *Monsters and Mad Scientists: a cultural history of the horror movie*, Oxford: Basil Blackwell Publishers.

Yamamoto *Akira* 1975 '*Nippon Chinbotsu* no imi' (The meaning of *Japan Sinks*), p. 191–96 in *Kokubungaku Kaishaku to Kyōzai no Kenkyū* 20 (4).

Part V

Popular Literature and Japan's Present

9

Murakami Haruki and Contemporary Japan

Aoki Tamotsu

Translator's Note

Best-selling novelist Murakami Haruki (born 1949) is problematic for Western scholarship on Japanese literature and mass culture. In Japan he is viewed as a so-called 'pure writer' (*junbungakusha*), roughly equivalent to what might be called a 'serious' author in the West. But in the United States Murakami has been billed almost from the beginning as a 'popular' writer. In part this is attributable to Murakami's style, in which the influences of Raymond Chandler, among others, are evident. But it is also proof of how, once borders are crossed, such categories can so easily change.

English-speaking audiences had their first taste of Murakami's work with *A Wild Sheep Chase* (Hitsuji o meguru bōken, 1982; English translation, 1989). There, Murakami began his experimentation with 'hard-boiled detective' fiction, a style of American literature which has fascinated him from early in his career, and remains a hallmark of his appeal even as his novels and satires are 'reexported'.

One of Murakami's trademarks is his manipulation of nostalgia. When, for instance, Murakami wishes to evoke the mood of the 1960s, he may draw upon the title of a song to bring the reader back to that time. Major Japanese critics have suggested that this technique points to an ironic view of history, for rather than evoke '1963' with a major historical event – for example, the Kennedy assassination – Murakami is apt to note it instead as the year 'The Girl From Ipanema' came out. In fact, Murakami often subverts the typically significant events of history in favor of observations drawn from the history of popular culture, typically American in character.

It is this salient conjuncture of a pop-cult past and a narrative present that cultural anthropologist Aoki Tamotsu interrogates in his essay presented here. Aoki, himself a member of Murakami's generation, is acutely aware of the tremendous influence exerted by American popular culture on Japanese youth in the 1960s. At the same time, he is at pains to demonstrate that the emergence of a youth culture based on two of the most prevalent American musical trends of the time – jazz and rock – created a cultural ideology which continues to inform the development of Japanese society through the period of 'rapid growth' in the 1970s and 1980s, and even to the contemporary moment.

Aoki analyzes the historical period in which Murakami writes, by examining the musical references found in Murakami's texts. He explores these pieces not merely as song titles, but as nostalgic triggers, tunes that play in the reader's mind to accompany the words on the page. Writes Aoki of one of Murakami's early pieces, 'the story works only if we manage to catch the faintly sad, nostalgic melody of Bacharach'. What emerges from his analysis is the idea that, beneath the 'sentimentality' of the Murakami text, there is a hard base of reality that examines the fatuousness of contemporary life against the backdrop of 1960s popular culture. For Aoki, then, catching the mood of the 1960s through musical references is ultimately the key to grasping the true significance of Murakami Haruki, as a chronicler not only of Japanese youth from the 1960s, but of the development and maturation of Japanese culture in the present day.

Matthew C. Strecher

* * *

Someone has said that Murakami Haruki only lightly irons his button-down cotton shirts before he puts them on. He must think that the secret to wearing shirts well – whether they are American Trad or Ivy – is to press them oneself. I do not know Murakami personally, so I have no way of knowing how his shirts look on him, but I can't help thinking that publicity like this must be great for selling his books. He may not have meant for it to be thus, but if there ever was good unintentional publicity, this is it.

In a similar way, Murakami's writing somehow attracts attention, seemingly without effort. Once you notice a work by him, you just have to read it. But there is always some process of selection at work here; somewhere, in the background, there is a reason behind our choice of what to read.

Consider, for instance, Murakami's recent collection of short stories, *A Slow Boat to China* (Chūgoku-yuki no Surō Bōto). Who can read a title like this without thinking of that old jazz favorite, 'Slow Boat to China'? It is one of those tunes that conjures up that sort of rootless nostalgia for the 'good old days' in America, or maybe in China – the kind of China that John Dewey knew, an image cherished by Americans at one time.

The title story concerns the protagonist's recollection of meeting three Chinese people, beginning with a Chinese primary school teacher in his seaside hometown when he was an elementary student. Next, he tells of his college days, and his acquaintance, through a part-time job, with a Chinese co-ed. Finally, he explains how he met the woman he would eventually marry. But only after re-reading this story did it finally dawn on me that the piece has nothing to do with Chinese people per se; they merely serve as milestones along the path taken by the protagonist from the 1960s to the 1980s. By the end of the story, we are left with nothing but this period of twenty years. And that is where the meaning lies. As the melody of 'Slow Boat to China' fades, an era is created, and for a little while we are reminded of our own journey down the same path. Among the many distinguishing features in Murakami fiction, his ability to awaken a historical moment for us is surely one of the most definitive.

In *The Kangaroo Condition* (Kangarū Biyori), yet another collection of short stories, one finds two works similar to those in *A Slow Boat to China*: '1963/1982 Girl from Ipanema' (1963/1982-nen no Ipanema Musume), and 'Are You Into Burt Bacharach?' (Bāto Bakarakku wa Osuki?). Although neither is a particularly striking story, the former centers on an exquisite Stan Getz album, and one can almost feel the *bossa nova* rhythm echoing through one. (It was, one recalls, thanks to the explosive sales of Stan Getz's albums that *bossa nova* became known throughout the world; a new era in jazz was created in the combination of his tenor sax and the gentle voice of Gilberto Astrud.) One major criticism leveled at Murakami's fiction centers on its almost overpowering sentimentalism. Yet, there is something undeniably vital in his work, a movement that is born from the music in the text. It is this movement which drives one to continue reading. Perhaps the works do strike one as a little precious at times, but one cannot help but embrace the dynamic musicality that drives the text forward.

In '1963/1982 Girl from Ipanema', the protagonist holds a conversation with the girl from Ipanema, only now the year is 1982.

Their conversation is light, fluid, yet tinged with a subtle gloom – like the high school hallway nostalgically recalled by the protagonist – which seems to hover about them. At the end of the work the protagonist comments, 'I felt that there *had* to be a knot someplace that would fasten me to myself. Surely sometime, in a strange place in some far-off world, I would run into myself'.

'Are You Into Burt Bacharach?' is another seemingly inconsequential story, this time about a man whose former part-time job was to exchange letters with lonely women. But the story works only if we manage to catch the faintly sad, nostalgic melody of classic Bacharach. Right from the title, the ballad plays subliminally, draws us on. But once again, by the end of the story, the reader is left with little more than the protagonist's nostalgic reminiscences of ten years past. 'In that one year,' he muses, 'I felt as if I'd aged two or three years, all at once.'

Music – mostly 1960s rock or jazz – plays in all Murakami literature. An intensely *aural* writer, the key to understanding Murakami's work lies in the sounds with which the texts reverberate. At the same time, when Murakami writes about the 1960s, one is conscious of the origins of our own contemporary moment, for the mood created in the 1960s seems to echo still today.

From the late 1950s through the early 1960s there was a renewed interest in jazz music in Japan. Things got started when 'Suzuki Shōji and the Rhythm Aces' teamed up with the singer Yanagisawa Shin'ichi, though the numbers they did were surely older still. 'Slow Boat to China' would also have been performed around this time. Jo Stafford and Nat Cole were big, and people used to talk about the 'velvet saxaphone of Stan Getz'. That same sophistication seems to be quite central to Murakami Haruki's writing style as well; all of his works somehow embody that ballad-like quality that marked the jazz music of the early 1960s. And, through that quality, he has captured part of what it meant to be a young Japanese during that time. It is important to note here that Japan in the 1960s is Japan before its period of 'rapid growth' (*kōdo seichō*). American influence was in many spheres immense, but once the difficult period of the 1960 *Ampo* (US – Japan Security Treaty) riots had passed, that influence turned almost entirely cultural.

In a sense Murakami's protagonist is symbolic of the freedom – or perhaps aimlessness – of jazz, perhaps of American culture in general. In 'A Slow Boat to China' the protagonist drops his lunch on the ground, and in a moment of distraction mutters to himself,

'So what? If I just brush away the dirt, I can still eat it'. This is how I remember the 1960s; if we were all 'dust in the wind', what was a little dirt to us? When the music of the 1960s plays, that dust seems to swirl up before me with each refrain. As these songs play subliminally through Murakami's stories, the same sensation is created, one of effortless nostalgia. In 'Twilight's Last Lawn' (Gogo no Saigo no Shibafu), the protagonist looks into his past, and discovers suddenly how distant it seems.

> When I was eighteen or nineteen, I used to cut lawns. Quite a while back, it was – maybe fourteen or fifteen years ago.
>
> Sometimes I can't help thinking, though, that fourteen or fifteen years isn't all *that* long. Jim Morrison had just recorded 'Light My Fire', and Paul McCartney was doing 'The Long and Winding Road'. Somehow it just doesn't seem like that long ago. I don't feel like I've changed all that much since then.
>
> No, that isn't true. I've changed a lot. Otherwise there are too many things I can't explain.

This is typically how Murakami sets off on a story; he'll begin with some seemingly pointless anecdote, out of which the story will grow. In this case, the protagonist tells of his recent break-up with his girlfriend, and his imminent plans to quit his job as a grass-cutter. From there he moves on to describe his last job, cutting the lawn at the home of a middle-aged woman. The job is in Kanagawa, a considerable distance from where the protagonist lives and, normally, works, but while he remarks on the distance, it does not especially bother him.

> There's not much to explain, really. I like going to distant places. I like cutting distant lawns in distant yards. I like looking at distant scenery on a distant road. But I guess no one is going to understand me if I explain it like that.

* * *

> 'Oh. Right. The lawn. What the hell *is* today, anyway?' she said in a brusque, manly way. . . . After cutting her lawn to perfection, I went inside, and found her sitting on the bed in her 'daughter's' second-floor room. There I had casual sex with her, and left the house.

Although Murakami's hero – this young man with the peristent belief that no one understands him – lives amidst a period of dynamic growth, from the 'dust' of the 1960s into the present moment, it is the portrayal of daily life in modern Japan that emerges from these stories. And while the presentation in fiction of ordinary, daily life may seem trivial – perhaps *is* trivial – readers nevertheless await each successive Murakami work in spite of this. Why this should be the case is no great mystery: it is precisely this triviality that marks the era so enthusiastically carved up in the Murakami text. His works reflect the mood of the moment in which they are set.

Of course, evoking the 'mood' of this twenty-year period means more than merely describing the trifles of daily life. Murakami examines with equal precision the increasingly urban atmosphere of living in Tokyo, as well as certain cultural 'artifacts'. Perhaps most notable of these 'artifacts' is the coffee shop (*kissaten*), which grew both in number and quality as time progressed.

As the 1960s turned into the 1970s, Tokyo underwent a change for the better; the city grew more orderly, and a highly distinctive, urban atmosphere pervaded the streets. This sensation could be felt even more strongly a short distance from the heart of the city. One saw it in the skylines of Aoyama, Roppongi, Kōjimachi, of Waseda or Shinjuku. Simultaneously, the coffee shop emerged as a symbol of this fresh atmosphere – indeed, one might credit these small establishments in part with the general amelioration of the city itself. Their emergence gave birth to the spirit of the era; their development was a kind of barometer for the city. One could use the coffee shop as an index to predict and interpret changes in the times.

This remains true today. There is nothing quite like sitting in a coffee shop on a sunny morning, a hot cup of coffee in front of you, even when you are depressed, broke, or both. Back in the 1960s I used to wish I could have a taste of what Hemingway's 'A Clean, Well-Lighted Place' must have felt like. Unfortunately, in those days you would never come across such a place. Nowadays reality often precedes imagination.

Murakami evokes a similar feeling of luxury in his depiction of a man sitting alone in a restaurant at an off-season hotel, sipping coffee one rainy morning. There, he encounters a young woman who leaves him with ambivalent thoughts.

> As I poured my second cup of coffee from the pot, a young woman entered the restaurant. She wore a pale blue cardigan

> over the shoulders of a white blouse, and a neat, knee-length navy blue skirt below. There was a pleasant clicking sound as she walked. It was the sound of top-grade heels striking a top-grade wooden floor. When she came in, the hotel restaurant suddenly *seemed* like a hotel restaurant. The waiters stood entranced. I felt the same way.

This scene represents in many ways a kind of fantasy world for many Japanese who lived through the 1960s – to enjoy solitary leisure in a place like that would have been a dream come true. Happily, that dream *has* come true in the 1980s, but not, it would seem, without a price. A sense of ambivalence permeates the world in which Murakami's protagonist lives out this 1960s fantasy. In the scene above, the woman in blue enters the restaurant and says something strangely suggestive, but ultimately the protagonist is left alone. His mood suggests an intense indifference; neither happy nor sad, replete nor empty, lonely nor loved, he simply exists. This is life in the 1980s.

As a modern man who lives in an atmosphere of such seeming indifference, the protagonist's character may seem difficult to grasp. Upon close examination, however, it is his intense morality that strikes one. In 'Are You Into Burt Bacharach?' the protagonist visits the woman with whom he has been exchanging letters, and has dinner with her. The woman approaches the protagonist suggestively, clearly offering herself. In the end, however, he merely thanks the woman for dinner and leaves. Looking back on this moment ten years later, the protagonist wonders if he made the right decision.

> Should I have slept with her?
> That's the theme of this story.
> I have no idea.
> The older I get, the more things there are that I can't figure out.

But is the protagonist truly as naïve as he would have the reader believe? To the objective eye, the matter is simple: Murakami's protagonist is *always* more stoic than is strictly necessary. Less confused than stubborn, he merely stands his ground, displaying a degree of self-control that creates specific parameters for his behavior. Within those confines, the protagonist may move more or less freely, but his essential character is one of self-denial. In this way he is perhaps suited to the fairy-tale world in which Murakami portrays him. Yet on a more sophisticated level, Murakami's moralistic hero displays a rugged individualism that ultimately proves satisfying to the reader. In his afterword to a translation of short stories by Raymond Carver, Murakami suggests that such individualism, expressed here as solitude, is the way of things to come.

> There is no need for me to explain the contents of these works. The world is as you have read it, and the events are just as you have seen them. The one motif to which I might direct the reader's attention is the violence that erupts at the moment when the fundamental solitude of a human being attempts (or attempts *not*) to interact with another person. The rugged natural scenery of the northern West Coast (Ken Kesey, by the way, is also a native of Oregon), and the inflexibility of the middle class background, combine to form the stage upon which the works are played out. In Japan, of course, such a combination is unlikely, for the middle class existence there is not yet so rigidly defined. However, this collection of Carver's stories might well be read as a foreshadowing of things to come.

From Carver's casual portraits of daily life, something radical, fiercely deviant, quickly emerges. It is something discernible in virtually any of his texts. At the same time, while Murakami examines this as a definitive trait in Raymond Carver, one comes to understand that, with certain modifications, it is a central element in his own work as well.

Yet even as Murakami portrays the isolation and morality of a man living in the twenty years of Japan's 'rapid growth' period, his protagonist's isolation is more a matter of self-restraint than of actual deviance. The Murakami hero is content with the isolation that is so much a part of contemporary life. His solitude at the end of the story, however, is neither wholly a matter of choice nor wholly one of circumstance, but a combination of the two. That is to say, circumstances naturally guide him in such a way that his own morality is maintained in the face of social pressures. He selects a manner of living which permits neither collapse nor pleasure-seeking. It is in the nature of this self-restraint that Murakami's protagonist never attempts to extend his own standards to govern others. He may attempt to interact with them, or not to do so, but his efforts are always non-violent. He lives in a world in which it is not only possible, but desirable, to avoid interference with others, and this is precisely the character of Japanese society during the twenty years of rapid growth.

Although he is no holdover, Murakami's protagonist clearly has deep roots in the 1960s. He recalls fondly the strains of jazz, and maintains even now a lifestyle of modest simplicity. Without definite goals beyond this uncomplicated existence, he nevertheless enjoys the benefits of society in an upward swing. Truly a man of moderation, he consistently locates the space between misery and joy in the contemporary moment.

In addition to Carver, Murakami has translated Fitzgerald's *My Lost City*, a work which combines Fitzgerald's waning desire to live with his disillusionment toward New York City. Murakami's view of Tokyo never quite reaches the depths of despair found in *My Lost City*, but in 'A Slow Boat to China' he permits the reader to glimpse his own disillusionment, his inability to locate a place for himself.

> Tokyo.
>
> One day, riding on one of the Yamanote Line's heavy railcars, even the city of Tokyo lost its reality . . . this was no longer a place for me. Someday all my words will disappear, my dreams will collapse, just as that bored adolescence I used to think would last forever had finally vanished. Everything dies, and I guess once the physical form is gone, all that remains is heavy silence and gloom.

Here, surely, is an omen that like Fitzgerald's New York, like Carver's 'fixed' middle class, the world in which Murakami's hero lives is growing increasingly inflexible and desolate. This is not, however, precisely the same disappointment of Fitzgerald's 'lost city', for in his assertion that Tokyo is 'no longer a place for me', the protagonist's disillusionment is not the result of facing *outward* toward the city; rather, it reverberates with the disenchantment of his own introspection. But all hope is not lost.

> Even so, I will lock away that tiny pride of the once devoted outfielder in the bottom of a trunk. I will go out to sit on the stone steps of the wharf, and wait for that slow boat to China to appear on the empty horizon.

All of which seems to amount to little more than the portrayal of an aimless lifestyle amidst a constantly shifting middle class. Murakami presents a self-portrait of the Japanese that is both piercing and sophisticated, of a people emerging from the 1970s shaped by rapid growth and development, yet grounded firmly in the 1960s. His is a portrait of a people born from the moderation of contemporary Japanese society.

I can remember some time back seeing the film version of Manuel Puig's *Kiss of the Spider Woman*, and being struck by the ambivalent feelings it stirred up in me. Amidst the endless discussions of 'male/female' surrounding the work, one has the impression of watching four or five films at once, connected yet distinct. By the end of the story, one can only stare hopelessly into the unfathomable abyss of sexuality and politics. In contrast with this, consider Murakami's response to Puig's work, as 'funny'. Without meaning to indulge in the usual clichés ('political gap', 'sexual gap', and so forth) about Japan and Latin America, there can be little doubt, reading this pronouncement, that the 'gap' between Puig's world and Murakami's is considerable, to say the least.

Unlike Puig's, Murakami's world is pleasant, even sentimental. He permits his readers to experience the cycle that fluctuates between quiet solitude, and bustling urban existence. To this extent his pleasant sentimentalism is not a bad thing. If, however, Murakami's intention is to chronicle a lost era, a lost generation, then the terms 'pleasant' and 'sentimental' take on entirely new significances which may not be at all positive. Murakami unquestionably portrays the everyday life of the average Japanese citizen; one is equally certain that his portrayal reflects both the maturation *and* the forfeiture of modern Japanese culture.

At the beginning of this essay I remarked that Murakami's shirts look good on him because he presses them lightly. The point is notable not merely for its publicity value, but because it suggests his willingness to labor with his own hands, and there is still something ultimately moral about manual labor. Such morality is, I think, rapidly fading from American culture.

It is easy to see America through Murakami. And if he has been influenced by America, I should say this is one of the more endearing things about him. It is only one more proof that contemporary Japanese society has matured.

And so go my thoroughly *un*-literary comments on Murakami Haruki.

10

Yoshimoto Banana Writes Home

The Shōjo in Japanese Popular Culture

John Whittier Treat

Giving up on future dreams
To dwell on rosy memories
Will make sure your best days
Are in the past

Nostalgia for an age that never existed
Nostalgia for an age that never existed
Jello Biafra, 'Nostalgia for an Age That Never Existed'

I am looking to the future with nostalgia.
Mayor Richard E. Daley

The Shining Season of the Shōjo, Never to Come Home Again
Cover blurb, *Tsugumi*

There is in Japan a very famous young writer who goes by the improbable name of Yoshimoto Banana. She is the daughter of Yoshimoto Takaaki, perhaps Japan's most influential, if maverick, postwar intellectual;[1] she is also the most important new novelist to debut in the late 1980s, familiarly known by a botanical pen name that insinuates something as perishable and consumable, as domestic and playful, as her father's high-cultural work is conversely massive, argumentative and almost unreadably serious. Born Yoshimoto Mahoko in 1964, a year whose Olympic spectacle is typically cited as proof of Japan's successful entry into the company of advanced capitalist nations, Banana, unlike Takaaki a generation earlier, has grown up in a late-twentieth-century Japan where pervasive talk of the tedium of life ('sono nani mo nasa', as she colloquially puts it [Banana 1989b:236]) contrasts with the turbulent national history that drove Takaaki's and his postwar generation's

Figure 1 'Shōjo are children. . . .'

critique of an intelligentsia faulted for the unfortunate results of its purported elitist insularity.

At the age of twenty-three Banana published her debut work *Kitchen* (Kitchin) in the November, 1987, issue of the literary journal *Kaien*. She immediately attracted the attention of readers and critics, and won that journal's annual prize for new writers. *Kitchen* is the story of a young college student, Sakura Mikage. Orphaned at an early age, Mikage is suddenly left completely alone in the world when her grandmother dies. She finds lodging with a young man named Yūichi and his mother Eriko, only to discover that Eriko is a transsexual and in fact Yūichi's father. This story, whose raw style is reminiscent of a teenager's diary, evokes what is commonly termed the 'unique world' of Japanese schoolgirls. One of the judges for the *Kaien* prize, senior novelist and critic Nakamura Shin'ichirō, said of *Kitchen* that

> This is a work written on a theme, and with a sensibility, that the older generation of which I am part could not have imagined. It is the product of an abandon completely indifferent to literary traditions. Its naive rejection of the very question of whether it does or does not conform to conventional concepts is precisely what makes it strike me as a new sort of literature.
>
> (Mitsui and Washida 1989:143)

Nakamura, while guarded in his praise, is nonetheless generous in thinking of Banana's writing as 'literature', in Japanese more than English a high-cultural appellation. Others have wondered. She has been labeled the cutting edge of the new Japanese 'minimalism', ultimate in the sense that she is the perfect pop-cultural disposable (*tsukaisute*) author, like the *manga* comic books with which she is legitimately compared (Shima 1988:152). The 'rejection' to which Nakamura refers includes the entire high-cultural pantheon: Banana's debts, she tells us herself, are to horror-novelist Stephen King and manga writer Iwadate Mariko (Banana 1989b:73–78, 122–32; 1990:197–98). But part of the critics' doubt over Banana's literary longevity hinges on the assumption that, like the popularity of such pop singers as the earlier 1980s sensation Matsuda Seiko, her teenage narratives cannot survive her own teenage years, that there is nothing to her stories apart from the guise she herself assumes as a shōjo novelist. This is an assumption that betrays a cynical hope on the part of some for such stories to fade quickly from view, and it is a cynicism defensively generated by the nervous crisis of intellectuals in Japan dating back to the mid-sixties, the years of Banana's own infancy.

In Japan today it is commonly said that more than half the submissions to the numerous new-writer prizes come from adolescents. Banana herself has stated that she wanted to be a writer from her earliest elementary school days. It was a desire, she says, just like wanting to become an 'airline stewardess' and thus presumably an ambition no more special (Banana 1990:116). But quite unlike every aspiring author, Banana's novels and collections of short stories and essays, and the motion pictures they have inspired, have been notably commercial. By 1990 her five hard-cover books had sold four million copies, and she is already available in English. Although it is readily assumed in Japan that the preponderance of her readers are women from high-school age to approximately thirty, one suspects that Banana's works, like the shōjo manga or 'teenage girls' comics' often indicated as the major influence on her themes and style, are enjoyed by readers of older ages and other genders as well (Mitsui and Washida 1989:9–54). Banana is, in the words of her critic Washida Koyata, 'without a doubt the number one [*nanbā wan*] writer of popular fiction today' (Washida 1990:440).

Critics, however, often view Banana and her success as final confirmation of a fundamental shift in how one is to understand 'culture' in Japan since the early 1970s, particularly 'literary culture'. Nakamura's bewildered and back-handed praise is one register of how Banana represents what older generations of writers have dreaded: the victory of popular, which is to imply non-oppositional, culture over the critical potential long (if anxiously) associated with *junbungaku*, or 'pure literature'. Nobel laureate Ōe Kenzaburō, a prominent voice on the left for intellectual literature committed to social change, has bemoaned for nearly two decades the irrelevancy of serious fiction for reading audiences in contemporary Japan. In the widely reprinted essay 'A Novelist's Lament' that appeared on the eve of Banana's debut, Ōe complained that 'Japanese intellectuals, including students at the major metropolitan universities, no longer look to serious literary writing for new models of the future' (Ōe 1986). What Ōe means when he uses words such as 'serious' and 'models' are the discourses of his own New Left generation raised on Sartre, Mao and James Dean and committed to the romance of the artist as high-brow disaffected rebel. Banana and a host of other young writers today such as Tawara Machi, Murakami Haruki and Takahashi Gen'ichirō comprise in the words of pop musician Nanba Hiroyuki the 'pure literature of the manga generation' in a reference to the comics that fairly dominate the print side of Japanese popular culture today and which raise the collective ire of many critics (Nanba 1991).

When asked if her famous father Takaaki inspired her to become a professional writer, Banana responded that on the contrary it was her reading of manga (Banana 1990:194). There are, however, certain familial coincidences. At the same time that Ōe was ruing the demise of intellectual, politically critical literature,

Takaaki was theorizing present-day Japanese culture as a 'complex indeterminacy', which is to say a culture without a fixed center or hierarchy. Instead, argued Takaaki, Japanese culture is now one in which diverse classes, subcultures and discourses circulate and contend with equal claims to legitimacy (Inamasu 1989:14). Yoshimoto father and daughter alike enlist in their respective analytical and fictional work certain postmodern qualities of contemporary life which, for better or worse, fundamentally depart from the presumptions of modernism and modernist literature. Banana refers to herself with no evident embarrassment as a 'popular writer' (*taishū sakka*). She boasts that her generation was 'raised on manga and TV. That's why we understand only those things that go fast' (Banana 1990:14, 269). Narratives spun out of speeding sound-bites, this postmodern textuality that Banana was both raised within and now reproduces in her own work cannot be countenanced as fully literary in the view of critics nostalgic for the times when writers believed themselves engaged in the work of a critical introspection that prepares consciousness for the prospect of social change. Banana's stories, given their idiomatic kinship with billboards, television commercials, pop songs and fashion magazines, appear to those critics as an unconditional capitulation to the forces of commercialization so often cited as the nefarious agent behind the production of popular culture, a charge familiar in the West at least since Theodor Adorno's famous essay on the depressing predictability of Tin Pan Alley's music.

The apparent victory of popular culture emblemized by Banana's success, and with it its unsettling postmodernist traits, have produced apprehensive fears among those intellectuals convinced of modernist high culture's unique stake in issues of human freedom and individual worth. But Banana has clearly generated an enthusiastic response among readers who heretofore lacked a body of fiction with which to empathize, and these readers are not solely adolescent women. One of her critics – both male and nearly middle-aged – has written of his and his wife's startling, exciting experience of identification with the vacuous ('nani mo nai') sense of life represented in Banana's books (Matsumoto 1991:16). Her fans are reportedly attracted to her works because they are 'easy to understand', written in a style both colloquial and 'real' (Mitsui and Washida 1989:107–8). Fans could only approve, however, if the 'world of girls' therein described is the idealized or ideological 'lived' experience of those fans themselves, and such experience can neither be simple nor insignificant. Banana's stories are not casually dismissible as the sentimental narratives we may or may not correctly associate with shōjo culture in Japan. Banana's romanticism is always qualified and amended, and while her characters are thoroughly assimilated into Japanese youth culture, they are not reductively 'pop' in the sense of lacking discrete individuality. Part of their appeal certainly does, however, lie in the way they mark a clean break with earlier 'pure' fiction valorized as 'intellectual' and a shift towards a fiction unapologetically and intimately targeted towards *anata*, 'you', i.e., the teenage woman and her cohorts, an audience and point of view never too removed from the center arena of contemporary Japanese public culture.[2]

Banana has defined her generation as that age cohort which 'came into contact with exactly the same kinds of consumer products'. Those commodities, in other words, define what is particular about the generation which is induced to consume them. Magazines, radio, above all television: in whatever direction one turns, the barely (and thus ambiguously) pubescent woman is there both to promote products and purchase them, to excite the consumer and herself be thrilled by the flurry of goods and services that circulate like toys around her. Banana recognizes that her own works are commodities, which is to say that they have a planned obsolescence – she has said, for example, that she wants all of her previously published books removed from the store shelves whenever she comes out with something new (Banana 1990:239, 279).

The modern concept of the shōjo coalesced in the late nineteenth and early twentieth centuries, when rapid economic change produced a social utility for 'adolescence', i.e., a period between childhood and adulthood during which labor is trained for its role in industrial culture. Horikiri Naoto dates the concept of a 'special shōjo world' to the Taishō period (1912–1924), when rising affluence permitted middle and upper-class families to send their daughters to girls' boarding schools, creating a youthful and all-female subculture. Before this time, such girls were routinely put to domestic work by the age of twelve or thirteen; after, at least for girls from certain class backgrounds, there was an extended period of adolescence that soon generated its own dedicated cultural milieu (Horikiri 1991:108–9). However, with the advent of Banana's generation the shōjo was rearticulated as a definitive feature of Japanese late-model, consumer capitalism. It was during Banana's infancy and youth that modern boutiques (known in Japanese as *fanshii bizunesu* 'fancy businesses'), brand-name marketing and western fast-food merchandising were introduced widely throughout Japan. The role of the shōjo in this service economy was not to make these products, but consume them (more precisely, to *symbolize* their consumption). The shōjo are, if you will, 'off the production line', lacking any real referent in the 'economy' of postmodern Japan. Until they marry, and thus cease to be shōjo, they are relegated to pure play as pure sign. It is in the interim of their shōjo years that these young women (and the young men that increasingly resemble them) participate in a uniquely *un*productive culture. They effectively signify sheer consumption, and as such cannot exist as wholly 'real' in an economy otherwise committed to creating value, be it in terms of goods and services, if one is an ideal man (*otoko*), or children, if one is an ideal woman (*haha*).

The word most often associated with this shōjo culture is *kawaii*, or 'cute'. This aesthetic value is directly linked to the consumer role that shōjo exist to play. A kawaii girl is attractive, and thus valorized, but lacks libidinal agency of her own. While others may sexually desire the shōjo – and indeed, another phenomenon in the Japan of the 1980s was talk of the *rorikon* 'Lolita complex' of adult heterosexual males – the shōjo's own sexual energy, directed as it is towards stuffed animals, pink notebooks, strawberry crepes and Hello Kitty novelties, is an energy not yet deployable in the heterosexual economy of adult life in Japan. But as a master-sign for economic consumption, the shōjo is indeed of immediate and profitable use: in some sense, anyone who consumes in Japan today is to that extent a 'shōjo'. Horikiri, for one, is aware of an ironic reversal that now marks contemporary Japanese culture:

> I wonder if we men shouldn't now think of ourselves as 'shōjo', given our compulsory and excessive consumerism, a consumerism that in recent years afflicts us like sleepwalking. We are no longer the shabby and middle-aged teacher Humbert Humbert who chased Lolita's rear-end in his dreams. We all have become the forever-young Lolita herself. We are driven night and day to be relentless consumers. . . . The 'shōjo', that new human species born of modern commodification, has today commodified everything and everyone.
>
> (Horikiri 1991:40–41)

It is important, given Horikiri's extended application of the term 'shōjo', to understand the word as one of difference rather than

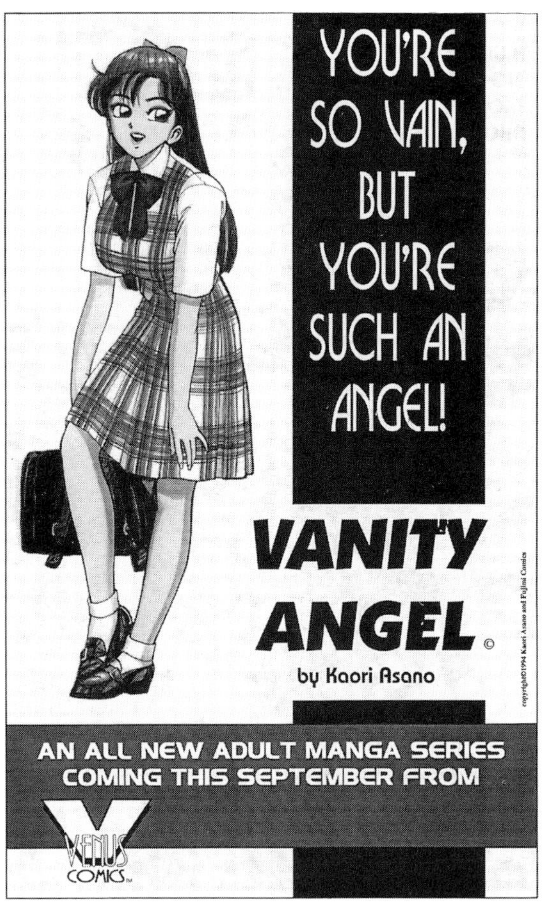

Figure 2 ". . . But adults like them, too"

identity. It is probably incorrect and certainly misleading to translate the term shōjo with any single English phrase. 'Young girl' is not only redundant but can refer to infants, and 'young woman' implies a kind of sexual maturity clearly forbidden to shōjo. In English, gender is binary – at every stage one is either 'male' or 'female'. But in Japan, one might well argue that shōjo constitute their own gender, neither male nor female but rather something importantly detached from the productive economy of heterosexual reproduction. Anthropologist Jennifer Robertson points out in an essay on the all-women Takarazuka troupe that 'Literally speaking, *shōjo* means a "non-quite-female female". . . . *Shōjo* also implies heterosexual *inexperience* and homosexual *experience*' (Robertson 1989:56) – presumably homosexual because the emotional life of the shōjo is essentially narcissistic in that it is self-referential, and self-referential as long as the shōjo is not employed productively in the sexual and capitalist economies.

Author Yoshimoto Banana herself is used to exemplify shōjo culture within its critical and media representations. Though now past her twenties nominally beyond the strictest upper age limit of the shōjo, Banana's own life is depicted as still thoroughly shōjo-like. As the signet sign of the shōjo, Banana is the first literary figure in Japan to achieve the status of an *aidoru* 'idol', a celebrity rank heretofore limited to such wildly popular shōjo singers as Matsuda Seiko. The aidoru's appeal lies not in any unique talent but instead in its purported lack: anyone is theoretically a potential Matsuda, or Banana, and it is that interchangeability and disposability – that 'commodification' – which makes the shōjo affiliate with the signifying processes of Japanese consumer capitalism. Just as the television aidoru is a proliferating reproduction of the cinema star (*sutā*), the fiction-writing (or more commonly, manga-writing) shōjo rebounds as a Xerox-copy toss-off of the *sakka* 'novelist.'

Given this absence of value that is now itself a value, it is easy to look upon Banana and what her success portends with disdain or even alarm. As is often said of popular culture in general, the shōjo phenomenon seems to celebrate the vapidness of our contemporary existences, as against the richness of human life attested to in such high-cultural artifacts as the high-brow or intellectual novel. Specifically the lament most often heard over shōjo culture since the 1970s is its apparently complete displacement of the overtly critical Japanese youth culture of the 1960s which, like it counterparts in Europe and North America, pointedly took issue with institutional power.[3] This remorse for the eclipse of the sixties' modernist counter-culture and the related trepidation before the rise of a complicit mass culture recall attacks made on the culture industry by European intellectuals before the Second World War, who held that the actual product of film, radio and advertising was the construction of a 'pseudo-individual' to purchase goods and services. In this critique, popular culture was identical with the dominant capitalist ideology, with the intent of defeating authentic selfhood and replacing it with pliant workers and consumers. As Theodor Adorno and Max Horkheimer wrote in 1944, 'the culture industry as a whole has molded men as a type unfailingly reproduced in every product' (Adorno and Horkheimer 1972:127). This view of popular culture, still current, usefully points to the relationships between cultural practices and modes of capitalist production, but reductively describes ideology as monolithic and finally irresistible.

In more recent decades, however, the analysis of popular culture has been enlivened with more complex and less static models of the relationship between ideology and mass culture. Rather than reduce consumers under popular culture to the mindless dupes of some omnipotent system, it now seems more illuminating to posit that within the matrices of popular cultural production and reception there are a plethora of opportunities for the rearticulation of the roles that might very well be intended for or assigned us. Within that dynamic set of discursive and non-discursive practices called popular culture a polyvalent 'we' construct for ourselves equally various and even contradictory meanings out of what may indeed seem to be the uniform products of mass culture. It is commonplace now, after the work of critics such as Fredric Jameson in the United States and Stuart Hall in Britain, both of whom elaborate ideas initiated by Antonio Gramsci, to look upon popular culture as the site of struggle for hegemony, a 'contested terrain' between the admittedly dominant ideological intentions for how we are to live within culture and the emergent ideological ways in which we may succeed in re-articulating that culture in our own diverse interests. If, as Jameson argues, popular culture is both 'ideological and utopian', then it is internally contradictory in a way that permits us some small space to position ourselves variously within it.

It is in this framework that I wish to read Yoshimoto Banana: as a phenomenon that on one level seems to celebrate the 'lifestyles' Japanese are encouraged to lead under its present and not wholly consistent consumer-capitalist logic, yet on another allows for an assessment of, and even resistance to, those same lifestyles. Banana's stories, no less than those of more conventional or canonical writers, permit their reader to interpret meaning and interpolate point of view, and it could even be argued that Banana's theme of the shōjo – an empty sign easily scriptable – represents a point of difference especially open to ideological contestation. Reading Banana while receptive to such questions should also free us to look at her success as not the baleful reminder of a moribund high culture, but as its own opportunity for studying how an emerging sub-genre of fiction positively affords readers the power to imagine themselves and their place as other than the constraints of everyday life might otherwise dictate.

Tsugumi

Yoshimoto Banana's most commercially successful work to date, the 1989 novel *Tsugumi* (Tugumi), is also her most paradigmatic. The character after whom the novel is named, Tsugumi, might be described as a stereotypical shōjo. Eighteen years old, she nonetheless is still physically skinny, flat-chested and small in stature; a 'kirei de wagamama' child – pretty but wilful. The first line of the novel tells us that she was a 'difficult child'; her 'quite proper outward appearance, like that of a doll lovingly made by God', belies a personality so easily capable of wanton meanness that others around her are both intimidated and vicariously thrilled. Who knows her best is cousin and closest friend Shirakawa Maria, and she serves as the novel's narrator. The two grew up together in the back rooms of the Yamamotoya, a traditional inn in a now rather dowdy seaside resort town on the Izu peninsula. Recently Maria's mother, who worked with the rest of her family at the inn, has moved to Tokyo to live with her lover, Maria's father. Maria, one year older than Tsugumi, has just begun college there. Their friendship remains close, despite not only the distance that now separates them but Tsugumi's cruel penchant for practical jokes and generally bizarre, indeed often militantly antisocial, behavior.

Tsugumi's true capacity for hazardous eccentricity is revealed in the climatic events of the novel. Maria has come back to the resort town to spend her first college summer vacation. She and Tsugumi soon meet a young man named Kyōichi. Tsugumi develops an innocent crush on him despite the fact he is the son of a commercial developer building a large modern hotel in the town, a hotel that everyone knows will put the smaller inns out of business. Tsugumi's father, in fact, has already decided to close the Yamamotoya and start a more modern inn elsewhere, perhaps in the mountains. The idyllic seaside childhood that Tsugumi and Maria spent in each other's company is about to end, although no reader at this point really knows just how soon, or how dramatically.

Kyōichi, too, has a pet dog, named Gongorō. One day Gongorō inexplicably disappears, and after a thorough search for him suspicion grows that a band of local boys, resentful of Kyōichi and his father's new hotel, has done away with the animal. Everyone blames the incident on the unavoidable delinquency of youth – everyone, that is, except Tsugumi. Her behavior grows increasingly erratic, the consequences of which are revealed one night when an aunt discovers an underground pit Tsugumi has secretly dug in the garden of her family's inn – a pit in which is found, in the nick of time, one of the local boys she had suspected of killing Gongorō.

Tsugumi's nearly homicidal stunt is explained away as a prank, but her physical and mental health, never good, is consequently diagnosed as serious enough to warrant a long hospital stay. Kyōichi and Maria stay in touch with Tsugumi and her family, and are assured that she is recovering. One day Maria receives a surprise phone. Don't read the letter from me you're about to get, Tsugumi ominously instructs; just throw it away. I'm much better now than I was – I didn't die after all. An intrigued Maria, of course, reads the letter as soon as it arrives.

When they were younger Tsugumi and Maria used to play a game of their own invention called 'ghost mail' (*obake posuto*). They would send each other letters supposedly from the spirits of dead people interred in a nearby cemetery. Once Tsugumi went too far by sending Maria a 'ghost' letter from a person over whom Maria still very much grieved, her recently deceased grandfather. The letter this time is also from a 'ghost' Maria is not quite ready to accept as such. It is from a Tsugumi who had, at the time of its composition, been planning for her own death. It is not clear whether what prompts this is a worsening illness or a decision to take her own life. Tsugumi writes her final farewells to Maria at considerable length, and with the last line of the letter – 'Anyway, I am happy to be able to die in this town. Take care' – the novel ends.

In a postscript Banana characterizes this novel as both autobiographical and nostalgic:

> Every summer I go to the western coast of Izu with my family. I have come to think of that one inn, in that one town, where we have gone for more than ten years, as my home. Somehow or other I just while away my summers there.

> The ocean, the walks, swimming, sunsets: I have written this novel based on my experiences of those summers stored away somewhere within me. If one day I were to lose all memories of myself and my family, I would be able to retrieve them by reading this book. You see, I am Tsugumi. What is naughty about her is naughty about myself.
>
> (Banana 1989c:236)

What *Tsugumi* retrieves for Banana is the memory of her family, but 'family' is precisely what could be termed the core problematic of this work. Contrary to what we might have expected to find in fiction directed towards an audience of adolescent women, there are no stereotypically perfect families in any of Banana's stories, unless they exist as images, dreams, copies or untrustworthy memories. In her 1988 novel *A Sad Premonition* (Kanashii Yokan), orphaned shōjo character Yayoi describes the fantasy of her adoptive family's life as 'a bright world of the sort of happy middle-class family you see in a Spielberg movie'. But that simile never approaches the real – Yayoi can only muse, 'if only somewhere, in some far-off place, I had a real family'. In another example of the American pop-cultural representation of the ideal set of social relations that frames Banana's work, the 1989 short story 'Night and the Night Traveler' (Yoru to Yoru no Tabibito) includes a character named Sarah who comes from a 'happy American family'.

The complement to the mythical or lost family is the unconventional – the so-called dysfunctional – family, of which there is a plenitude in Yoshimoto Banana. Already mentioned is the family in which *Kitchen*'s Mikage finds herself. Living with half-sibling/half-boy friend (and thus always potentially incestuous) Yūichi and surrogate mother/father transsexual Eriko (who very nicely blocks the Oedipal trajectory for anyone), Mikage can be neither 'sister' nor 'daughter'. The family is 'assembled' just as Mikage is 'found'. Blood ties and genealogy are less important than circumstance and simple human affinity. This is true of other Banana works where, as in many manga, characters are the illegitimate offspring of mistresses (*Tsugumi*) or orphans (*Kitchen*), or are compromised by any number of other potentially handicapping personal backgrounds. These characters invariably stumble upon or recruit alternative families for themselves. Feminist critic Ueno Chizuko observed of Banana's work that it typically 'describes the experience of a non-biological pseudo-family created by a young girl otherwise parentless' (Ueno 1990:30). These shōjo are alienated from their biological families because they discern no necessary link between the obvious fact that they are 'derived' from their (original) parents and themselves. These characters live in a different world or time frame from their parents, and thus also this way obviate the logic of the Oedipal triangle. With no sense of a familial history, the self cannot be the result of any genealogical 'process' at all. In *Kitchen*, for example, Mikage reflects upon her present moment and its radical dislocation from the past:

> Sometimes I realize that I used to have a family, a real family, but over time it grew smaller and smaller, until now I'm the only one left. When I think of my life in those terms, everything seems unreal. Time has passed, as it always does, in these rooms where I've grown up, but everyone else is gone. What a shock.
>
> It's just like science fiction. This vast, dark universe.
>
> (Banana 1988:153)

One might speculate that Banana's characters choose to assimilate their experiences in terms of popular culture (e.g., 'science fiction') because their pasts are only available in the form of its artifacts. Unlike previous eras, when often only our iconography was taken from the every-day and transported into the legitimated higher cultures we thought our authentic home, we and Banana now can be said to *live* in the popular. But what is specifically key here is Mikage's skeptical isolation, her awareness of her familial past as false. The father is always distant or missing entirely in Banana's stories. (Banana, perhaps not coincidentally, never makes explicit mention of her own father in her essays.) This means that the families from which her characters exit and the ones they enter cannot be exclusively patriarchal. Tsugumi's father, Tadashi, is so tangential to the novel that the one or two times he does briefly figure in a scene, it is comical. Maria notes that 'Uncle Tadashi has never spent much time with Tsugumi', and Tsugumi herself says of her father that she 'never felt that much love for him'. Nor is there much regret expressed over this lack. It is amply compensated for in the close relations that the two teenage women enjoy with each other.

Fathers are shadowy and ambiguous figures in much modern literature, and not just Japan's. The relative decline of the prestige of the patriarch is variously explained. It is common, for example, to hear argued that the nuclear family and its father has been rendered anachronistic with the advent of late capitalism. Sociologist Sodei Takako notes 'major shifts, from around 1965, in the attitudes and behavior of the Japanese with respect to marriage and the family' (Sodei 1985:81), and Banana, born at just that critical moment, has observed in an essay that the conventional household (*katei*) 'is completely disappearing' (Banana 1990:123). Our desires, according to this view, are no longer sublimated or organized within the frame of the Oedipalized family – excess, play and unbridled consumption are now to be encouraged rather than curbed. With the collapse of the father's authority, so falls the libidinal economy in circulation around him: a daughter will not first resent her father for his phallic power only to forego her desire to identify with him and form an erotic attachment. Like Tsugumi's father (who, it should be recalled, is closing his obsolete business), all fathers, their power and their appeal, are rendered moot.

This argument, of course, overlooks how patriarchal authority has been dispersed rather than dispensed with, but its linkage of the reduced role of the father with the rise of mass consumerism helps to make sense of Yoshimoto Banana's stories. *Tsugumi*, a work whose avowedly simple schoolgirl style has vexed critics, is richly complex in its postmodernist critique of the modern nuclear family. While the utopian symbolism of 'home' has certainly been used in Japanese fiction to romanticize the patriarchal family, the term also engages meanings and desires at a level of ordinary day-to-day life that are of a more open-ended and critical nature than any simplistic definition of ideology accommodates. In addition to Tsugumi's own family – one made up of women – there is Maria's family, or rather her multiple families. The daughter of Tsugumi's aunt and that aunt's adulterous married lover, Maria has grown up in a type of exile at the Yamamotoya inn, where she has spent her life as part of a feminine extended family in which both Tsugumi's father and her own are real but invisible. In an early memory that Maria long repressed, she recalls her mother crying on the phone with her father in Tokyo: into the warm happiness of that old-fashioned seaside inn, there only occasionally intrudes the uncomfortable reminder of the father. Eventually Maria's father divorces his wife and brings Maria and her mother to come live with him in Tokyo, which they do despite the great regret with which they leave their idyllic seaside life and cozy female companionship. One day Maria and her mother walk out of a Ginza department store and catch the scent of the nearby harbor, prompting them to confess to each other how they miss the sea and what it now symbolizes – living not with Papa but instead collectively with other women at the Yamamotoya.

This is not to say that life with Papa is miserable, only that that 'happiness', like Mikage's family, seems 'false'. The daily rhythms of the nuclear family seem rehearsed and thus ersatz. Maria describes her father, who at middle-age now very much enjoys the domesticity of having Maria and her mother close-by, as a 'My-home papa who has come home late'. He finally has what he has long wanted – a normal family with a child and a wife who stays at home. Maria, too, enjoys this new role for herself, but cannot shake the feeling that it is, indeed, a role and nothing more: 'We used to live in such a strange way that now the three of us are as affectionate with each other as actors would be in a scenario entitled the "Typical Happy Family"'; 'life', Maria concludes, 'is a performance'. This mood of alienation, of simulation, makes Banana's work both different from much other adolescent fiction and at the same time indicative of the uncanny sense of the basic incongruity of daily life with consciousness of it. The family in Banana is neither the site of the model home where the Oedipal struggle teleologically unfolds, nor is it the place where, now free of that struggle, the 'real' relations that should have obtained between family members are triumphed. Both 'family' and 'home' are tropes of 'everyday life', which is to say the ideological ground over which different subject positions constituted within (popular) culture contend. As terms that gloss the intersubjectivity of the myriad quotidian ways that human self-reproduction is welded to wider processes of social reproduction, 'family' and 'home' stage a crucial conversation, a negotiation between Banana's shōjo and their lived relations with the world that such words denote.

Whatever sort of biological family Banana describes, her narrators are 'there' for no other reason than because their parents or grandparents were 'there', and any worry over what sort of history produced their forebears is irrelevant to the narrative at hand. In other words the biological family is not governed by any necessarily discordant human relationships. It is, however, a unit that is threatened if not created by such stresses. Maria, for example, has a great apprehension about her father. She is understandably frightened of losing him again (he did, after all, divorce his wife in order to be with her mother and her) and, in a central chapter entitled 'Swimming with Father' (Chichi to Oyogu), she is both overjoyed and vaguely disturbed when her father comes to join her for a weekend while she is spending her summer vacation back at the Yamamotoya. Overlapping with the fear of her father drowning in the ocean is another fear: 'I don't really understand a single thing yet about the life we're leading in Tokyo now. . . . The Tokyo family feels like nothing but a dream . . . and father . . . is just one piece of that still distant dream'.

It is that summer back at the Yamamotoya that the idea of family assumes, albeit nostalgically, a more actual and authentic sense for Maria. It is interesting to speculate that life at the Yamamotoya – life not only within an extended rather than nuclear family, but within a family whose productive functions, those of running a traditional inn, have not been shifted outside the home – already represents a nostalgic pre-capitalist social formation that complements Maria's own elaboration of obsolete personal relations. Reunited with Tsugumi and Maria's cousin – Tsugumi's older sister – Yōko, Maria revels in the intimate, indolent summer reminiscent of the sort she remembers having before, back (only a year earlier) when she was the shōjo that the eighteen year-old Tsugumi still is. Into this reconstituted 'family' is introduced Kyōichi, a *shōnen* or 'teenage boy' who is nonetheless, like his brethren in contemporary Japanese comics, somewhat effeminate on one hand and somewhat sibling-like on the other. Tsugumi develops a crush on Kyōichi, but it is an innocent one not notably different from her affection for Maria. In fact when Tsugumi, usually deferential in front of boys, displays her real, i.e., impudent, self in front of Kyōichi, it must be because he is less a phallic threat to the utopian family of women than a feminized supplement to it. The pseudo-sibling relationship is always powerful in Banana's fiction: seldom sexual, never Oedipal, not anything but snug and non-threatening, the pseudo-sibling relationship engenders a kind of lateral parity that contrasts with the hierarchical schema of a patriarchal family organization. In fact Maria manages to re-conceptualize even her father as a 'brother'. That day swimming at the beach, Maria not only realizes that she is at heart still a shōjo but imagines her father a shōnen. The distance between father and daughter that prevents the family from attaining 'critical' nuclear mass also produces a non-erotic but nonetheless intense desire on Maria's part to enjoy her father's company in much the same way she does Tsugumi's. Maria's father complies with Maria's desires when he says to her,

'Gee, living this far apart makes my grown-up daughter seem like a girlfriend [*koibito*] to me'. 'Girlfriend' here is less a reference to any incestuous impulse than simply a cooperative response to Maria's imaginative yearnings for emotional relations devoid of adults (and the 'real world' they imply) and especially devoid of potentially disruptive adult males.

It is possible that this sort of horizontal brother – sister or boyfriend-girlfriend schema of social organization somehow suggests the shape of the modern household after the often-proclaimed break-up of the nuclear family. But to talk about a 'post-' nuclear family is still to talk about the family, and to accept the logic of the term. 'Family' is, in fact, a word that Banana uses repeatedly, albeit in a radically reworked sense. In an essay pointedly entitled 'Family' (Famirii) she reflects:

> Usually the world is a terribly difficult place to be, and lots of times we end up living our lives apart from each other. That's why the family is a fort built for us to flee into. Inside that fort both men and women become symbols, and there protect the home. I like that fact. I really think it's necessary, even when it's hard.
>
> (Banana 1989b:39–40)

This defensive concept of family, a response to the stresses of a modern life that demands the participation of each person in differentiated, specialized and scattered tasks, is one in which both genders become 'symbols', which presumably means we act out roles (such as 'mother' and 'father') that are certainly useful and expedient in 'protect[ing] the home', but are not by any means necessarily determined or inevitable for 'men and women'. The ideal family in Banana's stories, as I have indicated, is never a genetic given but instead a willed construct.[4] As critic Fujimoto Yukari has noted of Banana's work, 'There are only unconventional, abnormal families, but within those families there most certainly exists an individual will and liability in having made those choices' (Fujimoto 1991:315). Banana harbors no illusions about the permanence of such constructions. In 'Family' she adds:

> Wherever I go I end up turning people into a 'family' of my own. That's just the way I am, for better or worse, and I've got to live this way. What I call a family is still a group of fellow-strangers who have come together, and because there's

> nothing more to it than that we really form good relations with each other. It's hard for us to leave each other, and that bothers me. This happens to me constantly, and each time it does I think to myself that 'life is just saying good-bye'. But while it lasts there are a lot of good things, so I put up with it.
> (Banana 1989b:39)

This sense of family as something contingent, provisional and temporary finds its precise expression in *Tsugumi*. The family in *Tsugumi*, whether those from which Maria departs or those she enters, is always shifting and recombining. Insofar as Banana's discourse of the family, and its casual, de-naturalized and almost accidental character, can be extrapolated to apply to other essentialized units of social organization, it suggests at least a nascent critique of how processes of identification and differentiation may operate throughout the range of contemporary human communities.

Many of the relationships which Banana's shōjo enjoy with males risk becoming incestuous, as in the case of Maria and her father. But they never do become incestuous, in the sense of consummating in physical intercourse, if for no other reason than because the concept of the shōjo does not permit such relations. In *A Sad Premonition* that risk runs the highest, but even there sexual desire is finally deflected towards a self-gratifying and chaste narcissism. Yayoi falls in love with her younger brother, but goes no further than a single innocent kiss that she characterizes as 'perfectly natural, not immoral at all'. What she feels for Tetsuo are 'brilliant feelings of love, feelings that are both dense and light at the same time [and which] filled the small space between the two of them'. That such impossibly incestuous impulses, distributed liberally throughout Banana's work – as liberally as the theme of the troubled family – suggest they are parallel or even integral phenomena, and perhaps are further linked perhaps to the construction of a contestatory, non-familial identity for the shōjo. This identity repudiates the shōjo's exchange value in the kinship economy of the family, and produces in its stead a non-circulating narcissistic 'small space', a space which is no longer a momentary phase on route to an adult heterosexuality but a site of potential resistance to it. It is noted that young male characters in her fiction, the characters to whom the shōjo are emotionally attracted, are very shōjo-like themselves. Rather effeminate, prone to tears, and attuned emotionally to their shōjo friends, 'the males who appear in Yoshimoto Banana's fiction', as one critic has put it, 'do not seem to have much vitality' (Furuhashi 1990:83). This tendency recalls the similar representation of young men in the manga culture out of which Banana emerges, where they are often depicted as pale in complexion and sensitive in features. They indulge in shopping for designer goods, show interest in cosmetics, and devote themselves to pop aidoru. This depiction of both teenage men and women without key heterosexual difference points to an unproductive (in the sense that such relationships are incapable of producing value in the form of children) self-referentiality that qualifies the sign of the shōjo and that of the shōjo-like shōnen subsumed beneath it.

Nostalgia

It is this self-referentiality that anthropologist Ōtsuka Eiji interestingly sees as linking the concept of the shōjo to postmodern consumer capitalism (Ōtsuka 1991:64–65). But in the work of Yoshimoto Banana there is another important feature attending the shōjo that on one hand supports the contention that 1980s culture in Japan is a 'retro-culture', yet on the other hand may suggest that such retro-spection preserves the critical agency associated with the modernist culture for which older critics wax nostalgic. Tomoaki and Tomoko, the shōnen and shōjo in Banana's 1988 novel *Sanctuary* (Sankuchuari), are only just out of high school but already look longingly back on those years together. Tomoko, unhappy in her marriage, wishes 'I could return to when I was in high school'. In *A Sad Premonition* – a novel that Banana described while writing it as 'the story about the retrieval of lost memory' (Banana 1990:128) – Yayoi yearns for a childhood past she cannot recall. 'There is value in it precisely because it is completely gone', she muses quixotically. Yayoi represents that value in the person of Yukino, an older sister whom she had long believed to be her aunt:

> She hides something for which she is incredibly nostalgic. Anyone who has lost her childhood is capable of understanding that very well. Something far away, something deeper than the night, something longer than eternity.
>
> (Banana 1989a:154)

It is the search for that 'something' – the lost family in which Yayoi and Yukino were once 'home' – that provides the plot for *A*

Sad Premonition, whose title according to one critic 'describes Yayoi's process of retrieving the memory of her past' (Furuhashi 1990:83). Nostalgia (*natsukashisa*) is pivotal not only in this work but all of Banana's: critic Kamata Tōji calls it her writings' 'key word' (Kamata 1991:281), and writer Hikari Agata claims to find it in her every choice of imagery (Banana 1990:121). Nostalgia is certainly conspicuous in *Tsugumi*, and governs its plot as well as sentimental temper. Maria's constructed family that summer of her last visit to the Yamamotoya is already a memory even as she experiences it, a replay of a life not so much one that she ever led as the one she wishes to posit, nostalgically, as having led. The novel suggests an 'already always' nostalgia, postmodern in nature because it is so guilelessly simulated. 'This tale is a memoir of the last time I returned to the seaside town where I spent my girlhood', explains Maria on the first page of the novel, and that girlhood represented by Tsugumi, the perfect shōjo who will never grow up, will always be just that in Maria's mind. 'Tsugumi . . . never looked back at the past . . . there was never anything but "today" for Tsugumi'. It is Maria, and only Maria, who can have a past and a future as well as a 'today'. Maria, unlike Tsugumi, experiences nostalgia at every turn; nostalgia is the means through which she registers her existence. *Tsugumi* is a novel in which a young woman who has just crossed the line out of girlhood reproduces it by the exercise of a nostalgic false memory. That is why Maria recalls Tsugumi as a perfect shōjo. Tsugumi is an idealization that assumes more authority and power than what is reflected by that image presumably ever had.

But referents hardly matter here: Maria never really sees anyone or anything, only representations of people and places. Every description of something Maria yearns for is like a 'dream', or a 'painting'. Consequently all that Maria experiences is a 'memory' of the past communicated to her through the various artifacts and vehicles of nostalgia. The object of this nostalgia is what Maria wistfully calls her adolescent 'world free of troubles' (*mukattō no sekai*). 'Home', that for which Maria ceaselessly pines, is not where the nuclear family resides – Maria already has that in Tokyo – but that kawaii world made up of cousins, boyfriends and favorite pets. Maria is aware that this perfect world is not only gone, but was in fact never quite here to begin with: nostalgia, as one of its theorists has defined it, 'is the desire for desire' (Stewart 1984:23). Like her youth with which this world seamlessly overlaps, it is a role into which one steps and performs. Every action, from walking with boys on the beach to eating ice cream cones, makes reference only to what signified 'youth' in all its crystal perfection should be. The nostalgia which Maria deploys in order to produce this psuedo-utopia might be called a purposefully reflexive nostalgia. She describes, for example, her final summer vacation as having been in a 'separate world', a world 'even more intense than the real thing', a world as vivid 'as the dream a soldier has of his hometown on the eve of his death'.

The 'present' that Maria experiences that last summer is converted into the 'past' for which she is already, in some future-perfect way, nostalgic. When she returns to the Yamamotoya, she thinks to herself 'I knew that there was no way this could last forever'. She traverses a physical distance, that from Tokyo to Izu, in order to create a historical and nostalgic distance. This production of a past, which substitutes a temporal longing for a spatial separation, creates a loss that can never be retrieved but never wholly absent either. The 'ghost mail' game in which the two women receive letters in the 'present' from people who only existed in the 'past' reiterates the same relation that obtains between Maria's 'world free of troubles' and her nostalgia for it. Maria is already seeing the present from a future perspective that, while indeterminate, can only be different from the 'present' if it is not as good. These words 'present', 'future' and 'past' have scant secure reference beyond themselves: Yoshimoto Banana generates a youth (*seishun*) that could be anywhere, at any time, as an act of homage to a present that does not necessarily have to be 'now' or 'here'.

Banana's contemporary nostalgia lacks any determined past to validate it. An experience of the 'present' without a real-life referent, one that makes sense only as the much-vaunted empty signifier associated with postmodernity, is something that many Japanese intellectuals have considered, including Banana's father Takaaki. 'The character of the present is that it allows the social order created of massive, large-scale images to exist as a pre-existent stratum', he once wrote (Mitsui and Washida 1989:21), which I take to mean that it is the peculiar function of advanced capitalism, with the collusion of the mass media, to convert through the work of ideology the structure of our modern life into a sense of it as a moment we name the 'present'. In this analysis our lives are subordinated in a hegemony we cannot resist, or even recognize, because it is obscured behind a seemingly spontaneous 'now'. But daughter Banana's 'present' is not easily described as an ideologized 'pre-existent stratum', given how it is always constructed via a reflexive nostalgia. In much fiction, of course, a simulated youth is evoked longingly as the past from an adult, i.e. displaced, point of view. But *Tsugumi* is different. It is as if Banana, reversing the usual order, is describing 'now' as if it were 'then'. This is, for example, precisely what Banana's postscript in *Tsugumi* encourages us to think. In fact the novel's 'then' and its 'now' are separated by very little real chronological time. The reader seems encouraged to doubt the whole framework of time in the novel, and if the reader does indeed doubt, then an ironic reading and potentially one that resists the inevitability of growing up (and the burdens then assumed) becomes possible.

Banana commonly portrays herself – not least of all in *Tsugumi*, where she declares in the postscript that 'I am Tsugumi' – as the perfect shōjo. She typically downplays the fact that she is an adult and commercially successful novelist, but rather insists she is still much the child she cultivates in her fiction. In her essay 'Stephen King and Me' (S. Kingu to Watakushi), she claims to be incapable of writing anything other than a 'child's impressions' (Banana 1989b:73). The question arises why childhood and adolescence should be so idealized as a lost object at the expense of a future adulthood. At the end of *Tsugumi* the two main characters are meted out very different fates. Maria says of herself: 'I felt that inside of me some vague, amorphous sense of quiet determination came to fill me. For this moment, and from this place, I will go on living'. Maria's 'quiet determination' to have a future may be 'vague' and 'amorphous' because the nostalgic paradigm of present and past does not account for it, but it is still possible for precisely the reason that her reflexive nostalgia can cast the 'present' as desirous from the future, just as the past is desirous from the present. Tsugumi has a determination as well, but it is neither so quiet nor vague. In her farewell letter to Maria she writes: 'In any case, I am happy to be able to die in this town', the town itself a nostalgic sign of something past. Banana's stories are always full of deaths and near-deaths, but they seem to function less as important topics in themselves than as the means for dramatically punctuating youth not from adulthood but from what is 'not-youth', thus making her girlhood a neatly self-contained, self-referential object of desire for Maria. Death in Yoshimoto Banana's stories means that teenage women never have to be anything else, and that those who do survive, such as Maria, live only to 'remember' those women longingly. Maria will never forget Tsugumi or give up her nostalgic search for the lost object of her own shōjo past, because that would mean abandoning her narcissistically invested self-image.

In her essay 'A Death in Spring' (Haru no Shi) Banana says of herself something readers will recognize as true of Tsugumi:

> When I get really depressed I think I'd like to die. It's not like I want to leap into death or anything, but rather that I get unhappy at the very thought of tomorrow coming, that there isn't one thing that's any fun, that I'm disagreeable even to myself, that nothing inspires me. Life ends up being a real drag.
>
> (Banana 1989c:51)

The inability to imagine a future, and thus to deny oneself it, complements the impulse to convert the past, via nostalgia, into exactly what the present and (impossible) future are deficient in. Banana refers to this complementary link in another essay, 'The Moment of Happiness' (Kōfuku no Shunkan):

> What I call the 'moment of happiness' . . . is to be overflowing with the feeling that 'those days were the good days', days that later we idealize. But the 'moment of happiness', so intense that at the time we think 'I don't care if I die now', is a moment that cannot be recreated, and grows only dimmer with time.
>
> (Banana 1989b:59)

If happiness is the retroactive consequence of nostalgia, then Banana's point of view here is that of a person already nostalgic for nostalgia, one who now reflexively makes nostalgia available to critical scrutiny. Although it might be assumed that the readers of *Tsugumi* are themselves teenage women like Maria herself, in fact the novel was serialized in the Japanese edition of *Marie Claire*, a middle-brow women's magazine edited by the former staff of the now defunct literary journal *Umi* and marketed to the so-called 'office lady' in her early adulthood. The first audience for *Tsugumi* may well have ample incentive to review wistfully its adolescence recently terminated by the exigencies of either work or marriage at an age approximately Maria's.

The nostalgic relationship of Banana's characters to their everyday lives is replicated in the relationship that each Banana book constructs between the text and its audience. All her novels save one are narrated in the first-person. There is no where omniscient narration, nor any exchange of subjective perspective. This point of view also invariably governs the *atogaki* or postscript, found in every Banana book whether fiction or non-fiction. Each takes the form of a direct address by Banana to an assumed audience of fellow shōjo, and each describes the process of the writing of the book to which it is appended as a nostalgic exercise. *Tsugumi*'s postscript, for instance, recasts the novel as an *aide de memoire* that will serve to reconstruct nostalgically Banana's own happy youth and family. Such nostalgia is at root contradictory: what kind of longing could there be without the very memory that Banana fears losing? But nostalgia in Yoshimoto Banana is divorced from verifiable experience, and from the memory of such. Memory, lost or otherwise, is produced only through the experience of reading the novel. As Banana says in the postscript to her collection of essays *Songs From Banana Note*, 'I'll want to reread these after I reach that point in life called "middle-aged"' (Banana 1991:185). By placing such postscripts at the conclusion of her books, her stories and essays are situated within a simulated nostalgia anticipated from a future perspective, and within that nostalgia an imagined past is ideologically utopianized. Banana contends in *Sanctuary*: 'As soon as one unthinkingly takes a step forward in life, the place you were just a moment ago now looks as vivid as a flower-strewn stage'.

At the same time these postscripts, by virtue of their direct address of shōjo author Banana to her shōjo audience, are suggestively narcissistic. They are phrased like mawkish love letters, in a style that intimates close ties between Banana and her fans and fosters an extra-libidinal intimacy already a hallmark of the relations that her shōjo characters enjoy with each other or their shōjo-like boyfriends. This cozy familiarity is an extension of that produced in other discursive practices associated with shōjo culture. Ōtsuka Eiji, for example, claims that from the mid-seventies shōjo manga developed the practice of placing asides from shōjo narrators to their readers outside the caption boxes used to contain speech. In a move similar to that of Banana's postscripts, these manga establish a direct line of communication between shōjo character and reader in spaces outside the conventional graphic perimeters of the cartoon drawings.[5] Banana, addressing the importance of such manga to her work for precisely this feature, has confirmed that 'These manga contain the tacit understanding between both those writing them and those reading them that it's best if only girls understand what is going on' (Banana 1990:186).

The regular coincidence of nostalgia and narcissism in Banana's writings is unlikely either accidental or inconsequential. In the postscript to *A Sad Premonition*, a novel propelled by the narrator's desire to retrieve both her lost past and the love of her brother, Banana's writes, 'Looking back on it now . . . I am positive that [this book] will be a very important thing I will hold dear'. Both the narcissism and nostalgia collude to produce an emptiness; nostalgia by expressing the idealization of something gone, and narcissism by its pursuit for something 'else' already 'itself'. That both nostalgia and narcissism correspond in Banana's shōjo subject is significant. Just as shōjo comprises the empty sign – 'signs without substance' according to Ōtsuka Eiji – nostalgia is 'a sadness without object' (Stewart 1984:23) and by definition narcissism, too, conflates what is desired with whom desires.

It is in the home, that place which does not exist except in the nostalgic rehearsals with which popular culture represents it, where Yoshimoto Banana's nostalgia, narcissism, and shōjo self-referentiality are conjoined. When *A Sad Premonition*'s Yayoi and Tetsuo embrace to kiss, these three coincide: 'I could detect in Tetsuo that nostalgic scent of "home". I could smell the scent of the katsura trees of the home in which I grew up, the scent of the rugs, the scent of the clothing'. Her sibling-lover's body literally reeks of the metonymy for that lost but longed-for home whose memory is erased. The irony is that it is in the repressed narcissistic desire for her brother that the Hollywood version of the 'happy home' is retrieved. Later in this same novel Yayoi simultaneously realizes that she is both homesick (*hōmushikku*) and attracted to her brother, linking her two typically incompatible desires under the sign of her shōjo character. Similarly, in *Tsugumi* Maria's attraction to her friend and cousin Tsugumi, her former life at the inn and her playful flirtation with her stepfather all share an accommodation impossibly small were it not for her steadfast refusal to stop being a shōjo. It is there, in that refusal, that there may exist the agency with which this self-referential, empty sign of the shōjo proffers the option of meaningful reference after all. As Banana wrote in her postscript to *Kitchen*, 'I believe that growing up and overcoming one's problems are the records of the individual spirit, and that desire and possibility are everything'.

The Nostalgic Subject

Japanese popular culture in the 1980s is characterized, according to architectural historian Seo Fumiaki, by the 'uncertain, mercurial, elastic' qualities of shōjo culture, a culture that has 'excelled in its potential for creating emptiness' (Nishijima 1991:155, Seo 1991:159–75). The idea of emptiness, both as one associated with shōjo culture and Japanese postmodernity in general, is probably, alongside commodity, the key term in contemporary Japanese cultural criticism today. In what Mitsui Takayuki has termed the 'vacuity of the present', Yoshimoto Banana's work is held to symbolize the 'topos of the neuter, neutral sign' (Mitsui and Washida 1989:26). The concept of the shōjo itself has been schematized in similar terms: a category of being more discursive than material, an adolescent space without substantive or fixed subjective content, a point in the commodity loop that exists only to consume. Ōtsuka Eiji has written:

> The Japanese are no longer producers. Our existence consists solely of the distribution and consumption of 'things' brought us from elsewhere, 'things' with which we play. Nor are these 'things' actually tangible, but are instead only signs without any direct utility in life. None of what we typically purchase would, were we deprived of it, be a matter of life or death. These 'things' are continually converted into signs without substance, signs such as information, stocks or land. What name are we to give this life of ours today?
>
> The name is 'shōjo'.
>
> (Ōtsuka 1991:18)

The shōjo in its very referentless-ness is taken as emblematic of how contemporary culture manufactures and circulates images, information, concepts and discourses that in the aggregate constitute our experience of everyday life.

The ubiquity of nostalgia in Yoshimoto Banana and shōjo culture could be claimed as a demonstration of how our experience is, in fact, now thoroughly ideologized by the structures of what goes under the name, for lack of better, of 'late-model capitalism'. Whether as Japan's 'retro' boom that seeks to recall the allegedly carefree (American) 1950s, or as Banana's characters' yearning for a childhood or family that similarly never existed, such nostalgia would seem to prove that it is indeed a desire without object, a desire that is produced simply for desire's sake, and thus as narcissistic as the other key signs of postmodern Japanese culture. For wary critics, this nostalgia looms as politically retrograde whenever it idealizes the past rather than the future, and this is particularly true for that intellectual generation that came of age during the vehemently anti-nostalgic youth culture of the 1960s. This youth culture, remembered in parts of Tokyo as well as Berkeley by the phenomena of the hippie and the radical student, rebelled against precisely the consumer materialism that the youth culture today (the yuppie as well as the shōjo) seems to embrace and even celebrate. These critics, nurtured on the abstract and oppositional theories of Banana's father Takaaki, look at how the commodities of youth culture *are* youth culture today, and like theorists of popular culture before them, often read that culture reductively as the ideological accessory of modern capitalism and its affiliated superstructures.

Nostalgia, however, has been regarded differently by other critics in other contexts. Patrick Wright, for example, has characterized Thatcherism's revival of English nostalgia for empire as 'a nostalgia which, while it may indeed be differentiated according to the division of labor, also testifies in more general ways to the destabilization of everyday life' (Wright 1985:20). It is more than a coincidence that Yoshimoto Banana's nostalgia, too, seems focussed precisely where Japanese 'everyday life' is its most destabilized and fragile, and thus its claim to hegemony the most tenuous. Surely it is the function of nostalgia to supply what is lacking, or more correctly, to create a 'lack' that then demands a supplement. In the modernist organization of everyday life into the ostensibly opposed worlds of the 'individual' and 'society', the term 'family' has occupied a decisive intermediary position. Proposed as a kind of reconciliation of the two, and assuming the production of the new individuals needed for the reproduction of the social work force, the family has been the first arena of socialization. It is the oft-noted crisis of society today that families no longer carry out such socialization, just as it is the oft-noted crisis of Japanese literature that Yoshimoto Banana is the success she is. The nostalgic supplement of this obsolete family does not retrieve that family as much as it does in fact seal its fate.

In establishing an absence – in Banana, primarily the absence of the family as a unit of social production – nostalgia nonetheless requires that someone be invested with the agency to create it. The 'nostalgic subject', if I may theorize one, is a ideological subject produced in and by contemporary Japanese socio-cultural discourses. It is recognized by its equivocal accommodation with everyday life through a retreat into the past *and* by its resistance to that same life through its longing for another sort of life, one that never actually 'was' because no such life ever 'is'. In Banana's stories this particular nostalgia, reflexive and critical, for a shōjo such as Tsugumi who shows every sign of contesting authority and refusing to grow up into the role assigned for her may contribute to an emergent defiance to patriarchal ideologies that condition women (and by extension, men) for their use or exchange functions in the work and marriage economies.

There are those critics (perhaps nostalgic for a time when there was no nostalgia) who consider nostalgic behavior as based purely on the rationale that a culture which is organized along strongly utilitarian and materialistic lines makes loss, or failure to attain, values supporting this orientation (youth, beauty, productivity, the amassing of property) a threat that requires a search for gratification in the past. Nostalgia is deemed a sub-species of false consciousness that, in defiance of the logic of historical dialectics, looks longingly backward to obsolete social structures. Isn't it, it could be argued, reactionary to think that the future can only be worse than the past? Such questions were raised by the Frankfurt School, some of whom considered the practical agenda of mass culture to be the reconciliation of the masses to the status quo. More recently, the popularity of nostalgia in modern life has been attributed to a lost faith in the possibility of social change, prompting a retreat to the private enclave of the family and the consumption of certain retro styles. This is close to what Raymond Williams has called 'mobile privatisation', where a high standard of living and a wide range of consumer choices are allied with an inward-looking privacy. Such choices, Williams worries, are purchased at the cost of declining participation and confidence in our public and collective life (Williams 1982:188).

But what if what longingly for what was is itself a 'moment of happiness' that can suggest an undoing of the present, an opportunity for the future? In an early essay that considered Walter Benjamin's nostalgia for the nineteenth century, Fredric Jameson optimistically concluded:

> But if nostalgia as a political motivation is most frequently

> associated with fascism, there is no reason why a nostalgia conscious of itself, a lucid and remorseless dissatisfaction with the present on the grounds of some remembered plenitude, cannot furnish as adequate a revolutionary stimulus as any other.
>
> (Jameson 1972:68)[6]

As Jameson indicates, the stakes of nostalgia are destined to be high since they may well determine how we will connect ourselves with our future, insofar as an imagined future becomes feasible at the same moment as an imagined past. When Maria says near the end of *Tsugumi* that she 'will go on living' as a result of a 'vague, ambiguous' determination, her nostalgia for the present-as-past has produced a future that may yearn with desire for what went before, but does not feel governed by it. Unlike Jameson, who hopes for revolutionary change emerging from Benjamin's nostalgic romance with the past, we can hardly predict that Maria is going to go on to anything quite so dramatic or heroic. But neither can we conclude simply that the nostalgia for girlhood and its easy and innocent comradery, is not without its own potential for rescripting an adulthood left 'vague' and 'ambiguous' because it is so unsavory. We are admittedly left wondering whether the recovery of lost time which is achieved in nostalgia represents a retrospective deception or a retrospective insight. But it is precisely in that equivocation that the nostalgic subject functions as both a corroboration of the consumer culture that elitist critics mistrust, and the corrective imaginary for which Jameson hopes. Whether the recovery of that so-called 'lost time' is unreal or real remains an undecidable question as long as the nostalgia subject is constituted precisely where that boundary is contested.

In Banana's novel *Fleeting Bubbles* (Utakata), the two central characters – again, a near-incestuous pair of half-siblings, shōjo Ningyo and shōnen Arashi, who have long lived separately with one of each of their parents – dream of reuniting their family. But when Ningyo actually faces that possibility, her reaction is unexpected. 'I tried to imagine the scene. Father and mother and Arashi and myself, in that filthy house around a big table: it was unnatural, a bad nightmare, the portrait of a warm happy family in a dream that could never be' (Banana 1989d:49). Here is not so much nostalgia, as a nostalgia suddenly historicized and exposed. The irony here undoes the romance and supplants it with its own ideological critique. 'Unnatural' and as unreal as a 'portrait' or a 'dream', the nostalgic object of the 'warm happy family' momentarily but fatally loses its appeal. It is not unusual to hear popular culture today identified with a kind of macro-nostalgia in which there is no space we authentically occupy, and so that culture tries to fill the gap by manufacturing images of both home and rootlessness. (Banana's works are an obvious example, but so is *Little House on the Prairie.*) Yet as Banana's remarks on the modern family would seem to imply, the attempt can fail due to its sheer eclecticism, for if we can so easily invent and re-invent our cultural representations of 'home', then in fact we have effectively eliminated the need for the institution in the first place. Perhaps family values, in Japan as well as the United States, become a national issue only once they are irretrievable.

NOTES

1 For an introduction to Yoshimoto Takaaki's importance in postwar Japanese intellectual culture, see the late Lawrence Olson's 'Intellectuals and "the People": on Yoshimoto Takaaki'.

2 Much of the criticism of Banana's writing concerns itself with issues of its language and style, neither of which is held in universally high regard. However Matsumoto Takayuki, who notes the marked difference of Banana's writing from 'the formal language of "literature"' and its congruency with the language 'of the "comic book", of "animation", of "film", of "popular songs" and of "television"', also claims for it a 'contiguity with the sensibility of the everyday lives we lead' (Matsumoto 1991:16, 83). Ogasawara Kenji has dubbed Banana's close transcription of young people's speech as 'the new literary vernacular' (*shin-genbunitchi*), implying a shift underway in the language of Japanese literature as momentous as that which occurred in the Meiji period (Ogasawara 1990:147).

3 *Asahi Shinbun* cultural editor Nishijima Takeo, for example, darkly concluded that:

> Japanese culture in the 1980s was a culture that sucked everything in like a black hole, and let nothing out. No oppositional culture was established to provide an antithesis to the traditional one. Nor did any native culture develop to critique European or American culture. What did develop was only a retro-culture that cited mere convention.
>
> (Nishijima 1991:208)

4 In 1992 many newspapers carried an Associated Press report about a company called the Japan Efficiency Headquarters, which rents out, by the hour, 'families' on behalf of Japanese themselves too busy to

carry out the social obligations associated with being good sons, daughters-in-law, grandparents, etc. Its success attributed to 'disintegrating traditional family ties', Japan Efficiency Headquarters is testimony to creative entrepreneurship and its ability to commercialize, even commodify, the most basic human 'relations'.

5 Non-fiction writer Yamane Kazuma has argued it was at this same time that a new and distinct type-face – the rounded, child-like script derived from youthful handwriting and commonly seen in shōjo manga and associated commodities (such as notebooks, candy bars, etc.) typically purchased by teenage women in Japan – became prevalent. Yamane speculates that it became popular because it marks graphically the private discourses of adolescent female culture (Yamane 1986).

6 In Jameson's later writings, it should be noted, he has grown considerably less sanguine about the political prospects of nostalgia. Arguing that nostalgia must make us reflect upon 'the enormity of a situation in which we seem increasingly incapable of fashioning representations of our own current experience', he sees nostalgia replacing history with 'random cannibalization' (e.g., the fifties as an era of high school and hair grease, rather than of the Cold War and McCarthyism) in which 'the past as "referent" finds itself gradually bracketed, and then effaced altogether, leaving us with nothing but texts' (Jameson 1984:53, 66). But perhaps there can be nostalgia that functions like 'historicity', a concept offered in Jameson's more recent work and which is

> neither a representation of the past nor a representation of the future (although its various forms use such representations): it can first and foremost be defined as a perception of the present as history: that is, as a relationship to the present which somehow defamiliarizes it and allows us that distance from immediacy which we call historical . . . [W]hat is at stake is essentially a process of reification, whereby we draw back from our immersion in the here-and-now (not yet identified as a "present") and grasp it as a kind of thing.
>
> (Jameson 1989:523)

This distance that Jameson calls historical and which we then 'grasp' in order presumably to exploit for ourselves may, however, describe the nostalgic process in Yoshimoto Banana. What Jameson indicates, and what Banana may be read as attempting within the idioms of shōjo culture, is the historicization of nostalgia itself, a move that might lead to awareness of how we and our present are produced as subjects within and by nostalgia. The reified historicity that nostalgia in this formulation can lead to – the eccentric historicity of *Tsugumi* – is consequently not without utility, in the sense that it opens up the possibility of a changed relationship with the contemporary moment we inhabit. If reification, in Jameson's phrase, is 'defused and recuperated as a form of praxis', then the 'things' produced by reification, including Banana's 'youth' and the 'family', are things we can fashion for ourselves and in our own interests. 'At that point', concurring in Jameson's optimism, 'reification ceases to be a baleful and alienating process, a noxious side of our mode of production . . . and is transferred to the side of human energies and possibilities' (Jameson 1989:569).

REFERENCES

Adorno, T. W. and Max Horkheimer 1972 *Dialectic of Enlightenment*, New York: Seabury.

Fujimoto Yukari 1991 'Atsui ocha no kioku: "nichijōsei no shisō" to Yoshimoto Banana' (Memories of hot green tea: 'the ideology of the everyday' and Yoshimoto Banana), p. 303–17 in Hasegawa Izumi (ed.) *Josei Sakka no Shinryū* (The New Wave of Women Writers), Tokyo: Shibundō.

Furuhashi Nobuyoshi 1990 *Yoshimoto Banana to Tawara Machi* (Yoshimoto Banana and Tawara Machi), Tokyo: Chikuma Shobō.

Horikiri Naoto 1991 'Onna wa dokyō, shōjo wa aikyō' (Women have mettle, shōjo have charm), p. 108–28 in Honda Masuko *et al.* (eds.) *Shōjo Ron* (Essays on Shōjo), Tokyo: Aoyumisha.

Inamasu Tatsuo 1989 *Aidoru Kōgaku* (Idol Engineering), Tokyo: Chikuma Shobō.

Jameson, Fredric 1989 'Nostalgia for the present', p. 517–37 in *South Atlantic Quarterly* 88 (2).

—— 1984 'Postmodernism, or the cultural logic of late capitalism', p. 53–92 in *New Left Review* 146.

—— 1972 'Walter Benjamin, or Nostalgia', p. 52–68 in R. Boyers (ed.) *The Legacy of German Refugee Intellectuals*, New York: Schocken Books.

Kamata Tōji 1991 '"Atogaki" to "Natsukashisa"' ('Afterwords' and 'Nostalgia'), p. 278–90 in Hasegawa Izumi (ed.) *Josei Sakka no Shinryū*.

Matsumoto Takayuki 1991 *Yoshimoto Banana Ron: 'futsū' to iu muishiki* (Yoshimoto Banana: the unconscious 'ordinary'), Tokyo: JICC Shuppankyoku.

Mitsui Takayuki, and Washida Koyata 1989 *Yoshimoto Banana Shinwa* (The Myths of Yoshimoto Banana), Tokyo: Aoyumisha.

Nanba Hiroyuki 1991 'Yoshimoto Banana: "manga sedai" no jun-bungaku' (Yoshimoto Banana: the pure literature of the 'comic generation'), p. 319 in Hasegawa Izumi (ed.) *Josei Sakka no Shinryū*.

Nishijima Takeo 1991 *Kara-genki no Jidai: hachijū nendai bunkaron* (A Pseudo-Healthy Era: an essay on culture in the 1980s), Tokyo: Asahi Shimbun Sha.

Ogasawara Kenji 1990 *Bungakuteki Koji-tachi no Yukue* (The Whereabouts of Our Literary Offspring), Tokyo: Goryū Shoin.

Ōe Kenzaburō 23 November 1986 'A novelist's lament', *Japan Times*.

Olson, Lawrence 1978 'Intellectuals and "the people": on Yoshimoto Takaaki', p. 327–57 in *Journal of Japanese Studies* 4 (2).

Ōtsuka Eiji 1991 *Shōjo Minzokugaku* (Shōjo Ethnology), Tokyo: Kōbunsha.

Robertson, Jennifer 1989 'Gender-bending in paradise: doing "female" and "male" in Japan', p. 50–69 in *Genders* 5.

Seo Fumiaki 1991 'Toshi o Fuyū Suru Shōjo-tachi' (Shōjo who wander the city), p. 159–75 in Honda Masuko *et al.* (eds.), *Shōjo Ron*.

Shima Hiroyuki 1988 'Yoshimoto Banana wa Kakitsukerareru ka' (Can Yoshimoto Banana continue to write?), p. 152–55 in *Bessatsu Takarajima*.

Sodei, Takako 1985 'The fatherless family', p. 77–82 in *Japan Quarterly* 32 (1).

Stewart, Susan 1984 *On Longing: narratives of the miniature, the gigantic, the souvenir, the collection*, Baltimore: Johns Hopkins University Press.

Ueno Chizuko 1990 *Middonaito Kōru* (Midnight Call), Tokyo: Asahi Shimbun Sha.

Washida Koyata 1990 'Yoshimoto Banana no Shudai wa Shi' (Yoshimoto Banana's main theme is death), p. 400–03 in *Ushio* 373.

Williams, Raymond 1982 *Toward 2000*, London: The Hogarth Press.

Wright, Patrick 1985 *Living in Old Country: the national past in contemporary Britain*, London: Verso.

Yamane Kazuma 1986 *Hentai Shōjo Moji no Kenkyū* (Studies in Deviant Shōjo Orthography), Tokyo: Kōdansha.

Yoshimoto Banana 1991 *Songs from Banana Note*, Tokyo: Fusōsha.

—— 1990 *Fruits Basket*, Tokyo: Fukutake Shoten.

—— 1989a *Kanashii Yokan* (A Sad Premonition), Tokyo: Kadokawa Shoten.

—— 1989b *Painappurin* (Pineapple Pudding), Tokyo: Kadokawa Shoten.

—— 1989c *Tugumi* (Tsugumi), Tokyo: Chūō Kōronsha.

—— 1989d *Utakata/Sankuchuari* (Fleeting Bubbles/Sanctuary), Tokyo: Fukutake Shoten.

—— 1988 *Kitchin* (Kitchen), Tokyo: Fukutake Shoten.

Contributors

Aoki Tamotsu is a cultural anthropologist at Osaka University. He is the author of *'Nihon Bunkaron' no Hen'yō: sengo Nihon no bunka to identity* (Changing Theories of Japanese Culture: culture and identity in postwar Japan) and the 1985 *Culture Mass Culture*, from which his essay translated for this volume was excerpted.

Leo Ching completed a Ph.D. in Comparative Literature at the University of California, San Diego, in 1994. He is currently an assistant professor in Asian and African Languages and Literature at Duke University. He works primarily in the areas of Japanese colonial discourse and mass culture.

Brian Currid is a graduate student in the Department of Music at the University of Chicago. His research interests include queer(ing) popular musics, music in soul films, and the social history of recorded music.

Brian Moeran is a social anthropologist and Swire Professor of Japanese at the University of Hong Kong. He has lived and studied in Japan for more years than he can count and has written a number of books and articles on various aspects of Japanese folk crafts, pottery, media, advertising and popular culture.

Susan J. Napier is an associate professor of Japanese literature and culture at the University of Texas, Austin. She is the author of *Escape from the Wasteland: romanticism and realism in the works of Mishima Yukio and Ōe Kenzaburo* and the forthcoming *The Fantastic in Modern Japanese Literature: the subversion of modernity.*

Andrew A. Painter is currently teaching at Mukōgawa Women's University, conducting research on Japanese television audiences, and working on documentary and experimental video production.

John G. Russell, assistant professor of English at Gifu University in Japan, is the author of *Nihonjin no Kokujin-kan* (Japanese Perceptions of Blacks, 1991), which was designated as recommended reading by the National Library Association of Japan. Russell also served as consultant to Regge Life's *Struggle and Success: the African American experience in Japan* (1992). He is working at present on a study of the consumption of black culture in Japan.

Lise Skov is a cultural sociologist doing research on fashion. After having spent some years working on Japanese women's fashion and media, she is now studying innovation and imitation in fashion design in a global perspective. She is affiliated with the Department of Sociology and the Department of Japanese Studies, University of Hong Kong.

Matthew C. Strecher is a graduate student at the University of Washington. His doctoral thesis is on the works of Murakami Haruki, and his other research interests include the history of popular literature in modern Japan.

Alan M. Tansman, author of *The Writings of Koda Aya, a Japanese Literary Daughter*, has also published essays on critics Isōda Kōichi and Yasuda Yojūrō, as well as the writers Uno Kōji and Sholem Aleichem. He is currently at work on a book entitled *Images of Loss and Longing in 1930s Japan.*

John Whittier Treat is professor of Japanese at the University of Washington, where he teaches both literature and cultural studies. He is currently doing research for a two-volume history of modern Japanese literature entitled *Governing Metaphors: the imagination of modern Japan.*

INDEX

Note: All references are to Japan unless otherwise stated. Reference to illustrations are in bold type.